THE MORAL, SOCIAL, AND COMMERCIAL IMPERATIVES OF GENETIC TESTING AND SCREENING

THE AUSTRALIAN CASE

INTERNATIONAL LIBRARY OF ETHICS, LAW, AND THE NEW MEDICINE

VOLUME 30

The titles published in this series are listed at the end of this volume.

The Moral, Social, and Commercial Imperatives of Genetic Testing and Screening

The Australian Case

Edited by

MICHELA BETTA

Swinburne University of Technology,
Faculty of Business & Enterprise,
Melbourne - VIC - Australia

Springer

A.C.I.P. Catalogue record for this book is available from the Library of Congress.

ISBN-10 1–4020–4618–9 (HB)
ISBN-13 978–1–4020–4618–6 (HB)
ISBN-10 1–4020–4619–7 (e-book)
ISBN-13 978–1–4020–4619–3 (e-book)

Published by Springer,
P.O.Box 17,3300 AA Dordrecht, The Netherlands

www.springer.com

Printed on acid-free paper

Printed in the Netherlands.

TABLE OF CONTENTS

NOTES ON CONTRIBUTORS

Dr. MaryAnne Aitken is Group Leader in Genetics Education at the Murdoch Children's Research Institute at Royal Children's Hospital in Melbourne (Australia). Through her role she is affiliated with the Department of Paediatrics of the University of Melbourne and the Bruce Lefroy Centre for Genetic Health Research at Murdoch Children's Research Institute. With a background in molecular biology, nursing, and genetic counselling, she moved into genetics education in 1997. She has a keen interest in community education, public awareness, and genetic screening programmes and, as such, half of her time is devoted to providing an educational service to the community, while the other half is spent in a research capacity, evaluating the impact of genetics education programmes and the information needs of the community. She lives with her husband and four children in Melbourne.

Dr. Michela Betta is Senior Lecturer in the Double Degree Program Business and Humanities (Languages and European Studies) in the Faculty of Business and Enterprise of Swinburne University of Technology (Melbourne). She studied sociology, philosophy, and linguistics in Italy (Milan) and Germany (Frankfurt). She was awarded a Ph.D. from Johan-Wolfgang Goethe University of Frankfurt. Her main research areas are ethics and bioethics, moral philosophy, genetics and technology, and philosophy of science. In addition to having published extensively in scholarly journals and books, she has published a major study on embryonic research and family (*Embryonenforschung und Familie. Zur Politik der Reproduktion in Great Britain, Italy, and Germany*, Peter Lang Verlag Frankfurt/Paris/New York 1995) and a further book on human rights and technology (*Brauchen wir Menschenrechte?* Ulrike Helmer Verlag Königstein/Frankfurt, 2000). She has also published a collection of short stories (*Le Virtù del Camaleonte*, Maremmi Editori Firenze, 2006). Before moving to Australia she worked at Johan-Wolfgang Goethe University of Frankfurt, in the Faculty of Social Sciences and Political Analysis. She has lived in three different countries and speaks and writes in three languages.

Dr. Mrinal Bhave is Senior Lecturer in Biotechnology in the Faculty of Life and Social Sciences of Swinburne University of Technology. Her teaching is in areas of molecular biology, biotechnology, and genetics, across all grade levels of the Undergraduate Program. She also has a number of Ph.D. and Honours research students working in different areas of biotechnology. She has extensive experience in several different research fields involving human, animal, bacterial, and plant molecular biology. She feels passionately about the role of biotechnology in everyday life, and is amazed by the positive changes it is bringing, or can bring, but also shares the concerns of "common humanity" regarding some of the new developments.

Dr. Astrid H. Gesche is a multidisciplinarian, holding a Ph.D. from the Australian National University and four other postgraduate degrees in different areas. She worked as a senior research fellow at the John Curtin School of Medical Research at the Australian National University in Canberra and as immunologist and cell biologist at Flinders University, Adelaide (Australia) and the University of Mainz (Germany). She is now engaged in the Applied Ethics and Human Rights Program of the School of Humanities and Human Services, Queensland University of Technology (Brisbane), and works on ethics issues arising from technology, especially biotechnology, nanotechnology, and information technology. Her special research interests are in privacy, informed consent, indigenous rights, and the development of theoretical frameworks underpinning policy processes.

Dr. Richard Hil is Senior Lecturer in the School of Social Sciences at Southern Cross University. He has taught at the University of York, James Cook University, Sunshine Coast University College, and Queensland University of Technology. His main areas of interest are in youth justice, child and family welfare, and criminology. He is currently embarked on a study of poverty in the Coffs Harbour region. He is also completing books on crime and genetics, and institutional violations of the right of young people. In addition to having published extensively in scholarly journals, he has also edited a number of books and co-authored *Families, Crime and Juvenile Justice* (with McMahon, A.), *Discovering Risk*, and *Understanding Criminology* (both with Bessant, J. and Watts, R.).

Dr. Richard Hindmarsh is Senior Lecturer in Biopolitics and Environmental Policy in the Australian School of Environmental Studies, Griffith University (Brisbane). He previously lectured in Nature & Technoscience Studies and Contemporary Studies at the University of Queensland. He has a first class honours degree in Environmental Studies and a Ph.D. in Science, Technology & Society Studies, and has held an ARC Postdoctoral Research Fellowship. With his main research focus on the nature, politics, and implications of modern biotechnology, he has co-edited *Altered Genes* (Allen & Unwin, 1998; revised edition 2001, Scribe) and *Recoding Nature: Critical Perspectives on Genetic Engineering* (UNSW Press, 2004). His new book *Genetic Manoeuvres, Bio-utopian Visions: A New Politics of Life* will be published in 2007 by UWA Press.

Dr. Suzanne Jamieson has taught at the University of Sydney since 1990 after a career as a senior public servant and a trade union official. Since 1991 she has represented the National Pay Equity Coalition in national wage cases before the Australian Industrial Relations Commission and in the extensive litigation around equal pay for women in the New South Wales industrial jurisdiction. Her other principal research interest is in occupational health and safety, particularly as it affects women. She is a staff-elected Fellow of the University of Sydney Senate, sits on the Operations Review Committee of the Independent Commission Against Corruption, is a member of the NSW Anti-Discrimination Board and Director of the University's Celtic Studies Foundation. She likes to spend her spare time on her family's 40 acres of rock near Adaminaby in the Snowy Mountains.

Dr. Sylvia Metcalfe (Associate Professor) has a B.Sc. (Honours) and a Ph.D. in Biochemistry from the UK, with a broad background of biomedical laboratory-based research in London, New York, and Melbourne. In recent years, her focus has been on genetics education. She coordinates and teaches genetics to medical students, as well as other allied health and science students at the University of Melbourne. She is involved in developing genetics and ethics education resources, including a number of multimedia programs for schools, the community, and professionals. Her research interests include genetic understanding of health professionals and the community, implications of genetic technologies and counselling issues for families, and community genetic screening programmes. She is married and has two young boys.

Brian Opeskin has been a full-time Commissioner at the Australian Law Reform Commission since July 2000. He led the Commission's inquiry on the Judicial Power of the Commonwealth, and jointly led the inquiry into the protection of human genetic information, and into gene patenting and human health. He is now leading the inquiry into the sentencing of federal offenders. He has taught in the fields of constitutional law, federal courts, international law, and conflict of laws in the Law School of Sydney University, where he was an Associate Professor until July 2003. He has published many articles in these fields and has co-authored several books—*International Law and Australian Federalism* (1997), *The Australian Federal Judicial System* (2000), *Conflict of Laws in Australia* (2001), and *Australian Courts of Law* (4th edn., 2004). He has acted as a consultant to state and federal governments on issues of public health law and quarantine. He holds degrees in Economics and Law from the University of New South Wales, and a Bachelor of Civil Law from the University of Oxford. He was admitted as a barrister of the Supreme Court of New South Wales in 1989.

Dr. Enzo Palombo is Senior Lecturer in the Faculty of Life and Social Sciences and Head of the Environment and Biotechnology Centre at Swinburne University of Technology. His current roles involve teaching and research in clinical, applied, and environmental microbiology and biotechnology. He is author and co-author of over 50 papers in the fields of molecular and cellular biology of microorganisms, public health microbiology, and virology. He is an active member of the Australian Society of Microbiology (ASM), past-chair and honorary treasurer of the Victorian Branch of ASM, and member of the Australasian Society for Infectious Diseases.

Susan Pennicuik was the National Occupational Health and Safety (OHS) Coordinator for the Australian Council of Trade Unions from 1997 to 2004. She now works as a private consultant in matter related to social and industrial policies. Her role involves working with government and employer groups on national OHS policies and programmes, as well as consulting with, and providing advice and information to, unions and workers about national policies and programmes and on OHS issues in general. Sue has recently developed a website to assist both workers and employers to address alcohol-related issues at work in a fair and effective manner.

Dr. Lyn Turney is Lecturer in Sociology and researcher for the Australian Centre for Emerging Technologies and Society (ACETS) at Swinburne University of Technology. Lyn teaches in the areas of genetics and society, the sociologies of health and the body, and qualitative methods. Her Ph.D. and publications have been on women's experience of medical technology, in particular surgical sterilization. Lyn has also more recently published articles on issues concerning attitudes to DNA paternity testing, the ethics of revealing non-paternity discovered through genetic carrier screening, and the main reasons why people have a paternity test. She has also published articles on attitudes to stem cell research and the use of virtual focus groups in qualitative research and as an effective learning environment for student researchers. She is currently working on an Australian Research Council (ARC)-funded project examining the social impacts of DNA paternity testing.

Professor David Weisbrot has been President of the Australian Law Reform Commission since June 1999. He presided over the major inquiries into the protection of human genetic information, which culminated in the report *Essentially Yours* (ALRC 96, 2003), and into the intellectual property rights over genetic materials and genetic-related technologies (*Genes and Ingenuity: Gene Patenting and Human Health*, ALRC 99, 2004). He has also chaired the ALRC inquiries into the federal civil justice system; marine insurance; the distribution of federal judicial power; the use of civil and administrative penalties in federal regulatory jurisdiction; and the protection of classified and security sensitive information (*Keeping Secrets*, ALRC 98, 2004). He is an Honorary Professor in the Institute for Molecular Bioscience and the TC Beirne School of Law at the University of Queensland, and an Honorary Visiting Professor of Law at the University of New South Wales and Macquarie University. He is Vice-President of the Commonwealth Association of Law Reform Agencies (CALRAs), and elected member of the Human Genome Organisation (HUGO). He was previously Dean of Law and Pro-Vice-Chancellor of Humanities and Social Sciences at the University of Sydney. Prior to this position, he was a member of the Law Schools of the University of New South Wales and the University of Papua New Guinea, and a Commissioner of the New South Wales and Fiji Law Reform Commissions. In 2003, he was awarded a Centenary Medal by the Australian Government for "services to law reform."

MICHELA BETTA

ABOUT THIS BOOK

This book explores the controversial issue of the genetic testing and screening[1] of individuals and populations for personal and public reasons. The analysis opens with the controversy raised by testing and screening of life in its early stages. The question debated here is whether genetic manipulation or enhancement of embryos or stem cells is acceptable and desirable. Two lines of reasoning have been reconstructed that respectively defend the moral superiority of genetically non-manipulated human nature and the moral image of nurture, a contrast that remains unresolved. It appears that neither position has convincingly addressed the complexity of the new social and political relations made possible by the "new genetics,"[2] or the complexity of the self resulting from different forms of life and life-forms. New negotiations about the body and its social contexts have unveiled a new site within which an intensification or "disparagement" of the body and its spiritual dimension is now possible. The analysis then moves to a broader social, economic, and commercial field, in order to determine the context in which genetic screening of adults might have repercussions on fundamental social clusters such as healthcare, public and private insurance, work relations, and economic investments. In the course of this analysis, a new assemblage has been identified and described as the "genetic economy." This assemblage makes a resetting of bodily resources possible, which in turn will reinforce the role of the family and of family ties. In this context, health and insurance emerge as two of the fundamental social goods of the manipulating culture. The genetic economy will cause changes in the political agendas of western countries as well as impose another structure on distributive justice.

The first two chapters by Michela Betta serve to create the global context of genetic testing and screening, and introduce the reader to the complexity of the issue. They therefore remain embedded in a broader perspective. Chapter 1 confronts us with the ethical debate on the genetic manipulation of stem cells and embryos and the controversy caused by its regulation. The complexity of the issue is such that no single position is possible, and therefore a new system of distributive justice will be necessary in order to address different interests and styles, but also to reiterate the principle of *primum non nocere*, the obligation, first of all, to prevent harm. Chapter 2 explores the birth of a new economy based on bodily resources and territory. This new economy will open up options and possibilities in terms of the wealth and well-being of an emergent new social class and cultural style. The specific and empirical questions and policies elaborated upon in part II of the book will then help to contrast the global with the local, and to identify physical and social risks, policies and politics, and the practices that must be put in place or reinforced in order to protect fundamental rights. *The Australian Case* has identified fundamental and practical matters related to genetic testing and screening in Australia. The Australian authors have addressed important questions in terms of public policy and personal freedom.

Richard Hil and Richard Hindmarsh warn against the risk of an emergent genetic determinism in criminal law. The two authors assert that social policies must be freed from imperatives of control based on genetic data and knowledge, because this would reveal a form of genetic reductionism and attribute human behaviour mainly or entirely to genetic "make-up," "markers," "triggers," or "traits." Increasingly, the authors argue, violence, aggression, impulsivity, and hyperactivity have been linked to genetic factors. They describe the tendency to understand social problems in genetic terms as a "geno creep" or "backdoor eugenics" related to the recent renaissance of science, and occasioned in large measure by the rise of human genetics. They elaborate on how this branch of science manifests itself through subtle strategies capable of suggesting that life is governed by genetic composition.

David Weisbrot and Brian Opeskin elaborate on the work of the Australian Law Reform Commission (ALRC) and Australian Health and Ethics Committee (AHEC), presenting a detailed analysis of their promulgations in controversial issues related to "new genetics." Their extensive analysis focuses on comments and positions of different social actors, highlighting the conflict of interests that confronts the various social parties. Their narrative illuminates the legal, social, and commercial initiatives undertaken to respond to new challenges, and to the ALRC-AHEC recommendations. The authors expressly exclude the need for governmental intervention, instead calling upon the insurance industry, employers, and commercial sectors to develop responsible policies in matters related to genetic screening and testing.

Astrid Gesche describes the emergence of new agencies and databases that will play a major role in the incorporation of genetic technologies into the social and legal system. She has also identified the risks that such technologies may represent for children and adolescents, families, and minorities, when technocratic thinking takes precedence over personal rights. Her chapter on the "vulnerables" underlines the moral imperative to protect the rights, dignity, and personal freedom of all those who, for whatever reasons, are subjected to genetic testing.

MaryAnne Aitken and Sylvia Metcalfe have approached the issue of genetic testing and screening from an educational angle. The two authors are concerned with the creation of educational strategies and options capable of putting social groups in the position to understand and consequently use genetic screening as an empowering tool in a social context in which health is becoming a fundamental resource of well-being.

Enzo Palombo and Mrinal Bhave reiterate the essentials of a health system that coheres around genetic options, insisting on the fundamental importance of making parents and prospective parents familiar with the changing patterns of healthcare. The authors have stressed the need to reinvigorate the doctor–patient relationship in terms of inclusion and consensus.

Susan Pennicuik analyses the ALRC-AHEC recommendations on matters related to genetic screening in the workplace. She underlines the need to revise some of the recommendations formulated in the ALRC-AHEC final report, in order to guarantee that the use of genetic screening and testing in the workplace does not disadvantage employees. In her role as private consultant in matter related to industrial relations and social policies, Pennicuik discusses the ALRC-AHEC recommendations and laments that their Inquiry has perhaps taken too soft an approach towards employers.

Suzanne Jamieson has turned her criticism towards the Australian Unions themselves, in particular for failing to develop more substantial politics and policy direction regarding genetic testing and screening. This policy-vacuum, she argues, weakens the unions' position in terms of negotiations of new policies.

Finally, Lyn Turney challenges the ALRC-AHEC Inquiry by questioning its understanding of the value of private information and suggesting that in the genetic culture not only sexual relations but also the family as such might need to be redefined in order to address the complexity of relations that new genetic knowledge might bring about.

The central message resulting from the work of the Australian commentators and critics can be summed up as follows:

1. On the political level the Australian Law Reform Commission (ALRC) has been asked to set up an inquiry into genetic testing and screening and to formulate recommendations. The "Inquiry" is a point of reference for almost all the authors of this volume, as its formulations and recommendations have already had repercussions on commerce and private insurance, as well as on questions related to criminal law. These recommendations have reiterated the need to reinforce the responsibility of the market players and public agencies, but have unconditionally rejected genetic exceptionalism and state interventionism.
2. Genetic testing and screening may create new and subtle forms of control, unless clear policies are designed to protect the individual rights to privacy and personal freedom, as well as reiterate the moral interests of unborn life and born children not to be at the complete mercy of enthusiastic scientists, genetic enhancers, and parents. However, personal freedom is understood also as a consequence of an informed use of the new genetic testing technologies. These claims have been flanked by strong criticism against

emerging tendencies in criminal law, health, and social relations to address social problems in genetic deterministic terms, which lead to the creation of a criminal taxonomy based on genes.

3. On the educational, social, and organizational levels the need has been expressed to create the condition for more fluid and transparent information that will advantage all parties involved. The necessity to inform the individual as well as the public is the first condition for guaranteeing a fair treatment of questions related to public health, work, and ethnicity-related diseases. In particular, the authors coming from the science field have stressed the necessity of genetic testing and screening individuals and social groups in order to help them prevent diseases. However, every form of intervention must be flanked by educational and informative campaigns and supported by a clear and informed consent freely given by the parties involved.

From the perspective of public policy, the ALRC plays a major educational role, as it very often instigates a change of mentality in the important social, legal, and economic sectors targeted by its public inquiries. The ALRC enjoys strong support from the scientific and the political environment as well as the wider public. This support reveals a peculiar form of political and moral legitimacy placing it on a high pedestal equal perhaps to that of France's National Ethics Committee. The single but not insignificant difference is that the ALRC tends to keep state intervention at the lowest level, while the French Committee is notoriously pro-intervention.

The ALRC is an advisory body and has no direct role in implementing its recommendations. There is no requirement for the Australian Government to respond formally to ALRC reports, as is the case in some other countries. Among international law reform agencies, however, the ALRC is considered to have one of the most outstanding records of having recommendations turned into law and policy. In the case of genetic testing and screening, for example, the insurance industry, laboratories, the National Health and Medical Research Council (NHMRC), employer groups, and other major players were prompted to review and revise their own policies and practices both during and after an ALRC Inquiry. It appears, therefore, that the ALRC is Australia's major facilitator of consensus in controversial matters. In spite of this fact, some of the Australian authors question and criticize some key recommendations made by the Inquiry. This resistance must be addressed in the future public debate.

This volume makes an important contribution to the global governance of genetic testing and screening, because its authors have illuminated some of the most controversial aspects of this new technology. The chapters describe a country focused on itself, preparing for the major changes that lie ahead. Genetic testing and screening, especially of stem cells/embryos and of healthy individuals, will play a major role in the emergent proteomics period, the second phase of the bio-era. But the authors have also depicted a second, perhaps less aggressive, discourse that addresses the will to know, the necessity to collect data and samples in order to understand what is going on in cells or genes, to anticipate risks, to avoid risks, and to prepare for the worse by designing the best strategies. These concerns take another turn in the conclusive part of the book, which discusses the theoretical possibility that genetic testing and screening might also respond to the practices of a culture that has adopted biomedical analysis as a form of quest about itself. And it might be that this medical quest is related to a need for self-knowledge and ethical practices capable of bringing about a new form of self-governance, a personal politics of the care of the self.

NOTES

1 Here and in the following chapters the expression "genetic testing and screening" is used as a singular noun. Some authors use the expression "genetic testing" and "genetic screening" respectively indicating a practice that targets the individual and social groups. However, some of the commentators quoted by the authors exclusively use it as a plural noun.

2 In this volume the notion "new genetics" is put in inverted commas to underline its controversial meaning. Opinions differ as to what extent genetic science has reached a new level of knowledge. To some commentators and scientists this expression highlights a shift that has occurred in scientific practices leading from gene structures to gene and protein expressions. According to this assumption, "new genetics" results from a complex knowledge assemblage that combines different scientific and technological fields (see chapter 2 for more details). In addition, the editor has decided to adopt the term "healthcare" instead of "health care." The latter remains unaltered in quotations and references. Finally, a possible spelling conflict between the terms "centre" and "center" (American spelling) has been avoided by generally using the term "centre" but keeping the American spelling in quotation marks and references.

I. POSITIONING

MICHELA BETTA

FROM DESTINY TO FREEDOM? ON HUMAN NATURE AND LIBERAL EUGENICS IN THE AGE OF GENETIC MANIPULATION

1. THE REVOLUTION AND ITS REPERCUSSIONS

In his book on the fears plaguing the European cultures and societies between the 14th and 18th centuries, the French historian Jean Delumeau argues that the French Revolution would not have paved the way into the future or permanently removed the old fears from the collective mentality if it had not been progressively overcome by an economic and technological revolution (*si elle n'avait pas été progressivement doublée par une révolution économique et technique*[1]). A crucial aspect emerges from this quotation: The idea and belief that political transformations precede technological and scientific transformations, or that political changes create the conditions for their development and implementation. Historians have the inclination to read past epochs moving from codes and discourses embedded in political contexts and strategies. They tend, in other words, to read the past moving from one point, identified by them as a (revolutionary/epistemological) caesura, towards the present time, from which they write their facts. Such an approach is rooted in an understanding of scientific and technological changes as derivatives from political pragmatism. To this methodology the idea of progress is fundamental. It goes back to the 18th century. There the idea of a new society emerged which was considered capable of turning its own fate into a progressive improvement through rationality (enlightenment), revolution (Marxism), or "social evolutionism"[2] (liberalism). The validity of this grid has been recently questioned by an analytical approach that avoids describing history as a continuity of interconnected events initiated by political actions unavoidably leading to our present condition, and regulated by intelligible metaphysical rules. Fundamental to this analytic is the idea that people are embedded in a cultural rather than political system made of different fields of knowledge, also called codes.

> The fundamental codes of a culture—those governing its language, its schemas of perception, its exchange, its techniques, its values, the hierarchy of its practices—

Michela Betta (ed.), The moral, social, and commercial imperatives of genetic testing and screening. The Australian case, 1–24.

establish for every man, from the very first, the empirical order with which he will be dealing and within which he will be at home.[3]

Not only are citizens expected to respond to these codes but also policy-makers and scientists. Their actions—daily negotiations, political strategies, scientific practices, and technological projects—constitute the social field of a specific time. This empirical order becomes visible through scientific objects that enter the social and political space, irrevocably changing it, and with it also human *nature*. But these objects do not lie around waiting to be picked up by a political institution.

Since the 1970s we have been witnessing a transformation of social and cultural codes through practices that have introduced a different way of understanding our body, reproductive freedom, health and healthcare, family relations, and new forms of hazards and risks. All those social objects are embedded in an increasingly knowledge-oriented culture. Such a transformation has been made possible by a scientific and technological shift that transposed the conception of human life from the body to the laboratory. Some observers speak of *the new genetics* to describe a convergence of knowledge fields such as biology, computer science, chemistry, physics, and engineering. This collaboration has undoubtedly strengthened science and technology, leading to their intellectual supremacy in social and commercial fields.

The chapters in this book set out to study some of the effects caused by genetic testing and screening of adults for genetic risks, of criminals or suspected criminals, of children searching for their "natural" parents, of workers exposed to high-risk environments, and of ethnic communities in which some members carry specific disease-causing genes. An analysis such as this, however, cannot start without first initiating a broader reflection on the practice of genetic testing in the very early stages of human life, and the values we attach to it. This analysis will help us to identify the criteria that form our decisions and practices as well as social policies. By testing and screening during the early stages of human life, we mean conducting research on embryos or stem cells and pre-implantation genetic diagnosis (PGD). These two practices represent the initial stage of more extended testing and screening programmes.

This chapter will therefore deal with the controversy surrounding the effects of the "new genetics" on people, social relationships, and political institutions. It will investigate two discursive lines. The first questions whether recent claims for a more relaxed attitude towards liberal eugenics or freedom of choice are consistent with the cultural practices of our time, and therefore justified; the second investigates whether the criticism with which those claims have been rejected is consistent enough to justify a moral distinction between the logic of genetic enhancements and the logic of healing. Defenders of the first argument reject any form of genetic manipulation as an alien and external intervention. Their opponents argue that there is no moral difference between genetic treatment and eugenics/enhancement. But this debate is interesting for another reason. It reveals a methodological and practical gap between claims formulated by Australian and American philosophers and social scientists on the one hand, and claims coming from Europe on the other. It seems that diverging moral and ethical trajectories have been drawn with regard to fundamental questions related to reproductive rights, freedom of choice, and perception of personal health. The debate reflects two different positions and confronts us with two ways of articulating ethical and moral reasoning. The first is ascribed to traditional moral philosophy, while the second follows the principles of practical ethics. The general impression, however, is that we have irrevocably entered the post-metaphysical age of ethical reasoning. Such a shift seems to have been caused by the emergence of a different mode of understanding individuals' needs and expectations in a culture based on *diagnostic knowledge*. The following sections will investigate whether the language and reasoning of practical ethics are more successful in guiding individuals and regulative policies than classic moral philosophy.

2. CLASH OF CULTURES

In his 2001 book, *The Future of Human Nature*, the German philosopher Jürgen Habermas[4] attempts to come to terms with the fact that empirical thinking has taken precedence over theoretical reasoning. He speaks of an "acceleration of social changes" caused by technology and science that is escaping not only political control but also the guidance of old moral imperatives. He says: "[D]eontological theories after Kant may be very good at explaining how to ground and apply moral norms; but they still are unable to answer the question of why we should be moral *at all*."[5] What is the moral philosopher Habermas worrying about? In this text he tackles issues related to embryonic/stem cell research and PGD. This is new territory for Habermas, and his limited knowledge of the "facts" influences his reasoning, sometimes leading him to too hasty conclusions. The striking aspect of the ethical controversy surrounding those issues is undeniably the line dividing the European moral philosophical tradition and the practical ethical reasoning coming from Australia and America. The practical approach reveals a more flexible or liberal attitude towards genetic testing and screening and embryonic research. The divide is deeper than the balanced language game of morality seems to suggest. A 2001 colloquium in New York between Habermas and some of his transatlantic colleagues failed to resolve differences over theoretical and practical understandings of the consequences of genetic engineering.[6] They failed even in the rather modest attempt to reach, at least, a general consensus. Habermas could not convince his colleagues that stem cell research, PGD, and related forms of diagnosis and testing undermine the centrality of egalitarian universalism. His "failure," however, reveals a controversy and lack of communication that goes beyond philosophical terms. Habermas could but deepen the divide through his strong criticism: "This mode of undermining is as much loaded with practical consequences as it is free of theory."[7]

Old Europe is struggling in taking control over the moral debate. The fact that Habermas "responds" to reflections and claims formulated by Australian and American theoreticians is more than symbolic. In spite of the current insurmountable obstacles lying between old and new philosophical schools, Habermas refuses to consider his position as a sort of *Kulturkampf*: "I am not taking the attitude of a culture critic opposed to welcome advances of scientific knowledge."[8] What then are the causes that make morality and justice take their "own separate path from ethics"? To grasp the terms of this shift, it is necessary to dwell for a while on Habermas's position and to contrast it with the stance taken by Australian and American philosophers and social scientists. This controversy will help us to understand the degree of difficulty surrounding *diagnostic knowledge* as the ground on which genetic testing and screening and the related therapeutic and genetic-counselling society[9] are founded. The approach our culture will develop towards prenatal life will reflect the attitude towards, and values attached to, genetic testing and screening of adults.

Habermas sets a fundamental moral premise around which coheres his judgement on matters related to the "new genetics." The premise is that we constitute ourselves as subjects through transsubjective powers that install interpersonal relationships. These relationships rely on a natural foundation of the self-understanding of persons acting responsibly. It follows that there exists a correlation between the *grown* and the *made* or between the *nature we are* and the social equipment we give ourselves.[10] Now, according to Habermas, genetic engineering has invaded these two territories blurring the dividing line. Three consequences follow from this transformation:

1. The dynamic of the technological development is such that consensus cannot be asked or granted before genetic intervention takes place. It follows that consensus, which is one of the central regulatory categories of personal and public relationships, must be presumed. But although this consensus can be presumed in "the logic of healing,"[11] it might be refused when genetic manipulation has taken the form of an alteration of a personal genetic code to satisfy parental desires rather than to redress a contingency (illness). In other words: The moral distinction between prevention and eugenics is about to be disintegrated.
2. The problem is not an "overgeneralization of biological insights" but rather the weakening of the "sociomoral restrictions."[12] This weakening results from the powerful relation between three fields: Research reliant on capital markets for funding, pharmabusiness, and industrial location policies,[13] which put pressure on governments for medical and economic reasons.
3. The need to regulate "genetic engineering" must be addressed by a constitutional state in a pluralistic society that recognizes the fundamental principle of egalitarian universalism and personal freedom to "successfully be oneself." This freedom is rooted in a profound individual interest "in the success of one's own life project."[14]

3. PROGRAMMED PERSONS AND LIBERAL EUGENICS

Habermas assumes that interpersonal relationships emerge from communicative practices that people must intersubjectively share. These communicative practices install us as actors and agents who recognize the other's unique dignity. The communicative action that creates interpersonal relationships turns the actor or agent of the action into the first person of the communication process, and the other into the second person of the process. On this communicative level, an equal distribution of the communicative resources of the life world takes place that replicate themselves without the intervention of third agents or external forces. Habermas describes this form of communication as the "immanence of their autopoiesis."[15] The term autopoiesis describes the ability of things to replicate themselves without external intervention, that is to be self-referential. An example here could be cells or the genes whose differentiation processes seem to be governed by complex inner systems.

In acting according to the principles of equal universalism we express respect towards the personal freedom and dignity of every other individual. This dignity results from the wish to live according to a project grounded on the premise that each of us is the sole organizer of their own existence. The essential aspect here is that we identify ourselves with our life plan "without shame" because we understand ourselves as members of the human species who share "equal birth" or the life of "persons of equal birth." According to Habermas, this condition is now undermined by practices that allow an "auto-transformation of the species" through "self-instrumentalization" and "self-optimization." Programming genetic engineering would destroy the ability of the individual to understand oneself as equal to others in terms of his creation and birth.

> The programmed person, being no longer certain about the contingency of the natural roots of her life history, may feel the lack of a mental precondition for coping with the moral expectations to take, even if only in retrospect, the sole responsibility for her own life.[16]

What Habermas criticizes here is shared authorship over the biological composition of a person whose genetic structure was manipulated at an embryonic stage and allowed by new eugenics policies. He, therefore, unambiguously rejects the effects of "liberal eugenics" or, as he polemically says, its "programming enterprise." The term liberal eugenics has been disseminated and defended by Australian-born Nicholas Agar.[17] It describes a positive attitude towards genetic manipulation or enhancement. This is understood as equal to social manipulation (education and socialization). But before entering into that debate, I see here the need to further qualify Habermas's position with regard to what he calls genetic engineering. Habermas differentiates between "clinical attitude" and "deliberate quality control."[18] The clinical attitude is a relationship that we install with a human life incapable of giving personal consent for the changes that we, according to the logic of healing, consider necessary to improve or even make the existence of a potential human being possible. In this relationship, according to Habermas, we treat the specific human life—prepersonal human life, foetus, newborn—as a "second person." The person carrying out the treatment or the decision becomes the "first person" and he/she may assume that the patient preventatively treated would have given, and will later give, consent. But the logic of healing can also justify a dispositive that destroys that same prenatal life under certain circumstances. This is the case when genetic weaknesses cause insurmountable suffering for the future person and his/her parents as to make the elimination of that future life morally justified. Habermas is repositioning the compass, as, in his reasoning, negative eugenics emerges as a practice that reveals compassion, while positive eugenics or genetic enhancement is understood as a sign of power and contempt. Annette F. Timm has pointed out that this position underlines nothing but that "the true danger lies in the goal of positive eugenics."[19] In the past, negative eugenics had unanimously been condemned for the practices of physical elimination of "abnormal life." But now it seems morally more acceptable than the politics of enhancement through a genetic recomposition of the genome. The shift emerging from this new state of things is striking, and Habermas must undoubtedly take it for granted that it is rooted in a political order characterized by the lack of state coercion and racially biased practices, and the force of the laws that protect us from abuses. But Habermas does not engage in a debate concerning the new institutions that will guarantee fair decision-making processes.

Interestingly, Agar works from the same premises that genetic enhancement or liberal eugenics will have to be rooted in a regulated system. The label "liberal" works here as a guarantee that only those choices will be permitted that guarantee the absolute freedom of the persons to come. "I suggest a test to assess whether a particular use of enhancement technologies reduces real freedom."[20] Real freedom is reduced when the child is incapable of leading a successful life when his/her values oppose those of his/her enhancers. A judiciary system will have to then assess the parents' true intentions at the time they launch their application for genetic enhancement. Both authors believe in the protective power of a legal system rooted in a social and political context that guarantees freedom of choice, but poses some limits to private wishes. But how can a similar level of trust in the regulatory power of legal devices lead to so divergent a position in terms of freedom of choice and the distribution of genetic goods? The deliberate quality control emerging from genetic screening, according to Habermas, installs a relationship that treats life as a product. "This new structure of attribution results from obliterating the boundary between persons and things,"[21] where the person carrying out the intervention plays the role of a "third person" between parents and the (potential) child, bringing asymmetry in the communicative action. The uniqueness of each individual represents the ethical ground on which freedom is based; this is so because each individual is master over their own life project, which, again, rests on an unmodifiable genome.

According to Habermas and the European tradition from which he is articulating his passionate position, it is the equality of birth that makes us equal individuals whose lives have not been manipulated or manufactured by third parties.

The notion of being equal in birth and different in our attempts to successfully organize our own life projects gives moral significance to our life. Genetic screening, genetic manipulation, and genetic recomposition violate, Habermas argues, ethical freedom or the "ethical virgin soil"[22] on which the self-understanding of the species is erected. The major task that a constitutional state in a pluralistic society has to guarantee is therefore a regulation of the "diagnostic penetration and therapeutic control of human nature." This is the major critical point upon which the European moral philosopher moves against the philosophy of choice, alternatively called liberal eugenics.

> The program of liberal eugenics blinds itself to this task because it ignores the biotechnological dedifferentiation of the modes of actions.[23]

Here Habermas criticizes the terminology and position taken by Nicholas Agar in his 1998 article, *Liberal Eugenics*, but his reproach does not seem to have convinced his counterpart. Instead, it seems that the way philosophical and social scientists reason about the issues at stake differs according to their geographical location. Habermas's argument might give the impression that he and the philosophical tradition he belongs to is reacting against cultural patterns that have emerged in a different geographical context. But what are the terms of the controversy? Habermas thinks that through genetic manipulation the destruction of the ideal that we are born equal is made possible. This aspect acquires additional importance when the manipulation targets the stem cell line and the genome, and becomes irrevocable. Irrevocability undermines the power of "revisionary self-understanding" or the "reversibility to interpersonal relationships"[24] and cannot be compared, Habermas says, with what Agar calls social enhancement or manipulation through education. We find a similar sense of irreversibility when a disease is diagnosed for which no cure or treatments are given. The effects that the irreversibility of knowledge can have on people are comparable with the feeling of being locked in a genetic programme designed by science. Similarly to Habermas, the Americans, Buchanan, Brock, Daniels, and Walker, speak of being "locked in" by "parental choice"[25] but, interestingly enough, their concern is expressed exclusively against "communitarian eugenics," rather than liberal eugenics.

Habermas argues that the fate of socialization can somehow be modified through rejection of the skills, or refutation to live according to the social identity acquired in the social environment and provided by parents, family, school, tertiary education, and private tutoring. During the 2001 colloquium in New York, some critics rejected Habermas's interpretation arguing that a person whose genome was manipulated at an early stage could make the enhancement obsolete through an intervention that reinstalls the genetic traits originally eradicated by manipulation. This counterargument sounds a bit too extravagant, and less practical than the rejection of the effects of socialization. Agar's response is more articulated and challenging. He tackles three aspects of Habermas's analysis and deconstructs their assumed superior morality. Agar embeds his social approach in what he calls the "nurture principle": "If we are permitted to produce certain traits by modifying our children's environment, then we are also permitted to produce them by modifying their genome."[26] In saying this Agar reiterates the argument developed in an earlier publication about the impossibility of morally distinguishing educational from genetic manipulation or therapeutics from eugenic intervention. "Short of an argument that exposes a significant difference between the two sorts of traits, we should think of both types of modification in similar ways."[27] Responding to this challenge, Habermas reproaches the defenders of liberal eugenics for not yet having offered a moral justification for their request to allow genetic manipulation, and for having manipulated the language game of morality. Eugenic manipulation, in changing the language game, poses a fundamental problem, and, "therefore, liberal eugenics provokes the question of how to value morality as a whole."[28] What Habermas is suggesting here is that those who speak in favour of liberal eugenics are acting outside the limits of morality, directly or indirectly pushing the line of "globalized neoliberalism" as an explosive alliance between "Darwinism and free trade ideology."[29]

To this criticism Agar replies with three underlying aspects. First, he thinks that in reiterating the importance of the natural/genetic goods Habermas takes a stance that relies on "a genetic determinist view of development." Agar draws here on David Wasserman's criticism. Wasserman argues that Habermas's notion that educational manipulation or intervention is morally different because here the parents need the cooperation of their children, whereas genetic enhancement is a unilateral intervention, relies on an incorrect assumption about the "nature" of a child–parent relationship. "To the extent that parents shape the character and abilities of their already-born children, they do so largely at a time when those children are too young to contest their influence in any coherent or effectual way."[30] To illustrate the limited value of Habermas's position Agar defends the notion that genetic enhancement can be "less unilateral" as children and adolescents have "a say in whether the influence of the inserted gene gets matched with the environment." In fact, children or adolescents who have been receiving intelligence enhancement could refuse to go to school, or avoid using the potentialities by denying their expression, as often happens with educational enhancement, when young adults choose a different profession from the one planned and (expensively) paid for by their parents. Such rebellion could be flanked by additional, more technological, ways of limiting the expression of the inserted genes or of the enhancement through "direct control" over the gene promoters that serve as the on/off switch for its action. Through genetic intervention, the promoter could be delayed, or designed to activate itself only when a specific chemical is consumed, for example. Thus the carrier of inserted genes could decide whether or when they get activated.[31]

Second, Agar argues that by refusing to see the potentiality of the new genetics and new eugenics, Habermas behaves like those adults who, in spite of knowing—through genetic tests and screening—that their genetic structure predisposes them to particular health risks, maintain a fatalistic attitude towards their health and refuse to adapt to their status by following a special diet or eliminating known risks. "In thinking this way, they make the same mistake as Habermas."[32] The third level of the controversy is given by Habermas's reasoning that genetic manipulation or enhancement equates an interior intrusion, whose moral value is fundamentally different from an exterior intrusion through education or environmental measures. Agar rejects this moral distinction arguing that exercise can help a person to become a champion, but only if a certain genetic predisposition is given; or when a certain predisposition is given, one will turn into a champion only if the right exercise and environment are provided. The two environments have to be understood as morally equal. Accordingly, Agar argues in his 1998 article that "both genetic engineering and parent-administered environmental engineering by education or nutrition are externally driven attempts to improve capacities."[33] In his more recent book, Agar once again condemns the dichotomy between internally and externally driven enhancements, adding, however, a differentiation between internal effect and external intervention. Whatever type of intervention we pursue, its effects are internal in so far as they influence the way our genes work. This can happen by changing the letter of the DNA, by nutrition, or diet. However, dietary intervention does not change the genes, but "their expression." Agar refers to studies in the course of which it has been demonstrated that breastfeeding can improve the IQ of a person. The mother's milk contains docosahexaenoic acid (DHA), a polyunsaturated fatty acid (absent from cow's milk) that is a fundamental component of the membrane of the cells of the central nervous system, which is considered "to play a role in the transmission of signals within and between neurons." Deprivation of this acid might have some negative influence on our intelligence.[34] A good diet during pregnancy can also influence our genetic patrimony, as it can enhance the development of methylation, a chemical that gets attached to genes, and can therefore effect their expression. These internal effects are caused by external actions.

> When a genetic engineer adds DNA to an embryo, she introduces into the inside of an organism something that originates from outside of it. This manner of exterior intrusion takes place earlier than the exterior intrusion of an instructor teaching Latin vocabulary.[35]

Agar rejects Habermas's distinction between the morally acceptable exterior intervention and the supposed immoral internal intervention as an either/or approach that does not "match the reality of human development."

The controversy becomes more polarized when the debate targets the question of whether freedom is violated (Habermas) or reinforced (Agar) by the "new genetics" and liberal eugenics.

4. FREEDOM OR DESTINY?

Genetic screening and testing from the earliest stages of human development, and the knowledge and prediction of risk that they insert into social life, create the conditions for manipulating the individuals' genetic equipment. This practice is believed to influence the way people understand themselves, instilling a powerful relationship that irrevocably modifies nature. "Alien determination" is the term that Habermas uses to refer to a person's alteration of natural foundation by genetic engineers. Some critics reply here that a genetic alteration or manipulation does not intrinsically impede a person's self-understanding as a full member of the moral community. To this argument, Habermas responds that the question is not to be posed in terms of identity, but in terms of the self-evaluation of a "prenatally induced" fracture of an individual life development in so far as the person subjected to manipulation must share authorship about his/her life project. Habermas speaks of "persons of equal birth" to underline the equality of the condition of our existence. By birth he means, of course, not the way we come into the world, which could differ according to specific situations (Caesarean or vaginal birth), but the way we come into existence (conception). The expression "alien determination" is interesting, because it reminds us of a different historical situation. In his treatise *The Social Contract* (1762) Jean-Jacques Rousseau opens his reflections with the striking statement: "Man was born free, and he is everywhere in chains." In speaking of the "irrevocability of knowledge" through genetic manipulation, Habermas turns the terms of reference upside down. It seems now that man is born with a predetermined (genetic) destiny, which, according to his line of reasoning, means unfree.

> The danger for such a person is that she is no longer capable of understanding herself as the undivided author of her own life, and thus feels bound by the chains of the previous generation's genetic decisions.[36]

The fundamental change takes place between identity emerging from a given condition established by "nature," and identity emerging from a technological act. Habermas disqualifies the technological intervention as alienating the personal self-understanding of the particular life project of every single human being. In saying this he takes a stance in favour of human nature to which he seems to assign an a priori and absolute moral value. Consequently, human nature is to be understood as an unalterable reality that emerges from contingency—the encounter of sperm and egg (gametes), their fusion, and the resulting cells and embryo that will become a foetus, and finally a person (after birth) when certain conditions are given. Habermas may be right in noting the possibility that a person might feel "ashamed" when informed that he/she is the result of a genetic manipulation. Especially when such alteration ensues from the capricious will of the parents, rather than from a (medical) necessity, causing the young adolescent to have blond instead of brown hair, dark instead of blue eyes, resistance to fatigue instead of being subjected to biorhythms, with a strong memory instead of the usual ability to remember things. This "prenatal distribution of genetic resources" represents to Habermas a "redefinition of opportunities" that fixes the path of the individual's future life. Prior to manipulation, that future person would have had the choice to realize or not realize the opportunity given to him/her by nature according to his/her own life plan or choice. In Habermas's scheme the choices of the future persons are opposed to the choices of their parents and third persons qualified here as an alien intervention. He highlights the centrality of human nature and assigns a high moral value to a person's genetic structure, presupposing that a future adolescent will weigh it in the same way as the present generation does now. But who knows whether the genetic equipment of an individual will play any role as an identity-shaping device in the 23rd century? Indeed, there might be other criteria for the definition of uniqueness or belonging.

Habermas has not been able to offer any substantial argument that future generations will measure their levels of freedom by whether their DNA has been manipulated or not. Nor did the baby boomers regard the levels of our own freedom to author our own lives to have been significantly altered by the fact that our parents allowed third persons to vaccinate us. Insisting on the centrality of human nature, understood here as an unaltered genome, might however also lead to practices that Habermas himself would reject. Scientific studies of genes and DNA have increased awareness that genes and proteins might play a more fundamental role in human life than previously assumed. This may lead to the feeling that they have some influence on some of our actions and decisions. It is possible that this idea of the genes working on us might make us think that it is the genes that make us act unlawfully and cause harm to others. The risk could be that we overload the genes with responsibility for our actions. This means that the genes or our human nature could be understood as the catalyst that makes us do ugly things. In addition, the idea that we are what our genetic equipment is could also undermine our understanding of personal freedom. As Buchanan et al. express it: "The fear is that an increasing knowledge of how genes influence human behavior will undermine our conception of ourselves as free."[37] If I am guided by my own genes I have no choice and my destiny is inscribed in my genetic fate.

Habermas has chosen a risky line of reasoning indeed. The risk is that we become genetic determinists in our understanding of human nature if we place too great a moral value on what has been transmitted from generation to generation. It seems therefore that Agar has formulated a more accessible idea of what freedom might be in the age of genetic manipulation. "Goods of genetic engineering must be allocated to an individual in a way that improves prospects associated with all possible life plans—most especially the worst potential life plans."[38] Agar does not recriminate about interventions or enhancements that might increase intellectual abilities, the senses, or resistance to an illness. Habermas sees here a form of paternalistic control, but his criticism perhaps arises from a misunderstanding. In fact, he assumes that Agar and other representatives of liberal eugenics are open to every form of intervention. This interpretation, however, reveals a lack of patience, which is perhaps due to the fear that manipulation can turn into discriminated elimination. This seems to be a reflex originating from past evil. But fear alone cannot be the leading principle in the 21st century. Now, it seems that Agar's principle of nurture is more striking than Habermas's principle of the ethics of the species. Habermas considers everything that is not embedded in the principle of healing (treatment of illness) to be a violation of personal freedom, because we will not be able to understand ourselves as free individuals once we know that our genome has been manufactured or otherwise manipulated by a genetic engineer. But this verdict does not address many possibilities opened up by the "new genetics." Nor does it recognize that the idea of avoiding diseases or increasing the quality of life just might turn out to incense popular images about the ways that we want to live, threatening, according to Agar,

> to smuggle into individual choices substantive views about human worth. If so, citizens will end up being engineered in accordance with a dominant set of values after all, and the new eugenics will collapse into the eugenics of old.[39]

Agar argues that the protection of a child's right to an open future is equivalent to an obligation to "maximize real freedom." This means that whatever changes the parents think appropriate must be such that they guarantee the child's ability to choose a life plan completely different from the one the parents had envisaged for him/her. To guarantee this Agar differentiates between genetic goods that can be understood as "positional value" and genetic goods that are of "independent value." A positional value derives, for example, from a decision to add centimetres to height, whereas independent values could derive from an engineered resistance to flu. Positional values derive from a "winner-takes-all" mentality that reduces life to a competition, and therefore Agar suggests restrictions on the enhancement options parents will be able to choose from: "I propose that we limit the kinds of competitions that prospective parents can participate in."[40]

Habermas thinks that we belong to a generation where the *grown* and the *made* are two separate realities. However, it might be that the feeling of being "different" disappears as soon as genetic manipulation becomes a general or uniform practice conducted within the limits determined by the governing laws—much as, in the past, vaccines and vaccination became common practices. This is an interesting comparison because it reveals, more than other practices, the fragility of Habermas's methodological premise. The logic behind the practice of vaccination is that the body becomes infected with a virus in order to activate the memory of the immune system and prepare it for the dangers and health risks caused by infections. How can we describe this practice? It is a matter of fact that it cannot be ascribed to the realm of negative eugenics, as it does not eliminate (prenatal) life or suppress genetic threats in order to avoid later health hazards. Does it represent an enhancement, considering the weaknesses of human nature? Strictly speaking vaccines do not represent an enhancement either, because they potentially cause sickness, as the injected virus does. In fact, it seems that vaccines are posited between negative and positive eugenics. They are a cultural strategy that has helped the human species to survive for decades, defending itself against nature's challenges by adopting the principle of prevention through adaptation. Clearly, vaccines are not comparable with genetic manipulation of the germ-line cells. Nevertheless, their effects extend beyond the limits of a single generation; they are potentially transmittable to ensuing generations. What we transfer as parents is a healthy life. We pass on health that has been made possible through vaccines. However, in our hard times, vaccines alone cannot guarantee total health any more. Personal responsibility or rationality is also needed. Vaccines work best when they play a supportive role in a lifestyle guided by precaution and responsible behaviour. We realize what consequences a lack of caution and responsibility in matters concerning life and health can have when we look at figures of children born already infected by the deadly HIV virus.

This is an aspect neglected by Agar. It seems that genetic enhancement may alleviate the need for people to behave rationally; as risks are eliminated, so too is the need to be concerned about the way people lead their lives. Genetic enhancement seemingly promises to free the individuals from the responsibility for both themselves and their offspring. This is a crucial change, as people may come to rely on their genes rather than on their rationality, thus turning into little machines governed by an unknown process, while governments may feel detached from the imperative to provide health assistance and education. In fact, an engineered resistance against, for example, flu can boost our indifference towards particular health risks and increase the tendency to assume a passive attitude towards risks more generally.

One could, of course, reply that enhancing bodily functions through genetic manipulation might free us from some of our more onerous responsibilities and thus open new opportunities for more sophisticated actions. For example, if we become resistant to flu we might expose ourself to cold weather without getting sick. But what sort of benefit can we draw from that? It is a matter of fact that, in the pre-manipulation age, we do not catch a cold as long as we adopt the proper strategies or take good care of ourselves.

Of course, this option is not yet available for dealing with more complex forms of physical debilitation like cancer or Parkinson's. Here, some people seem to be destined to become sick because of a faulty genetic endowment. Genetic manipulation in this case might offer a new chance to live a "normal" life. If so, not to pursue a genetic treatment would be to act irresponsibly towards ourselves, but not towards the next generation, as cancer is not an infection that can be passed on to one's offspring, although the *probability* of hereditary genetic diseases remains. What can be genetically transmitted is a susceptibility or predisposition to cancer. The form of responsibility towards oneself is rooted in the logic of healing. Beyond the therapeutic aims the question of the responsibility turns therefore a bit more difficult. Here genetic enhancement seems to be guided by the principle: "If we can manipulate why not try to?" Any form of genetic manipulation that belongs to this order of things does not seem to enhance responsibility. Is responsibility important? It seems that it is still one of those principles through which we can measure the level of rationality inherent in our actions. Let us suppose that through a genetic enhancement I become very (not only in physical terms) strong—a sort of postmodern Achilles. How am I suppose to be governed and by whom? Undoubtedly, only by those who are as strong as I am or even stronger. This hierarchy would be ad infinitum and necessitate a decision to stop enhancing people beyond a certain degree. But who establishes the ultimate level? Mythology has avoided this dilemma by leaving a small part of Achilles' body vulnerable, and that will play a role when rational self-governance fails. Will we have to do the same in order to keep a minimal level of responsibility towards ourselves? A minimal moral standard towards society?

5. THE LANGUAGE OF THE MORAL GAME

Haberma's *The Future of Human Nature* is interesting for many reasons, one of which is the language he uses to advance his argument. Three terms or expressions especially deserve our attention: *species* and *species-ethics*, *pre-personal life* and its *preconditions*, and, of course, *human nature*. At first glance, they seem innocuous but upon closer examination they reveal another shifting of the compass' coordinates.

5.1 Species and Pre-personal Life

In Habermas's reasoning, the notion of the *species* appears more important than that of humanity; the latter term is mentioned only once in his text. To speak of species is not that self-evident. What we are witnessing here is the entrance of a category used in biological and scientific contexts into the philosophical and political discourse. But is it not a bit too risky to focus on the term "species" to justify the moral superiority of natural life compared to manipulated life? Referring to the genetic manipulation of pre-personal life, Habermas argues that the risks arising from this development can be best judged from the perspective of "the ethical self-understanding of the species." In setting his agenda, Habermas proceeds in a sequential way: He acknowledges the existence of what he calls a pre-personal life that has an ontological value because of its potential to become a future human and member of the species. This respect builds the preconditions of egalitarian universalism that is reflected in what he calls the equality of birth.

5.2 Human Nature

If Habermas's terminology appears a bit too deterministic, Agar's term "liberal eugenics" does not bring the methodological relief required by 21st-century society either. It reminds us of past wrongdoings, of strong political control over individuals and communities, and of the corruption of the scientific spirit. According to Agar and some other theoreticians,[41] the term "liberal eugenics" is embedded in the idea of a liberal society in which individuals are protected by the laws that establish and regulate their positive, individual rights to choose and live the lives they want to live. Agar expressly condemns "old eugenics" for its authoritarianism aimed at producing citizens "out of a single centrally designed mould." Instead, the "distinguishing mark of the new liberal eugenics is state neutrality."[42] This distinction, however, is insufficient to quell fears of a resurgent state authoritarianism. In fact, this terminology seems to emerge from a methodological assumption that reveals a certain automatism in reasoning. It is assumed that the eugenic paroxysms of the past were caused by the state and its biopolitics. A different state structure would therefore lead to different outcomes.

In fact, the interesting aspect is that "liberal eugenics" is a political term, which describes the political context in which scientific and medical practices are embedded. Conversely, "negative and positive eugenics" directly describe those practices. Agar is sensitive enough to avoid mixing up the two levels. In spite of this, however, his concept is linked to a precise political system. How can we define liberal systems? No single nation in the west would currently describe its own political system as illiberal. Is this a sufficient guarantee of personal freedom? This is not a rhetorical question. The term "liberal" evokes the idea that the individual is protected against the clutches of the state through a legal system that provides a political counterbalance.[43] There is a certain automatism that comes into play as soon as the terms "liberal" or "democratic" are invoked. This automatism is rooted in a general assumption that the legal system provides a balancing control over the political system through the judiciary.

In other words: It is the legal system of human and civic rights that gives sense to the idea of liberal democracies. Alexis de Tocqueville anticipated this condition in his 1835 book *Democracy in America*. There he argues that every sort of problem turns sooner or later into a legal problem. This is a tendency that also characterizes today's modern liberal democracies. It seems, therefore, that Agar's terminology makes sense only in a precise legal system. The basic features of that system were implemented two centuries ago and have been subjected to alteration and adaptation during the last two centuries in order to respond to cultural and scientific advancements. It seems reasonable to argue that the premises of that system rested on human nature as the common basis for its moral and ethical rules translated into laws. It is difficult indeed to imagine another sort of fundament. The claims of individual rights make sense only when they refer to common principles. The common principle is, for example, that our common humanity renders us equal in moral and therefore legal terms. Our personal experiences as members of specific cultures, on the other hand, legitimize claims that we are also different from each other and therefore need to acknowledge cultural differences through personal rights. The legal device called human rights unmistakably reflects this state of things.

If human nature is not the point of reference of liberal eugenics, what is the regulatory element that makes social relationships work and regulatory practices possible? If, as suggested by Agar, the regulative system is based on individual choices, however limited they might be, there is no common point of reference. Individual choice is not common choice. We could consider the freedom of the future/potential person as our point of reference. This seems to be Agar's suggestion. However, in so doing he introduces *potentiality* into the debate, contradicting one of the central assumptions made by the defenders of practical ethics since the mid-1980s. In those days it was argued that potentiality cannot be considered a regulative dimension of ethical issues related to biomedical research. John Harris, one of the most quoted representatives of practical ethics, once replied to the argument of potentiality defended by critics of embryonic research: "We will all, inevitably, die but that is, I suppose, an inadequate reason for treating us now as if we were dead." The Australians, Singer and Well, reinforced that point, arguing that the limits imposed on research because of potentiality are a gesture of authoritarianism. "There is a possibility of something going wrong at every stage, from the production of egg and sperm right through to the time at which there is a rational and self-conscious being."[44]

But the law has never taken potentiality as a regulatory element of social and public life. The only legitimate point of reference of the western legal systems is the person after birth—the rational healthy person who comes into completion at the age of 18. It follows that, if Agar founds his argument in defence of liberal eugenics on the advantages that this might bring to future people, he might run out of discursive munition when it comes to defending his reasoning or defining a framework for imminent manipulation laws. Similarly, the two Habermasian terms, "species" and "prepersonal life," become more problematic as soon as the notion of *human nature* comes into perspective. Habermas is, of course, embedded in a moral philosophical tradition that goes back to Aristotle and Kant, for whom human nature represented something unchangeable, and on which human beings did not have any power at all. The central argument is that human nature, because unchangeable, represents a common element to all human beings, and therefore constitutes the common basis of reference upon which respect and recognition are founded. Here, common sense or rationality becomes the way through which human beings express their universal equality. Starting from here, the genetic foundation or traits of human beings become the physical substrate on which the philosophical and ethical concept of human nature rests.

Habermas's insistence on the centrality of human nature expresses the fears that, as soon as the genetic traits are irrevocably modifiable, the "preconditions" for an understanding of human nature as a regulatory agency that installs a common humanity are lost. Consequently, we would put at risk the cohesive force of this ideal, and with it our ability to understand ourselves as equal and free. To stress the need to retain human nature as the "deontologically protected core of a future person," and to make it inaccessible to bioscience, Habermas reverts to the term "species," through which he hopes to evoke a stronger idea of what we are. In this move he also attempts to denounce negotiations or manoeuvres that try to accommodate technological and scientific advancements.

6. SCIENCE, THE LAW, AND THE INSTITUTIONS OF THE MANIPULATION ERA

Habermas's argumentation coheres around the idea of human nature that can claim moral power because of its immutable character. In the end, he argues that because human nature has always been intangible and untouchable it constitutes the basis of moral theory and a theory of justice. This is something Buchanan et al. have questioned. The American authors argue that a theory that understands justice and morality as derived from a conception of a fixed human nature cannot tell us whether the same justice and morality can allow us to alter our own nature. But Buchanan et al. do not engage in a debate on the common basis upon which the legal system of the past decades rested. Instead, they seem to overestimate trends that have emphasized "particularism" and difference against the egalitarian discourse. They, therefore, appear perhaps a bit too hasty in rejecting human nature by suggesting that it has not constituted an undisputed point of reference for past ethical theory.[45] In opposition to Habermas, however, Buchanan et al. predict that genetics will contribute to reinforce justice and "specifically to bring about a more just society."[46] This would mean that justice would have to include "natural as well as social assets" amongst the goods just institutions are expected to regulate. But the authors go a bit further in predicting that in the manipulation era we will have to "abandon the simple picture of justice being about distributing goods among individuals whose identities are given independently of the process of distribution."[47]

Will this change have consequences for life before birth? What seems indeed inevitable is that such a fundamental change cannot leave untouched the sociopolitical system in which it takes place. One of the consequences of this change will be a different perception of what human nature is. Buchanan et al. assume that genetics will introduce many changes, and consequently that there will be no "single successor to what has been regarded as human nature" till now.[48] But whatever these successors will be, they must posses the strong social cohesive force that characterized the idea of human nature till the 1970s in order to guarantee the functioning of society. Therefore, the question arises now of how to define the non-negotiable common principles on which respect and social relationships will have to rest and the legal system that they will have to refer to. Could this be common rationality? Rationality is what the Roman philosopher Seneca called a god, "a guest in a mortal body."[49] If we do not find a common point of reference, the risk might arise that individuals would not consider or treat each other as moral equals—a danger that Buchanan et al. cannot but think about. The necessity to be rooted in something superior is not satisfied by "genetic equality,"[50] because this principle does not commit us to any legal or ethical responsibility. In the post–human rights era, western countries are struggling to find their permanent centre of gravity.

This question is of fundamental importance. In fact, its definition might change the terms of reference of the institutions that guarantee the functioning of society, such as justice and distributive justice, individual and public responsibility of the agent, and the principle of *primum non nocere*, the obligation to first of all prevent harm. These three institutions represent the core of public and private life, in terms of law, social policies, and politics. The law and policies regulating individual choices and personal rights will therefore be challenged by the "new genetic science." As a consequence, a new political system will emerge from this historical shift.

7. POSITIONING AUSTRALIA IN THE ETHICAL DEBATE ON GENETIC PRENATAL MANIPULATION AND HUMAN NATURE

According to Aitken and Metcalfe (chapter 7), PGD and pre-implantation genetic manipulation (PGM) are currently allowed in Australia, especially to the benefit of a restricted number of families. The manipulation is done with the intent to help families with a history of genetic problems to circumscribe the effects of genetic inheritance. As also described by Palombo and Bhave (chapter 8), in 2003 a Tasmanian couple was given the green light for PGM of their in vitro embryo in order to escape an inherited immune deficiency disorder, the hyperIgM syndrome. The prospective child was to provide a healthy sibling as a bone marrow transplant donor for an affected brother. Australia can be considered the country that not only initiated a controversial bioethical debate on life before birth but also developed and implemented scientific practices targeting prenatal life. This goes back to the 1970s. Most of this credit goes to two scientists who worked in the same university, although in different areas of expertise. I am speaking here of the philosopher Peter Singer and of the embryologist Alan Trounson, who both worked at Monash University in Melbourne in the State of Victoria. In 1979 Peter Singer published his well-known book *Practical Ethics* (1979, Cambridge University Press), which repositioned the ethical discourse on fundamental questions related to life and death, animal rights, and the introduction of suffering as a moral category capable of providing moral justification for the elimination of human life before and after birth.

In the 1970s and 1980s the debate on practical ethics and bioethics was conducted above all in Australia and America and to some extent in the United Kingdom, although moral discussions in England always tend to revolve around utilitarianism rather than moral relativism. At that time, the rest of Europe was in the dark in relation to the new trends in the ethical debate on life and personal freedom that were taking place elsewhere, and which announced a shift towards a post-metaphysical approach to those questions. This debate is well known, and need not be reconstructed here. In the late 1970s, however, Australia was avant-garde not only in the ethical debate, but also in the scientific field, namely in the emerging biomedical laboratories. In the late 1960s Alan Trounson was one of the world-leading experts in animal in-vitro fertilization, as he managed to understand the sheep's ovulatory cycle and control the production of eggs by measuring the level of the egg-ripening hormones. In the early 1970s Trounson started working with the obstetrician Carl Wood, who was also located at Monash University in Melbourne. In 1973 Wood managed to produce the first IVF pregnancy, but because the embryo did not live beyond a few days,[51] this event remained unknown to the world. Trounson and Wood, however, produced the third IVF baby worldwide. The first was Louise Brown, born in London in 1978 as the result of the scientific efforts of the embryologist Robert Edwards and the gynaecologist Patrick Steptoe. In 1983 Trounson reported the birth of the first baby from a frozen embryo. Trouson was also the first scientist who used the technique of embryo biopsy by which a cell is removed from an eight-cell embryo to test for genetic defects.[52] Genetic testing and screening in the prenatal phase, also called PGD, is therefore a technology that has been developed and implemented in Australia.

Since then much has happened in terms of scientific achievements, legal regulations, and reorganization of the medical profession. And if the English scientists were the first in the IVF reproductive laboratories, the United Kingdom did not play a role in the second scientific wave concerning the stem cells. In fact, in 1998, exactly 20 years after the birth of the first laboratory child, Trounson and his Melbourne-based team were one of the three international scientific groups who identified human embryonic stem cells. The two other groups were located in the United States and led by James Thomson of the University of Wisconsin, and John Gearhart of Hopkins University in Baltimore.[53] Australia has also demonstrated an impressive productive energy in legislative terms, by the successful attempts to regulate and modernize the legal discourse and introduce a new dispositive into the emerging new medicine. In 1984 the State of Victoria passed the first bill in the world that sanctioned the treatment of in vitro embryos. In 1987 the State of Victoria passed an Amendment Act to respond to new research efforts. The first European law comparable with the 1984 bill and the 1987 amendment was the British Human Fertilisation and Embryology Act, which came into force in 1990. These scientific and legislative initiatives show that Australia has been extremely successful in paving the way towards the society of the 21st century. In the international debate on human nature and genetic manipulation, Australia is again part of the mainstream. This is not only because Australia is again articulating a new frontier through the debate on liberal eugenics but also because this country's entire approach towards medicine, health, and life is informed by the notion that prevention is better than cure. It is no wonder therefore that, with such a theoretical and scientific background, Australia is again a leading country in the genetic screening and testing technology.

And the chapters in Part II, *The Australian Case*, demonstrate how advanced the discussion and the policies already are. The Australian Law Reform Commission, perhaps the most prestigious regulatory dispositive the country has got to regulate technological advancements, social expectations, and modernization of its legislative tools, has already paved the way to some fundamental changes in terms of the legitimacy of such new technology. But also the legal, ethical, educational, and, of course, scientific conversations and discourses are already part of the quotidian life, and the following chapters on the risks of genetic determinism, paternity testing, workplace-related testing, genetic databases and migration, genetic education, and the health imperative are testimony of the advanced level of the public debate. The Australian scientists do not contest the potentialities inherent in the genetic testing and screening technology, but they do insist on the necessity to mitigate genetic determinism by strengthening the Kantian moral imperative according to which human beings are always ends of, never means to, something. They therefore warn that the technological fascination must not gain control over fundamental questions like inclusion, information, freedom of choice, and protection of the most vulnerable members of society.

One aspect that characterizes the Australian way of life is its preparedness to question given rules as soon as new options or possibilities become available. This reveals the innate exploratory style that governs the people and policies of this country, which, however, if it was guided by sole enthusiasm or entrepreneurial energy, could expose social life to risky enterprises. Undoubtedly, the most obvious virtue that ultramodern countries have to cultivate is the ability to maintain the fundamental and universal principles that govern cultural and social belonging intact by making them flexible. Only in this way will those countries be capable of properly reacting in case the new turns out to be ugly or even nasty.

NOTES

1. Delumeau, J. 1978. *LA PEUR en Occident. XIVe–XVIIIe siècles. Une cite assiégée*. Paris: Fayard.
2. Giddens, A. 1984. *The Constitution of Society: Outline of the Theory of Structuration*. Berkeley and Los Angeles, CA: University of California Press.
3. Foucault, M. 1994. *The Order of Things: An Archaeology of the Human Sciences*. New York: Vintage Book. [Les mots et les choses. 1966. Paris: Editions Gallimard]. xx.
4. Habermas, J. 2003. *The Future of Human Nature*. London: Polity Press in association with Blackwell. [*Die Zukunft der menschlichen Natur. Auf dem Weg zu einer liberalen Eugenik?* Frankfurt: Suhrkamp, 2001.] Interestingly, the title of the English version excludes the question that torments Habermas: Are we moving towards liberal eugenics? but it includes a postscript, missing in the German version, that reflects the dramatic tone of the debate between moral and practical philosophy.

[5] Ibid., 4.
[6] The colloquium on Law, Philosophy, and Social Theory was led by Ronald Dworkin and Thomas Nagel at New York University's School of Law.
[7] Habermas, ibid., 95.
[8] Ibid., 12.
[9] Brownlie, J. 2004. Tasting the witches' brew: Foucault and therapeutic Practices. *Sociology* 38(3): 515–532. Clarke, A. 2001. Genetic screening and counselling. In: Kuhse, H. and Singer, P. (eds.), *A Companion to Bioethics*. London: Blackwell, 215–228.
[10] Habermas, ibid., 22–44.
[11] Ibid., 44.
[12] Ibid., 21.
[13] Ibid., 17–18. Habermas, however, does not substantiate this aspect and it will therefore remain undiscussed in the present chapter.
[14] Ibid., 6–15.
[15] Ibid., 24.
[16] Ibid., 81
[17] Agar, N. 1998. Liberal eugenics. *Public Affairs Quarterly* 12(2): 137–155. Text reprinted in Helga Kuhse and Peter Singer (eds.). 1999. *Bioethics*. Malden, MA: Blackwell. Agar, N. 2004. *Liberal Eugenics*. Oxford: Blackwell.
[18] Ibid., 43 and 30, respectively.
[19] Timm, F.A. 2002. From the politics of fertility to liberal eugenics: what lessons can we learn from the case of twentieth-century Germany? Paper presented to the Comparative Program of Health and Society. Munk Centre for International Studies, 1 March, 20.
[20] Agar. 2004, ibid., 124.
[21] Habermas, ibid., 13.
[22] Ibid., 39. Here Habermas quotes the German Otfried Höffe who used the expression in a newspaper article for Die Zeit, 1 February 2001, titled "Whose human dignity?"
[23] Ibid., 44.
[24] Ibid., 14 and 63, respectively.
[25] Buchanan, A., Brock, D.W., Daniels, N. and Wikler, D. 2000. *From Chance to Choice*. Cambridge: Cambridge University Press, 177–178.
[26] Agar. 2004, ibid.
[27] Agar. 1998, ibid. 141.
[28] Habermas, ibid., 92.
[29] Ibid., 21. A claim that he never substantiates.
[30] Wasserman, D. 2003. My fair baby: what's wrong with parents genetically enhancing their children? In: Gehring, V. (ed.), *Genetic Prospects: Essays on Biotechnology, Ethics, and Public Policy*. Lanham, MD: Rowman & Littlefield, 99–110. Quoted in Agar. 2004, ibid., 117.
[31] Agar. 2004, ibid., 117–118.
[32] Ibid., 118.
[33] Agar. 1998, ibid., 149.
[34] Agar. 2004, ibid., 113–114.
[35] Ibid., 120.
[36] Habermas, ibid., 91–92.
[37] Buchanan et al., 2000, ibid., 91.
[38] Agar. 1998, ibid., 150.
[39] Ibid., 137.
[40] Agar. 2004, ibid., 129.
[41] For example, Kitcher, P. 1996. *The Lives to Come: The Genetic Revolution and Human Possibilities*. New York: Simon & Schuster. Glover, J. 1994. *What Sort of People Should There Be*? Harmondsworth, Middlesex: Penguin.
[42] Agar. 1998, ibid., 137.
[43] Betta, M. 2000. *Brauchen wir Menschenrechte?* Königstein/Taunus: Ulrike Helmer.

[44] Harris, J. 1983. In vitro fertilization: the ethical issues. *The Philosophical Quarterly* 33(132): 217–237. Singer, P. and Wells, D. 1984. *The Reproduction Revolution: New Ways of Making Babies*. Melbourne and Oxford: Oxford University Press. For more details see Betta, M. 1995. *Embryonenforschung und Familie. Zur Politik der reproduction in Gorssbritannine, Italien and der Bundesrepublik*. Frankfurt, Paris, New York: Peter Lang Verlag, 43–49.

[45] Buchanan et al. 2000, ibid., 90.

[46] Ibid., 59.

[47] Ibid., 63.

[48] Ibid., 93–95.

[49] Foucault, M. 1988 [1984] *The Care of the Self: The History of Sexuality*, Vol. 3. London: Allen Lane.

[50] Buchanan et al. 2000, ibid., 102.

[51] Finkel, E. 2005. *Stem Cells: Controversy at the Frontiers of Science*. Sydney: ABC Books, 112.

[52] Ibid., 113.

[53] Ibid., 5.

MICHELA BETTA

DIAGNOSTIC KNOWLEDGE IN THE GENETIC ECONOMY AND COMMERCE

1. ENTREPRENEURIAL SCIENTISTS

On 5 December 2002 the Australian Senate passed the Research Involving Embryos and Prohibition of Human Cloning Bill 2002, which regulates stem cell research. The bill introduces some restrictions with regard to the use of stored frozen embryos, which are not destined to be implanted. The bill states that only frozen embryos created before April 2002 can be used for research purposes, provided that the individuals whom these embryos relate to give their consent. The alternative to this restriction would have been no research at all, and this would have happened if the law had been stopped. The Australian scientists regarded the new law as a compromise that would undoubtedly slow down research, but not entirely stop it.

Here, it is perhaps worth noting that Australia is at the forefront in stem cell research, as one of its most prestigious scientists, the embryologist Alan Trounson and his team in Melbourne, have played a major role in the discovery of embryonic stem cells. That discovery was shared with two other US research groups: one led by the embryologist James Thomson (Wisconsin), and the other led by the embryologist John Gearhart (Baltimore). In terms of biomedical research, Alan Trounson is a strong player. In spite of this, the passage of the mentioned bill risked jeopardizing his reputation and consequently to ridicule the scientific work of many Australian scientists. Attached to that bill package was the allocation of $43.55 million granted by the Commonwealth Government and by the Victoria Government to Trounson and other Australian scientists working in the biomedical field for the creation of the National Stem Cell Centre. Surprisingly, in spite of being worldwide one of the most productive countries in stem cell research, politicians threatened to stop the research. During the bill debate in August 2002, Trounson spent time at the Australian Federal Parliament educating politicians by providing them with details concerning stem cell research, in an attempt to help them to formulate informed judgement about the scientific work performed in Australia. The ultimate goal was to see the law be endorsed by the majority of the parliamentarians and the allocation of the large public funding

Michela Betta (ed.), The moral, social, and commercial imperatives of genetic testing and screening. The Australian case, 25–52.

confirmed. To underline the potentialities of the new research, Trounson showed a video taken by two American scientists: John McDonald, Director of the Spinal Cord Injury Unit in Missouri; and Doug Kerr, the director of a research centre for the treatment of transverse myelitis in Baltimore.

The video documented a treatment administered to a mouse affected by transverse myelitis, a virus that puts the immune system into chaos making it attack a wrong target, for example a group of nerves in the spinal cord instead of a virus looming in that area. In the first sequence, the video recorded a mouse affected by that virus that left it paralysed. In the second sequence the video showed the same mouse using its hind legs after a treatment by which embryonic stem cells were injected into its spinal cord. Trounson used the video to reinforce the potentialities of stem cell research. An opponent of the use of embryo research, American scientist David Prentice from Indiana University, contradicted Trounson declaring that the cells used to cure the mouse were not embryonic stem cells, but germ stem cells taken from a 9-week-old aborted embryo. The peculiar scientific meaning of that difference, which was known only to scientists, caused a delay in the parliamentary debate and an unprecedented campaign against Trounson. The scientist was denounced for having shares in a private stem cell company, which was said to gain financial advantages from the passage of the law. The hysteria that followed made some public commentators portray scientists as greedy vampires exclusively interested in their own financial rewards. The law was then finally passed in December 2002 and the grant reconfirmed, which led to the formal establishment of the National Stem Cell Centre, now renamed as the Australian Stem Cell Centre (ASSC). The interesting aspect here lies at the terminological level. Germ stem cells are those cells that will form egg and sperm and have the potential to develop any other type of tissue, and are therefore considered pluripotent cells. Conversely, embryonic stem cells derive from in vitro embryos and are not necessarily germ cells. Some commentators and politicians spoke of fraud and private interests that were blinding the scientists. The scientists themselves replied that the mistake was due to the fact that many did not differentiate between the two types of cells. John McDonald, one of the two video authors, commented that when speaking of stem cells "people lump them in the same category all the time; it's a fine line."[1]

This anecdote reveals two conflicting lines. One is related to (scientific) rigour, and the second to the need for scientists to move forward as speedily as possible. It is indeed difficult to believe that a scientist of the calibre of Trounson, well known for his scientific stand, had overlooked such an important detail. Perhaps he thought of it, but then he must have considered it too difficult to explain, or too risky to introduce such a terminological differentiation, as the aborted embryo would have indeed captured the moral fantasy of politicians, and for certainty questioned the ethical stand of the research applied to the paralysed mouse. The other line is related to scientific passion. Undoubtedly, the public saw (and some admired) one of the world's most recognized scientists descending the way to Parliament in order to convince political parties and their lobbies of the necessity to let scientists do what they have been trying to do since the existence of the scientific method. The severity of some criticism formulated by politicians, journalists, and public commentators, who attacked Trounson on a personal level by alleging economic advantages for the scientist himself, was reminiscent of the Inquisition. Undoubtedly, Trounson did not contribute to an increase of trust towards bioscience. It is the latter aspect that instigates reflection, because those reactions seem to suggest that as soon as scientists get involved with commercial activities, they lose their scientific aura, and therefore their objectivity. This is an issue that is increasingly occupying the minds of some critics, in and outside the academic field, who are worried about an increase in scientific and commercial joint ventures. But does this preoccupation with science collaborating with commerce not derive from an instinctive mistrust towards commerce? Here the question arises of whether the expectations we hold towards science and medicine, namely to avoid any commercial involvement, do not originate from an old notion of medical science.[2]

This book opens with a quotation by the French historian Jean Delameau, who argued that the French Revolution would not have paved the way to modern society without technology and science, which means that politics alone cannot change society. But do science and technology not need an additional component to make knowledge transfer and implementation possible, i.e., to take scientific and technological progress out of the laboratories and make it available to the public? But how open are we towards scientists trying to commercialize their research in order to implement it on a large scale? Why do scientists have to become entrepreneurs? Do they do this just for money or in order to get recognition? Admittedly, the palpable lack of trust towards science in general and bioscience in particular is worldwide. In her 2005 book *Stem Cells: Controversy at the Frontiers of Science*, Australian scientist Elizabeth Finkel points the finger to punitive minds and political circles, which always insist on promoting negative spin when talking about science and scientific endeavours, especially in the "new genetics" and stem cell debate. In her reconstruction of the most salient moments of the emergence of the stem cell field, Finkel remarks: "Scientists were portrayed as amoral and only out to make big bucks."[3]

Finkel herself is a biochemist and a well-recognized scientific journalist. She worked as a research scientist for many years before becoming a writer. She has won many important prizes for medical journalism in Australia and abroad, and therefore she knows what it means to work as a researcher in a scientific environment. Finkel is perfectly aware of the constraints scientists are subjected to, in terms of financial support and social recognition for their efforts. She is an attentive observer of the Australian scientific culture and of its protagonists, and her interlocutors are the best researchers in the new field called biomedicine. Her work is highly productive, and her passion and partiality for the researchers very seldom escape her objectivity. Therefore, it is always worth trying to understand why such a profound connoisseur of the scientific scene sarcastically reminds us that "there are dragoons of ethicists, lawyers, conscientious scientists and activists who make medical ethics their livelihood."[4] She reproaches these people for having overlooked the shift that occurred in the scientific style and collective, not only in Australia but in many other western countries as well, leading scientists "through a cultural revolution that shed them of the bourgeois notions such as 'knowledge for knowledge's sake'."[5] This revolution, she argues, has catapulted them into the open social field. The reasons for this transformation of the scientific ethos are to be found in "the exigencies of the cash-strapped universities"[6] as well as in a new commercial approach of the international venture capital after the collapse of the dotcom economy. But the goodwill of the scientists does not seem to have been counteracted by equally enthusiastic commercial actors. According to Finkel, Australia would have a stronger position on the international level if it had not been for the lack of "business managers" capable of giving "wings to changes" in the global marketplace.[7]

This is also something that Manuel Castells reproached commerce and private companies for, namely their lack of vision and commercial courage.[8] But, as it often happens during cultural shifts, what to some gives reason to condemnation is to others motif of prize and support. This chapter deals with science and scientists as well as medical practitioners and their involvement with commercial partners. The author restrains from taking a stance against or for one position, but opens the chapter to different positions and interpretations of the trends we are currently witnessing. In an exemplary way, she explores the effects of emerging biomedical techniques that make the deposit and conservation of body parts in cell banks, specifically created for this purpose, possible. The umbilical cord blood (UCB) banks represent a successful encounter of two types of minds: the biomedical and the business. Other examples could have been chosen, but this one is interesting because—perhaps substantiating the criticism expressed by Finkel and Castells—it does not represent a big commercial risk. On the other hand, it opens the scene of one of the most intimate moments in private life to commercial actors. In fact, the UCB must be collected at the very moment of a baby delivery. Finally, the collecting and banking technique would not have been possible without testing technologies capable of excluding health risks from collected human genetic material. Genetic testing is therefore a central step in a healthcare practice that is increasingly oriented towards the creation of new forms of investments in health, while aiming, at the same time, at increasing society's ability to respond to health crises through private and public initiatives based on personal and bodily resources.

2. BODILY TERRITORY AND GENETIC TESTING

If genetic testing and screening in the early stages of human life confronts us with ethical dilemmas, questions, new social risks, and fears, all of which make increasingly difficult the formulation of policies that addresses everybody's interests and ethical expectations, the issues surrounding genetic testing and screening of adolescents and adults do not seem less cogent and difficult to govern. The discourse that accompanies local policies of genetic testing and screening can be articulated into two categories: the narrative of great promise and the narrative of concern.[9] The first maintains that the new predictive knowledge resulting from such tests is a social good whose distribution will positively change our approach towards our health and body. The second speaks of risks and the impossibility of finding a compromise based on common sense. These two attitudes are simultaneously present in the social landscape, reinforced by a "genohype" narrative that portrays benefits and risks associated with genetic research and genetic engineering. Who disseminates these words? According to a study undertaken by Tania Bubela and Timothy Cauldfield (2004):

> Only 15% of the newspaper articles and 5% of the scientific journal articles discussed costs and risks, whereas 97% of the newspaper articles and 98% of the scientific journal articles discussed the likelihood of benefits of research.[10]

The data collected by the two authors, however, seem to reflect the interesting trend whereby "the journalists may not always be the primary source of exaggerated claims." Moreover, they maintain a cool attitude towards the narrative of promise compared to the scientific divulgators of knowledge, who "may be inadvertent 'complicit collaborators' in the subtle hyping of science stories."[11] MacIntyre (1997) also comes to this conclusion. She argues that some of the most optimistic views about the potential power and benefits of genetic testing and screening are to be found in official reports, and not in the tabloid press as sometimes assumed.[12] The two studies suggest the emergence of two trends: first, the more optimistic reading of scientific research data comes from the scientific community itself; and second, the narrative of benefits and great promise has worldwide attracted more fans than that depicting risks and exaggerated expectations. How is this lack of balance to be interpreted? What are the forces driving this discourse? Before discussing this aspect, which is undoubtedly related to public policy and the regulation of new research, it is necessary to define the perimeter of our investigation through a discussion of the types of currently available tests and their repercussions on people. A methodological remark is necessary at this stage. In the course of this analysis we will be referring to both narratives, sometimes giving precedence to the discourse underlining risks, and sometimes to the enthusiastic discourse of scientific advancements. The uncertainties and potentialities of scientific advancements are such that a clear-cut stance does not as yet seem justified. In the following sections, the writer moves into the privileged position of an observer, trying to maintain as objective a style as possible.

3. PROBABILISTIC AND PREDICTIVE TESTS VERSUS A NEW DEFINITION OF ILLNESS

Diseases can be assessed according to a grid of four different categories of genetic tests:

- Disease/illness[13] caused by the defect of a single gene
- Multifactorial disease deriving from a combination of gene defects
- Disease deriving from chromosomal abnormalities
- Mitochondrial abnormalities manifest in the early stage of the DNA

These four categories create the territory on which genetic testing and screening is erected in order to install a new register of illness that will differentiate between predictive and preventive medicine. They are embedded in different testing practices that underline the function and purpose of the testing itself. The tests cover the following areas:

- *Diagnostic testing* (which formulates or reconfirms a diagnosis)
- *Presymptomatic testing* (which ascertains whether a healthy person has been subjected to a possible genetic mutation that will develop into a disease)
- *Predictive testing* targeting genetic susceptibility/predisposition (which detects risk factors that become active through exposure to specific environments or through gene interaction)
- *Testing to detect heterozygotes* (which detects carriers of genetic disease inherited from different factors)
- *DNA fingerprint* (which identifies a person by analysing specific regions of DNA)[14]

Although this register extends to different areas of the DNA and bodily geography, it seems reasonable to argue that diagnostic testing is the overarching technique with which all the others are related. In spite of this, it is not easy to define what a genetic test is. The more comprehensive definition goes back to 1996 when the American National Association of Insurance Commissioners tried to set the principles governing genetic testing and screening. The length of the definition, however, reveals the difficulty inherent in such a definition that, considering the possible advancements in diagnostic knowledge, may very soon become obsolete.

> Genetic screening or testing means a laboratory test of a person's genes or chromosomes for abnormalities, defects, or deficiencies, including carrier status, that are linked to physical or mental disorders or impairments, or that indicates a susceptibility to illness, disease, or other disorders, whether physical or mental, which test is a direct test for abnormalities, defects, or deficiencies, and not an indirect manifestation of genetic disorders.[15]

The formulation reiterates the peculiar nature of genetic testing and screening embedded in predictive and personalized medicine. Predictive medicine is probabilistic in so far as it singles out those at risk while they are healthy, but for that very reason is also difficult to quantify. Some powerful commentators have called upon these two aspects to criticize the validity of predictive medicine. A position paper submitted to the Conference of European Churches in October 2003 argues that genetic testing and screening causes a "reversal in the perception of time"—the future that has always been open and undetermined becomes a certainty through genetic prediction. A psychological consequence could be that people might live in preparation for the worse. "The final outcome, like a metaphorical cancer, invades every space and everything revolves around it."[16] According to this interpretation, genetic testing and screening seems to introduce a subtle change in the perception of illness: Whereas before genetic testing and screening medical doctors confirmed the presence of a state of illness, now their skills are directed towards the assessment of the "risk of illness." It is said that this transformation will have major repercussions on the relationship between doctor and patient.

Therefore, the European Churches identify here a shift of actions from beneficence to autonomy. Treating the patient is understood as the relation that installs beneficial effects, while the predicting of an illness presupposes "a looking further into the detail of the diagnosis, rather than just managing the illness or curing it." This new regime will also have repercussions on the principle that underlines our duty to respect the individual's autonomy, as this seems to become more important than the principle of beneficence. Furthermore, genetic testing is considered to indirectly target the family members of the persons who undergo the testing, extending diagnostic knowledge to larger social territories. It is likely that the Council of Europe had this in mind when they accorded "hybrid legal protection" or an intermediate status to the families and their members genetically related to the tested person. Such new legal definitions allow for distinguishing family members from third parties and, therefore, to ascertain their rights to know or not to know or to refuse the diagnosis.[17] Finally, here the European Churches see the emergence of a double register: one for those who are potentially sick, and another for those already "living with the reality of illness." Are the European Churches overestimating the psychological effects of genetic testing and screening? Are they assigning a passive role to people, especially in the way they understand their status as carriers of potential diseases and chronic illness? Is it possible that genetic testing and screening introduces new attitudes towards one's own physical status, demystifying illness and strengthening other factors?

The Churches themselves acknowledge this possibility by stating that "a person's moral and spiritual health are decisive components of bodily health." However, where people gain these strengths from is still an open question. Very often personal resources derive from strategies embedded in local and peripheral knowledge and experience. It seems reasonable to suggest that faith constitutes one of these resources, but faith may be only one option among many. Interestingly, in his 2003 essay "Faith and Knowledge," the philosopher Jürgen Habermas[18] suggests that in our postsecular societies faith is re-entering the social fields called upon by genetic engineering, revealing how transitional our secularization is. "Even in Europe... feelings towards secularisation are still highly ambivalent, as shown by the dispute over genetic engineering." Habermas reinforces faith as a personal resource to withstand "the depressing current events" caused by the "new genetics." This turn makes many sceptical of the profound sense of cultural pessimism that underpins his conclusions. Undeniably, genetic testing and screening introduces new regulatory elements in the strategies of every single person. The social effects of genetic diagnoses on people and their relationships are well encapsulated in the following statement:

> One friend says, "well, you aren't well", and I think, "well, but I'm not ill". So, if I'm not well, but I'm not ill, what am I?[19]

Given that genetic testing is predictive, the impossibility of pronouncing a final judgement might make people think of their illnesses in terms of perception of illness rather than physical impediment. Lowton and Gabe (2003) speak of four concepts of health perception used by people affected by cystic fibrosis, an autosomal recessive genetic disease, in the context of their daily activities. According to this grid, "health" is identified as "a normal state," as "controllable," as "a distressing state," and as "a release."[20] This approach is contrasted with the attitude adopted by people who accept their chronic physical illness as a fate. According to Bury (1991), chronically ill individuals tend to rely on a module that helps them to live with their condition, and follow three trajectories: coping, style, and strategy.[21] This approach is reflected in an attitude that aims at *managing* chronic illness and treatment. Perception and management of illness underline two different personal ethical approaches towards the sick self. A further discussion of these findings would go beyond the scope of the present analysis. This differentiation nonetheless underlines how a clear-cut definition of illness has never existed. People try to identify strategies that allow them to live their lives, however physically limited they might be, according to an idea of health that very often is cultural rather than medical, and very often profoundly rooted in an ethics of the care of the self. For that reason, some of the criticism that has accompanied genetic screening and testing from the very beginning of its emergence seems to be the product of ideological interpretations rather than ethnographic observations. Lowton and Gabe (2003) open up a new narrative line in the discourse of genetic screening and testing by saying:

> It is well known that the concepts of "health" and "illness" mean different things to different people and it may be here that difficulties in distinguishing between coping, style, and strategy lie.[22]

The two authors reveal that, although cystic fibrosis is considered a "child-killing disease," genetic testing has demonstrated that many previously undiagnosed adults appear to have a milder form of it. What are the consequences of genetic testing and screening and the diagnostic knowledge that this technology installs in the social field? Is genetic testing and screening extending the radius of control? Does it represent a threat to social cohesion and personal identity? The European Churches do not of course adopt this position,[23] and in their paper they underline the importance of predictive medicine in terms of policies of prevention. And it is not by chance that they refer to the recommendations of the British Human Genetic Commission that introduces the discourse of "genetic solidarity and altruism," a sort of genetic welfare state or common genetic territory on which the health of future society can be erected. The notion of the sharing of genetic information is reinforced by the exhortation to show "respect for the person, which implies observing the principles of respect of the privacy of the individual and the confidentiality of personal genetic information, as well as the principle of free consent and non-discrimination."[24] In their position paper the European Churches reiterate two principles that they believe should facilitate the regulation of genetic testing and screening. The first underlines the notion that human beings are "equal with regard to risk," and the second that our "collective ignorance is fundamental to our solidarity." The fact that predictive medicine can now push forward the limits of knowledge, and thus allow us to see those "who are more at risk than others," is said to undermine the system of fundamental solidarity.[25] This contention will be further investigated in Section 4.

4. FROM GENETICS TO PROTEOMICS—THE LONG-STANDING COLLABORATION BETWEEN COMMERCE AND LIFE SCIENCE

What do we actually mean when we speak of genetic tests? The International Genetics & In Vitro Fertilization (IVF) Institute, the world's largest provider of infertility treatment and genetic services, offers a range of tests addressing different problems. These include, testing for immigration purposes, DNA profiling, self-service paternity testing, full paternity testing, contract paternity, and infidelity testing. The latter test involves "an easy-to-use and inexpensive kit to detect semen on clothing or related items," which costs $210 per item.[26] This institute and its services embody a new relationship between the cellular and the social level of knowledge, or between the local (the collection of material deriving from cells, genes, eggs, sperms, and proteins) and the global (services that can be marketed and ordered globally). This relationship installs a new bodily and cellular geography that can be best described using the Foucauldian term of biopolitics and the emerging term of diagnostic geopolitics. Biopolitics revolves around the body, its regions, and the new enhancement regimes. Diagnostic geopolitics creates registers and classifications according to an idea of well-being that allows for the creation of new clusters: genetically healthy persons, at-probable-risk persons, at-risk persons, sick persons. Diagnostic geopolitics finds its expression in the biobanking projects currently undertaken in the United Kingdom, Iceland, Estonia, and Japan which aim at transforming countries into repositories of the genetic information of a country and its people. At this stage, we can maintain that this new relationship between the bodily local and the diagnostic global reveals a redefinition of cultural patterns and social regions in which health professionals, economists, scientists, medical practitioners, genetic counsellors, families, and individuals are renegotiating personal rights and reorganizing their genetic resources and well-being.

4.1 Profit or Care?

In his 1999 article, *Genetic testing and therapy: A pathway to progress and/or profit?*, Robert F. Rizzo[27] opens his analysis with the uncompromising statement that "genetic testing and therapy are in the process of becoming enterprises propelled by the profit motive for the creation of an industry of multibillion dollar proportions." Rizzo's article targets the US healthcare system that has reached an exasperated level of budgetary management of primary care services. The US-managed health service seems to highlight fundamental contradictions of the healthcare system itself, especially when healthcare has to cope with genetic testing and screening and therapy. We will dwell a little on Rizzo's analysis embedded in social economics, and try to understand the angle from which he formulates his criticism. A clear sign of the enterprising nature of modern healthcare systems is a technological mentality that seems to penetrate even the thinnest interstices of the doctor–patient relationship. This development appears to be as unstoppable as it is inexplicable, as "it is difficult to sort out what motivates the use of technology in every instance." One reason is the intended benefit to patients. However, Rizzo refers to a number of studies which suggest that aggressive—highly technological—care and treatment have "often resulted in poor survival rates.... This has also been true of neonatal intensive care of infants with minimal brain function."[28] But the application of technology in medicine seems also to derive from a productive collaboration between physicians, hospitals, research scientists, and medical industrial corporations—all of whom benefit financially from the use of technologies. This network is gaining predominance, especially in the field of biotechnology in which history seems to be "repeating itself in the collaboration of commercial interests and medical research"[29] propelled by the profit motive.

This analysis has been confirmed by successive studies such as that by Australian scientist, Nicolas Rasmussen (2004). Rasmussen has identified a special biotechnology relationship between drug firms and academic biomedicine. His discussion of two cultures "brought together by perceived mutual advantage" seems to confirm Rizzo's thesis of the profit motive. Interestingly, Rasmussen also speaks of a perception of common interests, which, perhaps not intended in the way they are perceived, for that very reason, cause "deep clashes" in the values of the two cultures[30]: the pharmaceutical industry and the academia. But where does the profit motive come from? According to Rizzo,[31] it arises out of a fundamental transformation of healthcare into a commodity that introduces market practices into the medical profession and its establishments. New biotechnologies such as genetic testing will increase the level of intervention and with it also health costs, causing the healthcare system to reach "a deeper level of crisis than it is now experiencing." Rizzo exclusively refers to the US healthcare system that is controlled by different forms of managerial strategies such as health maintenance organizations (HMOs), independent practices associations (IPAs), preferred provider organizations (PPOs), point-of-service plans (POSs), and prepaid group practices (PGPs). The common element of these diversified private regulatory systems is capitation. There are two forms of capitation contracts. In the first, primary care capitation contract physicians work under tight budget guidelines and receive pay for each treated patient, which covers the visit, in-office tests, and other minor procedures. Additional budgetary subforms cover emergency, X-rays, referrals to specialists, admissions to hospital, all of which are paid under "fee-for-service." This is because specialists themselves, despite also being subject to budget constraints, are paid for each service provided. A second form of capitation contracts for primary care accords high monthly salaries to physicians who are ultimately responsible for referrals to specialists and hospitals. Here Rizzo sees room for negotiations between different interests, as "*capitated* physicians can reap larger profits by staying under budget," because "capitation provides financial incentives to treat less."

It is generally believed that the historical shift that led to capitation was caused by the creation of medical savings accounts (MSAs), a sort of self-insurance in which individuals are given the opportunity to use funds deposited into their insurance accounts to shop for the best and most economical care. The social economist Rizzo argues that there is no better example of the pervasive influence of the marketplace mentality in the healthcare system, as the savings accounts turn patients into consumers.[32] But what is the problem with being a consumer instead of a patient? "From a consumer's perspective, tests, drugs and other medical procedures are much less attractive than clothes, cars, homes, vacations and luxury goods."[33] The profit motives and the marketplace mentality are turning primary healthcare service into goods that can be bought according to an individual's budget rather than his/her needs. The changes are pervasive as they install the idea that healthcare as such is an economic good produced by an industry.

4.2 Biomedicine and Commerce—Merchants of Life?

It is undeniable that medical science has been attracting the attention of big money since the beginning of the 20th century. But what in the early 1900s seemed to constitute largely philanthropic moves into the healthcare system—think of the American Carnegie and Rockefeller foundations—has now turned into corporate interests. It seems that the current corporate interest in healthcare coheres around five targets: (1) discovery and sequencing of genes related to diseases (genome and DNA); (2) identification of biochemical markers; (3) ascertainment of function and role of the proteins (proteomics); (4) provision of genetic testing; and (5) development of (individual) drug therapies (pharmacogenomics). These five strategies take place concurrently and are interrelated to each other. At present, we are in the genomics phase, but the limited geography of the DNA will soon be overcome by the need to extend territory exploration into the proteins and their functions as well as expressions. Indeed, drug therapy will be successful only after a coherent classification of proteins and the creation of a new taxonomy has taken place. This scientific taxonomy could lead to the installation of different social regimes defined by different understandings of the power of cellular life. At present, we are witnessing financial manoeuvres directed towards large investments of companies into the promising market potential of diagnostic testing on individuals without symptoms. According to some European analysts, proteomics will be the successor of the genomic era, as it "has already supplanted genomics."[34] These sharp market observers speak of genomics as a first wave and proteomics as the second wave of the bio-era. That such a shift has begun is said to be demonstrated by already existing "powerful technologies that allow data to be stored, analysed, and interpreted."[35]

From the point of view of targets and effects, proteomics and pharmacogenomics are interrelated, in so far as they refer to the study of genes and proteins in a person's genome that determine a certain drug reaction. According to Aitken and Metcalfe (chapter 7), the "pharmacogenomic future is one where a person would be screened for a host of gene variants before being prescribed medications." As the two authors maintain, this emerging rational approach towards prescription of medication "is set to become an integral part of medical practice." Developments towards "individualized prescribing" seem to confirm a shift from the hospital, as the curative place of the past, to the laboratory, as the place in which disease can be predicted and its treatment tailored to the needs of the individual person, who therefore will turn into a customer rather than a patient. Through this historical shift the laboratory will turn into a privileged medical scene capable of permeating healthcare policies and social life.[36]

Another significant aspect that highlights the changes in bioscience and biotechnology and related applications is the emergence of new commercial actors that are about to replace the chemical companies of the past. Rizzo (1999) believes that free enterprise and the profit motive in healthcare will invigorate inventiveness and risk-taking, and create "new industries in research and applications."[37] Some commentators speak of "the industrialization"[38] of healthcare, which is understood as a rational system that aims at creating the conditions of predictability, quality control, and an inclusion of cost–benefit reasoning. This would reflect a "rationalized" industry that maximizes the utilization of personnel with minimum expenditure of resources. The healthcare industry is related to biotechnology. According to Bock et al. (2001), one-fifth of the new drugs originating from biotechnology already represent 5% of total pharmaceutical sales. The United States and Japan are dominating the European market, while US firms seem to be an invincible force in terms of innovation and innovative drugs. In 1999 its global market participation reached 40% of the total world market for prescribed drugs. This commercial and economic net is spun by new commercial actors called Amgen, Chiron, Biogen, and Genzym, small firms that are "securing an increasing proportion of the global pharmaceutical market"[39] and perhaps completely replacing acronyms like BASF, Hoechst,

Merck, Roche, Dupond, and Cyba. Genomics is said to have the potential to create completely new industrial clusters and activities, and therefore to replace existing industries.[40] Nicolas Rasmussen, who has written extensively on the moral economy of drug companies from a historical perspective dating back to the 19th century, speaks of the pharmaceutical industry as a

> powerful presence in academic life science, in the form of both the giant multinationals that sell drugs and the smaller "biotech" firms that supply them with some of their new products.[41]

This collaboration goes back to the first decades of the 20th century, as accurately underlined by Rizzo (1999) and Rasmussen (2004). However, the two authors differ in their interpretation of the reasons why this collaboration has turned into such an extensive business since the 1920s. Rizzo seems to suggest that scientists pursue profits no matter how compromising this attitude might be for their moral status and their professional standing. In the course of this development, Rizzo contends, physicians have become "more dependent on pharmaceutical companies for the application of research through drug therapy, becoming the bridge for the marketing of the industry's products with both parties reaping the financial benefits."[42] Instead, Rasmussen[43] has elaborated on the moral dilemmas that have accompanied the emergence of a new collaboration between the emerging pharmacologic industry and the medical researchers in American society and culture since the 1900s. Rasmussen's historical reconstruction, while exclusively referring to the American case, can be applied to western countries in general. It was inevitable after World War I that the role of scientists in academia be reorganized, and that they open up their scientific establishments to external forces such as industries.

Rasmussen, however, seems to read these developments in rather pessimistic terms. He underlines that "according to the original ethos prevailing among US preclinical scientists devoted to the research ideal, ethical standards had declined between the 1890s and 1930s."[44] Rasmussen's interpretation of the transformations that occurred in the academic environment during the previous century, leading to an extensive collaboration with the industry, seems to be influenced by a purist attitude.

It could be worth investigating the reason for that collaboration. Can it be that a transformation of society, caused by the entrance of the idea of social welfare into political calculations, made it necessary to create the conditions of a more practical collaboration between academia and industry, in order to guarantee a safer production and distribution of drugs? Is this collaboration perhaps foremost due to the emerging mass society and mass consumers? A different reading of the development would therefore place the scientists in a different light—between Rizzo's voracious scientists and Rasmussen's utilitarian researchers. At the beginning of the previous century, with the US pharmaceutical field dominated by numerous private medical colleges that produced a glut of physicians with inadequate education, especially in science, modernizing seemed unavoidable.[45]

This modernization was intended to curtail the number of patent medicine makers with a poor academic background, and to impose new marketing practices on drug companies. The notion of the "ethical drug firms" emerged. However, only those firms that labelled active ingredients and marketed through the medical professions earned this title.[46] The necessity of selling more scientific drugs to the public made the ethical drug firms look for more productive collaborations with academic scientists and physicians and, consequently, invest more in research. These collaborations, however, did not always form smoothly. For many scientists at the beginning of the previous century, intellectual reputation was the scientist's salary. In addition, "academic disrespect for business ran especially high."[47] Although both cultures perceived the fresh wind of the medical reform, "commercial involvement" of pharmacologists and physiologists was considered "inconsistent with ethical codes," which were understood as "requiring disinterestedness and full disclosure of scientific findings." In spite of this resistance, Rasmussen identifies a "blossoming of collaborations between academic life science and ethical pharmaceutical firms" throughout the 1930s. "Materially, what drug firms chiefly wanted from laboratory researchers was access to new scientific drugs that could readily be marketed."[48]

According to Rasmussen, this collaboration, which must be understood as the pharmaceutical firms assuming control over scientific findings, manifested in three different ways: (1) exclusive access to the practices and knowledge of the academic researchers; (2) exclusive rights to use the name of a compound, made famous by the scientists who discovered it, as a trademark (this strategy led to the discovery of insulin in 1922 as a result of the collaboration between the University of Toronto and the drug firm Lilly); and finally (3) patents taken by individual scientists. Of these three strategies, the patents became the more successful for scientists and their universities, and therefore their preferred form of collaboration between science and commerce/economy. This, however, does not mean that patents were easily introduced as a self-rewarding device. As Rasmussen maintains, patents on medical products were especially controversial among physicians. Indeed, they were forbidden in France and by the American Medical Association, and regarded by many as inconsistent with the Hippocratic oath. To make them morally acceptable a new discourse was introduced in the scientific practices, one that underlined the notion that patents in the name of public protection were morally acceptable, as they could "protect the public from bad medicine." A scientist working for the University of Toronto wrote in 1922:

> I can see no more reason why the man that separates the active constituent of the pancreas should not share financially as much as the man that makes a new wireless telephone.[49]

Rasmussen interprets this statement as a utilitarian argument in favour of "inventing for the general benefit." The quotation of course unveils the active role played by scientists in shaping the patent culture of the previous century.

This prompts Rasmussen to conclude his impressive article with a note of subtle criticism:

> Indeed, patenting trends among academic life scientists in especially competitive fields during the interwar period may not have been entirely due to industrial pressures. Academic scientists seem to have placed exaggerated value on patenting, at least in the view of drug firms, which sometimes would have preferred special access to know-how or exclusive use of trade names.[50]

It seems, therefore, that science rather than commerce has created patents and their successful system. And if scientists preferred them to other forms of reward, there must be a reason beyond simple utilitarianism. Perhaps patents can be understood as a particular surviving strategy pursed by scientists in a historical phase dominated by a cultural shift in the context of which scientists were beginning to lose their privileged position. It might be that the emergence of the mass university and with it different fields of knowledge increased the level of competition.[51] In the 1930s,

> few topics were as important to physiologists and biochemists in the period as hormones and vitamins, molecules that appeared to account for many of life's processes. The importance of these substances made discovering and purifying them especially competitive.[52]

It seems therefore that being an entrepreneurial life scientist in the 1930s was a necessity rather than a choice. In the changing economy of the 20th century, with its managerial commerce, new cultural codes become installed by practices that would prepare the scientific field of biology and biochemistry for the "new genetics."

4.3 Healthcare Contra Marketplace? Three Contradictions

Patents still represent the most coherent way of ascertaining research activities and results. According to Bock et al. (2001), between 1985 and 1997 the United States had a sixfold increase of pharmaceutical patents, whereas Japan and the European Union only doubled their number. In 2001 more than 75% of pharmaceutical firms listed on stock markets were US-owned. In 2001 there were already 800 patents on genetic tests in the United States,[53] which will by now be on the market. In spite of these trends, genetic testing, on its own, represents only a small portion of total market and potential market (healthcare benefits) compared to, for example, drugs (pharmacogenomics and proteomics). But if genetic testing and screening is embedded in a larger field, e.g., biopharmacology, its importance seems to be steadily increasing. In addition, the cultural and social effects of genetic testing and screening appear to be irreversible, as it represents the first steps towards a universal redefinition of human nature, well-being, healthcare, and the social and legal policies that will accompany their implementation. In his 1999 article, Rizzo describes the current phase as transitional, but one leading to "universal genetic testing and therapy."[54] Some medical practitioners and scientists rely on an imminent trend towards the screening of "entire populations or specific subgroups for genetic information."[55] Population screening as a public policy was first established by the World Health Organization (WHO), and was erected on three fundamental principles:

1. The identification of individuals who are at risk of specific disorders (the aim here is to develop preventive policies)
2. The identification of subgroups that need medical attention because of those specific disorders (public prevention)
3. Intervention to benefit the tested individual/individuals

This grid covers testing on an individual level and screening as group intervention in the name of public health. But this policy, created to reshape healthcare strategies and intervention on a global level, encounters problems on a local level. These problems might be caused by an intrinsic contradiction of the economic and commercial strategies that have permeated the healthcare system of the world's largest economy. An understanding of these problems may help others to avoid the same mistakes. It is worth noting, at this stage, that genetic testing and screening and therapy allow a special form of access to the personal data of an individual. The information collected through this intervention is unique, because it is related to the person undergoing a test and consequently also to his/her family or ethnic group. Therefore, it is generally suggested that special care must be taken in order to avoid exploitation of the data in terms of social exclusion from insurance policies, health insurance, and employment.[56] But, because the information resulting from the tests might leave the person in a sort of limbo in terms of risks and real health status, the repercussions of genetic testing and screening also need to be addressed on a psychological level. For that reason Annas et al. (1995) speak of DNA information as "a personal diary" of a highly private nature with the potential to affect all aspects of individual life.[57]

In addition, genetic testing and screening has installed a system in the context of which diagnosis is not always related to treatment, in so far as not all diagnosed diseases can currently be treated. The consequences here are enormous for the counselling field, as demands for more counsellors will emerge in order to deal with the sense of confusion that a diagnosis might create in a person and his/her family. Other difficulties could emerge once parents claim the right to have their offspring genetically tested. How is society to regulate these issues? Can parents demand a genetic test for their children without their children's consent? Additional problems might be caused by the fact, recognized by scientists as well, that genetic tests are not infallible, that errors can occur on biological, clerical, and/or laboratory levels—the so-called false negatives or false positives that might influence a diagnosis. The commentator, Rizzo, wonders whether our society and its healthcare system are prepared to provide the support and protection to individuals who avail themselves of the tests. "In a society noted for law suits for malpractice and negligence in informing, counselling faces a formidable task."[58]

Rizzo identifies three fundamental contradictions that the US healthcare system will have to face as soon as genetic testing and therapy become some of the most basic services of primary care—basic because they are strictly related to pharmacogenomics or personalized medicine and drug therapy. The first contradiction is that managed care will increase the risk of malpractice liability as "under capitation, managed care will be incapable of meeting the demands of genetic testing, diagnosis and counselling, because they demand more contact with patients."[59] The second contradiction seems to be caused by the "industrialization" of healthcare, which aims to rationalize the sector in economic terms. But it is not clear whether the economic principle of minimal costs and maximum profit can be successfully applied to healthcare. This vision might instead increase "the financial risks of physicians and put them squarely in the business world."[60] Again the question arises as to whether physicians will be able to offer the care that genetic testing and therapy require. The third contradiction is related to health insurance and the possibility that the insurance industry might refuse to sell life or health insurance to individuals identified as high-risk, or may attempt to charge higher premiums. In October 2000 insurance companies in the United Kingdom gained permission to ask for genetic tests results. This permission was subsequently withdrawn as many observers anticipated that this move would lead to the creation of a "genetic underclass" of people unable to buy health or life insurance. However, some observers suggest that no obligation of disclosure of genetic test results could represent a high risk for the insurance industry itself, because it would undermine the principles and fundamental understanding of the insurance industry. The issue related to the Australian insurance industry and disclosure of genetic information will be explored by Weisbrot and Opeskin (chapter 6).

Another problem, according to Rizzo, is that due to the costs of genetic tests and therapy, a price regulation could make many companies look for more competitive markets, in turn causing an increase in insurance costs. The employers could also decide to discontinue the group plans for their employees. This makes Rizzo conclude that whether health insurance is less regulated or stringently regulated, "the system will be unable to cope with genetic testing and therapy."[61] Here Rizzo is indicating that health insurance systems need to be controlled in such a way as to positively respond to social rather than commercial and economic imperatives. Does this make sense to the insurance industry? This question will be addressed in Section 5. At this stage, it seems that two fundamental consequences derive from the introduction of genetic testing and screening and therapy into western healthcare systems: the uncertainty surrounding the treatment of diseases diagnosed by genetic tests; and the increasing need for counselling, which will require state intervention in order to govern the social, ethical, and psychological problems related to genetic medicine. This is an extraordinary change in an economic and social order in which we have been witnessing widespread state deregulation since the 1980s. It seems, therefore, that the genetic economic and commercial order resulting from free market ideology has created new conditions for strong state regulation or governmental intervention. The governance of genetic testing and therapy will question the fairness of the marketplace as the only regulatory dimension. It might follow here that "wherever health-care turns, it has to contend with the marketplace mentality."[62] Rizzo seems intuitively correct in identifying a clash of cultures between medical health practices and commerce.

5. INSURANCE INDUSTRY AND GENETIC TESTING

Since the emergence of issues related to genetic testing, the public debate has been dominated by different attempts to address health insurance and the responsibilities of the insurance industry. This debate has produced the peculiar situation in which consumer activists have promulgated a definition of insurance as "a vehicle to meet community goals," or in other words as a societal way of reducing social risks. This approach is of course opposed to that of the actuarial profession and private industry, both of which see insurance as "an economic institution opposed to an instrument of social policy."[63] The ultimate goal of the insurance field is to distribute risks according to a list of classification variables generally known as risk and discrimination. Now some commentators and consumers' representatives maintain that genetic information cannot be included in that list. The insurance industry, on the other hand, replies that suppressed information regarding genetic questions might create discrimination among the insured and lead to an increase in premiums levels.

> When there is suppression of information, as would occur, for example, if insurers were forced by law to ignore genetic information in classification, and if the insurers were forced to charge the same rate to insured persons who are known to have different expected loss costs, then the insurance pricing not only might be viewed as "unfairly discriminatory" to the group of lower-expected-cost persons but also would encourage more hazard and adverse selection against the insurer.[64]

The authors quoted above add that the consequences of suppressed genetic information would be disastrous for the industry, as it might even threaten the solvency of insurers. Other commentators put it more bluntly: "If insurers are forbidden under any circumstances from using genetic information to adjust premiums, then we are on the highway to eliminating insurance."[65] Undoubtedly, genetic testing represents a challenge for one of the oldest businesses of modern economy and commerce. According to Brockett et al. (1999), the debate on the restriction of accessing genetic information and the resulting indiscriminating distribution of risks among low-risk and high-risk groups result from a flawed understanding of the insurance field. The authors believe that social demands are led by a welfare expectation that aims at transferring wealth from one group to another. "While this may be desirable from a societal perspective, it must be debated whether insurance is the most appropriate mechanism to achieve this wealth transfer."[66] Brockett has written extensively on the effects that the "new genetics" will have on insurance and workplace relations, and he has also debated the necessity to differentiate between the interests of the industry and those of the individuals and social policymakers (2001, first published in 1973). "From the perspective of the insurers, who view themselves as financial intermediaries, the ultimate rationale for using . . . genetic-based information for classification purposes is economic."[67] This fact has also been reiterated by Weisbrot and Opeskin (chapter 6), who maintain that the ALRC-AHEC Inquiry into insurance practices and genetic information in Australia has rejected the notion of genetic exceptionalism, through which some would like to justify a revision of insurance practices and more incisive state intervention. Although the two authors understand that claims for more control are influenced by fears that the insurance industry could discriminate against certain prospective individuals threatened by genetic predispositions, they argue that such discrimination is more prone to happen in America than in Australia. They, therefore, reject claims that the insurance industry should not be allowed to ask prospective clients to undergo genetic testing.

The stance taken by consumer groups advocating the prohibition of genetic testing for any type of insurance has been criticized as deriving from the belief that because healthcare is a right, so also must healthcare insurance be. The debate is still open. The US Senate passed Bill S. 1053 in mid-October 2003, the *Genetic Nondiscrimination Act*, which protects the privacy of genetic information and prevents health plans, insurance carriers, and employers from discriminating on the basis of genetic information. The bill is still awaiting action from the US House of Representatives, and many signs suggest that no decision will be taken in the next months. Many observers see the political wait-and-see approach as a welcome delay to the decision-making process regarding genetic testing, genetic information, and insurance industry. Most western countries do not as yet have any clear legislation on genetic testing in place. In the last 15 years, some American states imposed a moratorium on the use of genetic information for insurance purposes, and in 1995 the Netherlands and the United Kingdom followed. The United Kingdom has reviewed a previous decision to accord access in order to avoid the emergence of a two-class regime in the insurance field, but this political strategy does not seem to satisfy the industry. According to Brockett et al.:

> The states that disallowed classification in genetic testing issues have raised privacy rights and employees' concerns onto a higher pedestal while invalidating the business concerns of insurance companies.[68]

The authors believe that this trend has blurred the lines between social programmes and insurance companies, with the genetic testing issue transformed into an argument against insurance. Genetic testing and screening and therapy are undoubtedly a challenge for public policies as they reflect an emergence of conflicts deriving not only from a reorganization of the risks allocation system but also from a new understanding of what risks are in the genetic economy and commerce. Interestingly, this debate seems to overlook the fact that genetic testing provides ways of assessing predispositions and susceptibilities, but by no means concrete diseases. If illness is defined according to genetic information rather than expression of illness, we might all turn out to be somehow high-risk-insured, as the probability of an illness does not say anything about its genetic mutation. Nevertheless, genetic information is becoming a source and a reference not only for medical practitioners, healthcare managers, and the insurance industry but also for new investors and the new economy.

6. THE GENETIC ECONOMY AND COMMERCE—A NEW ORDER

In his 1988 book *Embryo Handel* (Trading Embryos), the Swiss author and academic researcher Samuel Stutz[69] posed the question that many had been thinking about since the creation of the first IVF laboratory embryo in 1977/78. Stutz asked whether the laboratory structure of the new biomedicine would transform embryos into raw material for the medical and pharma industry.[70] Since then, this question has occupied the minds of many biotechnology critics, as the biolaboratory opens up another site in the economic and commercial system in which genetic resources are more easily acquired. Stutz did suggest that a sort of illegal trade was already taking place in the late 1980s, one capable of giving research laboratories what needed for the advancement of their research activities. The author singled out Australia as one of the western countries that most eagerly cultivated a utilitarian approach towards the use of embryos and foetuses for research purposes, turning its scientists into merchants of life. Since then, however, new regulations and genetic laws have been introduced in western societies to make it more difficult to trade genetic resources as raw material, although this does not necessarily mean that the illegal economy, which is the other side of the coin, has been completely defeated. The fears expressed by many critics that the bioscience and biotechnological field will enter new collaborations and alliances with industry and commerce intuitively reflect what has been acknowledged over the years: that genetic material—stem cells, embryos, cells, genes—is profitable raw material. And analyses projected towards the future reinforce this sense of repositioning of the compass in terms of the creation of wealth using genetics and bodily resources. In their 2002 article "Genomics and Social Science," Harvey et al. propose a series of forecasts that describe the genomic era and the cultural system in which it is embedded. The authors, however, do not engage in a debate about definitions, and admit to using the expression *genomics* in rather general terms, as at the time of writing, it might already be superseded by "proteomics" or "the post-genomics era."

Proteomics is the science of the gene and protein functions, as they are used in healthcare, agriculture (genetically modified [GM] food), stem cells research, organization and work, and other emerging fields like biomining and bioremediation (environment). Proteomics represents a caesura in so far as "there is a great distance between a nucleic acid sequence and gene expression," and for that very reason the possibility is given that "the concept of a gene itself will fall."[71] Undoubtedly, Hil and Hindmarsh (chapter 3) would argue here that the term gene will fall anyway, and not only because of scientific advancements that make proteins (gene expression) more important than the gene itself. According to the two authors, the connotations attached to genes reveal the political machinations to which that term has been exposed. This would justify speaking of gene as "a fuzzy" term to underline that it lends itself to many uses, especially in criminal law and in disciplinary techniques targeting children. As Hil and Hindmarsh say:

> Above all, there is readiness to assert the primacy of biological factors in crime causation, and to assert that "criminality" can be found in constitutional features rather than in socio-economic, cultural and political contexts. On such questionable premises are based futuristic notions of screening for such fuzzy concepts as the "crime gene."

This controversy reminds us of the precariousness of terms in a changing social and economic order, and of the consequences that that precariousness may have for cultural habits. But what are the consequences of genomics/proteomics for economy and commerce? According to Harvey et al., certain developments seem to indicate that public sector investments in genomics could overtake those going to NASA in the United States. Individual medical profiling, the creation of drugs genomically tailored to individuals, is said to lower the overall costs of drug production and diminish the demand for most drugs. Drugs will also be combined with staple food (nutriceuticals) and create different styles of consumption. A new framework of risk assessment in terms of individual and public risks will boost the insurance industry.[72] Harvey et al. wonder whether the changes that are occurring in industry and global gross domoestic product (GDP) through biotechnology will make it necessary to change classic assessment methods. "Do statistics measures need to be modified to cope with changing structures and relationships?" In other words: "How do you calculate the value of genomics-based research and development (R&D), and the economic returns to R&D investments?" or "How is economic and financial risk assessed in relation to genomics-related externalities, such as environmental degradation, public opinion, biodiversity, and human health?"[73]

An investigation of the emergence of a new banking system illustrates the vastness of the changing economy and commerce. Since the emergence of the first (egg and sperm) donor banks in the late 1970s, the cell, zygote, and embryo banks in the 1990s, and now the establishment of human tissue banks, the notion of investment has undergone a fundamental change. Currently there are 400,000 frozen embryos deposited in different US embryo banks. The critic Lori Anderson suggests that this would be enough to create an entire new city.[74] The general impression is that an increasing number of people create term deposits on their genetic material. One of these new forms of investment in genetic resources is the *umbilical cord blood* (UCB), which apparently contains a high number of stem cells and is generally described as "the mother of all blood cells."[75] The stem cells of the UCB have the potential to turn into different types of blood cells that could be used to regenerate bone marrow after intensive chemotherapy. According to Gesche (chapter 4) the UCB technology in Australia has led to the creation of the National Cord Blood Network, which includes 11 collection centres. Given that Australia's population scarcely reaches the 20-million mark, this is an impressive network of blood stem cells and DNA, which Gesche compares with other genetic databases that collect genetic samples to create new and "commercially useful cell lines," from which "substantial financial profit" can be expected.

It is worth dwelling on the significance of this new form of banking in terms of a reorganization of commercial and economic activities in the genetic field. To begin with, it seems reasonable to argue that the notion of "the new economy" makes sense not only in informatics but also when referring to the genetic economy and business that is transforming the relations between production, profit, physical enhancement, and body.[76] Authors Rusinko and Sesok-Pizzini (2003) reveal the fundamental relationship between the new economy and its new raw material when they maintain that UCB stem cells are readily available as a by-product of birth, making them less ethically and politically controversial than embryonic stem cells.[77] But why does UCB banking represent a fundamental element of a new economy, rather than just another technology to be added to the list of the biotechnologies that are already shaping and modifying the social space? Rusinko and Sesok-Pizzini argue that UCB is an innovation that is embedded in a technological community framework.[78] This technological community framework is constituted by three chronological and interdependent activities: R&D functions (given by basic research, financing, education, and training); institutional functions (legitimation, regulation, and technology standards); and, finally, proprietary functions (applied R&D, testing, manufacturing, and marketing).

These functions and subfunctions represent a technological community in which central roles are played by corporate interests, social expectations, public governance, grants and financial support, educational establishments and networks of practitioners, proprietary knowledge (patents) and profit, genetic testing for safety reasons, manufacturing of final products, and customer information and selling strategies. The institutional functions are given by the policies that legitimate and govern the members of the technological community. That the UCB banking necessitates such an apparatus in order to move from an innovative stage to applied knowledge and finally proprietary knowledge is due to the special human aspects related to this form of system that collect this "raw material" during the birth or soon after the placenta has been expelled from the female body. It is an emergent economic practice that commodifies a highly intimate part of private social life. The UCB banking represents an economy of the body and, as such, it requires a different way of penetration and regulation of the human territory. In addition to that, specific questions arise concerning ownership, privacy, and transferability and use of the stem cells in the cases in which the UCB derives from an abortion.[79] Who owns the UCB—the child from whom the placenta was taken or the parents? If the UCB is donated to be used on patients external to the family, additional forms of genetic testing of cells and genetic testing and screening of the donor are necessary to avoid the transmission of genetic diseases. In this case, privacy questions emerge connected with informed consent and safety. If the UCB stem cells derive from aborted foetuses, the ethical issue are said to be less cogent; however, a question of safety arises when spontaneous abortions reveal foetal anomalies that must be coded in the stem cells.[80]

But what do UCB banks do? They collect, analyse, test, and store the cord and its cells for the donor and his/her family for later use in case of disease and invasive operations. Usually, this sort of banking is defined as private UCB banking, because its services are exclusively directed to the donors and their family members, and the potential UCB beneficiaries must pay a fee for the initial storage. According to Rusinko and Sesok-Pizzini (2003), the largest of the commercial UCB banks, Viacord Inc., charges $1,500 and an annual storage fee for the duration of the storage contract ($95). But a very large non-profit system has also emerged, called natural family planning (NFP) UCB banking, in which the donors do not have exclusive use of the stored cord. Here the donors and their families have no precedence over other customers. The NFP UCB banks collect a fee ($15,300) only when the UCB is used for transplant, and the NFP fee is paid by the public sector.[81] When the UCB is used for research purposes, no fee is required.

The most striking aspect of the genetic economy and commerce is that, contrary to what it is generally assumed, many projects and technologies related to the "new genetics" are publicly funded. Interestingly, the private sector is increasingly capitalizing on (perhaps exploiting) the knowledge provided by "government-funded research and on the expertise of researchers in academic institutions, many of which are publicly funded."[82] The first research activities on the use of stem cells deriving from UCB started in the United States in the 1980s and were primarily federally funded and directed to NFP UCB laboratories and banks. According to Rusinko and Sesok-Pizzini, the National Heart, Lung, and Blood Institute of the National Institute of Health (NIH) has invested millions of dollars to support a network of research, transplant centres, and UCB banks in the United States. The first privately funded UCB bank appeared in the 1990s "due to the profit potential in UCB collection and storage for individuals and families."[83] In the mean time numerous UCB banks have been created such as the London Cord Blood Banks (LCBB) which belong to the National Blood Service, the latter of which has invested £4 million in this public service in recent years. There are also private UK Cord Blood Banks, a business venture of the US New England Cord Blood Bank Inc. Other banks are an emanation of transplant or blood centres, like the New York Blood Center, the Eurocord (a cooperative of clinical trials groups), and the Placental Blood Program.

The private UCB banks store stem cells for family use, while the NFP UCB banks do so for public use. However, studies seem to confirm that transplants from relative to relative have a higher success rate than donor transplants. These results have prompted the creation of a Cord Blood Registry in the

United States (2001) storing cord blood stem cells for family members. These cells "might allow a patient to obtain a new blood and immune system as healthy as that possessed at birth in case of need, and other family members might also receive the same protection."[84] It seems that, through the technological transformations that are currently taking place, family ties, and perhaps family in general, emerge as invigorated and stronger (in genetic-economic terms) and more disciplined (in biopolitical terms) than ever. Finally as Rusinko and Sesok-Pizzini confirm, there are already patents related to UCB in the United States, Europe, and Japan.[85] The "new genetics" and genetic economy and commerce reveal a very interesting network of actors that goes beyond the social clusters of the past. It seems that the medical and scientific profession has irrevocably entered into new forms of alliances and commercial fields in order to respond to demands coming from both personal and public interests. This shift perhaps also results from a second repositioning of the scientific and medical profession. If in the past medicine was regarded as a high-standard profession, and the medical professionals as a sort of priest-caste that pronounced their sentences in terms of hope or lack of hope, they now seem able to narrate a different story that takes the individuals away from the realm of fate and into that of action. The narrative of prediction is reminiscent of the ancient practice of foretelling dangers in order to prepare individuals for the challenges looming in the future.

This new way of approaching risks might lead to a different attitude towards the self, a sort of care of the self that is embedded in a different knowledge culture in which the private and the public are intrinsically connected to each other. But who are the guardians of this knowledge? The Australians, Otlowski and Williamson (2003), argue that "doctors must be the gatekeepers of the new genetic knowledge."[86] As explained by Weisbrot (chapter 5), there seems to be a need to give medical doctors and practitioners decision power in matters related to the disclosure of, or denied access to, genetic information. This is what emerged from the recommendations that the Australian Law Reform Commission and Australian Health and Ethics Committee (ALRC-AHEC) have formulated in the final report resulting from their inquiry into the protection of human genetic information in Australia. It seems, therefore, that through genetics doctors reposition themselves in the social sphere as mediators between the interests of the individual and those of the family, groups, society, as well as economy and commerce. Considering the myriad of new actors operating in the genetic economy, it seems reasonable to cultivate a privileged relationship with the physicians, who have been the most trustworthy allies of women, children, and human beings for many centuries.

But now the question arises of whether they can be trusted to the extent of being considered the owners of genetic knowledge. Perhaps here lies the most challenging task for public policy, policymaking, and politics, for the governance of the new genetics will succeed only when we come to a shared definition of who is the morally legitimate owner of genetic knowledge. And at this stage everything seems to point to the ethical self.

As argued in the preceding chapter, new laws and policies regulating individual choices and personal rights must be formulated in order to create the conditions of shared principles capable of facing the challenges of new genetic science and technologies. As a consequence, a new political system must arise from the historical transformation that we are witnessing, one that expresses a social policies framework in which the ethical self and its social, cultural, and economic activities are embedded.

What the social policies framework in the genetic society will look like is still an open question, as no definitive decisions have been made in terms of governance of biotechnologies and proprietary knowledge emerging from the "new genetics." Some commentators, e.g., Gottweis (1998), exhort policymakers to consider the necessity to develop conditions of reinvigorating old institutions and creating new institutional bodies capable of ensuring a high degree of tolerance of, and respect for, the variety of socially available policy narratives and interpretations of realities in the field of social policies. Gottweis understands this multiplicity of different positions as an expression of the postmodern condition of our culture characterized by an "irreducible pluralism." The postmodern style of policymaking could be guaranteed through the creation of "public spaces" within the confines of institutional politics and policies that allow for the "articulation of alternative readings of genetic engineering." This approach would institutionalize what Gottweis calls "the micropolitics of boundary drawing" between politics, the economy, and science.[87]

But, as Fisher (2003) suggests, a changed way of understanding policymaking and, consequently, policy analysis necessitates a different political framework removed from "technocratic policy analysis." The author privileges a post-empirical approach to policymaking oriented towards "an understanding of the discursive struggle to create and control systems of shared social meanings." At this stage, Fisher argues: "If politics does not fit into the methodological scheme, then politics is the problem."[88]

NOTES

1 Finkel, E. 2005. *Stem Cells: Controversy at the Frontiers of Science*. Sydney: ABC Books, 101.

2 Betta, M. and Clulow, V. 2005. Healthcare management—training and education in the genomic era. *Journal of Health and Human Services Administration* 27 (1): 465–500.

3 Finkel, ibid., 259.

4 Ibid.

5 Ibid., 134.

6 Ibid.

7 Ibid.

8 Castells, M. 2001. *The Internet Galaxy: Reflection on the Internet, Business, and Society*. Oxford: Oxford University Press, 22. "The Internet did not originate in the business world. It was too daring a technology, too expensive a project, and too risky an initiative to be assumed by profit-oriented organizations."

9 MacIntyre, S. 1997. Social and psychological issues associated with the new genetics. *Philosophical Transactions of the Royal Society of London* 352: 1095–1101.

10 Bubela, T. M. and Caulfield T. A. 2004. Do the print media "hype" genetic research? A comparison of newspaper stories and peer-reviewed research papers. *Canadian Medical Association Journal* 170 (9): 1399–1400. The authors investigated 26 newspapers from four countries or 627 newspaper articles reporting on 111 papers published in 24 scientific and medical journals.

11 Ibid., 1404.

12 MacIntyre, ibid., 1095.

13 For the purpose of this chapter I will use the terms illness and disease interchangeably without specifying their semantics or differences originating from local/peripheral knowledge.

14 For more details on available tests see Genetics & IVF Institute at <http://www.givf.com>.

15 American Council of Life Insurance, 1996. The need for genetic information insurance. Statement of the American Council of Life Insurance presented to the National Association of Insurance Commissioners Genetic Testing. Working Group of the Life Insurance (A) Committee on 3 June 1996. White paper. Washington, D.C. Quoted in Brockett, P. L., MacMinn, R., and Carter, M. 1999. Genetic testing, insurance economics, and societal responsibility. *North American Actuarial Journal* 3 (1): 1–20, 3.

16 Author unknown. 2003. Genetic testing and predictive medicine. Conference of European Churches. Commission for Church and Society. Working Group on Bioethics, 1–13, available at <http://www.cec-kek.org/English/BioethicGeneticTesting.pdf>. Cited 7 July 2004. The following quotations refer to this article.

17 Ibid., 6.

18 Habermas, J. 2003. *The Future of Human Nature*. London: Polity Press in association with Blackwell. [*Die Zukunft der menschlichen Natur. Auf dem Weg zu einer liberalen Eugenik?* Frankfurt: Suhrkamp, 2001.] Interestingly, the English version contains a postscript, and the essay on faith, which are missing in the original German version, in which Habermas seems to argue that in the genetic era philosophy is moving towards religion. A controversial move indeed. I refer here to pp. 102–103.

19 Lowton, K. and Gabe, J. 2003. Life on a slippery slope: perceptions of health with cystic fibrosis. *Sociology of Health & Illness* 25 (4): 289–319, 298.

20 Ibid., 296.

21 Bury, M. 1991. The sociology of chronic illness: a review of research and prospects. *Sociology of Health & Illness* 13 (4): 451–468. Quoted in Lowton and Gabe, ibid., 291.

22 Ibid., 315.

23 Catholic and Protestant Churches have never absolutely condemned technological and scientific research—of course after Copernicus and Galileo. In the debate concerning IVF, genetic research, and cloning, the Churches have maintained an open position that reveals their will to avoid the mistakes of the past. Even the abortion debate has demonstrated how stratified and sophisticated their argumentation is, which should not be confused with the sectarian fighting among some of its members. For a detailed analysis of the official documents and position taken by the Churches in the genetic debate, see Betta, M. 1995. *Embryonenforschung und Familie. Zur Politik der Reproduction in Grossbritannien, Italien, and der Bundesrepublik Deutschland.* Frankfurt, Paris, New York: Peter Lang Verlag, especially 147–163.

24 Author unknown, ibid., note 6, p. 10, available at <http://www.cec-kek.org/English/Bioethic GeneticTesting.pdf>.

25 Ibid., 12.

26 See Genetics & IVF Institute at <http://www.givf.com>. The institute's main offices and laboratories are in Fairfax, Virginia. The services offered include egg donors, the world's largest group of sperm banks, and one of America's most active pre-implantation genetics testing centres. Cited 14 September 2004.

27 Rizzo, F. R. 1999. Genetic testing and therapy: a pathway to progress and/or profit? *International Journal of Social Economics* 26 (1/2/3/): 109–133, 109.

28 Ibid., 113.

29 Ibid., 112.

30 Rasmussen, N. 2004. The moral economy of the drug company–medical scientists collaboration in Interwar America. *Social Studies of Science* 34 (2): 161–185, 162.

31 In the following paragraph I will refer to Rizzo's analysis on pp. 113–118.

32 For a philosophical analysis of the transformation of patients into consumers through the emergence of the biotechnological laboratory, see Betta and Clulow, ibid.

33 Ibid., 129.

34 Bock, A.-K., Ibarreta, D., Lheureux, K., Libeau, M., and Nilsagård, H. 2001. Data is destiny: health care and human genomics. *Foresight* 3 (4): 377–388, 378.

35 Ibid., 378.

36 Betta and Clulow, ibid.

37 Rizzo, ibid., 109, 117–188.

38 Kleinke, J. D. 1997. The industrialization of health care. *Journal of the American Medical Association* 278: 1456–1457. Quoted in Rizzo, ibid., 117–118.

39 Bock, ibid., 381–382.

40 Harvey, M., McMeekin, A., and Miles, I. 2002. Genomics and social science: issues and priorities. *Foresight* 4 (40): 13–28.

41 Rasmussen, ibid., 161.

42 Rizzo, ibid., 112–113.

43 Rasmussen, ibid., 164.

44 Ibid., 178.

45 For the following reconstruction of the modernization of American medicine towards "scientific medicine" I will draw on Rasmussen's historical analysis on pp. 163–174.

46 A trend that we are currently witnessing with the increasing attempts to discipline the biomedical laboratories and new genetic firms by requesting them to label genetically modified food or the exact ingredients of genetic drugs. The debate that originated out of GM food labelling and genetic drugs labelling, and which is currently taking place in all Western societies, confirms that we are in the middle of a dramatic reorganization of the pharmaceutical and healthcare system, as well as of the production systems of primary goods (food/agriculture) and distributive justice.

47 Rasmussen, ibid., 166.

48 Ibid., 168

49 Ibid., 172.

50 Ibid., 177.

51 Perhaps current grants and grant applications can be classified in the same way, namely as a means by which scientists, especially social scientists, collaborate with governments or bureaucracies, such as the European Union which is still a supranational state, in order to secure much needed money for their academic activities, and to take part in the governance process. For governments grants are a form of scientific cooptation that does not evoke the same negative feelings as political cooptation of intellectuals and scientists. The effects, however, might be the same.

52 Rasmussen, ibid., 179.

53 Bock et al., ibid., 384.

54 Rizzo, ibid., 117.

55 Khoury, M. J., McCabe, L., Edward, R. B., and McCabe, M. D. 2003. Population screening in the age of genomic medicine. *The New England Journal of Medicine* 348 (1): 50–58, 50.

56 The effects of genetic testing in the workplace have been a cause of concern to many observers. In spite of this, no national policies seem to have been created in order to manage this new form of employee–employer relation. The unions, not only in Australia, have failed to produce any coherent policy in the field. The following literature underlines the necessity to anticipate at least some aspects linked with testing employees. MacDonald, C. and Williams-Jones, B. 2002. Ethics and genetics: susceptibility testing in the workplace. *Journal of Business Ethics* 35: 235–241. French, S. 2002. Genetic testing in the workplace: the employer's coin toss. Duke Law & Technology Review, May 9, available at <http://www.law.duke.edu/journals/dltr/articles/2002dltr0015.html>. Cited 6 July 2004. Jinks, A. M. and Daniels, R. 1999. Workplace health concerns: a focus group study. *Journal of Management and Medicine* 13 (2): 95–104. Draper, E. 1998. Drug testing in the workplace: the allure of management technologies. *International Journal of Sociology and Social Policy* 18 (5/6): 62–103.

[57] Annas, G. J., Glantz, L. H., and Roche, P. A. 1995. *Guidelines for Protecting Privacy Information Stored in Genetic Data Banks*. (The Genetic Privacy Act and Commentary). Boston, MA: Health Law Department, Boston University School of Public Health. Quoted in Rizzo, ibid., 127.

[58] Rizzo, ibid., 123.

[59] Ibid., 115.

[60] Ibid., 118.

[61] Ibid., 125.

[62] Ibid., 129.

[63] Brockett et al., ibid., 9.

[64] Ibid., 5.

[65] Fisher, N. L. 2004. Genetic testing and health insurance: can they coexist? *Cleveland Clinical Journal of Medicine* 71 (1): 8–9, 9.

[66] Brockett et al., ibid., 7.

[67] Brockett, P. L. and Tankersley E. S. 2001 [1973]. The genetics revolution, economics, ethics, and insurance. Beauchamp T. L. and Bowie N. E. 2001 [1973]. *Ethical Theory and Business*, 6th edn. Englewood Cliffs, NJ: Prentice-Hall, 310–318, 311.

[68] Ibid., 17.

[69] Stutz, S. 1988. *Embryo Handel*. Bern: Zytglogge.

[70] The question of selling human bodily parts is not new, but it is acquiring increasing importance. See on this topic Kolnsberg, H. R. 2003. An economic study: should we sell human organs? *International Journal of Social Economics* 30 (10): 1049–1069. Kolnberg develops economic scenarios and outcomes related to the selling of human organs particularly focusing on pricing and profitability in relation to donor benefit. In the end, the donors do not seem to benefit at all.

[71] Harvey et al., ibid., 23.

[72] Ibid., 23.

[73] Ibid., 16–17.

[74] Anderson, L. 2004. Rasche Lösungen, magische Pillen. *Gen-Ethischer Informationsdienst* 165 (August/September): 38–40.

[75] Rusinko, C. A. and Sesok-Pizzini, D. A. 2003. Using a technological community framework to manage new medical technologies: the case of umbilical cord blood (UCB) banking. *Journal of Health Organization and Management* 17 (96): 399–421.

[76] Not only human bodies are meant here but also the entire genetic body of nature comprehensive of animals and plants.

[77] Rusinko and Sesok-Pizzini, ibid., 400.

[78] The authors draw on the theoretical model of the technological community framework developed by Van de Ven, A. H. 1993. A community perspective on the emergence of innovations. *Journal of Engineering and Technology Management* 10: 23–51.

[79] Yang, M., Kuo, T. R., and Murphy Jones, R. 2003. The marketing strategies analysis for the umbilical cord blood banking service. *International Journal of Health Care Quality Assurance* 16 (6): 293–299, 294.

[80] Ibid.

[81] Rusinko and Sesok-Pizzini, ibid., 409.

[82] Buchanan, A., Brock, D., Daniels, N., and Wikler, D. 2000. *From Chance to Choice: Genetics and Justice*. Cambridge: Cambridge University Press, 4.

[83] Ibid., 406.

[84] Yang et al., ibid., 294.

[85] Rusinko and Sesok-Pizzino, ibid., 406.

[86] Otlowski, M. and Williamson, R. 2003. Ethical and legal issues and the "new genetics." *Medical Journal of Australia* 178: 582–585.

[87] Gottweis, H. 1998. Governing molecules. *The Discursive Politics of Genetic Engineering in Europe and the United States*. Cambridge, MA, and London: MIT Press, 9, 27, 336–338.

[88] Fisher, F. 2003. *Reframing Public Policy: Discursive Politics and Deliberative Practices*. New York: Oxford University Press, 2–5, 12–13.

II. THE AUSTRALIAN CASE

RICHARD HIL AND RICHARD HINDMARSH

BODY TALK: GENETIC SCREENING AS A DEVICE OF CRIME REGULATION

Considerable controversy has accompanied the emergence of human genetics and its offshoot, behaviour genetics, over recent decades. The tendency in some quarters to engage a form of genetic reductionism—i.e., attributing human behaviour mainly or entirely to genetic "make-up," "markers," "triggers," or "traits"—has raised concerns over the possible implications of this way of thinking about human affairs. Violence, aggression, impulsivity, and hyperactivity have been linked variously to genetic factors. While few if any geneticists would be brazen or foolhardy enough to talk about a "crime gene," it has nonetheless become clear that certain genetic markers have been linked with certain problematic and aberrant conduct—markers that may be screened for in a future, arguably dystopian society. This form of "geno creep" or "backdoor eugenics" is the subject of this chapter. By this we mean the tendency for genetic reductivist accounts to filter into, and perhaps dominate, explanations of phenomena that previously might have been interpreted in alternative ways. This is a subtle mode of incrementalism founded upon the recent renaissance of science, and occasioned in large measure by the rise of human genetics (also referred to as the "new genetics"; see below). The growing ascendancy of this branch of science, and its application to human affairs, comes not through brazen and totalizing claims but through subtle appeals to science and the assumption that life is governed through genetic composition. We critically examine the underlying assumptions of this form of reductivist approach and raise questions about its possible implications for certain populations. We draw particular attention to the connection between genetics and attention deficit hyperactivity disorder (ADHD) and to the way this "condition" has been explained as a result of genetic predisposition. We begin, however, with a brief foray through the history of biological explanations of crime and criminality with the purpose of highlighting a way of taxonomic and classificatory thinking that continues to the present day. The origins of such thinking are to be found in the rise of science during the 17th century and later the disciplines of the 19th century that privileged biological rather than other competing explanations of crime and criminality.

Michela Betta (ed.), The moral, social, and commercial imperatives of genetic testing and screening. The Australian case, 53–70.

1. CRIME, SCIENCE, AND THE CREATION OF THE CRIMINAL "OTHER"

The "scientific" study of crime and criminals emerged as a formally constituted discipline towards the end of the 19th century. Similar scientific accounts of "criminals" had already occurred in the 17th century, if not before. But the impetus provided by the growing fear among the "respectable" classes of threat and disorder, along with the general commitment to "scientific progress" introduced with the Enlightenment, ushered in an era of intense empirical activity concerning crime and other social problems. This followed in the wake of other areas of inquiry, such as mathematics, physics, and natural philosophy, where counting, measurement, and classification had become the hallmarks of scientific practice, and the empirical foundation for what was regarded as acceptable "knowledge" about the world and the place of people in it.[1] Numerous philosophers and reformers thus sought new ways of approaching questions of crime and punishment that contrasted with the arbitrary and brutal practice of the past. Criminology came to the fore during the late 19th century as a scientific project dedicated to the government of certain populations. Based on rigorous, although ultimately flawed, empirical studies of "criminals," Italian army physician, Ceseare Lombroso (1913), put forward the first major criminological explanation of crime.[2] Lombroso's attempt to explain the origins of crime and criminality as an expression of biological inferiority rested on the Darwinian assumption that human behaviour resulted from certain evolutionary processes, which, in effect, rendered some people more "developed," "advanced," and "civilized" than others—a form of chauvinistic thought evidenced later in the works of eugenicists.

Drawing on positivist methodology (which recognizes only positive facts and observable phenomena), Lombroso conducted elaborate studies of human skulls. His attention was drawn most enthusiastically to the skull shape of an infamous criminal named Vilela. Lombroso concluded from his studies that the criminal was "born" rather than "made," and that the most serious criminals displayed various "primitive" facial and bodily features that distinguished them from others. Jaw size, skull shape, eye defects, large ears, and lips typified the "atavistic" offender. For Lombroso and others, the "discovery" of the biological origins of crime was something of a Holy Grail. In scrutinizing the skull of Vilela, Lombroso declared:

> I found in the skull of a brigand a very long series of atavistic anomalies, above all an enormous middle occipital fosea and hypertrophy of the vermis analogous to those that are found in inferior vertebrates. At the sight of these strange anomalies the problem of the nature and origins of the criminal seemed to be resolved; the characteristics of primitive men and of inferior animals must be reproduced in our times.[3]

Lombroso's reference to "atavistic abnormalities" and his apparent "discovery" of characteristics similar to "primitive men" and "animals" revealed much about his working assumptions. Above all, he held the staunch belief that the origins of crime could be discovered from the inherited characteristics of the individual criminal. Such thinking proved a convenient way of promoting the value of scientific inquiry in unravelling the secrets of the social world; it also installed a profound sense of difference between "criminals" and others. Nowhere in this narrative, however, was there an appreciation of the socially constructed and contested nature of categories like "crime" and "criminal"; nor was crime considered or situated in historical, social, economic, or political contexts. Rather, crime and criminality were seen as artefacts of the biological world, and the task facing scientists and law enforcers was simply to identify and classify those who constituted a danger to others.[4] Although Lombroso was later to refine his theory, citing, for instance, the role of some social factors in influencing the expression of biological traits, he nonetheless adhered strongly to the notion of the atavistic criminal.[5]

Although widely criticized for his views, Lombroso's brand of "biological positivism" was to dominate criminological thinking for at least three decades.[6] Perhaps the most significant challenge to the empirical conclusions drawn by Lombroso was in the work of the English prison medical officer, Charles Goring. Goring set out to examine Lombroso's proposition that criminals could be clearly distinguished on the basis of inherited constitutional factors like skull shape, eye colour, ear size, jaw lines, and so forth. In a meticulous study that took over a decade to complete, Goring compared a group of convicts to a group of unconvicted persons (the latter including university undergraduates, hospital patients, army officers, and rank-and-file soldiers in the Royal Engineers). Yet, after having scrutinized various physical characteristics (head height, width, circumference, symmetry, nasal contours, eye and hair colour, left-handedness, and so forth), Goring was unable to discern any real constitutional differences when he compared various criminals and non-criminals. Nonetheless, when it came to "mental ability," Goring found evidence of inherited shortcomings, and he further discerned differences in stature and body weight. Such differences, Goring argued, supported the view that criminal conduct was largely the product of nature rather than nurture.

The works of Lombroso and Goring (among others) thus embraced a human-centred biological way of thinking about crime and its causes. In practical terms, all that remained to be done was to measure the nature and extent of inhered difference and then to recommend a rigorous programme of intervention in order to sift the "criminal" from the "law abiding." Premised on the supposed "objectivity" of "scientific method," this project amounted basically to a "criminology of the other," designed for purposes of intellectual interest as well as the practical management of certain populations.[7] The eugenicist impulse was never far from the criminological surface. As Rafter commented, "[T]he continuing dispute over whether criminology's main goal should be to help control crime or to produce knowledge with no direct use-value can ... be traced to criminal anthropology—to some of its proponent's subordination of criminology to eugenics."[8]

2. CRIME AND THE "RACIALLY UNFIT"

A central feature of the eugenicist movement (which flourished from the mid-19th century onwards) was the belief that without radical intervention "racial fitness" (a notion propounded by Darwin) would be compromised by the growing ranks of the "feckless," "idle," "alcoholics," "mentally defective," "degenerates," and—worst of all—"criminals." Based on the "scientific" proposition that the fundamental characteristics of human kind were passed down (differentially, of course) from one generation to another, this view led to practices aimed at achieving "racial hygiene/fitness" through clinical methods of "selective breeding."[9] Importantly, such a programme required a more rigorous and practical form of population measurement and analysis than had been previously conducted by statisticians like Adolphe Quettelet (1796–1874). In seeking to measure differences between populations, Quettelet drew on the publication of French national crime figures to support his views on "normal distribution" and "standard deviation."[10] This laid the foundations for countless classificatory projects that were linked to criminological inquiry. Additionally, this tradition of intense statistical inquiry was further evidenced in meticulous empirical studies of the poor by social reformers and philanthropists like Jeremy Bentham (1748–1832) and, later, the prodigious Henry Mayhew (1812–1887).

However, the fusion between biological explanations of crime (via the notion of "heritability") and organized statistical knowledge relating to discrete populations became expressed most powerfully in the empirical works of Francis Galton (1822–1911) and Karl Pearson (1857–1936) in England, and of Charles Davenport (1866–1944), George Yule (1871–1951), and Havelock Ellis (1859–1939) in the United States. In his energetic (some might say feverish) devotion to the study of "individual differences," Galton proposed that scientific method could be used to identify the "racially unfit" and all those who strayed from the "racial centre."[11] Like many of his devoted followers, Galton took the white upper classes as his taxonomic yardstick of racial superiority and contrasted the respectable classes with the aberrant qualities of the lower (criminogenic) "orders." Viewed as an expression of biological inheritance, eugenicists thus regarded criminality and other "disorders," "abnormalities," "conditions," and "maladies" as closely related to the qualities and characteristics of a "lesser stock." As Ellis observed:

> The criminal... in some of his [sic] most characteristic manifestations, is a congenitally weak-minded person whose abnormality, while by no means leaving the mental aptitude unimpaired, cruelly affects the feelings and volition so influencing conduct and rendering him an antisocial element in society.[12]

Eugenicists, however, observed that although biological factors took precedence in the aetiology of crime, social factors too played their part in such behaviour. Yet while heated debates took place about the relative weight given to biological and other factors, it was argued that a programme of "social hygiene" based on an appreciation of heritability could to some extent *mitigate* or *arrest* the worst effects of "racial pollution." At its most radical this programme involved surgical interventions such as vasectomies, lobotomies, abortions, and sterilizations. It further involved a range of "assessments" and "treatments." These included the IQ test, provision of maternal and child welfare programmes, epidemiological studies of disease patterns, medical testing of children, birth control, and clinics for sex education. Also, mental hygiene movements to medicalize the treatment of both mental illness and physical and mental disability, sexually transmitted disease (STD) clinics, campaigns to abolish slums and the provision of quality public housing, and the study, diagnosis, and treatment of juvenile delinquency.

The apparent scale of the "problem" of inherited criminality (or "racial unfitness") faced by governments was evidenced in the 1929 deliberations of a British Parliamentary Committee on Mental Deficiency, which estimated that there were 350,000 "mental defectives" in the United Kingdom. According to the Committee the number of "defectives" had doubled since 1908 and included "insane persons, epileptics, paupers, criminals, unemployables, habitual slum dwellers, prostitutes, inebriates, and other social inefficients"—all drawn, typically, from those "persistently below the average income and social character."[13] The proposition that criminals and other "defectives" and "inefficients" could be distinguished biologically from "normal" and "law-abiding" persons has continued to hold sway to the present day. Underpinning this proposition is the simple, yet apparently persuasive idea that crime and other forms of antisocial behaviours are passed on from one generation to another. Organic and constitutional theories of crime have tended to go in tandem. Constitutional theories of the body have proved particularly appealing as a way of explaining *predisposition* to crime and delinquency. Sheldon's typology of "body types" that equated "mesomorphic" (muscular, large chest, heavy-boned) body types with delinquent and violent tendencies,[14] followed by Glueck and Glueck's, and later Hans Eysenck's, endorsement of the same,[15] illustrated the connection often drawn between bodily constitution and behaviour, and by implication, genetics, and criminality.

Consider, for instance, Eysenck's following confident assertion: "There seems little doubt that mesomorphic physique and high andromorphy are positively correlated with delinquency, and that ectomorphy is negatively correlated with delinquency."[16] Eysenck then made explicit the genetic connection: "There is a *strong genetic component* to the development of different types of physique, *although environmental factors also play a somewhat minor part*, and this suggests that personality features associated with physique will also be found to differentiate criminals and non-criminals, perhaps partly on a genetic basis" (our emphasis).[17] Here we see a continuation of a tradition of "scientific" thought that has its origins in the anthropometric work of Galton, Pearson, and others. Above all, there is readiness to assert the primacy of biological factors in crime causation, and to assert that "criminality" can be found in constitutional features rather than in socio-economic, cultural, and political contexts. On such questionable premises are based futuristic notions of screening for such fuzzy concepts as the "crime gene." Questionable, not only biologically with contested notions of "the gene"[18] but because of all the claims of impartiality and objectivity, exhaustive longitudinal studies and manipulation of large population data-sets, biological studies of crime, and the theories that flow from them are easily critiqued. Perhaps the main problem facing genetic explanations of crime and criminality is the tendency to disregard social and other factors, and to treat "crime" as if it were a self-evident truth. Rarely is the socially constructed nature of "crime," "crime rates," and "criminality" viewed as problematic; nor is any attention given to the differential nature of policing. Such shortcomings necessarily render genetic explanations of crime problematic, even where there is a nod towards environmental factors or to the vague terrain of "other things being equal." Invariably this is achieved by reducing complex social, economic, and cultural questions to something vaguely known as "background" or the "environment." These entities are frozen in time and space and rendered obscure to anyone seeking a more complex explanation of human behaviour.

3. THE GREAT GENETIC HOPE: THE XYY CHROMOSOME

From time to time biological theorists claim to have discovered the genetic Holy Grail of crime causation. One such case is the discovery of the XYY chromosome. During the 1960s and 1970s, the XYY chromosome theory provided an important impetus for genetic explanations of crime and criminality. A 1965 study of 197 "subnormal" male prisoners found evidence of an additional Y chromosome among a cohort of violent and aggressive men.[19] Another study concluded that an additional chromosome produced extreme psychopathy and led to criminalization at a young age, usually for crimes against property.[20] Later studies linked other "variables" to the additional chromosome, such as tallness, "low intelligence," and epilepsy.[21] Despite the great promise of the XYY theory—indeed, it was considered pivotal to biological arguments about crime—it soon fell into disrepute once its methodological and theoretical shortcomings were identified. These included "scientific" abstractionism (avoiding a wide range of relevant sociocultural and economic considerations concerning crime), individualism, and an overacceptance of official categories like "crime" and "criminality."[22] Such problems, however, failed to deter other related theories from rising to the explanatory surface. For instance, a study conducted by the Institute of Child Health in London concluded that girls with an absence of an X chromosome (Turner's syndrome) were likely to display all manner of antisocial behaviours.[23] Again, such assertions were reductionist because they were made irrespective of social and personal circumstances, and without any appreciation of the socially constructed nature of crime and other forms of behaviour.

4. TWIN AND ADOPTIVE STUDIES

A most well-known attempt to demonstrate the biosocial origins of crime was Mechnick's study of adoptive children in Copenhagen.[24] He found that sons with natural and adoptive parents with criminal records possessed a greater chance of becoming criminal themselves. More significantly though, those sons whose biological parents had criminal records, but whose adoptive parents were law-abiding, were more likely to be registered criminal than those in converse situations. Mechnick concluded that inherited genetic factors, while not acting directly upon the individual, nonetheless rendered the subject more susceptible to criminal influence and therefore to a life of crime. According to Mechnick, susceptible persons have an autonomic nervous system that renders them unable to respond as quickly as others to certain stimuli. Thus, as a result of slow arousal, their ability to learn, and to control aggressive or antisocial behaviours, is significantly impaired. Initially, this theory proved highly persuasive. However, its methodological shortcomings (poor replication techniques, statistically insignificant findings) and other problems (such as the odd assertion that criminality is inherited largely from maternal genes—a gender traditionally less crime-prone than males!) soon raised doubts about its validity.[25] Parallel attempts to draw on studies of identical and fraternal twins have also run into difficulties, mainly on the grounds that they take little or no account of complex social, economic, and political factors. Despite assertions that identical twins exhibit a greater "susceptibility" to crime than fraternal twins, such studies have not managed to successfully disentangle biological from social factors.[26]

Another source of support for genetic theories of crime arose from a number of twin and adoptive studies conducted mainly in the United States during the 1960s and 1970s.[27] Here, attention was focused on whether similar sorts of behaviour were displayed in cases where siblings of natural parents were separated from each other. According to Ellis (in a somewhat uncritical review of sibling studies), the most persuasive support for a link between genetics and crime came from adoption studies. He concluded:

> [T]o the degree that causal statements can ever be made with finality in science the adoption studies carried out [over the last decade] seem to be making the following cautiously worded pronouncement about the involvement of genetics in criminal behaviour possible. Significant amounts of the observed variation in human tendencies to behave criminally appear to be the result of some genetic factors, presumably pertaining to the functioning of the nervous system (at least for the variations observed in criminal behaviours other than those describable as victimless and status offences).[28]

Ellis' cautious conclusion was, however, tempered somewhat when he noted that despite the "weight of accumulating evidence" indicating a connection between genetics and crime, the criminological theorizing around this "remains *embarrassingly primitive* [our emphasis] with respect to offering an adequate explanation for such evidence. In other words, no prominent contemporary criminological theory... specifically predicts that both genetic and environmental variables are involved in criminal behaviour aetiology."[29] Again, what characterizes these studies is a tendency to abstract biological conclusions from any sort of social, economic, political, or cultural explanation. Crime is thus viewed as an objective indicator of aberrant behaviours confined to discrete populations: a line peddled repeatedly by constitutional theorists of crime. Bereft of historical context, such conclusions are thus drawn from a narrow band of empirical indicators suitable mainly for purposes of narrow "scientific" measurement and classification.

5. GENETICS AND VIOLENT AND ANTISOCIAL BEHAVIOUR

The attempt to integrate the study of biology with the social sciences during the 1970s resulted in several fields of inquiry under the umbrella of sociobiology.[30] Predictably perhaps, this attempt to fuse biology with the social sciences aroused controversy.[31] Nonetheless, the many epistemological problems that beset this project failed to deter natural scientists from continuing to embark (in ever greater numbers) on research that purported to demonstrate a link between genetics and human behaviour in the field of "behaviour genetics." The emergence of the new genetics—a project devoted to the study of the genetic origins of various human and other "conditions," especially in relation to cognitive and behavioural manifestations—and the renewed credibility accorded to science have galvanized such work over recent years. Much attention has been focused on the link between genetic predisposition and violence and aggression. Yet, researchers searching for the biological origins of violence and aggression are generally cautious about the influence of genetics on such behaviours, even though they proceed on the basis that genetic differences can be detected, and that some people are more prone to these troubling outcomes. The linkages drawn between genetics and violence and aggression are subtle, but they are connections nonetheless and are expressed through a range of discursive indices that talk obliquely about "predispositions," "orientations," or "general tendencies."[32] Conveniently, this allows for the possibility of genetic explanation while at the same time acknowledging "environmental" factors. Human behaviour is thus seen as an interaction between genes and the environment, although the "trigger" for certain behaviours is usually located in the former. Over recent years, numerous studies have attempted to identify the biological and other factors that predispose some individuals to violent and aggressive conduct. Genetic factors said to lead to such behaviours include variation in neurotransmitter function, variation in thyroid hormone receptor function (leading to ADHD), variation of dopamine (the D4DR "thrill-seeking" gene) and serotonin, high levels of testosterone, or mutation in the gene coding for the enzyme monoamine oxidase.[33]

6. ADHD AND THE SPECTRE OF EUGENICIST THOUGHT

Let us return in more detail to the issue of ADHD in order to illustrate the way in which discursive assumptions find their way into genetics discourse. ADHD is seen by a number of educational psychologists, psychiatrists, and medical practitioners as a major problem requiring the use of personal and pharmaceutical interventions. As noted by researchers in the journal *Educational and Child Psychology*: "Australia is caught up in the current ADHD epidemic. The impact is being felt by families, schools, doctors and mental health practitioners alike."[34] Despite such claims, it has become abundantly clear that ADHD is a highly controversial category that evades easy definition. Despite the massive (and highly lucrative) promotion and dispensation of psychotropic drugs in Australia, America, and Britain to children experiencing this "disorder," this discursive notion is slippery and therefore tends to mean vastly different things to different people. Like the notion of the "gene" it is a fuzzy concept. In a devastating critique of the "scientific" use of the term ADHD, a North American psychologist and scholar, Bob Jacobs, observes:

> History has taught us the lesson of the "Big Lie". Whole societies have brought into ideas and concepts that have later proven to range from baseless to maniacal. Reading with any sort of open mind through the voluminous literature on the topic of ADHD in the early 21st century, one cannot help but be reminded of reading through treatises on slavery in the 18th century. How could something so horrible and so egregious be happening in a "civilized society"? Why didn't these people take a hard look at what they were doing?[35]

Jacobs continues:

> I have no doubt that someday people will look back on the massive drugging of children in Australia and America in the same way. ADHD is a catchall description of childhood behaviour invented by people sitting around a table who stood to benefit by the diagnosis professionally and financially. Virtually any child who has been a problem for an adult could qualify for this "diagnosis", and be declared "sick" in the absence of any medical, scientific or organic findings whatsoever. Yet despite the indisputable fact that no one has been able to tell us what ADHD actually is, millions of parents, teachers and doctors are accepting it without question and supporting the use of powerful cocaine-like drugs in children. Meanwhile, pharmaceutical companies are reaping hundreds and millions of US dollars in profits. When dissidents speak out they are ignored, discouraged or attacked with the viciousness historically characteristic of those profiting from a "Big Lie".

What Jacobs is alluding to here is not only the way in which the category ADHD has come to serve certain sectional interests but also how the term has been uncritically absorbed into the current vernacular of behavioural "conditions," especially in the sphere of education. Further, Jacobs suggests that ADHD is not simply a contested term that lacks clarity and universal application but also enmeshed in a range of other interests linked to the accumulation of corporate profit. The use of this category may serve to discriminate against some of the most disadvantaged of social groups, such as children and young people with intellectual disabilities. Given the questionable nature of ADHD it might be expected that geneticists would be mindful, indeed hypercautious, of its contested nature and application to disempowered subjects. In fact, the reverse is the case.

Take, for example, an article published in the *Journal of the American Academy of Child and Adolescent Psychiatry* entitled "Adoptive and Biological Families of Children and Adolescents with ADHD."[36] The article reports on comparisons of ADHD and other "psychiatric" problems in three groups: adoptive first-degree relatives of children with ADHD; biological first-degree relatives of children with ADHD; and first-degree biological relatives of control subjects with ADHD. The researchers found high rates of mood and anxiety disorders among biological relatives, but not among adoptive carers. "This finding," state the authors, "is consistent with results of prior family studies of ADHD and provides further support for the idea that these other psychiatric disorders in ADHD families are variable manifestations of the genes that influence ADHD."[37] Invariably, such studies tend to take the category of ADHD for granted and to regard it as a self-explanatory and objective category. Little or no attempt is made to question the socially constructed nature of the concept, or to question the differential ways in which it is applied to various populations of children and young people. This is scientism at its most questionable and potentially dangerous. This is further the case if genetic screening for a claimed disposition to ADHD emerges. The idea that certain populations can be distinguished and classified for purposes of intervention and "treatment" on the basis of the most spurious of discursive categories should be of major concern to anyone involved in this field of inquiry.

7. VIOLENCE AND AGGRESSION

Violent and aggressive behaviours have long been associated with genetic influences. The release of chemicals such as testosterone are said to predispose some individuals to periodic outbreaks of violent and aggressive conduct.[38] With unerring confidence, Galton suggested that there are clear biological and genetic determinants of crime, associating crime much more often with men than women. He concluded: "[G]enes almost certainly do play a part in some aspects of criminal behaviour and the question now is not whether to accept the idea of an inborn tendency to crime, but how far it goes in explaining criminal behaviour."[39] This sense of explanatory certainty, however, is undermined somewhat by a number of sociocultural considerations with respect to violence and aggression. As noted previously, there is, first of all, the awkward question of what exactly constitutes these behaviours? Such actions are not as obvious as they might first appear and might again be the end result of complex socially constructed processes that depend on who is involved, and when and where they occur. The sociocultural meanings and definitions associated with such terms inevitably render them problematic. Additionally, as in the case of categories such as ADHD, much depends on who defines or "diagnoses" particular actions as violent and aggressive. This is no cheap semantic point but rather goes to the very heart of concepts that are frequently used as "objective" indicators of human behaviour. This applies to concepts such as "dangerousness," "risk," and "antisocial," all of which are subject to differential interpretations and meanings.

If there is a need to remind ourselves also of how definitions and thinking vary over time, one might ask the following: Who would (other than the totally insensitive or naive) now employ the terms "maladjusted," "retarded," "handicapped," or even "spastic" to refer to people with disabilities? Or who would support the description of school pupils as "educationally subnormal" (ESN), as occurred in the 1950s and 1960s in England? While on the matter of definition, it could be argued that what we define as "violence" or "violent conduct" is commonly understood as direct and interpersonal action that harms others. This in itself begs a number of additional questions like what does "direct" mean? Could, for example, the order by the current US President to bomb Afghanistan or Iraq, knowing full well that this would produce civilian causalities (or "collateral damage"), be regarded as an act of violence? Perhaps it is indeed time to test the genetic links between the actions of various US presidents, dictators, and despotic leaders to determine the origins of *their* behaviours. We might even go as far as seeking to identify the genes of scientists who have repeatedly, over the course of recent history, perpetrated often highly significant harms against all sorts of unknowing, vulnerable, and trusting subjects? Or is this, again, just wishful thinking?

In our view, proponents of genetic explanations of criminal behaviour are often just too quick to dismiss or overlook definitional matters. Further, they are prone to leap to conclusions in the face of credible alternative explanations. Take, for instance, Galton's above argument that the disproportionate number of male offenders *necessarily* reveals a certain sort of genetic predisposition. To fully explain this, one would need to discuss a range of issues such as the culture of aggressive masculinity, situational and context-bound definitions and meanings of violence, as well as various strategies and techniques of policing and regulation that contribute to the criminalization of certain individuals. To leap into genetic explanation is, to put it mildly, premature. It could be further argued that much genetic work proceeds precisely because it chooses to ignore the complexities associated with certain discursive categories. To question the conceptual scaffolding upon which scientific studies are founded would be to dislodge the investigator from a position of empirical confidence. Indeed, many studies exist because they select what they choose to ignore or analyse. Whatever else the field of behaviour genetics reveals, it is a preparedness to regard certain concepts central to its scientific project and to regard them as objective and consensually agreed artefacts suitable to the business of empirical inquiry.

8. SCIENTISM, KNOWLEDGE, AND POWER

The belief that science and scientific method can lead to the discovery of certain truths has been seriously questioned, not least of all by Michel Foucault. This form of epistemological imperialism, as Midgely terms it,[40] has led in some cases to the deliberate obfuscation or ignorance of other competing perspectives on human conduct. Arguably, the completion of the Human Genome Project and various other developments in the field of biotechnology have given rise to a reassertion of faith in science as the ultimate arbiter of reliable and verifiable knowledge. Why the science of human genetics has made such inroads into contemporary thinking is a complex matter, although bioscientific explanation appears to offer a refurbished Enlightenment hope that progress and social order can be achieved through continuation of the modern scientific medium. And yet, despite all the promises, hopes, and portrayals of progress, doubts over genetic technologies have been conspicuously present. Debates over human cloning and designer children,[41] other reproductive technologies, genetic "cures" for conditions and diseases like alcoholism, drug addiction, schizophrenia, and depression, the "commodification" or "bar-coding" of the human body,[42] along with problems associated with genetic testing and screening (such as accuracy and privacy) all highlight the many anxieties attendant in this field. Links drawn between genetics and "stupidity," and even "ugliness" (as suggested by John Watson), are particularly worrying indicators of some types of discriminatory thinking in this area. As David Suzuki and Joseph Levine noted a decade ago:

> [T]he past twenty years have seen a revival of the false dichotomy between genes and environment and a swing in the scientific pendulum towards hereditarianism. Today there are ongoing searches for rogue genes that cause alcoholism, manic depression, criminality, language presidency, intelligence, and sexual orientation. In part, this shift is understandable. The tools of molecular biology have pinpointed genes at work in evolution and disease, so why not apply the same techniques to behaviour?[43]

Suzuki and Levine add that scientists often have little appreciation of the consequences that ensue from their "findings":

> Many scientists are—or profess to be—unaware of how easily scientific claims, even uncertain ones based on tentative and preliminary results, can be used to "explain", and hence justify, why individuals or some groups of people prosper while others languish.

This form of differentiation in which groups and populations are selected out on the basis of genetic diversity harks back to earlier taxonomic ways of thinking. While contemporary behaviour geneticists may balk at being likened to 19th-century eugenicists, there is little doubt that the rush to "scientific explanation" can result in potentially dangerous processes of classification that border on neo-eugenicism. By this we mean that there is a tendency among new geneticists, like their eugenicist predecessors, to engage in a form of classificatory practice that may result in the selecting out of certain populations on the basis of genetic "predisposition" towards certain odd or aberrant behaviours. Much of their work relies on an intellectual screening out of many other explanations (socio-economic, political, and cultural) and a ready acceptance of various assumptive categories. Like eugenicists, exponents of genetics delight in the discovery of classificatory difference that is attributable not to the world of human relations but rather to genetic "markers," "traits," and "triggers." Clearly, it is not sufficient merely to assert that human genetics is benign or aimed solely at improving the quality of life since such claims have been made by some of the most interventionist and intrusive of scientists.

What matters here, though, are the consequences of particular ways of thinking about the origins of human behaviour and the complex interactions between genetics and "the environment." Any such account will be incomplete without due attention to issues of power and of how knowledge is socially constructed and transmitted in the context of a differentiated society. The fact that geneticists have intervened so assertively in various aspects of human behaviour, and that their "findings" and "discoveries" have been so sympathetically regarded by governments eager to address the "problem of crime," suggests that their work is linked closely to the imperatives of regulation and control. If this is the case, as we suggest, then at the very least it behoves scientists in this area to consider, and consider closely the discursive categories that underpin their work. What is abundantly clear in any given area of human behaviour is that it is obviously naive to ignore the social, political, and cultural contexts in which such behaviour originates and occurs. No amount of recidivist thinking can deny that human experience is embedded in such contexts and that power, privilege, and status play a central part in this experience.

For example, there is an abundance of literature that locates the origins of schizophrenia in social and cultural contexts,[44] with Gene Watch UK highlighting the regulatory connection:

> In the UK, Afro-Caribbean people are disproportionately more at risk of being detained by the police or courts under the Mental health act and diagnosed as schizophrenic than any other group, leading some to argue that the label operates as a mechanism of social control.

Importantly, Gene Watch UK adds:

> The complexity of mental and behavioural processes—coupled with the subtleties of the gene–environment interaction—mean the simplistic links between such conditions and one or several genes are inaccurate and potentially dangerous. This is because such oversimplified links can fuel discriminatory claims that one ethnic group may be somehow "mentally inferior" to another and this, in turn, could lead to potentially oppressive practices against particular social groups.[45]

One of the primary dangers of such classificatory reductionism is that it not only avoids the complexities of human life and the interaction between genes and the social environment but it also gives rise to the possibility that certain groups are singled out for medical or social intervention. That such a logic might be applied—indeed is already being applied—to those deemed "criminal" or "antisocial" is readily apparent by the tendency of some exponents of crime genetics to take certain categories and propositions for granted. In the area of criminal justice, behaviour genetics has thus come to play a subtle yet highly influential role in seeking to explain aberrant conduct. There is of yet no forthright claim to be found about a "gene for crime" or a "crime gene" and few would deny some interaction between genes and the environment. And yet links are being made between certain behaviours and genetic markers and in this case "the environment" seems to conveniently slide out of explanatory contention. In multicausal accounts—those that weave together a host of factors and variables—these genetic indices are joined together to form a powerful explanatory nexus that is often difficult to resist, not least because of the enduring faith placed in the scientific method of genetics. In some quarters there has been talk of entire populations of the "genetically unfortunate" languishing in prisons, while others see various degrees of criminal tendency and predisposition among the aggressive, violent, and hyperactive as directly attributable to genetic make-up. Such accounts rarely if ever acknowledge the contested nature of categories like crime and criminality, or antisocial conduct for that matter. Nor do they point to the complex sociopolitical or cultural processes that render some populations (rather than others) likely candidates for criminalization.

9. CONCLUSION

In the current climate of risk-based management and assessment in which wide nets are cast to trawl for those who appear more "crime-prone," it is hardly surprising that such a receptive ear has been given to the taxonomic possibilities of genetic thought, and thus of genetic screening for claims of genetic conditions of crime and antisocial behaviour. The individualization of crime by locating its origins in the body rather than contexts external to it provides the perfect foundation for the science of human genetics to flourish in a system that seeks supportive scientific truth claims to legitimate actions to manage "problem populations," and to buttress existing regimes of power and governance. Against the backdrop of this would-be bio-utopia of a crime-free world[46] lies the dystopian discourse of treating the body like a text, a *password*, providing a document for decoding, categorizing, selection, and discipline suitable to the imperatives of the existing social order. In this worst case scenario, genetic screening as a device of nominating the body as the key site of crime and antisocial behaviour becomes also a diversionary device for the more apparent—and interrelated—reasons for crime and antisocial behaviour such as poverty, alienation, joblessness, lack of educational opportunity, injustice, community disempowerment, discrimination, or abuse and neglect. In short, the policy narrative underpinning genetic screening is that crime is simply a technical, *not* a social, problem, a problem that is to be "deleted." The result is that genetic screening becomes a regulatory device for the legitimation of discrimination and oppression, a "regulatory legitimizer" for the existing order, one that is far removed from any current portrayal of benevolence.

NOTES

1 Worster, D. 1994. *Nature's Economy: A History of Ecological Ideas*, 2nd edn. Cambridge: Cambridge University Press, 406. Also Hindmarsh, R. and Lawrence, G. 2004. Recoding nature: deciphering the script. In: Hindmarsh, R. and Lawrence, G. (eds.), *Recoding Nature: Critical Perspectives on Genetic Engineering*. Sydney: UNSW Press.

2 Lombroso, C. 1913. *Crime: Its Causes and Remedies*. Boston, MA: Little, Brown.

3 Cited in Roach Anlue, S. 1996. *Deviance, Conformity and Control*. Melbourne: Longman Cheshire, 11.

4 Ibid., 14–15.

5 Ibid., 17–18.

6 Taylor, I., Walton, P., and Young, J. 1973. *The New Criminology: For a Social Theory of Deviance*. London: Routledge & Kegan Paul, 39

7 Garland, D. 1997. Of crime and criminals: the development of criminology in Britain. In: Maguire, M., Morgan, R., and Reiner, R. (eds.), *The Oxford Handbook of Criminology*. Oxford: Oxford University Press.

8 Rafter, N. 1992. Criminal anthropology in the United States. *Criminology* 30 (4): 525–545, 526.

9 Kevles, D. 1985. *In the Name of Eugenics*. Los Angeles, CA: University of California Press.

10 Taylor et al. ibid., 37.

11 Kevles, ibid., 5.

12 Ellis, H. 1901. Cited in Kevles, ibid., 56.

13 Cited in Kevles, ibid., 112.

14 Sheldon, W. 1949. *Varieties of Delinquent Youth*. New York: Harper & Row.

15 Glueck, S. and Glueck, E. 1950. *Unravelling Juvenile Delinquency*. New York: Harper & Row; Eysenck, H. 1989. *Crime and Personality*. London: Paladin.

16 Eysenck, ibid., 41.

17 Ibid.

18 Fischer, E. 1997. The archetypal gene: the open history of a successful concept. In: Wirz, J. and Lammerts van Bueren, E. (eds.), The future of DNA. Proceedings of an International Conference about Presuppositions in Science and Expectations in Society, 2–5 October 1996, Goetheanum, Dornach, Switzerland: Kluwer Academic Publishers, 35.

19 Jacobs, P., Brunton, M., Melville, M., Brittain, R., and McClermont, W. 1965. Aggressive behaviour, mental subnormality and the XYY male. *Nature* 208: 1351–1352.

20 Price, W. 1966. Criminal patients with XYY sex chromosome complement. *The Lancet* 1: 35.

21 Morgan, P. 1978. *Delinquent Fantasies*. London: Temple Smith, 343.

22 See Taylor et al., ibid.,, 45–56; Roach, ibid., 14.

23 See Higgins, E. 1997. Study links men's bad behaviour to what's in their genes. *The Weekend Australian*, 14 June.

24 Mechnick, S. 1977. A bio-social theory of the learning of law abiding behaviour. In: Samoff, A., Mechnik, S., and Christensen, O. (eds.), *Biosocial Bases of Criminal Behaviour*. New York: Gaizner; see also Mechnick, S., Muffit, T., and Stack, S. (eds.). 1987. *The Causes of Crime: New Biological Approaches*. Cambridge: Cambridge University Press.

25 Ackers, R. 1994. *Criminological Theories: Introduction and Evolution*. Los Angeles, CA: Roxbury, 80–81.

26 Ibid., 81.

27 For a general review, see Ellis, L. 1985. Genetics and criminal behaviour: evidence through the end of the 1970s. In: Marsh, F. and Katz, J. (eds.), *Biology, Crime and Ethics: A Study of Biological Explanations for Criminal Behaviour*. Cincinnati, OH: Anderson Publishing, 69–81.

28 Ibid., 81.

29 Ibid., 82–83.

30 See Breuer, G. 1982. *Sociobiology and the Human Dimension*. Cambridge: Cambridge University Press; Hinde, R. 1987. *Individuals, Relationships and Culture: Links Between Ethnology and the Social Sciences*. Cambridge: Cambridge University Press; Alcock, J. 2001. *The Triumph of Socio-Biology*. Oxford: Oxford University Press.

31 See Midgley, M. 2003. *The Myths We Live By*. London: Routledge.

32 Fishbein, D. 1990. Biological perspectives in criminology. *Criminology* 28: 27–72, 42.

33 Brunner, H. 1993. Abnormal behaviour associated with a point mutation in the structural gene for monoamine oxidase A. *Science* 262: 578–580; Booth, A. and Osgood, W. 1993. The influence of testosterone on deviance in adulthood. *Criminology* 31 (1): 93–117;.Van den Oord, E. 1994. A study of problem behaviourism 10- to 15-year-old biologically related and unrelated international adoptees. *Behaviour Genetics* 24 (3); Cook, E. 1995. Association with attention deficit disorder and the dopamine gene. *American Journal of Human Genetics* 56: 993–998; Cloninger, C., Adolfsson, R., and Svrakic, N. 1996. Mapping genes for human personality. *Nature Genetics* 12 (1): 3–4; McGuffin, P. and Thapar, A. 1997. Genetic basis of bad behaviour in adolescents. *The Lancet* 350 (9081): 885; Demott, K. 1995. Personality disorders may be genetic. *Clinical Psychiatry News* 27 (12): 27; Hudziak, J., Rudiger, L., Neale, M., Heath, A., and Todd, R. 2000. A twin study of inattentive, aggressive, and anxious/depressed behaviors. *Journal of the American Academy of Child and Adolescent Psychiatry* 39: 469–476. See also Taylor, L. 1984. *Born to Crime: The Genetic Causes of Criminal Behaviour*. Westport, CT: Greenwood Press; Gunn, J. and Farrington, D. (eds.). 1985. *Aggression and Dangerousness*. London: Wiley.

34 Atkinson, I., Robinson, J., and Shute, R. 1997. Between a rock and a hard place: an Australian perspective on education of children with ADHD. *Education and Clinical Psychology* 14 (1): 21–30, 21.

35 Jacobs, B. 2002. *Queensland Children at Risk: The Over Diagnosis of "ADHD" and the Overuse of Stimulant Medication*. Brisbane: Youth Affairs Network Queensland, 4.

36 Sprich, S., Biedenman, M., Crawford, H., Mundy, E., and Faraone, S. 2000. Adoptive and biological families of children and adolescents with ADHD. *Journal of the American Academy of Child and Adolescent Psychiatry* 39 (11): 1432–1437.

37 Ibid., 1435.

38 Galton, D. 2002. *Eugenics: The Future of Human Life in the 21st Century*. London: Abacus, 155.

39 Ibid.

40 Midgley, ibid.

41 See Love, R. 2004. Deleting sadness? clones and designer babies. In: Hindmarsh, R. and Lawrence, G. (eds.), *Recoding Nature: Critical Perspectives on Genetic Engineering*. Sydney: UNSW Press; see also Rowland, R. 2001. The quality-control of human life: masculine science & genetic engineering. In: Hindmarsh, R. and Lawrence, G. (eds.), *Altered Genes II: The Future?* Melbourne: Scribe.

42 See Pigem, J. 2002. Barcoding life. *New Internationalist* 349 (September); Gray, C. 2002. *Cyborg Citizen*. London: Routledge.

43 Suzuki, D. and Levine, D. 1994. *Cracking the Code: Redesigning the Living World*. Sydney: Allen & Unwin, 222.

44 See Gene Watch UK. 2001. Human bio-collections: who benefits from gen-banking. *Gene Watch UK Briefing*, 14(April):4.

45 Ibid., 2.

46 For the coinage of the term "bio-utopia" and discussion, see Hindmarsh, R. 2007. *Genetic Manoeuvres, Bio-utopian Visions: A New Politics of Life*. Perth: UWA Press.

ASTRID H. GESCHE

GENETIC TESTING AND HUMAN GENETIC DATABASES

Genetic databases would not exist without the input from donors. Their samples and their associated information are the foundation of their existence. Genetic databases contain very personal, sensitive information and, if misused, could lead to any number of potential harms for the donor. Consequently, the operation and use of genetic databases should meet the highest ethical standards backed up by effective regulations and legislation. The aim of this chapter is to first describe genetic databases and their function before turning to two of the most controversial ethical issues that surround genetic databases, namely privacy and informed consent, and describe how the Australian Government has so far responded to these challenges. It will close by turning to an explicit example, the National Criminal Investigation DNA Database (NCIDD), which is one of a web of databases overseen by the CrimTrac[1] agency of Australia.

1. WHAT ARE HUMAN GENETIC DATABASES?

Human genetic databases can be defined as a collection of genetic samples, data, and associated information from which genetic inferences can be drawn. Their number is increasing and so are their collections. The size of human genetic databases varies, from relatively small to fairly large. At present, Australia does not have large-scale human genetic research databases like the Islandic deCODE database,[2] which contains genetic samples and associated data from the entire Islandic population, the Estonian Genome Project database,[3] which embraces one million individuals, or the UK Biobank,[4] which has approximately 500,000 individuals on its register. However, this is about to change. Researchers at the Western Australia Institute for Medical Research are constructing a vast genetic epidemiology database, the Western Australian Genetic Epidemiology Resource (WAGER). Already, the collection contains more than 17 million records of highly sensitive personal information from Western Australia's 1.98 million residents.[5] The database is being constructed from linkages within and between various WA statutory collections (e.g., birth and death registrations; hospital

Michela Betta (ed.), The moral, social, and commercial imperatives of genetic testing and screening. The Australian case, 71–94.

and mental health services; cancer notifications; electoral rolls), population research databases, data systems, and health surveys—records that may go back up to 30 years. In general, three large types of genetic databases exist: genetic registers; human genetic research databases; and human tissue collections (Table 1). Genetic registers usually address only one particular type of heritable disorder and any possible subtypes. This focused purpose contrasts with human genetic research databases (HGRD). The latter term covers a range of databases for different research purposes, which often allow for data mining and linkage analysis within and across databases. The third large group of genetic databases comprises the human tissue collections maintained by pathology laboratories or hospitals. These collections are not being stored primarily for use in research. The value of these large depositories of human tissue lies in their potential secondary uses.

In Australia, genetic databases are located throughout the country in academic or government institutions, teaching and research hospitals, and private and public research organizations. One of the better-known genetic research databases is the Westmead Tumour Bank of the Children's Hospital at Westmead (Sydney) in New South Wales (NSW). At present, the tumour bank holds approximately 16,000 samples from 1,600 children covering 50 different childhood cancers and their subtypes and is accessible to a wide range of researchers in Australia and abroad.[6] Australian genetic data is also entered into international human genetic research databases, such as the one connected to the GenomEUtwin project,[7] which analyses 80,000 European twins and other population cohorts to determine specific genetic and non-genetic factors in health problems ranging from obesity and migraine to coronary heart disease and longevity.[8] In reality, any facility where human tissue, including blood, is being stored has the potential to become a type of DNA database. These inchoate genetic databases could be highly valuable for research, since they constitute long-established and large depositories of genetic samples and information, often from unique classes of patients. Two such sources of inchoate genetic databases are the pathology archives and the Guthrie card (newborn screening card) collections. Millions of patient samples and records are kept in pathology archives maintained by hospitals, public and private research organizations, and private pathology laboratories.[9] They are stored for a variety of reasons, from quality assurance testing and patient management to re-testing of samples and research.[10] Similarly, a few million Guthrie cards are held in hospitals across the country.[11] Guthrie tests are conducted on all newborn babies in Australia and screened for phenylketonuria and other mainly metabolic diseases. The test is performed by pricking the heel of the newborn and spotting a small drop of blood onto blotting paper before submitting the blot for further analysis. The Guthrie test cards with their blood spots are then stored in the hospital's archives. The blood spot is a genetic sample containing genetic information and could be used for genetic studies. Since DNA is very stable in dried blood, interest in Guthrie cards as a potential resource for genetic studies is increasing.

Table 1. Types of human genetic databases and their purpose

Type and focus of genetic database	**Purpose**	**Examples**
Genetic registers Usually only address one disorder or closely related disorders	1. Reference list of people or families with known genetic abnormalities 2. Clinical or therapeutic role for those listed 3. Monitoring of outcomes of therapies or services provided 4. Research tool 5. Risk analysis, including risk management for other family members	Cystic fibrosis Huntington's disease Fragile X syndrome Duchenne muscular dystrophy Marfan syndrome Familial cancers, e.g., hereditary bowel cancer
Human Genetic Research Databases Methodical or systematic diverse collections of genetic samples and genetic health data and other health information Descriptions of DNA Genealogies	Research, such as: 1. Study into the cause of diseases and disease subtypes 2. Pharmacogenetic studies, investigating the relationship between drug reactions and genetic status 3. Epidemiological genetic studies, examining environmental causes of diseases with genetic component 4. Studies into the prevalence of genes in populations 5. Linkage and association studies of clinical, personal, and genetic information within and across databases 6. Collection and mapping of genetic sequence information 7. Elucidation of gene function	Selection of Australian databases: WA Genetic Epidemiology Resource (WAGER) Tissue bank maintained by the Peter MacCallum Cancer Institute Menzies Centre for Population Research (Tasmania) Selection of non-Australian databases: deCODE genetics (Iceland) Estonian Genome database Biobank (UK) Biobank (Japan) CARTaGENE (Quebec) Medical Biobank (Sweden)

(*Continues*)

Table 1. Types of human genetic databases and their purpose—Continued

Type and focus of genetic database	**Purpose**	**Examples**
Human Tissue Collections Inchoate databases, such as archived pathology collections, Guthrie card collections; population screening programmes, cord blood storage facilities; other tissue repositories	Archival purposes Forensic and law enforcement purposes Parentage and other kinship testing Transplantation and therapeutic purposes	Private and public pathology laboratories across the country; private firms, such as Cryosite (Sydney), which store cord blood of newborns

2. THE VALUE OF GENETIC DATABASES

The value of genetic databases depends on their function. For example, genetic research databases have clinical as well as commercial value. Their clinical value comes from their ability to cross-link data derived from personal, genetic, clinical, and other information and from using the linked data for specific investigations. For instance, cross-linking data and information from disparate databases could become useful for individual or population profiling, identifying linkages between gene sequences and illnesses, investigations into the interactions of genes with their environment, pharmacogenetic studies to determine why some patients tolerate one drug better over another, forensic purposes, kinship testing, or genealogical studies. Each of these options uses human genetic databases in unique ways and with countless, still unfolding possibilities.

The commercial value of genetic databases is similarly important. New biotechnology products may emerge from discoveries made using the stored patient samples and associated information. For example, a certain gene sequence coding for a protein isolated in a patient might be identified as being significant in the development of disease or other phenotypic manifestations, because if absent, mutated, or produced in subnormal levels, the person may become ill. If the researchers can isolate, purify, and characterize the protein, and if their subsequent research leads to patents and new pharmaceutical drugs, the initial isolate of the patient would have become a powerful and valuable commodity. Likewise, should a tissue sample originally provided by a tissue donor be used to create a new and commercially useful cell line, substantial financial profits can be expected.[12]

Should donors have a right to control the use of their samples? Should they have a right to a share of the ownership benefits in the case where an intellectual property right results from the research? In Australia, it is not clear whether property rights would attach to human tissue;[13] indeed, it may be "unlawful to provide financial benefits in exchange for tissue donation."[14] The Australian Law Reform Commission (ALRC) suggested in their 2004 discussion paper on gene patenting that the donor might be able to enter into contractual arrangements with researchers, which could result in some other form of benefit-sharing.[15] Others disagree with this interpretation. For example, in a submission to the ALRC discussion paper on gene patenting, the Queensland Government asserted that it is not the donation that is patentable, but the invention resulting from it, because it is the invention not the donation that is important for patenting, since the patenting system rewards a researchers' "expertise, skill, time and expense."[16] It believes that no special benefit-sharing provisions for donors of genetic samples/information should be necessary.[17]

3. IS GENETIC INFORMATION SPECIAL?

Is genetic information different from medical information? The opinions are divided,[18] but many people would say "yes." It is different because:

- It focuses on particularity and difference.
- It is inextricably linked to a person's identity, which, at least at present, cannot be altered.
- It may provide critical probabilities concerning a person's future health.
- Genetic information may even point towards certain behavioural traits, such as intelligence, sexual orientation, anxiety, or aggression, adding layers of complexity.

History has demonstrated all too often that the aforementioned traits carry with them the spectre for possible moral and social disadvantages, such as prejudice, racism, discrimination, stigmatization, and even victimization. While discrimination on the grounds of a person's genome is unlawful under Australia's current racial, sex, and disability legislation, and would breach Australia's international human rights obligation, the potential for disadvantage cannot be dismissed and is particularly high for employment and insurance.[19] Others, however, disagree. For them, genetic information is not different from any other medical information. They regard genetic information as speculative in the sense that genetic testing provides a person with information whether a mutation is present or not; but rarely is it able to shed light on specific information about disease progression or the severity of disease.[20]

Issues regarding genetic information may also project themselves in other ways. Firstly, since in many instances genetic abnormalities and their manifestations cannot yet be treated or cured, people may want to remain ignorant of their condition as long as possible and continue with their normal life. This may be especially true for individuals who are afflicted by so-called late-onset genetic diseases, such as Huntington's disease, where symptoms often do not appear before the person is between 30 and 50 years of age.[21] Secondly, genetic information is of interest not only to the individual but also to familial information (within defined limits of probability), since genetically related family members share a proportion of a common gene pool. This means that the same abnormalities that are observed in an individual may also be present in other close relatives. Thirdly, as individuals are embedded in a number of family relationships, it is not uncommon that individuals with genetic diseases may wish to keep their own genetic test results private so as not to burden other family members with unfavourable news.

4. GENETIC DATABASES AND PRIVACY

In their celebrated seminal article of 1890, "The Right to Privacy," Warren and Brandeis defined privacy as a legal right that emanates from a natural right to life, property, and freedom. They understood privacy largely in terms of "the right to enjoy life,—the right to be let alone."[22] Over time, a number of additional definitions developed. For example, in bioethics, privacy may mean "a state or condition of physical or informational inaccessibility."[23] It may also refer to the protection of dignity and autonomy of an individual and as providing choice—choice to authorize or decline access to a person and to personal information.[24] Another branch of privacy deals with information privacy. *Information* privacy is "the interest of an individual to control, or at least significantly influence, the handling of data concerning him[self] or herself."[25] Today, personal information is stored in computerized databases. With respect to computerized databases, Spinello (1995) has long recognized four major challenges:

- Potential for data to be sold to unscrupulous vendors
- Problems with the trustworthiness and care of data collectors
- Potential for data recombination to create detailed, composite profiles of individuals
- Difficulty of correcting inaccurate information once it has been propagated into many different files[26]

These challenges remain unresolved and have become of concern for genetic databases as well. Genetic samples and genetic information are collected and stored in genetic databases located in hospitals, pathology laboratories, and public and private research organizations. Genetic databases can be a source of harm as well as of benefits. Harm can result from breaches of privacy that may compromise a person's autonomy and self-determination; it could lead to possible exploitation of individuals or groups of individuals when, for example, pharmaceutical for-profit companies use the information without equitable compensation, which could lead to discrimination or stigmatization, as mentioned above. However, the same scenario might be interpreted as benefit. Being able to link genetic information to drug responses might lead to more specific and effective drugs with fewer side effects.[27] Sometimes is may be necessary to use and work with an extensive set of personal data for the benefit of the larger population. For instance, learning more about the link between genetic make-up and illness is a major population health benefit in itself. It may also result in new diagnostic, prevention, or treatment mechanisms. Another example could be chosen. When population studies reveal correlations between environmental exposure, such as cigarette smoke, and the development of certain cancers, such as lung cancer, the correlations may not necessarily establish cause and effect; thus, other biochemical and/or genetic evidence may be needed to explain the epidemiological findings.[28] However, without access and the ability to cross-link a large number of samples and associated data, researchers may not be able to properly investigate a possible genetic link to certain diseases.

What are some of the practical steps that are undertaken to protect the privacy of individuals? The research genetic database at the Menzies Centre for Population Health Research located in Hobart, Tasmania, compiles genealogical data from genetic samples and health information provided by donors. In addition, it collects other personal information, such as biometric data (height and weight), medical and clinical family history, pathology blood test results, and any other additional family information. Samples are obtained from a number of sources: (1) volunteers who respond to a media or other advertising campaign for a certain study or who are made aware of the study by their clinician; (2) collaborating researchers or clinicians; (3) disease-based registers; or (4) mandatory registers.[29] On arrival at the Menzies Centre, samples are de-identified (the names, addresses, and dates of birth are removed), coded with a unique identifier and stored in various depositories and databases. Samples remain, however, potentially identifiable. This way researchers can cross-link genetic and non-genetic information to verify or interpret data and for data mining. It also enables them to remove participants from the collection and update the collection, if necessary. Risks to privacy can occur at any stage of the continuum, from data entry and the de-identification or re-identification of samples to data mining, and to forwarding and interpreting of data. At any one point, there is ample room for intentional and unintentional privacy breaches. Who is accountable for the privacy of data? Who is responsible for any resulting harm to the donor? The cross-linking of databases is of particular concern, because

> Linkages ... create privacy concerns, as the combination of samples and information can yield new information in itself. Collections may build up a more comprehensive picture of an individual's health than is held in any other form,

> such as by linking detailed genealogical information with the health records of a number of family members and data derived from testing genetic samples.[30]

Another risk to privacy comes from more mundane sources: errors made (intentionally or not) by the data entry operators. Unauthorized hackers have also been reported to gain access to databases and occasionally to even modify data. In our computerized world, morality in hyperspace is ethereal; data are easily manipulated at the touch of a button. The chances for perpetrators being caught are low.[31] Who is responsible for errors? At present, the questions still await satisfactory answers. An investigation into issues relating to genetic information and privacy and responsibility led two of Australia's most respected independent federal organizations, the Australian Law Reform Commission (ALRC) and the Australian Health Ethics Committee (AHEC) of the National Health and Medical Research Council (NHMRC), to conclude that Australia's current health privacy legislation, and its existing ethical principles and guidelines, are insufficient to protect the genetic privacy of people and that major collections lack appropriate governance and accountability.[32,33] They tabled a report in Parliament in May 2003, making 144 recommendations, most of which the Australian government subsequently adopted either fully or partially in late 2005.[34]

5. AUSTRALIA'S PROVISIONS REGARDING GENETIC DATABASES AND PRIVACY

In Australia, a mixture of sometimes overlapping legislation, guidelines, and standards regulates the collection, storage, and use of genetic samples and information and the disclosure of such information held in genetic databases.[35] The following is intended to provide some insights into the complexity of privacy legislation as they relate to health information and databases. It does not purport to be complete.

Firstly, at the Commonwealth public sector level, the privacy of health information is covered by the Privacy Act 1988, especially its Information Privacy Principles (IPPs),[36] which contain information regarding the collection, storage, access, use, and disclosure of personal health information. The intention of the Privacy Act 1988 is to give individuals greater control over their personal information. It covers all health services, including private hospitals, health professionals and insurance companies that hold health-related information. The Privacy Act 1988 was amended on 21 December 2001 via the introduction of privacy provisions for the private sector. They are set out in the Privacy Amendment (Private Sector) Act 2000,[37] which comprises ten Privacy Amendment (Private Sector) Act 2000 (National Privacy Principles [NPPs]).[38] The amendments now also oblige private sector organizations to operate under similar privacy provisions and under similar data protection mechanisms as the public sector. The amendments made it possible for public sector organizations to outsource private health information or health services to private contractors, since data transfer between private and public sector organizations had to comply with equally secure data protection provisions.[39] Both, the IPPs and the NPPs make an important contribution towards a more uniform and consistent national health information legislation in the future. The NPPs outline the minimum standard expected for handling personal information by private sector organizations. For example:

- NPP1 states that individuals must be informed of the purpose of the collection and can only collect information that is relevant for a specific function.
- NPP2 directs that personal information must not be used or disclosed for a purpose other than the primary purpose of the original collection. Individuals may generally consent to the use or disclosure of their genetic information for secondary purposes, e.g., medical research.
- Exceptions exist for both NPP1 and NPP2.
- NPP4 regulates that personal information must be stored in such a way that it is protected against loss, use, disclosure, modification, and unauthorized access.
- NPP6 allows individuals whose health information is being collected to correct information.
- NPP10 provides that, generally, sensitive information can only be collected with the consent of the individual.

An organization must also use reasonable steps to destroy or permanently de-identify health or personal information when it is no longer needed for the original purpose. Unfortunately, the NPPs only apply to information collected after 21 December 2001 and are as yet largely untested. This means that they do not protect the privacy of samples and data collected through private organizations before the cut-off date. Furthermore, the new private sector privacy laws apply generically and have not been especially designed for the protection of genetic information and for regulating the storage, use, or transfer of genetic tissue samples.[40] Apart from the Commonwealth sector and the private sector, a further set of provisions relate to special State and Territory government bodies and local governments.[41] They are not covered by the Privacy Act 1988 and follow their own legislation instead.[42] A large number of institutions fall under this category, including public hospitals, public sector health administrators, and other state, territory, or local government health services. The patchwork of legal regulations was highlighted by the ALRC inquiry, which recommended harmonizing information and health privacy legislation nationally. Another shortfall in the present legal framework concerns the current definition of "personal information" and "record." It is not clear whether a genetic sample can be defined as personal information. A genetic sample that is not labelled with a name or other unique identifier would not fit the definition of "personal information" and thus would not be protected by the Privacy Act 1988 (Cth). This, however, changes as soon as the sample is labelled, because it is then protected indirectly through its association with the label. Similarly, the ALRC asserts that it remains unclear whether a genetic sample can be interpreted as a "record," defined to mean "information stored or recorded by means of a computer."[43] If it can, and this is far from certain, a further layer of protection under the Privacy Act would exist. The above issues still remain unresolved.[44]

Privacy of genetic information is not only a legal matter. Privacy is also important from an ethical perspective. In the biomedical context, ethical guidance is provided by non-legislative means, such as the National Statement on Ethical Conduct in Research Involving Humans (the National Statement)[45] of the NHMRC. The National Statement explicitly notifies researchers that they must inform the person of their intention to store the genetic sample/information and that they must protect the confidentiality and privacy of stored genetic information. Where specific information stored in separate databases is to be linked for specific purposes, an institutional human ethics research committee should, but does not have to, oversee the de-identification, linking, and re-identification process. Yet, despite these ethical, legal, and regulatory provisions, privacy of genetic information cannot be guaranteed. Instead of introducing even more legislation, the inquiry opted for recommending that the NHMRC should take a lead and amend the National Statement in such a way that it provides more specific and more detailed ethical guidance on genetic databases. The Inquiry also suggested improving transparency, accountability, and data protection by establishing a public register of human genetic databases in order to "provide that no genetic research under the *National Statement* can be conducted using information from a database unless it is duly registered."[46] A public register could also function as some form of quality control entity, by providing the AHEC with the option to monitor "the kinds of research being conducted using the samples and information" contained in the databases.[47]

As a third major measure, the inquiry suggested the establishment of a "gene trustee" system. The gene trustee would operate as an independent third party and would control codes and information that identify and link data and samples. It is hoped that this separation of information and samples would increase transparency and integrity, which "may become increasingly important in allaying public concern about the privacy, ethical and other implications of the continuing development of research databases." It may also assist in better monitoring and correcting breaches of privacy.[48] Any breaches of genetic privacy can be pursued by making a complaint to the Federal Privacy Commissioner. The Office of the Federal Privacy Commissioner is an independent office with a brief to protect, amongst others, the privacy of personal information held by federal and ACT government agencies, and by all large private sector organizations and service providers. It also provides them with policy guidance and advice on privacy.[49] In contrast to the breaches of genetic privacy, breaches that relate to genetic discrimination can be referred to the Human Rights and Equal Opportunity Commissioner, who will follow the Human Rights and Equal Opportunity Commission Act 1986 (Cth).[50,51] However, redeeming invasions of privacy is difficult in Australia. As the High Court of Australia found, "there is no enforceable general right to privacy in Australian common law; there is no tort of invasion of privacy; and enforcement of rights to privacy must be based on statute."[52]

6. AUSTRALIA'S PROVISIONS REGARDING GENETIC DATABASES AND INFORMED CONSENT

Genetic databases can be used to store very specific genetic tissues and data, for example, from patients with colon or breast cancer. The samples and data are often shared with other researchers, usually under rules set out by institutional ethics committees. One such set of rules refers to the informed consent process, which is central in medical and human research ethics. Consent can be manifested and implied. The *Guidelines to the National Privacy Principles* (2001) explain:

> Express consent is given explicitly, either orally or in writing. Implied consent arises where consent may reasonably be inferred in the circumstances from the conduct of the individual and the organization.[53]

For example, if a patient on his/her own accord visits a doctor to have a blood sample taken for his/her regular blood sugar screening, consent to taking the sample would be implied. In Australia, informed consent is guided and protected by both ethics and law.[54] At present, the federal Privacy Act 1988 (Cth) as well as the NPPs, in particular the *Guidelines to the National Privacy Principles*,[55] and the Australian NHMRC *National Statement on Ethical Conduct in Research Involving Humans* (1999),[56] all provide guidance on how to obtain consent and what the consent process should entail. The *National Statement*, which does not specifically deal with human genetic databases, stipulates that individuals must receive information about the specific purpose,[57] methods, demands, risks, discomforts, and outcomes of a procedure. Their consent must be given voluntary and without inducement or coercion. Researchers must also inform the donor about whether the genetic material and the genetic information is going to be stored for yet unspecified future research,[58] or whether it is to be disposed of at the end of the research.[59]

Human genetic tissue is also covered by the Human Tissue Acts operating in each State and Territory, which again are generic in application. They, too, neither comprehensively cover genetic databases nor make any specific provisions, which would regulate the storage, use, or transfer of the genetic tissue sample.[60] They do, however, direct that the consent process must include a statement giving information about what is going to be done with the sample once the research has been completed.[61] The ALRC inquiry came to the conclusion that the existing regulations regarding the informed consent process and genetic databases are insufficient to protect the individual and that more specific guidance on obtaining consent should be provided and the government suggesting that these matters should be taken up by Australia's National Health and Medical Research Council (NHMRC).[62]

7. THE PRACTICE OF INFORMED CONSENT AND SUGGESTIONS FOR TRANSFORMATIONAL CHANGE

A person can only give consent to a specific procedure if competent and after having obtained full information about it, including risks, benefits, and alternatives. Rather than being simply a matter of signing consent forms in order to comply with bureaucratic legal requirements, as it seems to be practised in many institutions at present, obtaining consent should be a *process* of shared, transparent decision-making, an expression of care that gives patients choice and autonomy. The outcome of any intervention should be in the best interest of the person. Giving consent should also be voluntary. Australian human genetic research databases have a number of different consent procedures in place. For example, the Westmead Tumour Bank in Sydney seeks consent for unspecified future research in a two-step process. The first step entails the following clause:

> I understand and agree that blood, urine, and other samples may be taken for the diagnosis and treatment of myself/my child. Any unused part of the sample may be retained for future research.[63]

The second step occurs at a later stage (*retrospective consent*), when the parents have coped somewhat with the traumatic diagnosis that their child has been diagnosed with childhood cancer. At that later date, parents will be fully informed about the Tumour Bank and that their child's samples, genetic tests, and other medical information are being stored for subsequent research. At that point, parents are told about their right to have the specimens that were collected in step one withdrawn from the tissue bank.[64] The two-step process at the tumour bank is laudable. But is it sufficient? Each person, the researcher as well as the patient, is embedded in social relationships and touched by specific circumstances that shape and limit their free choices and influence their consent.[65] Since the initial contact between child, parent, and specialist healthcare provider is usually at a critical stage of the patient's illness, consent at that stage might readily be forthcoming. Even though a two-step process may be in place, acute care patients and their parents may still not be in a position to freely give their consent for future research, given that the child is faced with acute serious health problems, which demand all their attention. They might also want to establish a good rapport with the child's carers and thus might choose to comply with what is requested of them. Can parents at that point in time fully appreciate the long-term implications of their consent? In addition, would they not find themselves in an unequal power relationship that can exacerbate their dependency? Is it therefore possible that acute care patients and/or their parents are in a vulnerable position, which might see them agreeing to protocols and procedures they may not normally agree to?

The informed consent process usually contains a provision allowing potential research subjects to refuse participation or to withdraw from the research at any time, and the tumour bank is a good example. But is it realistic to assume that the children's parents are truly free to make a choice one way or the other, given their disempowered and vulnerable state? Could the consequence of these limitations translate into a practice where on paper the patient (or his/her guardian) may be competent to accept a procedure, but in practice incompetent to refuse it? These are just some of the still unresolved difficult ethical questions.[66] However, there may be room for transformational change to adapt the current practice of seeking consent to the realities of genetic databases. What suggestions could be made? It is suggested here that one should move away from primarily signing forms and insist that the consent process becomes a meaningful *process* of information sharing and negotiation. Furthermore, one could expand on the normal provisions found in consent forms. For example, one could indicate upfront that the tissue sample and the associated information might have some commercial value for the researcher or other commercial entity. One could allow the patient to choose for which area of research he/she is willing to provide a genetic sample/data. One could provide information about what will happen to the sample/information should the database be sold or passed on under licence. Furthermore, one could provide feedback on what will happen if a genetic database owner becomes bankrupt, or is taken over by another Australian or non-Australian company or seeks access to foreign markets. In addition, the consent process could address potential abuse of genetic data/information and the kind of remedies that would be available, should any abuse become apparent.

Finally, when a person has consented to be part of a specific research project, the researcher should not assume that the patient samples/data could be used for other research as well. Respect for the autonomy of the patient and the integrity of the researcher–patient relationship demand that new consent should be asked for, regardless how cumbersome this may be. Even though asking individuals for renewed consent for different procedures might be burdensome, the practice should not be broken. This is relevant for genetic databases that have been developed from existing collections unrelated to genetic research in clinics and pathology laboratories. The ALRC-AHEC Inquiry is especially cognisant of the need for reform in this area for unspecified research:[67]

These changes ought not to be too cumbersome. Drawing a parallel with good business practices, one could argue that since genetic databases will increasingly become associated with commercial enterprises, the same care that management of commercial enterprises afford valued clients should extend to the relationship between genetic database owners and genetic "donors".

Privacy and the consent process are also at the core of genetic database operations that lie outside the medical arena. In the Australian context, the NCIDD is such an example. Section 8 exemplifies how privacy has been eroded and how the informed consent process can be misunderstood and potentially harm innocent, vulnerable persons.

8. DNA FINGERPRINTING AND FORENSICS

DNA databases have their foundation in clinical medicine or clinical research. Increasingly, their value is being recognized in other areas as well. For instance, for forensic and law enforcement purposes, genetic databases may assist with identifying victims or suspects of violent crimes. They may help in profiling and tracking certain individuals. They may be used for searches of missing persons. The millions of Guthrie cards stored in hospital archives constitute a useful resource for such purpose, enabling the matching of samples collected in an investigation.[68] According to the Privacy Commissioner of NSW, since 1996 more than a dozen requests to use the newborn screening cards have been made, mainly to identify bodies or to assist in a murder inquiry.[69] Forensic DNA testing usually involves a comparison between two bodily samples containing nuclear DNA (blood, semen, hair, skin, urine, bone marrow, saliva, sweat, buccal cells, tears, and others) in order to verify whether or not they came from the same person. The testing method used is a special type of genetic testing called DNA fingerprinting. DNA fingerprinting has been used to confirm that Dolly, the Scottish sheep, was a true clone of the 6-year-old ewe that provided the nucleus.[70] It was also used to identify the victims of the terrorist attack on the World Trade Center in New York in 2001 and again in the terrorist bombing of the Sari Nightclub in Bali in 2002, and the Asian Tsunami of December 2004.

DNA fingerprinting relies on molecular genetics and population genetics. It is based on either single nucleotide polymorphism (SNPs) or short sequence repeats (STRs) that are different in length. Such sequences are said not to encode protein, and thus are believed not to affect the phenotype of a person. Population genetic statistics are then applied to determine the probability of two individuals from a given population having the same pattern for all the DNA sequences examined.[71] Humans are 99.9% identical with respect to their DNA sequence. However, 0.1% equalling 3 million differences still occurs. A match occurs when at least 6 allelic values match and no more than 2 allelic values do not match.[72] Although DNA profiles are established from non-coding sections, the sample itself contains all coding and non-coding regions. It is a complete sample on which in theory any number of identifiable genetic tests could be done. DNA fingerprints are stored in Australia's NCIDD, managed by the CrimTrac agency.

9. CRIMTRAC AND THE NATIONAL CRIMINAL INVESTIGATION DNA DATABASE

The CrimTrac agency was established on 1 June 2000 within the Commonwealth Attorney General's Office in Canberra. Its original objective was to integrate and share police information more effectively across Australia's nine State and Territory police jurisdictions. Its initial brief was to set up three new databases, each able to link to the other. These new databases are the national automated fingerprint database (NAFIS), the Police Reference System (CPRS), and the DNA database (NCIDD). The NAFIS database compares conventional normal fingerprints against a database of 2.8 million existing ten-prints. Ten-prints are fingerprints of all ten fingers and are taken either by inking and rolling the fingertips onto a paper fingerprint card or by scanning the fingertips with a scanner. Fingerprints can be scanned at 39 special data "workstations" situated throughout the country, and then uploaded and compared with those held in the primary NAFIS database in Canberra. In addition to its fingerprint files, NAFIS houses the world's largest automated palm print database (4.8 million). The second database is the CPRS. It contains:

- Apprehended and domestic violence orders
- Court notices and orders
- Criminal records
- Warrants
- Charged persons
- Persons of interest
- Facial features and images (mugshots)
- Stolen vehicles
- Vehicles of interest and driver information
- Person warnings[73]
- Missing persons
- Firearms licences
- A firearm register
- A paedophile database[74]

The third, and most far-reaching database is the NCIDD. It has been in operation since June 2001. It contains digital DNA profiles from offenders, suspects, and other forensic DNA genetic testing operations. It is anticipated that together the three databases will perform approximately 50,000 searches annually. Considering the potency of these databases the Acting Privacy Commissioner of Australia's Attorney-General's Department warned against "function creep," a term used in privacy literature to indicate a process in which a tool introduced for one specific application is later on applied to new, and usually more extensive, sets of applications. In a letter to the Forensic Procedures Review Committee, Johnston (2002) writes:

> Once an information resource exists, in this case in the form of DNA samples acquired to create profiles or in the form of the profiles themselves recorded in databases, arguments based on utility or cost effectiveness are frequently cited as a basis for expanding the range of possible uses including research. These proposals seriously undervalue the importance of trust in relation to the way our society processes personal information such as that derived from DNA.[75]

This is of particular concern in relation to DNA testing on so-called volunteers in criminal investigations. In criminal investigations, two categories of people can be tested for DNA: volunteers and non-volunteers (such as prisoners or suspects). Volunteers have to give their informed consent to testing, non-volunteers can be forced, if necessary. In some circumstances, e.g., in cases of high media interest, so-called volunteers might feel coerced into DNA testing. This would lead to the paradox scenario, where a person is compelled to prove his/her innocence, instead of a prosecutor proving a person guilty.

10. ETHICAL ISSUES ARISING FROM THE NATIONAL CRIMINAL INVESTIGATION DNA DATABASE

In 2000, an elderly woman in the small Australian township of Wee Waa, NSW, was sexually assaulted. In the wake of this assault, police asked the township's approximately 500 male residents between the ages of 18 and 45 to volunteer a DNA sample for analysis to eliminate suspects and to identify the likely perpetrator. It was Australia's first mass DNA screening for forensic purposes. Farm labourer Stephen James Boney, 44 years of age, was one of the men tested.

> Ten days after submitting to the test, as police waited for the results of the samples to come back, Boney suddenly entered Wee Waa police station, saying he wanted to confess, that the pressure from the inevitability of eventually being caught by DNA had got to him.[76]

Since then, a number of other mass screenings have taken place.

Only 2 years later, another well-publicized mass screening took place, this time in Bundaberg, Queensland. It occurred in the wake of the death of a female British backpacker in June 2002 who was robbed and believed to have fallen or to have been pushed from a bridge. When male DNA was found on the bridge, this time close to 2,500 men and boys living in the vicinity of the bridge were asked to provide a DNA sample. It has been reported that the male population of Bundaberg was told by police that they would record the name of any person who refused to submit to DNA fingerprinting. The case for requiring DNA samples from violent convicted criminals might be compelling, especially since many have high recidivism rates. It is not uncommon that offenders convicted for say burglary or robbery may later be arrested on other violent charges such as assault or sex crimes. It might be that the problem does not so much lie with whether or not a convicted criminal should be compelled to provide a genetic sample for profiling, but with the informed consent process. Similar to other genetic databases, consent is a major issue. A police officer can ask a person for a DNA sample if he/she is reasonably sure that the person committed a serious offence. The suspect has to be informed about the forensic procedure in accordance with strict guidelines and must be given an opportunity to discuss the test with the officer. Before a bodily sample is taken for forensic DNA testing, the suspect must give his/her informed consent.

Three issues can be isolated. Firstly, unlike in medical situations, where the providing of a genetic sample cannot be enforced without informed consent, a convicted criminal *cannot* refuse DNA testing. If he/she refuses, a magistrate or judge can order a non-invasive DNA fingerprinting. No consent is needed. Secondly, in Wee Waa as well as in Bundaberg, considerable pressure was put on the male population to submit to genetic testing. In Wee Waa it may have been community pressure, in Bundaberg perhaps police pressure, which compelled people to conform. In both cases the informed consent process does not seem to have been truly voluntary or free from coercion. In fact, one could deduce that the enforced procedures in both cases make a mockery of the consent process, which has a distinguished and proven track record in medical practice. In cases where consent can be overridden, it is recommended that the protocol governing the NCIDD database remove the clause referring to consent.

The different standards applying to the same terminology in medicine and in law enforcement are problematic. While acknowledging the possible benefits of mass screening, such as enhanced efficiency in criminal investigation, the possible harms cannot be overlooked. Apart from the still high economic cost involved in testing a large number of people and maintaining the results in a database, even if only for a short time until the investigation is complete, the infringements into a person's right to privacy, dignity, and liberty, and assumption of innocence, may be substantial.[77] Furthermore, the practice of apparently pressuring individuals and coercing them into compliance as seen in Wee Waa and Bundaberg are unethical. It is highly unlikely that such practice would be tolerated in the medical context, where the principle of free and voluntary consent means giving consent without coercion, manipulation, or persuasion and forms one of the fundamental principles in medical ethics.[78] A third problem with "voluntary" mass DNA screening arises from the fact that family members share genetic information. Since DNA fingerprints of people convicted of an indictable offence will be included in a forensic database, and genetic information is familiar, the NCIDD stores not only information about the offender but, by default, also DNA information about his/her other family members. Thus, in terms of human rights or personal freedom, the potential repercussions can be enormous. Is it ethical (and/or politically acceptable?) for the Australian Federal Police (AFP) to perform mass DNA screenings for profiling and eliminating potential suspects? Undoubtedly, DNA fingerprinting can be most helpful. However, to fingerprint large sections of a population almost as a matter of course in order to perhaps find one or two suspects does not seem to be justified, either on economic or on moral grounds. In addition, even though DNA fingerprinting may presently only use so-called non-coding sequences[79] that do not appear to be associated with phenotypic manifestations, it is more than likely that in the future researchers may become aware that the former non-coding regions will have defined and distinguishable functions.

11. AUSTRALIA'S PROVISIONS REGARDING ITS NATIONAL CRIMINAL INVESTIGATION DNA DATABASE

DNA testing for forensic purposes in Australia is protected by legislation and largely guided by Part 1D of the Crimes Act 1914, which deals with forensic procedures. Forensic sampling information storage is also controlled by Australia's privacy principles, the latter demanding consent, secure storage of information, de-identification of samples, and destruction of DNA material when they are no longer needed. All steps, from the informed consent process to the disclosure of information in DNA database systems like the NCIDD of CrimTrac are covered. The CrimTrac authority had its first audit in 2002. The audit revealed that oversight and accountability is wanting. For instance, at the time of the audit, the agency had no processes in place to monitor and check the accuracy of data entry. In the same year, Part 1D of the associated Crimes Act 1914 was also reviewed and criticized, because Part 1D "defines destruction of samples as the removal of the means of re-identification while allowing the samples themselves to be preserved for purposes which are undefined,"[80] leaving the option open to re-identify the samples for other purposes at a later stage. Australia's National Criminal Investigation DNA Database is of special importance, because it, together with the other two databases, can evolve into a new national identification system similar to the current ubiquitous tax file number. In Australia, the tax file number (TFN) is used as an identifier when dealing with the Tax Office and other Commonwealth government agencies. Individuals are also required to pass their TFN to their employer and they may provide their TFN to financial institutions. If they do not, tax or interests are being "deducted from their income or interest payments at the highest marginal rate."[81]

Over time, a large portion of the Australian population will have been added to CrimTrac's database system. Would this lead to a two-tiered power system where all individuals turn into suspects and the government into controllers? The constantly expanding database system might also be used/abused in the future for reasons unrelated to the original purpose for which the samples were collected. The same problems that were identified earlier in the context of medical genetic databases would apply here. There is the danger of abuse. Perhaps it is preferable to give the primary oversight of the forensic genetic database to an independent agency, which is different from the AFP. The NCIDD can become far more invasive than the "Australia card" proposal of 1985–1987,[82] which sought to introduce a multipurpose national identification scheme on all individuals and organizations. The proposal was highly controversial and galvanized the population into action until its repeated defeat in 1988 in the Senate.[83] In contrast and unfortunately, the NCIDD is not discussed in public at all, even though it might evolve into a far more invasive identification scheme than the "Australia card" ever intended to be.

12. CONCLUSION

The initiative of the Australian Government and the thorough recent inquiry of the ALRC and the NHMRC into genetic testing have been an excellent opportunity for Australians to begin to discuss genetic testing and to review current practices. The inquiry uncovered many weaknesses and gaps and made numerous recommendations for improvements, especially in regard to transparency and administrative and regulatory oversight. It even went so far as to recommend the introduction of a new criminal offence for persons who surreptitiously obtain genetic material for parentage testing without the consent of the person (this topic is taken up in chapter 11). As we learn more about the benefits, risks, and consequences of genetic testing, the ethical, social, and legal implications will become clearer. Regular reviews such as the one undertaken in Australia will lead to an ethically more aware public and better regulatory and legislative actions and pave the way to maintain us as civil society. But the process is still incomplete. The cross-linking of data with little or no input from the individuals whose data are entered, with no mechanism in place to ensure the trustworthiness and care of data entry, with limited possibility to correct inaccurate data across a variety of databases and across a number of jurisdiction—national and international—still makes us vulnerable as individuals. At present, data and samples can be sold to any number of untold vendors under licence. The sharing of personal samples and data kept in genetic databases with "business partners," corporations, and government agencies with which database owners might enjoy a strategic relationship must become more transparent. Donors need to know upfront what might be done with their donations. The reality at present is that even if donors consent freely to the processes and actions, the unequal knowledge base, capacity, and power relationship between donor and receptor makes donors still vulnerable to exploitation and harm.

We have reached a point where society must ask the question: How much personal data collection is tolerable or acceptable? Genetic databases, despite their undisputed benefits, can create inequality in power relationships, can violate civil claims to confidentiality of personal information, and can breach the principle of information security. How do we minimize the loss of privacy and how do we as society make certain that robust informed consent procedures are followed? A just society must do everything it can to ensure that the individual person can either control, or at least significantly influence, data that concern himself/herself.[84] Privacy and consent are important as prerequisites to exercise freedom and self-determination. When privacy and consent are threatened, our dignity as human beings is threatened. When our dignity is threatened, we become vulnerable people, vulnerable to exploitation, discrimination, stigmatization, and victimization. Do we submit to a technological imperative? Is it dehumanizing to treat people as genetic codes wrapped in some social environment and identifiable by some significant biological markers? Are we in the process of treating people like manufactured goods? Where is the ethical and social impact assessment? Where is the public debate about DNA databases, DNA profiling? We need to be aware that genetic testing, irrespective of how valuable and useful it is, can harm people in unexpected ways. In chapter 11 (this volume), I discuss three areas of potential harm and vulnerability: genetic testing for paternity confirmation, immigration, and Aboriginality.

NOTES

1 CrimTrac agency, About us, available at <http://www.crimtrac.gov.au/aboutus.htm>, cited 3 May 2004.

2 deCODE Genetics, Homepage, available at <www.decode.com>, cited 8 April 2004.

3 Estonian Genome Foundation, Genome Project, available at <www.genomics.ee/index.php?lang=eng&show=20>, cited 8 April 2004.

4 The UK Biobank, available at <www.ukbiobank.ac.uk>, cited 8 April 2004.

5 Australian Bureau of Statistics, 2005. Population by age and sex, Western Australia—electronic delivery, available at <http://www.abs.gov.au/Ausstats/abs@.nsf/0/a4d377caaa8b667fca256d81007eb5b7?OpenDocument>, cited 11 September 2005.

6 Ibid.

7 GenomeEUtwin, Homepage, available at <http://www.genomeutwin.helsinki.fi/>, cited 15 April 2004.

8 For a discussion on cross-national research collaborations, human gene banks, ownership, and the consent process, see Maschke, K. J. 2005. Navigating an ethical patchwork—human gene banks. *Nature Biotechnology* 23 (5): 539–544.

9 McEwen and Reilly, 1994, cited in Gesche, A. 2001. Genetic testing: a threat to privacy. In: Hindmarsh, R. and Lawrence, G. (eds.), *Altered Genes II: The future?* Melbourne: Scribe, 105.

10 For example, genetic patient information and karyotypes are kept for 3 years, microscope slides for 5 years; DNA extracts for molecular genetics minimum 1 month (but can be retained at the laboratory's discretion); bone marrow slides and reports and frozen section tissue samples for 20 years. National Pathology Accreditation Advisory Council, 2002. *Guidelines for the Retention of Laboratory Records and Diagnostic Material.* Canberra: Department of Health and Ageing, available at <http://www.health.gov.au/npaac/pdf/retentionlab.pdf>, cited 2 May 2004. How many are stored in pathology laboratories? No figures are available for Australia, but Barlow-Stewart (2001) reports that in 1999 US pathology archives held 282 million genetic samples and information about these samples.

11 The Guthrie cards are stored for a period of up to 25 years. National Pathology Accreditation Advisory Council, ibid.

12 An oft-cited case is the *Moore Versus Regents of the University of California Case*, where Moore sued the University of California, which patented a cell line derived from his tissue sample. In this case, the Supreme Court of California found that Moore did not have a property right over his tissue, only a right to be informed about what the researchers intended to do with his tissue. Cited in Australian Law Reform Commission, 2004. Gene patenting and human health. Discussion Paper 68, section 3.65. Canberra: SOS Printing Group.

13 Australian Law Reform Commission, 2004. ALRC 99: genes and ingenuity. Gene patenting and human health. Ibid., section 3.63.

14 Ibid.

15 Ibid.

16 Ibid., section 3.70.

17 For innovative recent suggestions of how to equitably balance the interests of researchers and donors, see Bovenberg, J. 2005. Whose tissue is it anyway? *Nature Biotechnology* 23 (8): 929–933.

18 See the debate in Levine, C. 2001. *Taking Sides: Clashing Views on Controversial Bioethical Issues*, 9th edn. Guilford: McGraw-Hill/Dushkin, 214–226.

19 Gesche, A. 2001. Genetic testing: a threat to privacy. In: Hindmarsh, R. and Lawrence, G. (eds.), *Altered Genes II: The future?* Melbourne: Scribe, 105–110.

20 Ibid., 216–218.

21 Australian Huntington's Disease Association NSW Inc. Frequently asked questions (FAQ) about Huntington's disease, available at <http://www.ahdansw.asn.au/information/faq_onset.html>, cited 1 September 2004.

22 Warren, S. and Brandeis, L. 1890. The right to privacy. *Harvard Law Review* 5 (5), available at <http://www.lawrence.edu/fast/boardmaw/Privacy_brand_warr2.html>, cited 1 September 2004.

23 Beauchamp, T. and Childress, J. 1994. *Principles of Biomedical Ethics*, 4th edn. New York: Oxford University Press, 406.

24 Ibid., 407, 410.

25 Clarke, R. 2000. Roger Clarke's dataveillance and information privacy Pages, available at <http://www.anu.edu.au/people/Roger.Clarke/DV/index.html>, cited 2 February 2004.

26 Spinello, R. A. 1995. Privacy in the information age. In: Spinello, R. A. *Ethical Aspects of Information Technology*. Englewood Cliffs, NJ: Prentice-Hall.

27 National Center for Biotechnology Information, 2004. One size does not fit all: the promise of pharmacogenomics, available at <http://www.ncbi.nlm.nih.gov/About/primer/pharm.html>, cited 30 April 2004.

28 Lewis, R. 2003. *Human Genetics: Concepts and Applications*, 5th edn. New York: McGraw-Hill.

29 Menzies Research Institute Homepage, available at <http://www.menzies.utas.edu.au>, 1 September 2004.

30 In Australian Law Reform Commission, ALRC 96 *Essentially Yours: The Protection of Human Genetic Information in Australia*, Chapter 18, available at <http://www.austlii.edu.au/au/other/alrc/publications/reports/96/>, cited 12 April 2004.

31 Eder, P. 1994. Privacy on parade. *The Futurist* 28: 38–42. Cited in Gesche, ibid., 103.

32 ALRC 96, ibid., 9 of 22.

33 The ALRC is a permanent, independent federal statutory corporation that provides advice to government on federal laws and legal processes. Some of its aims are to "simplify and modernise the law" (Australian Law Reform Commission Homepage. No date. About the ALRC, available at <http://www.alrc.gov.au/about/index.htm>, cited 3 September 2004). The NHMRC is Australia's most respected supporter of health and medical research and an important funding body. It is also an independent statutory authority that allocates Commonwealth funding for medical research, provides guidelines and advice on matters relating to human health, health care, public and medical health research, and health ethics, and promotes community debate on certain issues. The AHEC, a subcommittee of the NHMRC, inquires into ethical issues and, from time to time, develops and reviews highly influential ethics guidelines relevant to specific issues (National Health and Medical Research Council Act 1992), available at <http://scaleplus.law.gov.au/html/pasteact/0/379/0/PA000130.htm>, cited 7 July /2004.

34 In February 2001, the Attorney-General and the Minister for Health and Aged Care asked the ALRC and the AHEC to jointly inquire into primarily four areas of human genetic information: the protection of privacy of genetic samples and genetic information; the prevention of unfair discrimination from the use of genetic samples and genetic information; the balance of different ethical considerations across a number of different context; and the possibility that changes to the current regulatory framework may be required (ALRC 96, ibid., Terms of Reference; also Opeskin, B. 2002. Ten signposts to better law reform in relation to human genetic information. Conference paper. Einshac and the Istituto di Psicolgia Conference, Rome, 21–22 March, available at <http://www.alrc.gov.au/events/speeches/BRO/20020322.htm>, cited 8 July 2004.

35 ALRC & NHMRC, 2002. Protection of human genetic information: discussion paper 66. Canberra: Commonwealth of Australia, section 15.34.

36 The Office of the Federal Privacy Commissioner. 2004. Information privacy principles, available at <http://www.privacy.gov.au/publications/ipps.html>, cited 30 April 2004.

37 Privacy Amendment (Private Sector) Act 2000, available at <http://www.privacy.gov.au/publications/is15_02_print.html>, cited 15 April 2004.

38 The Office of the Federal Privacy Commissioner, National Privacy Principles, available at <http://www.privacy.gov.au/publications/npps01.html>, cited 15 April 2004.

39 Office of the Federal Privacy Commissioner. 2001. Health Information and the Privacy Act 1988, available at <http://www.bordergp.org.au/PCP/DOCS/Health%20Info%20and%20 Privacy%20Act%201988.pdf>, cited 1 September 2004.

40 The NPPs were compiled for *general* application across all private sector organizations. While NPP6 and NPP10 make reference to health information, the principles are not intended to be specific to genetics. Consequently, they do not provide specific guidance on privacy issues related to genetic testing and genetic databases. In addition, any reference to genetic information would have been premature, given that the major ALRC/NHMRC inquiry into the protection of human genetic information was still underway.

41 For example: Health Records Act 2001 (Vic), Health Records and Information Privacy Act 2002 (NSW), Health Records (Privacy and Access) Act 1997. Cited in Skene, L. Genetic testing and privacy rights. Conference. *The Body as Data.* Melbourne, available at <http://www.privacy.vic.gov.au/dir100/priweb.nsf/download/493EFC9F05D954F6CA256DE-C0002A88B/$FILE/Loane%20Skene%20paper.pdf>, cited 30 April 2004.

42 Ibid.

43 Cited in ALRC 96, ibid., Sections 8.11 and 8.12.

44 Australian Law Reform Commission and Australian Health Ethics Committee Report *Essentially Yours: The Protection of Human Genetic Information in Australia*: Government Response to Recommendations, <http://www.ag.gov.au/agd/wuagdhome.nsf/All Does/Df.C5F37153385647CA2570CA0076BC77? Open document, 20 March 2006>

45 NHMRC. 1999. National statement on ethical conduct in research involving humans, available at <http://www.nhmrc.gov.au/publications/pdf/e35.pdf>, cited 15 April 2004.

46 Ibid.

47 Centre for Law and Genetics, *Submission G255*, 21 December 2002, ALRC 96, ibid.

48 ALRC 96., ibid.

49 Furthermore, the Privacy Commissioner also comments on proposed legislations and inquiries, which deal with privacy issues. The Office of the Federal Privacy Commissioner Homepage, available at <http://www.privacy.gov.au/about/index.html>, cited 3 September 2004.

50 Skene, L. Genetic testing and privacy rights. Conference. *The Body as Data.* Melbourne, available at <http://www.privacy.vic.gov.au/dir100/priweb.nsf/download/493EFC9F05D954F6CA256-DEC0002A88B/$FILE/Loane%20Skene%20paper.pdf>, cited 30 April 2004.

51 "Cth" indicates Commonwealth law.

52 Australian Broadcasting Corp versus Lenah Game Meats Pty Ltd 185 ALR 1. Cited in ALRC & NHMRC, 2002, ibid., 228.

53 Office of the Federal Privacy Commissioner, 2001. *Guidelines to the National Privacy Principles.* Sydney: Office of the Privacy Commissioner.

54 Mappes, T. A. and DeGrazia, D. 2001. *Biomedical Ethics*, 5th edn. Boston, MA: McGraw-Hill, 100.

55 Office of the Federal Privacy Commissioner, 2001. *Guidelines to the National Privacy Principles.* Sydney: Office of the Privacy Commissioner.

56 The Australian National Health and Medical Research's Council. 1999. *National Statement on Ethical Conduct in Research Involving Humans.* Canberra.

57 Ibid., Paragraph 15.6.

58 Ibid., Paragraphs 16.10(j), 16.12, and 16.16.

59 Ibid., Paragraph 16.10(k).

60 Cited in ALRC 96, ibid.

61 No uniform Human Tissue Act exists. Each Australian state has its own Act. For example, in New South Wales, the Human Tissue Act 1983 applies, in Queensland it is the Transplantation and Anatomy Act 1979, and in Victoria it is the Human Tissue Act 1982. Cited in ALRC 96, ibid., Chapter 18, 18 of 22.

62 Ibid.

63 Children's Hospital at Westmead Tumour Bank, *Submission G276*, 17 December 2002. Cited in ALRC 96, ibid., Chapter 18.

64 D. Catchpoole, Head, Tumour Bank, The Children's Hospital at Westmead. Email to the author on 4 May 2004.

65 A careful analysis of informed consent in the clinical setting can be found in: *The Values Underlying Informed Consent*. Reprinted from President's Commission for the study of ethical problems in medicine and biomedical and behavioral research, making health care decisions, Volume one: Report (1982), 2–6, 41–45. Cited in Mappes, T. A. and DeGrazia, D. 2001. *Biomedical Ethics*, 5th edn. Boston, MA: McGraw-Hill, 97–103.

66 In Levine, C. 2001. *Taking Sides: Clashing Views on Controversial Bioethical Issues*, 9th edn. Guilford, CT: McGraw-Hill/Dushkin, 2–19, Levine provides transcripts of two opposite views on informed consent in medicine: the proponent view is taken by R. M Arnold and C. W. Lidz (cited in: Informed consent: clinical aspects of consent in health care. In: Warren T. Reich. (ed.), *Encyclopedia of Bioethics*, Vol. 3, rev. edn. New York: Simon & Schuster, and the opponent view is taken by R.M. Veatch (from "Abandoning Informed Consent," *Hastings Center Report* (March–April 1995).

67 See note 30.

68 See note 30.

69 NSW Privacy Commissioner, Correspondence, 4 June 2002. Cited in ALRC 96, ibid., Chapter 19.

70 Lewis, ibid., 269.

71 Lewis, ibid., 269–270.

72 Commonwealth Ombudsman and the Privacy Commissioner, refer earlier notes.

73 Mobbs, J. D. 2001. Crimtrac-technology and detection. Paper presented at the 4th National Outlook Symposium on Crime in Australia, New Crimes or New Responses. Canberra, 21–22 June 2001.

74 Ibid.

Johnston, A. 2002. Acting Privacy Commissioner. *Letter to Forensic Procedures Review Committee Secretariat*, 11 September 2002, available at <http://www.law.gov.au/www/criminaljusticeHome.nsf/0/314E5AA2F814BC9CCA256C400017F7C3?OpenDocument>, cited 4 May 2004.

75 National Institute of Forensic Science. Forensic Fact File—DNA Profiling.

76 <http://www.nifs.com.au/FactFiles/DNA/case.asp?page = case&title = DNA%20Profiling>, cited 3 September 2004.

77 Guillén, M., Lareu, M. V., Pestoni, C., Salas, A. and Carracedo, A. 2000. Ethical-legal problems of DNA databases in criminal investigation. *Journal of Medical Ethics* 26: 266–271, available at <http://jme.bmjjournals.com/cgi/content/full/26/4/266>.

78 See the discussion on forms of influence with regards to informed consent by Beauchamp, T. L. and Childress, J. F. 2001. *Principles of Biomedical Ethics*, 5th edn. New York: Oxford University Press, 94–98.

79 Each individual carries a unique set of genes, made up of two strands of deoxyribonucleic acid (DNA). Each strand of DNA is composed of active segments that code for functional protein, and seemingly inactive, non-coding regions of DNA. These non-coding regions contain repeated sequences of DNA base pairs, called variable number tandem repeats or VNTRs. The uniqueness of these VNTRs provide the markers of identity known as a DNA fingerprint (Thieman, W. J. and Palladino, M. A. 2004. *Introduction to Biotechnology*. San Francisco: Pearson Benjamin Cummings, 170).

80 National Institute of Forensic Science. Forensic Fact File—DNA Profiling.

81 The Office of the Federal Privacy Commissioner. No date. *Tax File Numbers*, available at <http://www.privacy.gov.au/act/tfn/>, cited 3 September 2004.

82 Clarke, R. 1987. Just another piece of plastic for your wallet: the "Australia card" scheme, available at <http://www.anu.edu.au/people/Roger.Clarke/DV/OzCard.html>, cited 1 May 2004.

83 Schweik Action. 1995. The Australia Card. Surveillance conference papers. Wollongong, November 1995, pp. 19—20, available at <http://www.uow.edu.au/arts/sts/research/surveillance/Schweik.html>, cited 5 September 2004.

84 Clarke, R. 2000. Roger Clarke's Dataveillance and Information Privacy Pages, available at <http://www.anu.edu.au/people/Roger.Clarke/DV/index.html>, cited 2 February 2004.

DAVID WEISBROT

THE IMPERATIVE OF THE "NEW GENETICS": CHALLENGES FOR ETHICS, LAW, AND SOCIAL POLICY

1. THE JOINT INQUIRY INTO THE PROTECTION OF HUMAN GENETIC INFORMATION

On 29 May 2003, in the Australian Parliament, the then Attorney General of Australia, the Hon Daryl Williams AM QC MP, and the then Minister for Health and Ageing, Senator the Hon Dr. Kay Patterson, launched the report *Essentially Yours: The Protection of Human Genetic Information in Australia*.[1] The launch represented the culmination of a major, 2-year inquiry by the Australian Law Reform Commission (ALRC) and the Australian Health Ethics Committee (AHEC)—a principal committee of the National Health and Medical Research Council (NHMRC). The Report was the product of an extensive research and community consultation effort—the most wide-ranging and comprehensive consideration of the ethical, legal, and social implications of the "New Genetics" ever undertaken. The Terms of Reference for the inquiry ("the Inquiry") directed the ALRC and AHEC to consider, with respect to human genetic information and the samples from which such information is derived, how best to:

- Protect privacy
- Protect against unfair discrimination and
- Ensure the highest ethical standards in research and practice

The Inquiry then applied these basic concerns across a wide range of contexts, reflecting the growing breadth and impact of the New Genetics in modern society, extending to:

- Ethical oversight of scientific and medical research[2]
- Provision of clinical genetic services[3]
- Collection, storage, analysis, and use of DNA samples by law enforcement authorities[4]
- Use of genetic information in insurance underwriting[5]
- Use of genetic information by employers[6]

Michela Betta (ed.), The moral, social, and commercial imperatives of genetic testing and screening. The Australian case, 95–124.

- Use of genetic information by immigration authorities[7]
- Management of tissue banks, genetic registers, and human genetic research databases[8]
- DNA parentage and kinship testing[9]
- Role of genetic information (if any) in the construction of racial, ethnic, and cultural (including Aboriginal) identity[10]
- Use of genetic testing and information in sports.[11]

From the beginning, the Inquiry recognized the need for extensive public involvement and widespread consultation, engaging the general community as well as the recognized experts and interest groups. To this end, the Inquiry released a substantial Issues Paper[12] and a 900-page Discussion Paper[13] to promote public education and debate; conducted a series of 15 open forums in all capital cities and the major regional centres; initiated well over 200 meetings with interested parties in Australia and overseas; and received nearly 350 written submissions. In accordance with the ALRC's standard practice, the Inquiry also established a broad-based, external Advisory Committee—a reference group that included leaders in the fields of genetic and molecular biological research; clinical genetics and genetic counselling; public health and community medicine; indigenous health; public health administration; community and professional education; employment and industrial law; human rights, privacy, and anti-discrimination law; and insurance and actuarial practice. A separate Working Group on law enforcement and evidence was also established, with experts on forensic medicine, DNA profiling, policing practices, and criminal law (prosecution and defence).

2. BALANCING INTERESTS OR VINDICATING RIGHTS?

Many of the public submissions to the Inquiry employed the language of absolute rights. However, achieving justice in this complex area is not susceptible to a simple vindication of individual rights. Careful consideration of the legal and policy issues thrown up by the use of genetic samples and information requires a wide range of interests to be balanced. Although relatively easy to articulate in the abstract, achieving the proper balance is difficult in practice, since various interests will compete and clash across the spectrum of activity. For example, as discussed throughout ALRC 96, human genetic information has a powerful familial dimension. The Inquiry noted that human genetic information calls from *before* the cradle and lasts well *beyond* the grave—an individual's genetic information usually will reveal information about, and have implications for, his/her parents, grandparents, siblings, children, and generations to come. Or it may reveal that the person is not biologically related to his/her social relatives—another sensitive matter that may or may not have been known or openly disclosed. Thus, there may be circumstances in which an individual's presumptive right to privacy, and to the confidentiality of the doctor–patient relationship, may be called into question by the competing needs of genetic relatives. Similarly, a balance needed to be struck in a number of other areas in order to recognize and accommodate wider social interests that transcend individual ones—e.g., in the compulsory acquisition of DNA samples by law enforcement authorities; the ability of researchers to gain a waiver of individual consent requirements; the imposition of restrictions on employers from requiring genetic testing and information from their employees; or in limiting the ability of a person to initiate parentage testing without the knowledge and consent of the child and the other parent.

3. THE REJECTION OF "GENETIC EXCEPTIONALISM"

A threshold question for the Inquiry was whether we should embrace notions of "genetic exceptionalism"; i.e.,

> the idea that genetic information is so fundamentally different from, and more powerful than, all other forms of personal information that it requires different and higher levels of legal protection.[14]

The initial public policy responses to the New Genetics largely followed this approach, most clearly represented by the work of professors Annas, Glantz, and Roche of the Boston University School of Public Health, who produced the influential Model Genetic Privacy and Non-Discrimination Bill, which was introduced into the Australian Parliament by Senator Natasha Stott Despoja in 1998, in a first attempt to raise consciousness and stimulate public debate about these issues in Australia.[15] In the words of professors Annas, Glantz, and Roche, "genetic information is uniquely powerful and uniquely personal, and thus merits unique privacy protection."[16] This approach is predicated on the basis that one's DNA amounts to "a coded probabilistic future diary, [which] describes an important part of a person's unique future."[17] Now that the novelty of dealing with the New Genetics has passed, however, the Inquiry firmly concluded that an "inclusivist" approach was much preferred, in which the Commission (a) refrained from making artificial and unproductive distinctions between "genetic" and "non-genetic" information; and (b) adapted existing laws and practices to meet the special features and challenges of genetic information, rather than creating new, specialist regimes. For example, the Inquiry was determined to build upon what the Australian community has learned in recent years from dealing with the challenges of HIV-AIDS—in terms of privacy, non-discrimination, and non-stigmatization, as well as in terms of community education, the importance of pre- and post-test counselling, the mandating of best practice in laboratories, and sensible and effective public health administration. Similarly, the Inquiry preferred to adapt existing privacy laws and safeguards, as well as existing anti-discrimination laws and watchdog bodies, rather than recommend the establishment of new ones dedicated only to disputes arising out of a person's real or perceived genetic status. Finally, the Inquiry was careful to avoid accepting notions of "genetic essentialism" or "genetic determinism," or to incorporate these directly or indirectly into policies and practices.[18]

4. KEY GENERAL RECOMMENDATIONS

The extraordinary breadth of the issues raised by the New Genetics, coupled with the rapid advances in the science and technology, meant that significant law reform would not likely be achieved via an omnibus "Human Genetics Act." Rather, the Inquiry endeavoured to develop a sophisticated mix of strategies and approaches, including some legislative amendments and regulations; official standards and codes of practice (such as those promulgated by the NHMRC and the Office of the Federal Privacy Commissioner); industry codes and best practice standards;[19] education and training programmes (ranging from community education through to continuing professional education and specialist medical training); and better coordination of governmental and intergovernmental programmes. Thus, the 144 recommendations contained in ALRC 96 are addressed to 30 different "actors" *besides* the Australian Government. For this reason, the ALRC included an "Implementation Schedule" for the first time in one of its reports, to make clear the lines of responsibility for implementation of the various recommendations and to facilitate subsequent monitoring of the resulting activity (or lack thereof).

Apart from those dealing with privacy and discrimination laws, which are dealt with in detail below, the key recommendations in ALRC 96 included the following:

- A standing Human Genetics Commission of Australia (HGCA) should be established to provide high-level, technical, and strategic advice to Australian governments, industry, and the community about current and emerging issues in human genetics, as well as providing a consultative mechanism for the development of policy statements and national standards and guidelines in this area.[20]
- The protection of the integrity of the individual warrants the creation of a new criminal offence to prohibit an individual or a corporation from submitting another person's sample for genetic testing, or conducting such testing, knowing (or recklessly indifferent to the fact) that this is done without the consent of the person concerned or other lawful authority.[21]
- Ethical oversight of genetic research should be strengthened by ensuring that all genetic research complies with NHMRC standards; better supporting Human Research Ethics Committees (HRECs); providing more guidance to researchers and research participants about ethical best practice; developing new rules to govern the operation of human genetic research databases; and tightening reporting requirements.[22]
- An ethical dimension should be added to the accreditation standards of the National Association of Testing Authorities (NATA), Australia,

and only accredited laboratories should be permitted to conduct genetic testing for health and medical purposes. The Therapeutic Goods Administration (TGA) should be empowered to regulate genetic testing devices that may be provided directly to the public.[23]

- As a matter of priority, Australian governments should develop strategies designed to assess and respond to the need for increased and adequately resourced genetic counselling services.[24]
- As a general rule, employers should *not* be permitted to gather and use predictive genetic information except in rare circumstances, e.g., where this is necessary to protect the health and safety of workers or third parties, and the action complies with stringent standards developed by the HGCA and the National Occupational Health and Safety Commission (NOHSC).[25]
- DNA parentage testing should be conducted only with the consent of each person sampled, or pursuant to a court order. In the case of a child who is unable to make an informed decision, testing should go ahead only with the consent of both parents, or pursuant to a court order.[26]
- Australian governments should develop national minimum standards with respect to the collection, use, storage, destruction, and index matching of forensic material (and the DNA profiles created from such material) in order to facilitate an effective national approach to sharing DNA information for law enforcement purposes. No inter-jurisdictional sharing of information should be permitted except in accordance with these national minimum standards.[27]

5. THE PATCHY REGULATORY FRAMEWORK

The current methods of regulation and conflict resolution in this broad field in Australia involve a patchwork of federal, state, and territory laws; official guidelines; personal and professional ethics; institutional restraints; peer review and pressure; oversight by public-funding authorities and professional associations; supervision by public regulatory and complaints-handling authorities; private interests; free market pressures; and occasional media scrutiny and exposés. The complexity of Australia's federal system adds substantially to the difficulties in describing, much less reforming, law and practice in this field. For example, the Commonwealth and each State and Territory has enacted a statute—sometimes more than one—that touches on privacy interests in human genetic materials and information. Similarly, there are nine different legislative regimes governing forensic procedures involving the collection, analysis, use, and databasing of genetic information—as well as many protocols and agreements signed among Australian governments to facilitate interjurisdictional sharing of such information. The Inquiry's brief was to scrutinize the existing regimes, and then tailor them—where necessary, and to the extent possible—to the particular needs and demands of genetic testing and information. In some instances, the Report has recommended new forms of regulation to address existing gaps. Successfully fulfilling this brief has involved not only providing adequate protections against the *unlawful* use of genetic information but also putting into place measures and strategies aimed at ensuring a higher order goal: that where such information may be used lawfully, it will be used properly, fairly, and intelligently.

6. PRIVACY PROTECTION

As noted above, one of the central concerns for the Inquiry, as specified in the Terms of Reference, was to determine whether the existing regulatory framework is adequate to protect the privacy interests of Australians in relation to human genetic information (and the tissue samples from which such information readily may be derived)—and if not, what changes are needed. Consequently, the Inquiry examined the operation of the Privacy Act 1988 (Cth) as amended (including the private sector provisions) in this area, as well as the parallel statutory provisions in the States and Territories. While human genetic information has some special characteristics that distinguish it from other forms of health information—especially in terms of its ubiquity and durability, and the familial dimension[28]—genetic privacy issues are usually similar in nature to those applicable to information privacy generally and, in particular, to the privacy of medical records and other sensitive health information. The Inquiry concluded that, while some weaknesses in the existing legislative privacy framework could be identified, they would best be addressed through changes to general information and health privacy laws (in particular the Privacy Act) and practices, rather than through the development of a new regulatory framework dedicated to the protection of genetic information. Again, after some considerable deliberation, the Inquiry rejected "genetic exceptionalism" as an organizing principle for reform in this area.[29]

6.1 The Privacy Act 1988

The Privacy Act is intended to protect the personal information of individuals and to give them control over how that information is collected, used, and disclosed. The legislation sets out certain safeguards that government, private sector organizations, and individuals must observe, and also gives individuals rights to access and correct their own personal information. Under section 6(1) of the Privacy Act, "personal information" is defined as "information or an opinion (including information or an opinion forming part of a database), whether true or not, and whether recorded in a material form or not, about an individual whose identity is apparent, or can reasonably be ascertained, from the information or opinion." For the purposes of the private sector provisions (see below), the Privacy Act also creates a special category of "sensitive information" and gives this a higher level of protection.

Sensitive information is defined in section 6 as "information or an opinion about an individual's racial or ethnic origin; political opinion; political association membership; religious beliefs, affiliations or philosophical beliefs; professional or trade association membership; union membership; sexual preferences; criminal record; or is health information about an individual." "Health information" is separately defined in section 6 as:

(a) information or an opinion about:
   - (i) the health or a disability (at any time) of an individual; or
   - (ii) an individual's expressed wishes about the future provision of health services to him or her; or
   - (iii) a health service provided, or to be provided, to an individual; that is also personal information; or

(b) other personal information collected to provide, or in providing, a health service; or

(c) other personal information about an individual collected in connection with the donation, or intended donation, by the individual of his or her body parts, organs or body substances.

In keeping with the pattern of legislation in most of the western world, the Privacy Act contains privacy safeguards set out in a number of Information Privacy Principles (IPPs) and National Privacy Principles (NPPs). The IPPs cover collection, storage and security, use, disclosure, and access to "personal information", which is found in a "record." The "golden rule" operating in this area is that personal information may only be collected and stored with the consent of the individual concerned, and may only be used for the purpose for which it was collected. An alleged breach of the IPPs may give rise to an investigation by the federal Privacy Commissioner, who has powers under the Privacy Act to make determinations—which only may be enforced by the Federal Court after a new hearing. The Commissioner also can initiate investigations without a complaint and has powers to seek injunctions. In addition, the Commissioner has the power to audit the handling of personal information by Commonwealth agencies. Initially, the privacy protection afforded by the IPPs extended only (with limited exceptions) to the personal information handling practices of a federal government "agency," but the Act was extended to the private sector commencing 21 December 2001—including such entities as private hospitals, doctors and other health practitioners, and insurance companies. Private sector organizations must comply with the NPPs, which set out how to collect, use, and disclose personal information, maintain data quality, keep personal information secure, maintain openness, allow for access and correction of personal information, use identifiers, allow anonymity, conduct transborder data flows, and collect sensitive information. Some of these principles are similar to the IPPs; however, among other differences, the NPPs contain special provisions for "sensitive information," a subset of which is "health information."

Under the Act, organizations and industries can develop their own privacy codes (for approval by the Privacy Commissioner), which must provide privacy protection of at least equivalent standard to the NPPs; where they do not do so, the NPPs apply as the default position. Small business operators—defined by section 6D as those with an annual turnover of less than $3 million—have extensive exemptions from the Privacy Act. However, all organizations or individuals that provide health services and hold any health information (except in an employee record) are subject to the private sector provisions, regardless of their size and income. Due to the broad definitions used in the Privacy Act, health service providers are not limited to hospitals, medical practitioners, and others traditionally considered to be part of the healthcare system. Such organizations and individuals may include gyms and weight loss clinics. Alternative medicine practitioners, pharmacists, mental health professionals, optometrists, and social welfare and counselling service providers also would be considered to be health service providers, whether the service is provided face to face, over the phone, via mail order, or through the Internet. However, small business organizations that provide no health services, but merely collect and store health information on behalf of others, probably would not be caught by the Privacy Act.

Under Australia's federal arrangements, most state, territory, and local government bodies are not covered by the Privacy Act—including public hospitals and other health service providers. Similarly, private sector health service providers working under contract for a state, territory, or local government agency are not covered by the Privacy Act. In all such cases, the applicable practices and protections must be found in the relevant state or territory privacy legislation, although in many cases these apply similar principles to those in the federal law.

6.2 Consent and the Collection and Use of Genetic Information

Most genetic information about identifiable individuals is obtained from the taking of family medical history or from medical genetic testing, whether diagnostic or predictive, carrier or prenatal. Therefore, such genetic information would likely fit within the definition of health information. Diagnostic testing most clearly counts as health information, since it is information about the health of the individual. Family history and predictive testing would generally also qualify, since it is "information or an opinion about the health or disability (at any time) of an individual" in terms of section 6 of the Privacy Act, even where it deals only with probabilities. The Federal Privacy Commissioner's *Guidelines on Privacy in the Private Health Sector* (2001) state that health information includes "genetic information, when this is collected or used in connection with delivering a health service, or genetic information when this is predictive of an individual's health." For the same reason, genetic information provided to insurers or employers also may constitute "health information," even though it is not taken for clinical or therapeutic purposes.

The position becomes less clear with respect to other forms of genetic testing. There are circumstances in which genetic information may not be health information as defined in the Privacy Act. For example, carrier testing might fall outside the definition of health information, since it is not information about the health or a disability of "an individual." That is, the health of the test subject is not at issue—the information is about the health of future children. In Victoria, the Health Records Act 2001 (Vic) section 3(1) addresses this by defining health information to include "personal information that is genetic information about an individual in a form which is or could be predictive of the health (at any time) of the individual *or any of his or her descendants*" (emphasis added). Other forms of genetic information that may not fall within the definition of health information include genetic information collected and used to establish parentage or for the purposes of forensic investigation.

NPP 1 provides that an organization must not collect personal information unless the information is necessary for its functions and must collect personal information only by lawful and fair means and not in an unreasonably intrusive way. Individuals must be informed about various matters such as their access rights, the purposes of collection, and to whom the organization usually discloses information of that kind. In general, an organization must collect personal information about an individual only from that individual, rather than from any third party.

The Federal Privacy Commissioner's *Guidelines on Privacy in the Private Health Sector* state that there are three key elements involved in seeking consent to use health information in particular ways: (1) consent must be provided voluntarily; (2) the individual must be adequately informed; and (3) the individual must have capacity to understand, provide, and communicate his or her consent. Consent is of particular importance in the collection of genetic information, as compared with most other forms of health information, given the special characteristics of genetic information and the ethical considerations involved in decision-making about genetic testing. For consent to be truly voluntary, there must be no undue pressure or coercion. On one view, an individual's consent may not be voluntary and valid if the individual is denied some benefit or is disadvantaged in some way because he/she refused consent. These dimensions of consent may become relevant when considering the application of the NPPs to genetic testing by an employer, prospective employer, or for insurance purposes. NPP 10 contains provisions dealing specifically with collection of health information for the purposes of providing health services. Under NPP 10, a health provider generally must not collect sensitive information (including genetic and other health information) unless the individual has consented. However, NPP 10 then sets out a number of specific circumstances in which an organization may collect sensitive information without consent, including: where collection is required by law; in specified circumstances relating to the provision of health services; and in circumstances related to public interest, such as for research relevant to health and safety—providing that collection is carried out according to certain professional rules of confidentiality.[30]

As noted, some collection of information necessary for research or statistical purposes may be done without an individual's consent—but only where obtaining consent is impracticable, de-identified information would not be suitable, and the collection is carried out in accordance with guidelines issued by the NHMRC and approved by the Privacy Commissioner under section 95A of the Privacy Act. NPP 2 provides generally that an organization must not use or disclose personal information about an individual for a purpose other than the primary purpose of collection (i.e., for a secondary purpose). NPP 2 then sets out a range of circumstances in which an organization may use or disclose personal information for a secondary purpose, including: where the secondary purpose is related (or *directly* related in the case of health and other sensitive information) to the primary purpose and the person would reasonably expect such use or disclosure; where the individual has consented to the use or disclosure; and in circumstances related to public interest, such as for research relevant to health and safety and for law enforcement purposes. The Privacy Commissioner's *Guidelines on Privacy in the Private Health Sector* provide a range of examples of secondary purposes for which the use or disclosure of personal information would usually be permissible without consent, provided it is within the reasonable expectations of the individual concerned. These include sharing information with other health service providers within a multidisciplinary healthcare approach. Other directly related secondary purposes may include many activities or processes necessary to the functioning of the health sector, including use or disclosure in connection with: providing an individual with further information about treatment options; billing or debt recovery; an organization's management, funding, service-monitoring, complaint-handling, planning, evaluation, and accreditation activities; addressing liability indemnity arrangements, e.g., in reporting an adverse incident to an insurer; disclosure to a clinical supervisor by a psychiatrist, psychologist, or social worker.

6.3 The Familial Dimension of Genetic Information

Genetic records often contain information about the biological relatives of the individual to whom the information primarily relates. For example, in most genetic studies a "pedigree" is drawn. This involves the identification of a number of family members, some of whom may be quite distant in terms of their social relationship. The pedigree is likely to be essential to derive the mode of inheritance and, from this, the range of disorders that might apply to the genetic family and the person being tested. Privacy laws are largely built around the protection and vindication of individual rights. A key issue for the Inquiry was whether the familial or collective nature of genetic information also requires recognition as a basic element of the privacy protection regime. This would involve a shift away from the "rights model" towards a more "medical model", based primarily on what doctors consider best practice in providing medical care for patients and their families. Control of genetic information would be "shared" among genetic relatives.

> On this model, people would not have the ultimate right to "control" their information and the use of their tissue taken for genetic testing (though the nature and use of the information and tissue will be fully discussed at the outset before testing is undertaken); and doctors will have a special role in providing and imparting genetic information that may appear contrary to their traditional obligation to maintain patient confidentiality.[31]

This model for regulating genetic information, if adopted, would lead to quite different constraints being placed on the collection and disclosure of genetic information than those currently applicable under the Privacy Act. As a general matter, under existing law, the collection of information about genetic relatives without their consent is not permitted. By long tradition, of course, doctors have collected from patients a family medical history, which contains personal information about a large number of persons without their individual consent. Following the extension of the Privacy Act to the private sector, doctors sought (through the Australian Medical Association) an exemption from the Act in this regard; the Privacy Commissioner agreed and granted a Public Interest Determination permitting doctors to continue this routine practice without running foul of the Act.

More controversial, however, are issues of access to and disclosure of genetic information to relatives. Under the Privacy Act, disclosure of genetic information, other than for the primary purpose of treating the person tested, is generally only permitted with the consent of that person. However, in some circumstances, the disclosure of genetic test information could allow the prevention of serious health consequences in genetic relatives—e.g., where an individual's test results are positive for mutations linked with colorectal cancer or breast cancer. Ideally, and in many instances, the patient will consent to informing relatives, so that they may seek their own medical advice, including screening. Where consent is not obtained, in most circumstances (where disclosure is not for the primary purpose of collection or for a directly related secondary purpose), a health services provider may only disclose personal information to a relative if this is necessary to lessen or prevent a serious and imminent threat to an individual's life, health, or safety (NPP 2.1 (e)(i)). However, a familial *predisposition* to cancer or other genetic conditions generally would not be regarded as a sufficiently *imminent* threat to justify disclosure in breach of a patient's wishes. In its 1997 report and proposed ethical guidelines, the Cancer Genetics Ethics Committee of the Anti-Cancer Council of Victoria recommended that patients should no longer be able to prevent the disclosure of such relevant genetic information to their relations.

> It is as *members of families* that they are at risk, and because of family history which they share with many others that they may end up having a genetic test. The condition is necessarily shared, and the diagnosis of it necessarily implicates their relations.[32]

The proposed familial cancer guidelines suggested that where it becomes necessary to inform relatives of a genetic risk, the patient will first be asked to consent. If the patient objects, the information may be disclosed in de-identified form so that the relative is informed that the mutation exists in the family but not about the patient's identity or genetic status (even though these may be able to be inferred).[33] How significant the genetic risk must be in order to justify disclosure without consent under the guidelines is not entirely clear. The familial nature of genetic information also raises access issues. The High Court of Australia has ruled that neither common law nor equity confers a general right of patient access to medical records.[34] However, since December 2001, the Privacy Act (NPP 6) provides individuals with a statutory right, subject to some limited exceptions,[35] to access their own personal information upon request, and to correct the information if it is not accurate, complete, and up to date. (It may be particularly important to provide the individual with an opportunity to discuss his/her genetic health information when he/she seeks access to it, in order to help prevent the information being misunderstood or taken out of context—both special dangers with genetic information, especially predictive information).

Where a person is being assessed or treated for a genetic condition by a medical practitioner, the starting point under the Privacy Act is that the person has a right of access to the genetic records collected by the medical practitioner. However, these records may contain information about the family as a whole, including information about non-paternity as well as the genetic status of other individuals. Where the information relates to a genetic relative who is not a patient of the practitioner, the obligation to provide access to the genetic relative under the Privacy Act may conflict with a practitioner's legal and ethical duties of confidentiality with respect to his/her patient. NPP 6 provides that access may be refused to the extent that "providing access would have an unreasonable impact upon the privacy of other individuals." Therefore, in some circumstances, a medical practitioner may be entitled to refuse access to part of the records. The practitioner could also provide access in ways that do not have an impact on the privacy of another person, e.g., by removing the other person's identifying details or getting his/her consent to the release of his/her information.

The familial cancer guidelines provide for a presumption that genetic relatives should have access to genetic information and genetic samples in order to be able to assess their own risk.[36] Providing more flexibility with respect to access and disclosure has implications for preserving an individual's "right *not* to know." This principle may have particular application to genetic testing because of the predictive power, or perceived predictive power, of genetic information in relation to a person's long-term health experience and other physical and behavioural characteristics. Under the Privacy Act the "right not to know" is protected to some extent by requiring that, in most circumstances, genetic testing will not be permitted without the informed consent of the individual concerned. The National Statement on Ethical Conduct in Research Involving Humans requires that research participants be asked, at the time of giving consent, whether or not they wish to receive the results of the tests that relate to them as individuals.[37] However, protecting the right not to know becomes more problematic in the clinical context. As the Cancer Genetics Ethics Committee has observed:

> [W]ith a condition like FAP, in which virtually all who carry a gene mutation develop cancer, and in which the cancer may be prevented, the strong presumption should be that the relatives will be grateful for being warned. The same presumption should not be made in a cancer such as breast cancer, where the risk of developing cancer . . . is less than 100% and there is no assurance of a successful medical intervention.[38]

6.4 State and Territory Privacy Laws

New South Wales (NSW) is covered by comprehensive public sector information privacy legislation that extends protection to health information held by public hospitals and other public health service providers.[39] Other regulations protect the confidentiality of health information held in the records of private hospitals, nursing homes, and day procedure centres.[40] Some state legislation also covers health information held in the private sector. The most comprehensive is the ACT's Health Records (Privacy and Access) Act 1997, which regulates the privacy of public and private sector health information. In Victoria, the Health Records Act 2001 applies health privacy principles to all personal information collected in providing a health, mental health, disability, aged care, or palliative care service and all health information held by other organizations. All States have legislation relating to the administration of public health services and most of this legislation contains provisions to protect the confidentiality of health information obtained by public sector health administrators in the course of their employment.[41] Recognizing the need for a robust health information privacy framework—particularly given the Health*Connect* initiative, which involves the creation of a nationally linked electronic public health database, incorporating state and territory health records—the Health Information Privacy Working Group of the Australian Health Ministers Advisory Council (AHMAC) has promoted the establishment of a nationally consistent set of rules for the handling and protection of health information in both the public and private sectors. A draft National Health Privacy Code has been submitted to the Australian health ministers in July 2005 for consideration.

6.5 Other Domestic Privacy Protection

Decisions about collection and disclosure also must be taken with regard to other relevant legislation, the law, and ethics of medical confidentiality and to clinical and ethical guidelines. For example, the use and disclosure of genetic information collected for clinical purposes is constrained by obligations of doctor–patient confidentiality. Disclosure that is permitted by the Privacy Act may nevertheless constitute a breach of professional ethical obligations. Similarly, researchers who collect genetic information are subject to ethical duties of confidentiality and will have obligations under research guidelines issued by the NHMRC. Unauthorized disclosure of genetic information for law enforcement purposes (i.e., DNA profiling information for evidence in criminal proceedings or for inclusion in the National Criminal Investigation DNA Database [NCIDD]) may breach provisions of the Crimes Act 1914 (Cth).

6.6 International Regulation of Genetic Privacy

The United Kingdom's Human Genetics Commission has undertaken a useful survey of laws relating to the protection of genetic information, covering Australia, Canada, the United States, Germany, the Netherlands, and Sweden.[42] The United States relies on a patchwork of state and federal laws, with the first comprehensive federal standards for health privacy established in 2001, when the US Department of Health and Human Services issued regulations under the Health Insurance Portability and Accountability Act 1996 (USA).[43] As a general matter, most western jurisdiction countries have general information privacy (data protection) legislation—some of which distinguishes between health information and other personal information. However, there are few national laws dealing specifically with protection of personal *genetic* information.[44] In part, this no doubt represents a delay in governments catching up with the rapid advances in genetic science and technology. But, as discussed above, this delay also seems to embody a rejection of the notion of genetic exceptionalism, and to manifest a preference to regulate this area according to general laws and practices rather than creating a new regulatory device. In Australia, the ALRC-AHEC Inquiry noted:

> Given the plethora of existing regulation relating to the privacy protection of genetic information, it seems more appropriate to amend existing legislation to ensure that issues of genetic privacy are adequately covered rather than to add another layer of complexity by enacting genetic privacy legislation.[45]

The Inquiry concluded that while "genetic information has some special characteristics that distinguish it from most other forms of personal information,"

> genetic privacy issues and reform options are often similar to those applicable to information privacy generally and, in particular, to the privacy of medical records and other health information.[46]

7. RECOMMENDED CHANGES TO PRIVACY LAW

In ALRC 96 the Inquiry recommended a number of amendments to the Privacy Act aimed at improving the protection of human genetic samples and information. These include (and are discussed in further detail below):

- Amendment of the definitions of "health information" and "sensitive information," expressly to include human genetic information about an individual[47]

- Extension of the definition of "health information" to include information about an individual who has been dead for 30 years or less[48]
- Extension of the coverage of the Privacy Act to all small business operators that hold genetic information or samples[49]
- Extension of the Privacy Act to cover identifiable genetic samples[50]
- Creation of a right of an individual to access his/her own body samples for the purpose of medical testing, diagnosis, or treatment[51]
- Creation of a right of an individual to access genetic information or body samples of his/her first-degree genetic relatives, where such access is necessary to lessen or prevent a serious threat to his/her life, health, or safety[52]
- Permission for a medical professional to disclose genetic information about his/her patient to a genetic relative, where this disclosure is necessary to lessen or prevent a serious threat to an individual's life, health, or safety[53]
- Amendments to ensure that employee records containing genetic information are subject to the protections of the Privacy Act.[54]

7.1 DEFINITIONS OF "HEALTH INFORMATION" AND "SENSITIVE INFORMATION"

The Inquiry was of the view that genetic information should receive the heightened protection afforded to health and other sensitive information under the Privacy Act, but that the existing definitions of health information and sensitive information do not provide the desired level of protection for all genetic information. As noted above, there are circumstances in which genetic information may not amount to "health information"—either because the information is not about health, disability, or the provision of a health service (as in the case of parentage or forensic testing, where the focus is on identification), or because it is not about the health or disability of an existing individual (as sometimes may be the case with genetic carrier testing, where the information is primarily about the health of future children). There is also a range of non-health genetic information that falls outside of the definitions of sensitive information, in particular parentage testing done by commercial laboratories. Submissions to the Inquiry generally supported proposals to amend the Privacy Act to ensure that all genetic information is treated as health information or other sensitive information under the Act. After considering definitions in other health information privacy legislation, the Inquiry recommended that the definition of "health information" be amended to include "genetic information about an individual in a form which is or could be predictive of the health of the individual or any of his or her genetic relatives" (whether or not it was collected in relation to the health of, or the provision of a health service to, the individual or a genetic relative).[55]

The word "predictive" was not intended to bear the technical meaning used in some clinical contexts, but was chosen for the purpose of consistency with existing Australian statutory definitions. The term "genetic relative" was considered more appropriate than the term "descendants" used in some other formulations, in order to encompass genetic information about an individual's siblings, parents, and forebears. It was also considered necessary to amend the definition of "sensitive information" to include human genetic *test* information, in order to cover genetic information derived from parentage, forensic, and other identification testing that is not predictive of health.[56]

7.2 Coverage of Genetic Samples

The Inquiry's Terms of Reference specifically referred to the privacy of "human genetic samples and information." A distinction is made between the genetic "sample" (the biological sample—blood, tissue, saliva, etc.) and genetic information that may be derived from the sample by PCR technology[57] and DNA analysis. In common with most other "data protection" laws internationally, the Privacy Act does not cover genetic samples, even where these are identifiable to an individual (e.g., where the container has a name or identifier attached). With the exception of NSW, no other Australian jurisdiction applies IPPs explicitly to body samples. There was broad support among those consulted for extension of the Privacy Act to cover identifiable genetic samples in the submissions and in the extensive national consultations conducted by the Inquiry partners. ALRC 96 identified a number of reasons why protection for genetic samples should be covered by privacy legislation:

- Genetic samples are closely analogous to other sources of personal information that are covered by the Privacy Act and should be protected by rules that are consistent with those applying to the genetic information derived from samples.
- There are gaps in the existing framework for protecting the privacy of individuals from whom genetic samples are taken or derived.
- These gaps may be remedied if the NPPs or a set of similar privacy principles were to apply to genetic samples.
- No circumstances have been identified in which applying the Privacy Act to genetic samples would lead to adverse consequences for existing practices involving the collection and handling of genetic samples.[58]

The Inquiry made a number of recommendations about extending coverage of the Privacy Act to provide enforceable privacy standards for handling genetic samples, including:

- Amending the definition of "personal information" and "health information" to include bodily samples from an individual whose identity is apparent or can be reasonably ascertained from the sample[59]
- Amending the definition of "record" to include a bodily sample[60]
- Making provision for an individual's right to access his/her own bodily samples, through a nominated practitioner, for the purpose of medical testing, diagnosis, or treatment[61]

- Making provision for an individual's right to access bodily samples of his/her first-degree relatives, through a nominated practitioner, where access is necessary to lessen or prevent serious threat to his/her life, health, or safety, even where the threat is not imminent.[62]

7.3 Access to Genetic Information of First-Degree Genetic Relatives

As discussed above, genetic information may allow inferences to be drawn about persons other than the individual to whom the information most directly relates—especially about genetic relatives. In some circumstances, the disclosure of genetic information has the potential to prevent serious health consequences for genetic relatives by encouraging screening, which allows for the early detection and treatment of inherited genetic disorders. While it is desirable that disclosure to genetic relatives is normally made by, or with the consent of, the patient—and while acknowledging that confidentiality is a cornerstone of the doctor–patient relationship in western medicine—it became clear to the Inquiry that a range of circumstances exist in which this does not, or sometimes cannot, occur. The Inquiry concluded that there was a need to amend the Privacy Act to broaden the circumstances in which doctors and allied health professionals may use or disclose genetic information to prevent threats to life, health, or safety. It was considered that the existing "serious or imminent threat" test, included in the NPP 2.1(e)(i), is too restrictive in the context of shared genetic information. The Inquiry recommended that the Privacy Act be amended so that use or disclosure of genetic information by a health professional be permitted where the health professional believes that the use or disclosure is necessary to lessen or prevent a serious threat to an individual's life, health, or safety, even where such threat is not imminent—e.g., where a genetic test indicates a familial predisposition to breast cancer or colon cancer. ALRC 96 noted that this amendment could be achieved by one of the following options:

- Amending NPP 2.1(e)(i) to change the "serious and imminent threat" test to a more flexible formulation that accommodates predictive genetic health information
- Enacting a new NPP 2.1(e)(iii) to permit organizations to exercise a discretion, subject to guidelines issued by the NHMRC and approved by the Federal Privacy Commissioner, to disclose an individual's genetic information to a genetic relative where such disclosure is reasonably believed to be necessary to lessen or prevent serious harm to any individual.[63]

Although option 1 may be easier to articulate, there were some concerns that this would have implications beyond the context of genetic information—i.e., by permitting disclosure of *any* personal information in the regulated circumstances. The Inquiry ultimately did not recommend one or other of the options, stating that further professional and community consultation should be conducted by the NHMRC to determine the preferred course of action. Consistently with this position, the Inquiry recommended that genetic relatives should have a limited right of access on their own initiative.[64] This right should be exercisable only in relation to familial genetic information about the siblings, parents, or children of the individual (first-degree genetic relatives). Access should be provided by making the information available to the requester's nominated medical practitioner or genetic counsellor, who can explain the clinical relevance of the information obtained for the individual. Where an organization (such as a genetic register or tissue bank) receives a request for access to genetic information about an individual's genetic relatives, it should be obliged to seek the consent, where practicable, before determining whether to provide access. Access should be refused where the provision of such genetic information would have an unreasonable impact upon the privacy of the individual. To assist with implementation of this recommendation, the Inquiry recommended that the NHMRC should develop guidelines for health professionals in dealing with such requests.[65]

7.4 Deceased Individuals

The Privacy Act currently does not cover genetic information about deceased persons. This may be contrasted with the position under the health privacy laws of Victoria and NSW, and with the AHMAC Draft National Health Privacy Code, all of which extend to personal information about individuals who have been dead for not more than 30 years. The Inquiry considered it desirable to amend the Privacy Act to cover genetic information about deceased individuals because of the implications that the collection, use, or disclosure of this information may have for living genetic relatives, and adopted the 30-year period to ensure consistency with the position in Victoria and NSW.[66] The Inquiry also accepted the view put in submissions that the Privacy Act should include provisions for decision-making, either by a next of kin or an authorized person, regarding health information of deceased individuals.

7.5 Employee Records

The Inquiry found that the privacy protection affording personal information—including health information—which is held in the employee records of the private sector, is very limited, and recommended that the Privacy Act should be extended to cover employee records.[67] Previous inquiries into privacy protection had indicated concerns about the "employee record" exemption from the private sector provisions of the Privacy Act.[68] While the Australian Government's expressed preference has been to deal with the privacy of an employee's personal information in workplace relations legislation, the ALRC believes that the current provisions of the

Workplace Relations Act 1996 (Cth) do not provide the scope to protect adequately the privacy of employee records. While there is no contemporary evidence that Australian employers are ordering genetic tests or seeking access to genetic test information, there is little doubt that the pressures to use such information will intensify as the reliability and availability of genetic tests increase, and as the cost of testing decreases in the next few years.[69] There certainly are incentives for employers to utilize genetic information when it becomes more cost-effective as an aid in reducing workers' compensation and other insurance costs, minimizing sick leave and engaging in OH&S and civil liability risk management strategies. Several cases have already emerged internationally (although fewer in Australia) in which employers have demanded genetic information or genetic testing, or have surreptitiously obtained such information.[70]

A number of submissions expressed serious concern about the lack of privacy protection currently provided for sensitive information—particularly genetic information—held by private employers.[71] It is notable that the Australian Chamber of Commerce and Industry (ACCI), which has in the past strongly supported the existing employee records exemption, acknowledged in its own submission that there is room for special provision to be made with respect to sensitive genetic information held by employers.

7.6 Small Business Operators

Under the Privacy Act, some small business operators are excluded from the definition of "organization," and are therefore entirely exempt from the operation of the Act. The exceptions include any organization that is providing a "health service" and holds health information. However, the Inquiry noted that a small business that is not a health service provider but nevertheless holds health information can remain exempt from the Act—such as where a business stores genetic samples or acts as a genetic data repository, but does not itself provide a health service.[72] Concerned that this loophole poses a potential risk to the privacy of both the individual concerned and his/her genetic relatives, ALRC 96 recommended that all small business operators that hold genetic information should be subject to the provisions of the Privacy Act, whether or not they provide a health service.[73]

8. ANTI-DISCRIMINATION LAW

Anti-discrimination legislation exists at the federal, state, and territory levels in Australia.[74] At the federal level,[75] the major pieces of legislation include the Sex Discrimination Act 1984 (Cth) (SDA), the Racial Discrimination Act 1975 (Cth) (RDA), the Disability Discrimination Act 1992 (Cth) (DDA), and the Age Discrimination Act 2004 (Cth) (ADA). In addition, the Workplace Relations Act 1996 (Cth) contains provisions that prohibit discrimination on a range of grounds with respect to the termination of employment.

8.1 International Context

None of these Acts specifically addresses discrimination on the basis of genetic status. However, in recent years the international community has been turning its attention to this matter in some detail. The UNESCO Universal Declaration on the Human Genome and Human Rights 1997 recognizes that

> research on the human genome and the resulting applications open up vast prospects for progress in improving the health of individuals and of humankind as a whole, but . . . that such research should fully respect human dignity, freedom and human rights, as well as the prohibition of all forms of discrimination based on genetic characteristics.[76]

While the Declaration is not a binding legal instrument, it is evidence of growing international concern and an indication of the general approach of the international community in this area. Article 2 of the Declaration states:

> Everyone has a right to respect for their dignity and for their rights regardless of their genetic characteristics. That dignity makes it imperative not to reduce individuals to their genetic characteristics and to respect their uniqueness and diversity.

Article 6 goes on to declare:

> No one shall be subjected to discrimination based on genetic characteristics that is intended to infringe or has the effect of infringing human rights, fundamental freedoms and human dignity.

The Council of Europe's Convention on Human Rights and Biomedicine, which is a legally binding instrument and has been signed and ratified by 15 countries to date, gives a clear indication of the approach adopted in Europe in relation to this issue. Article 11 states that any form of discrimination against a person on grounds of his/her genetic heritage is prohibited.[77] It is against this background that the Inquiry was asked to consider whether the protection offered by existing legislation in Australia is adequate.

8.2 Basic Framework of Australian Discrimination Law

Despite some differences in detail, all anti-discrimination legislation in Australia embodies the same basic paradigm for identifying unlawful discrimination. For discrimination to be unlawful, an act or omission must:

- Be based on one of the grounds or attributes set out in the legislation, such as sex, race, age or disability
- Fall within an area of activity set out in the legislation, such as employment or the provision of goods and services
- Result in some harm or less favourable treatment, whether by direct or indirect discrimination
- *Not* fall within an exception, exemption, or defence.

The requirement that *unlawful* discrimination must be based on one of the grounds or attributes specified in the legislation means that the statutory definitions become crucial to the operation of the law. These grounds vary from jurisdiction to jurisdiction, and include race, sex, sexuality, pregnancy, marital status, parental status, age, disability, religion, political belief or activity, and trade union activity. If a person is discriminated against on the basis of an attribute that is not listed in the legislation—e.g., intense personal dislike—the victim has no remedy under anti-discrimination law. The exceptions, exemptions, and defences to anti-discrimination provisions mean that, in some circumstances, it is not unlawful to treat some people differentially and disadvantageously, even on the basis of specified attributes. For example, as discussed in detail in the next chapter, it is not unlawful under the SDA or the ADA for an insurer to discriminate on the basis of sex or age in the terms on which an insurance policy is offered if the discrimination is based on reasonable actuarial and statistical data—so that women with longer average life spans, and younger people, may pay lower premiums than men, and older people. In the same way, the DDA does not simply require that employers and others disregard a person's disability. Employers and others are expressly required to make reasonable efforts to accommodate disabled individuals so that they are, for example, able to perform the job, despite their disability—but they are not required to take extraordinary steps.

Australian law recognizes that discrimination may be direct or indirect. Indirect discrimination—or "adverse impact" discrimination, as it is sometimes called—is less obvious and more difficult to identify, because it focuses on the unreasonable consequences of the discriminator's action rather than on the particular attributes of the person towards whom the action was directed. For example, many metropolitan police forces have abandoned minimum height requirements in recent years—because these had an adverse impact on women and on persons from certain ethnic backgrounds. Although it is conceivable that a complaint of discrimination on the basis of genetic status could be based on race (e.g., by a carrier of Tay–Sachs disease or sickle cell anaemia, which run predominately in people of Jewish or African ancestry, respectively) or gender (e.g., by a female with a genetic mutation for breast cancer or a male with fragile X syndrome), most such actions are likely to arise under the DDA, and the remainder of this discussion focuses on the provisions of that Act.

9. THE DISABILITY DISCRIMINATION ACT

Section 4(1) of the DDA defines "disability" to a high level of specificity, to include:

(a) total or partial loss of the person's bodily or mental functions; or
(b) total or partial loss of a part of the body; or
(c) the presence in the body of organisms causing disease or illness; or

(d) the presence in the body of organisms capable of causing disease or illness; or
(e) the malfunction, malformation or disfigurement of a part of the person's body; or
(f) a disorder or malfunction that results in the person learning differently from a person without the disorder or malfunction; or
(g) a disorder, illness or disease that affects a person's thought processes, perception of reality, emotions or judgement or that results in disturbed behaviour;
and includes a disability that:
(h) presently exists; or
(i) previously existed but no longer exists; or
(j) may exist in the future; or
(k) is imputed to a person.

Under the DDA, disability discrimination is prohibited in employment, education, access to premises used by the public, provision of goods, services and facilities, accommodation, buying land, activities of clubs and associations, sport and the administration of Commonwealth government laws and programmes.[78] A product of its time, the DDA was designed to apply to unlawful discrimination based on a person's physical disability, mental illness, intellectual disability, or HIV-AIDS positive status ("the presence in the body of organisms capable of causing disease or illness")—but there is no express reference to genetic status. There is general agreement among experts in this field of law that the existing definition of disability covers genetic conditions that are manifested by current symptoms. Such symptoms may result, for example, in the partial loss of a person's bodily or mental functions (paragraph (a)) or in the malfunction of a part of a person's body (paragraph (e)). Under these paragraphs it is not necessary to consider the cause of the disability, only the effect on the individual.

The more difficult question is whether the definition in the DDA (and in other anti-discrimination legislation) is wide enough to encompass discrimination on the basis of genetic status where a person is presently asymptomatic. The DDA does refer to a disability that "may exist in the future" or is "imputed to a person," as well as to past or present disability. However, the difficulty with the definition is that paragraphs (h)–(k) must relate to a type of physical or mental manifestation in the less helpful terms of paragraphs (a)–(g) of the definition. Put in other words: Could a genetic mutation that increases a person's risk of heart disease be construed to be an "organism capable of causing disease or illness" (paragraph (d))? Or might it be considered a "malfunction, malformation or disfigurement of a part of the person's body" (paragraph (e))? It is more likely that discrimination on the basis of a genetic mutation that increases the risk of a person developing a particular disorder is covered by paragraph (j) of the definition of disability, coupled with paragraphs (a), (b), or (e). To take the case of a genetic mutation that increases the risk of heart disease, under the DDA the "disability" does not arise directly because of the person's present genetic mutation, but because that mutation indicates that a "partial loss of the person's bodily functions" (paragraph (a)) "may exist in the future" (paragraph (j)). In short, the disability is not the genetic mutation itself but the possible future expression of that mutation through the malfunctioning of a part of the person's body. But given the structure of Australian anti-discrimination law, with its emphasis on the characteristics presumed or imputed to apply to people who fit one of the specified grounds or attributes, there must be some uncertainty about the application of such laws to acts or omissions based on the use or interpretation of predictive genetic information.

9.1 Proposed Changes to Deal with Genetic Discrimination

Some of the key stakeholders, including the acting federal Disability Discrimination Commissioner and the NSW Anti-Discrimination Board, submitted to the Inquiry that the existing definition in the DDA adequately covers discrimination on the basis of genetic status.[79] However, there was a widespread view—including from peak associations representing doctors, lawyers, trade unions, insurers, genetic support groups, and geneticists—that it would be better to amend the DDA to clarify this point beyond doubt.[80] The NSW Anti-Discrimination Board acknowledged that "there is a strong public interest rationale for making such coverage explicit in anti-discrimination legislation," since such a clarification would:

- Reflect the current state of the law under the DDA and ADA
- Have an educative effect
- Serve a symbolic function in clarifying that such discrimination is unlawful conduct under anti-discrimination law
- Provide certainty regarding people's rights and responsibilities under anti-discrimination law.[81]

The Inquiry agreed with this approach, and recommended that, in order to provide a consistent approach to addressing genetic discrimination, the DDA and related laws and regulations[82] should be amended to make clear that they expressly apply to discrimination based on genetic status.[83] Consistent with its general approach in eschewing genetic exceptionalism, the Inquiry rejected suggestions,[84] and precedents from some other jurisdictions,[85] calling for a new, dedicated Genetic Discrimination Act. As with privacy laws, the Inquiry concluded that it would make for better policy and practice to deal with the issues within the existing regulatory framework—but with recommendations for amendments to anti-discrimination laws as well as other safeguards.[86]

10. A CRIMINAL OFFENCE FOR NON-CONSENSUAL TESTING?

The Inquiry expressed serious concern about the potential for non-consensual collection and analysis of DNA samples—e.g., by private investigators; employers; insurers; government agencies (except as authorized by statute, such as police officers conducting forensic procedures); journalists; or a parent with a doubt about the paternity of a child. Given the ubiquity of genetic samples (in blood, saliva, semen, tissue, hair, etc.), the rapid advances in the science and technology, and the growing availability and decreasing costs for DNA analysis, there is greatly increased potential for activities that threaten the legitimate privacy interests of individuals. The Inquiry found, for example, that a significant level of non-consensual DNA paternity testing already exists in Australia, conducted outside the auspices of the Family Court, and often by laboratories that are not formally accredited for this purpose.[87] The ALRC expressed appropriate caution about suggesting the use of criminal sanctions in regulating a field of activity where civil penalties or administrative remedies—or ethics or education—may be enough to secure routine compliance. However, the Inquiry was sufficiently alarmed about the privacy implications of the widespread non-consensual collection, testing, and analysis of DNA to propose that bold step. Accordingly, the Inquiry recommended in ALRC 96 that the protection of the integrity of the individual warrants the creation of a new criminal offence, to prohibit an individual or a corporation from submitting another person's sample for genetic testing, or conducting such testing, knowing (or recklessly indifferent to the fact) that this is done without the consent of the person concerned or without other lawful authority—such as a court order, statutory authority, or ethics committee approval for genetic research.[88]

11. CONCLUSION

The Inquiry's experience in dealing with the Australian public confirms the local and overseas literature with respect to the social ambivalence to the rise of the "New Genetics."[89] There is certainly considerable optimism about the potential for genetic research to produce important medical breakthroughs in the diagnosis, treatment, and prevention of terribly debilitating diseases, as well as leading to the development of whole new fields of medicine, such as gene therapy, regenerative medicine, and pharmacogenomics. And although it may give pause to some civil libertarians, it was also clearly evident that there is strong support in the general community for the collection and use of DNA by law enforcement authorities. At the same time, there is a palpable anxiety about some of these developments, prompted by the rapid pace of change, and aggregating a range of concerns about the loss of control; fears about the beginnings of "genetic determinism" or perhaps even eugenics; and some doubts about the ability of public authorities to regulate effectively in this area.

Beyond the implications for the health and well-being of individuals, the New Genetics also gives rise to questions as fundamental as what it means to be "human." It is noteworthy that Professor Francis Fukuyama's *Our Posthuman Future: Consequences of the Biotechnology Revolution*[90] contains a plea for strong government regulation of the biotechnology sector—this coming from a normally conservative advocate for small government, limited regulation, and free markets. It does not appear that Australians have lost faith in the capacity (or willingness) of government to regulate biotechnology effectively in the public interest. In part, this is a result of good management, but no doubt it is also the result of good fortune, in so far as Australia has not suffered the sort of public health crises or major scandals that sap public confidence—as has happened in Europe and North America.[91] This leaves open a precious window of opportunity for Australian governments and policymakers to lay down a sound policy platform in advance of these problems emerging.

A central concern of the Inquiry was to place a very high premium on the dignity of the individual. Thus, as discussed above, ALRC 96 recommended that we must take the concept of "informed consent" seriously—including outside of medical research and doctor–patient relationships, such as when it is used in the context of criminal law and procedure—and even to the extent of *criminalizing* the non-consensual testing of a person's DNA without lawful authority.[92] The Inquiry was determined to be vigilant in resisting notions of genetic essentialism or genetic determinism, or incorporating these into policy or practice (however unwittingly).[93] Human beings are worth more than the sum total of their genetic sequence—they are not "gene machines." Similarly, the Inquiry was careful not to develop policy and practice based on any notions of "genetic exceptionalism." Among other things, this strongly influenced the recommendations described above regarding privacy protections and anti-discrimination laws, as well as insurance underwriting law and practice (considered in detail in the following chapter). Since its release, ALRC 96 has been gaining significant attention around the world—including in the United States, Canada, the United Kingdom, New Zealand, China, Korea, and Japan, as well as in international forums organized by the World Health Organization (WHO), the United Nations Educational, Scientific and Cultural Organization (UNESCO), the Organisation for Economic Cooperation and Development (OECD), and the Human Genome Organisation (HUGO).

In his keynote address opening the Symposium on Human Genetics and Global Healthcare at the XIX International Congress on Genetics, which took place in Melbourne in July 2003, Dr. Francis Collins, Director of the US National Human Genome Research Institute and head of the international public consortium that conducted the Human Genome Project, described ALRC 96 as "a truly phenomenal job . . . placing Australia ahead of what the rest of the world is doing."[94] At the same conference, Justice Michael Kirby of the High Court of Australia, first Chair of the ALRC and member of both UNESCO's Bioethics Committee and HUGO's Ethics Committee, praised the "breadth and quality" of the report and hoped that "Parliament will examine the proposals and not simply put them into the 'too-hard' basket."[95] Similarly, Senator Natasha Stott-Despoja, the member of the Australian Parliament with the most abiding interest in this field, described ALRC 96 as "an extraordinary accomplishment," providing a "world-leading platform for policy development," and called for prompt Government action to implement the report's key recommendations.[96] Speaking of the final report Canadian commentator Professor Trudo Lemmons, of the University of Toronto, has written:

> The balanced and sensible approach conveyed by the title is found throughout the two-volume report and is a reflection of the impressively thorough background work on which it is based.... The final report has benefited from an impressive set of interviews, discussions, and submissions from individual scholars, various organisations and interested citizens from all over the world. The way in which the authors have managed to integrate these contributions is remarkable.[97]

Thomas Murray, Chair of the Human Genome Project's first Ethical, Legal, and Social Issues Working Group and currently head of the Hastings Center (for bioethics) in New York, has acknowledged:

> Despite the difficulties the quest for comprehensiveness must have posed, the ALRC and AHEC have done an extraordinarily fine job of explaining the science, identifying what is important for the people of Australia, and offering sensible advice.... In its thoroughness, its candour, and its analytical depth, *Essentially Yours* sets a standard for advice to the public and policy makers on how to understand and protect genetic information.[98]

While kind words about the quality of ALRC 96 are much appreciated by the participants in the Inquiry, much more important will be the take-up of its recommendations by the key stakeholders, including the Australian Government. There are already some very positive signs. In the May 2005 Budget, the Australian Government provided A$7.6 million over 4 years to establish a new Human Genetics Advisory Committee (HGAC)—an independent, expert advisory body—as a principal committee of the NHMRC,[99] fulfilling the central recommendations in ALRC 96.[100] In making this appropriation, the Government noted:

> Rapid developments in human genetics and related technologies are likely to provide substantial benefits for Australians, particularly for health. However, there are many complex social, legal, ethical and scientific issues that arise from these technologies. The new advisory body will ensure that these matters receive careful assessment. The advisory body will consider the impact of new technologies and provide advice on how they might best benefit Australians.[101]

The establishment of the HGAC will ensure that the government, regulators, industry, and the general community can expect to receive ongoing, high-level, technical, and strategic advice, providing a strong platform for policymaking in a rapidly changing environment. Not least, the HGAC will provide national leadership in managing the process of change in relation to human genetics, including engagement of the public on these issues, and provide a forum and a consultative mechanism missing since the end of the ALRC-AHEC Inquiry in mid-2003. Media reports also have confirmed that a "whole-of-government" reply to ALRC 96 is in the final stages of preparation, for release later in 2005, which will provide a detailed response to all of the relevant recommendations for government action or leadership on issues.

Finally, as discussed in detail in the following chapter, the insurance industry has been active in reviewing its practices and developing new policies, procedures, literature, and training programmes in direct response to the findings and recommendations contained in ALRC 96.

NOTES

1. Australian Law Reform Commission, 2003. *Essentially Yours: The Protection of Human Genetic Information in Australia* (ALRC 96).
2. Ibid., Part D.
3. Ibid., Part F.
4. Ibid., Part J.
5. Ibid., Part G—explored in further detail in the following chapter.
6. Ibid., Part H.
7. Ibid., Chapter 37.
8. Ibid., Part E.
9. Ibid., Chapter 35.
10. Ibid., Chapter 36.
11. Ibid., Chapter 38.
12. Australian Law Reform Commission, 2001. *The Protection of Human Genetic Information.* Issues Paper 26.
13. Australian Law Reform Commission, 2002. *The Protection of Human Genetic Information.* Discussion Paper 66.
14. ALRC 96, paragraph 3.41.
15. Ibid., paragraph 3.42. See Australian Law Reform Commission, 2001. *The Protection of Human Genetic Information*, Issues Paper 26, paragraphs 2.27–2.29 for a discussion of this Bill, and its consideration by a Senate committee. For the committee report, see Senate Legal and Constitutional Legislation Committee, 2002. *Provisions of the Genetic Privacy and Non-discrimination Bill 1998*. The Parliament of Australia, available at <www.aph.gov.au/senate/committee/legcon_ctte/genetic/index.htm>, cited 21 August 2002. The Bill was restored to the Senate *Notice Paper* on 14 May 2002.
16. Annas, G., Glantz, L., and Roche, R. 1995. Drafting the Genetic Privacy Act: science, policy and practical considerations. *Journal of Law, Medicine and Ethics* 23: 360, 365.
17. Ibid., 360.
18. See ALRC 96, especially paragraphs 3.64–3.77 on the "Dangers of genetic essentialism."
19. Such as the policy on genetic testing developed by the peak life insurance body, the Investment and Financial Services Association: see below.
20. ALRC 96, Chapter 5 and Recommendations 5-1–5-9.
21. Ibid., Chapter 12; see also discussion below.
22. Ibid., Part D, Chapters 13–17.
23. Ibid., Chapter 11.
24. Ibid., Chapter 23.
25. Ibid., Part H, Chapters 29–34.
26. Ibid., Chapter 35. In those cases in which agreement cannot be reached—e.g., because a mature child or a person with parental responsibility withholds consent or is unavailable—a court may authorize testing, after taking the child's interests into account. In order to ensure high ethical standards and technical competence, DNA parentage testing should be conducted only by NATA-accredited laboratories, operating in accordance with the specific accreditation standards in this area. Information about the availability of genetic counselling should be provided to the parties.

[27] Ibid., Part J, Chapters 39–46.
[28] Ibid., Chapter 3 on "Is genetic information special?"
[29] Ibid., Chapter 3 on "Is genetic information truly exceptional?"
[30] The Privacy Commissioner has noted that these professional rules must be binding on the health service provider (i.e., the breach will give rise to adverse consequences) and must be established by a competent health or medical body, such as medical boards recognized in federal, state, or territory law.
[31] Skene, L. 1998. *Patients' Rights or Family Responsibilities? Two Approaches to Genetic Testing*. 13–14, unpublished, appended to Research Committee of the NHMRC, Submission 39 to *Senate Legal and Constitutional Legislation Committee Inquiry into the Provisions of the Genetic Privacy and Non-discrimination Bill*, 26 May 1998.
[32] Cancer Genetics Ethics Committee, 1997. *Ethics and Familial Cancers*. Anti-Cancer Council of Victoria, Paragraph 10.18.
[33] Ibid., Guideline 16.
[34] *Breen versus Williams* (1996) 186 CLR 71.
[35] NPP 6 provides some limited circumstances in which health providers may withhold genetic and other health information, including where providing access would: pose a serious threat to the life or health of any individual; have an unreasonable impact upon the privacy of other individuals; or be unlawful or prejudice various law enforcement interests.
[36] Cancer Genetics Ethics Committee, 1997. *Ethics and Familial Cancers*. Anti-Cancer Council of Victoria, Guideline 13.
[37] National Health and Medical Research Council, 1999. *National Statement on Ethical Conduct in Research Involving Humans*, Paragraphs 16.10 and 16.15–16.16.
[38] Cancer Genetics Ethics Committee, Guideline 16. FAP refers to "familial adenomatous polyposis," a form of inheritable colorectal cancer.
[39] *Privacy and Personal Information Protection Act* 1998 (NSW).
[40] *Private Hospitals Regulations* 1996 (NSW); *Nursing Homes Regulation* 1996 (NSW); *Day Procedure Centres Regulation* 1996 (NSW).
[41] See, e.g., *Health Administration Act 1982* (NSW); *Health Services Act 1988* (Vic); *South Australian Health Commission Act 1976* (SA).
[42] Crosby, D. 2000. *Protection of Genetic Information: An International Comparison*. London: Human Genetics Commission.
[43] *Health Insurance Portability and Accountability Act 1996: Standards for the Privacy of Individually Identifiable Health Information* 45 CFR Part 164, 1996 (USA).
[44] Ibid., 78. The Dutch *Personal Data Protection Act 2000* does make specific reference to genetic privacy.
[45] ALRC 96, paragraph 7.63.
[46] Ibid., paragraph 7.65.
[47] Ibid., Recommendations 7-4 and 7-5.
[48] Ibid., Recommendation 7-6.
[49] Ibid., Recommendation 7-7.
[50] Ibid., Recommendations 8-1 and 8-2.
[51] Ibid., Recommendation 8-3.
[52] Ibid., Recommendations 8-4 and 21-3.
[53] Ibid., Recommendation 21-1.
[54] Ibid., Recommendations 34-1 and 34-2.
[55] Ibid., Recommendations 7-4 and [7-82].
[56] Ibid., Recommendation 7-5.
[57] The polymerase chain reaction method, which greatly amplifies DNA to enable analysis.
[58] Ibid., paragraph 8.3.
[59] Ibid., Recommendation 8-2.
[60] Ibid., Recommendation 8-2.
[61] Ibid., Recommendation 8-3.
[62] Ibid., Recommendation 8-4.
[63] Ibid., Recommendation 21-1, and see paragraph 21.88.

64 Ibid., Recommendation 21-3.
65 Ibid., Recommendation 21-4.
66 Ibid., Recommendation 7-6, and see paragraphs 7.84–7.91.
67 Ibid., Recommendation 34-1. Again, due to the Inquiry's Terms of Reference, this recommendation applies only to *genetic* information contained in employee records. However, the Inquiry identified a number of concerns about other forms of personal health and medical information contained in employee records, and the report contains another recommendation urging that this issue be given further consideration in a broader context: Recommendation 34-2.
68 Including the House of Representatives Standing Committee on Legal and Constitutional Affairs and the Senate Legal and Constitutional Legislation Committee in their respective considerations of the *Privacy Amendment (Private Sector) Bill 2000*.
69 Dr. Francis Collins, Director of the National Human Genome Research Institute and Head of the Human Genome Project, has predicted that within 10 years, and perhaps within 5, a person will be able to provide a sample and soon afterwards collect a CD-Rom spelling out his/her full, 3.3 billion letter, genetic sequence.
70 See ALRC 96, Part H: Employment, especially Chapters 29–30.
71 Ibid., Chapter 34.
72 Smyth, T. 2002. Protecting human genetic information and its use. *Health Law Bulletin* 10 (6): 64, 66.
73 ALRC 96, Recommendation 7-7, and see paragraphs 7.99–7.104. The Office of the Federal Privacy Commissioner supported the removal of the exemption for small businesses holding health information, but was concerned that limiting the reform to "genetic information" would introduce "unnecessary complexity into the regulatory framework applying to small businesses." The Inquiry was limited in the breadth of its recommendation by the Terms of Reference. However, if the definition of "health information" were amended specifically to include genetic information (as outlined above), this would achieve the underlying aims of the recommendation.
74 Each state and territory in Australia has its own anti-discrimination regime and each Act contains its own insurance exception; see: *Discrimination Act 1991* (ACT) section 28; *Anti-Discrimination Act 1992* (NT) section 49; *Anti-Discrimination Act 1977* (NSW) section 49Q; *Anti-Discrimination Act 1991* (Qld) sections 74, 75; *Equal Opportunity Act 1984* (SA) section 85; *Anti-discrimination Act 1998* (Tas) section 44; *Equal Opportunity Act 1995* (Vic) section 43; *Equal Opportunity Act 1984* (WA) section 66T.
75 The federal laws make reference to a wide range of international instruments, as well as "matters external to Australia" (in the case of the DDA and SDA) and "matters of international concern" (in relation to the DDA)—not least to help ground the exercise of federal power in this area in the Commonwealth's responsibility for "external affairs" under section 51(xxix) of the Australian Constitution.
76 Universal Declaration on the Human Genome and Human Rights, UNESCO, available at <www.unesco.org/ibc/en/genome/projet/>.
77 *Convention for the Protection of Human Rights and Dignity of the Human Being with Regard to the Application of Biology and Medicine* (opened for signature 4 April 1997, ETS No 164; entered into force on 1 December 1999).
78 Discrimination on the ground of genetic status may, potentially, arise in many of these contexts. However, consistently with the emphasis in the Inquiry's Terms of Reference, and with the level of concern expressed in submissions, ALRC 96 focused mainly on discrimination in employment and insurance.
79 See ALRC 96, paragraph 9.80.
80 Ibid., paragraph 9.81.
81 Ibid., quoting Anti-Discrimination Board of NSW, *Submission G157*, 1 May 2002.
82 Such as the Human Rights and Equal Opportunity Commission Act 1986 (Cth) and the Workplace Relations Act 1996 (Cth). The ALRC also made a parallel recommendation that the states and territories should consider harmonising their anti-discrimination legislation, and other relevant laws, in a manner consistent with the recommendations in the report: Recommendation 9.5.

[83] ALRC 96, Recommendation 9-3.
[84] Ibid., paragraph 9.50.
[85] Ibid., paragraph 9.51.
[86] Ibid., paragraph 9.55.
[87] Ibid., Chapter 35.
[88] Ibid., Recommendation 12-1; and see generally Chapter 12.
[89] See, e.g., ALRC 96, paragraphs 4.12–4.17.
[90] Fukuyama, F. 2002. *Our Posthuman Future: Consequences of the Biotechnology Revolution*. New York: Farrar Straus & Giroux.
[91] Only 45% of Europeans agreed with the statement that their governments regulate biotechnology well enough, compared with 29% who disagree and 26% who are not sure: Eurobarometer 52.1, The Europeans and biotechnology, available at <www.europa.eu.int/comm/research/quality-of-life/eurobarometer.html>, cited 19 February 2003.
[92] ALRC 96, Recommendation 12-1.
[93] See ALRC 96, especially paragraphs 3.64–3.77, on the "Dangers of genetic essentialism."
[94] Quoted in ALRC *Media Release*, ALRC work praised at World Genetics Congress, available at <http://www.alrc.gov.au/media/2003/mr0714.htm>, cited 14 July 2003.
[95] Ibid.
[96] Ibid., see also similar remarks made in the Parliament, *Hansard*, 11 May 2005, available at <http://www.aph.gov.au/hansard/senate/dailys/ds110505.pdf>.
[97] Lemmons, T. 2003. Why regulate the new genetics? *Reform* 83 (Spring): 41, 41–42.
[98] Murray, T. 2003. Essentially yours: a review. *Reform* 83 (Spring): 47, 50.
[99] This will require amendment of the National Health and Medical Research Council Act 1992 (Cth), to provide for the establishment, membership, and role of this new principal committee, which will join the Australian Health Ethics Committee, the Embryo Research Licensing Committee, and others.
[100] ALRC 96, Recommendations 5-1–5-9.
[101] Australian Government, Department of Health and Ageing, Leading Australia's health into the future, available at <http://www.health.gov.au/internet/budget/publishing.nsf/Content/health-budget2005-hbudget-hfact6.htm>, cited 10 May 2005.

DAVID WEISBROT AND BRIAN OPESKIN

INSURANCE AND GENETICS: REGULATING A PRIVATE MARKET IN THE PUBLIC INTEREST

1. EMERGING CONCERNS ABOUT GENETIC DISCRIMINATION BY INSURERS

As detailed in the preceding chapter, the Australian Law Reform Commission (ALRC) and the Australian Health Ethics Committee (AHEC) conducted a comprehensive, national inquiry into the ethical, legal, and social implications of advancing genetic science and technology, leading to the publication in 2003 of the report *Essentially Yours: The Protection of Human Genetic Information in Australia.*[1] One of the major topics in the report—and, indeed, one of the major precipitating factors in the establishment of the joint inquiry—was the emerging public concern about the operation of genetic testing and information in the context of insurance underwriting. Studies were conducted in 1999 in Australia by genetic counsellor Dr. Kristine Barlow-Stewart[2] and postgraduate law student David Keays, based on anonymous responses received from survey forms distributed by clinical geneticists and genetic support networks in Australia and New Zealand.[3] Genetic discrimination, defined in these studies as less favourable or adverse treatment because of a positive genetic test result, was reported with respect to a wide range of genetic tests.[4] Most of the allegations of genetic discrimination touched on insurance, of which 45 cases were reported with respect to life insurance, income protection insurance, trauma insurance, superannuation, or health insurance.[5] The actions complained of involved loading premiums, denial of requested increases to pre-existing coverage, and direct refusal to provide any insurance coverage.[6] The Barlow-Stewart and Keays studies suggested that in many cases the discriminatory decision or action was inappropriate, and based on misinformation or a lack of understanding of genetic information and the nature of genetic disorders. The allegations of genetic discrimination received widespread media attention in mid-2000.

Michela Betta (ed.), The moral, social, and commercial imperatives of genetic testing and screening. The Australian case, 125–164.

2. THE PARALLEL INQUIRY INTO THE EFFECT OF COMPETITION LAW IN THIS AREA

In August 1999, the Investment and Financial Services Association (IFSA), whose membership accounts for virtually all of the life insurance industry in Australia, lodged applications with the Australian Competition and Consumer Commission (ACCC) in relation to its draft policy on genetic testing. The ACCC was asked to grant an authorization under national competition laws for IFSA's draft policy on genetic testing.[7] Briefly, the critical aspect of IFSA's draft policy (contained in clauses 2 and 4) was that member insurers could ask individuals to disclose existing genetic tests for the purpose of risk assessment, but that member insurers could not initiate any genetic test on applicants for insurance—directly or indirectly, such as through the offer of lower than standard premium rates for individuals with "good" test results.

As discussed below, the ACCC considered this matter in stages between 1999 and 2003, initially inclining towards *not* granting an authorization, but ultimately accepting—with express reference to the findings and recommendations of the Inquiry in ALRC 96—that the public benefits of the policy outweighed the effects of any reduction in competition.

3. THE USE OF GENETIC INFORMATION BY AUSTRALIAN INSURERS

3.1 The Australian Insurance Industry

Insurance in Australia is commonly divided into three categories: life, health, and general insurance. Life insurance encompasses a variety of products, including policies that provide payment upon death, continuous disability, or trauma. Health insurance provides payment for the provision of hospital and ancillary medical and health services. General insurance covers matters not addressed by either life or health insurance, such as product liability, travel, professional indemnity, sickness, and accident. Across the full range of products, general insurers in Australia collected \$16.5 billion in premiums and paid \$11.4 billion in claims for the year up to September 2002. During the same period, life insurers operating in Australia received \$41 billion in premiums and paid \$38.5 billion in claims.[8] During the 2001/02 financial year, private health insurers collected \$7.2 billion in contribution income and paid over \$6.5 billion in benefits.[9] Genetic information is of greatest significance in relation to insurance policies that rely on the collection and use of health information, require an assessment of an applicant's risk of mortality or morbidity, and are mutually rated. In practice, this includes the following:

- Term life insurance, which provides for the payment of an agreed lump sum in the event of death of the insured[10]

- Income protection (or disability income) insurance, which provides for regular sums to be paid while an insured is unable to work due to sickness or injury[11]
- Trauma (or crisis) insurance, which provides for the payment of an agreed lump sum if the insured person is diagnosed with one of a list of specified conditions, such as a heart attack, cancer, or stroke within a specified period[12]
- Sickness and accident insurance, which provides for payment of a lump sum or periodic payments to cover losses or expenses incurred as a result of accidental injury or sickness
- Travel insurance, which provides for the payment of agreed sums to cover losses or expenses incurred in the course of travel, including medical expenses.

The largest part of the personal insurance business in Australia is undertaken by the life insurance industry, either as a component of superannuation or as voluntary, mutually rated, life insurance. At the time of the inquiry, there were 42 registered life insurers in Australia, of which six were reinsurance companies—however, not all registered life insurers are active and several do not operate in the mutually rated market. Superannuation funds almost always provide insurance cover for their members against death and disability. Premiums collected for insurance provided as a component of superannuation comprise 87% of total insurance premiums collected by life insurers. Generally, in relation to large superannuation funds, a modest level of cover is provided on automatic acceptance terms and is not mutually rated. The only entry requirement is that the person covered be fit enough to attend work on the start date.

In its submission to the Inquiry, the Australian Life Underwriters and Claims Association explained:

> In group life insurance, the necessity for underwriting is less strong because of the law of large numbers and the reduced likelihood of adverse selection. With group life insurance, an insurer can take the bad risks, knowing that there will be enough good risks in the entire pool of lives insured to balance the portfolio and allow profitability.[13]

However, where a person is self-employed, employed by a small business, or wishes to seek a higher level of insurance cover than that offered on automatic acceptance terms, the insurance component of superannuation would be mutually rated. It is important to draw a distinction between mutually rated and community-rated insurance. Community rating is the basis of Australia's public and private health insurance systems—contrary to the position in the United States, for example. Under the National Health Act 1953 (Cth), private health insurance contracts are required to be community rated: in setting premiums, or paying benefits, funds cannot discriminate on the basis of health status, race, sex, sexuality, use of hospital or medical services, or general claiming history. Although this risk is shared collectively across the entire pool of the insured, actuaries and underwriters nevertheless collect health information to determine the overall premium that insurers must charge to sustain the pool. The Australian Government provides an annual subsidy of over $2 billion to maintain premiums at a reasonable rate, and also employs a number of disincentives to discourage younger and healthier people from leaving the pool.

Because Australian private health insurers are prevented from using health information to assess individual risk, the use of genetic information in relation to health insurance does not raise the same issues as the use of genetic information in relation to other personal insurance products. For this reason—especially in tandem with the comprehensive public healthcare system available to all Australians through Medicare—the Inquiry focused its discussion and recommendations on mutually rated insurance products. This is in stark contrast with the position in the United States, which lacks a comprehensive public healthcare system like Medicare, and where private health insurance is extremely expensive (and, in practical terms, usually only available through group schemes offered as a salary package item by employers).

In mutually rated insurance, the particular characteristics of applicants are taken into account when assessing the risk the applicant will bring to the insurance pool. In its submission to the Inquiry, IFSA set out four fundamental principles that underlie the provision of voluntary mutually rated insurance in Australia. These are:

1. Spreading risks across large groups
2. Charging a premium that reflects the risk
3. Pooling of similar risks
4. Equal access to information[14]

Characteristics such as an applicant's age and sex will almost always be considered relevant to assessing risk—although the Race Discrimination Act 1975 (Cth) prohibits any distinctions being drawn on the basis of race, even where these might be supported by reliable actuarial data. Depending upon the type of insurance, other factors such as occupation, lifestyle, family medical history, current health condition, and genetic test results also will be relevant. In order to assess fairly the risk that each applicant brings to the pool, insurers require access to all the information known to the applicant that is relevant to the risk. In mutually rated insurance, the price that the insured pay for insurance is proportional to the risk they bring to the insurance pool.

3.2 "Utmost Good Faith" and Duties of Disclosure

Insurance contracts fall into a special category of contracts that are based on the principle of "utmost good faith". One element of this principle is that the applicant has a special duty of disclosure, first under common law[15] and more recently under legislation. The Insurance Contracts Act 1984 (Cth) largely replaces the common law on the duty of disclosure in relation to the types of insurance that were of interest to the Inquiry, and requires disclosure on both sides. Section 22 requires the insurer to inform the applicant clearly and in writing (usually in the insurance brochure and application) about the general nature and effect of the duty of disclosure. Section 21 of the Insurance Contracts Act requires the applicant to disclose to the insurer all relevant information that is known, or which reasonably ought to be known. In practice, disclosure usually occurs when applicants for insurance fill in the form or proposal provided by the insurance company. The insurer can then use this information for underwriting (or risk-rating) purposes, determining whether to accept the insurance application and, if so, on what terms. An insured person is only required to disclose matters during the course of the contract if there is a specific provision in the contract to that effect.[16] Because of the guaranteed renewable nature of life insurance policies, applicants are only risk-rated once—before the contract is entered into. Risk factors, including genetic information, that become known to the insured after the contract has been entered into need not be disclosed. However, some other risk-rated insurance products offered by general insurers, such as sickness and accident policies, must be renewed periodically (usually annually) and there is a duty to disclose relevant information at every renewal point.

Under section 21(2) of the Insurance Contracts Act, an applicant is not required to disclose certain matters such as those that diminish the risk, are of common knowledge, are already known to the insurer, or ought to be known to an insurer in the ordinary course of its business. The Insurance Contracts Act also provides that in some cases the insurer can be held to have waived its right to disclosure from the applicant, e.g., where the insurer has not taken steps to investigate obviously incomplete or inaccurate answers provided by the applicant. The insurer may raise non-disclosure as a defence when an insured person makes a claim under a life insurance policy. Under section 21(2), if the insurer can show that the person failed to disclose relevant information, it may:

- Avoid the contract from its inception if the non-disclosure or misrepresentation was made fraudulently
- Avoid the contract within 3 years if the insurer would not have entered into the contract except for the non-disclosure
- Vary the contract within 3 years by substituting the sum insured (including any bonuses) according to a statutory formula.

3.3 Risk-Rating and Underwriting

Australian insurers classify applicants into four general risk categories: "standard," "non-standard," "deferred," or "declined". "Standard" is the insurance risk benchmark for a policy. Applicants who fall into the standard risk grouping—which amounts to roughly 95% of life insurance applicants in Australia—have no particular adverse risk factors that warrant a premium loading. Insurance may be declined when the insurer determines that the risk that the applicant would bring to the pool is too high to accept, at least for a realistically affordable premium. Life insurance is rarely declined—but where it is, this is usually with respect to applicants with serious health impairments or extremely hazardous occupations or hobbies. Alternatively, an insurer may decline the insurance proposal at the time of underwriting, but offer the applicant an opportunity to have the application re-rated at a future date; for example, this may be the case where a risk factor is expected to reduce or stabilize over time, whether naturally or as a consequence of therapy. Insurers also may accept an application, but attach certain "non-standard" conditions, such as: the temporary or permanent imposition of a percentage increase in the cost of the policy ("premium loading") to account for the additional risk; the specification of certain matters that the insurer will not cover ("exclusions"); limitations placed on the duration of the insurance cover (e.g., where a person may be at significant risk of developing a late-onset disorder); or a specified reduction of the sum that will be paid in the event of a claim.

Actuaries produce the "standard" premium rate tables for insurers, with the rates based on the best risk statistics available and loadings added for expenses and profit—which requires informed judgment about both risk and strategic/competitive factors. Actuaries rely on various sources of data to determine the pricing appropriate to different risk classifications, including Australian aggregate life insurance industry statistics, the company's own experience, and medical and overseas statistics. Major business failures among general insurers (most notably Australian insurance giant HIH) have occurred in Australia in recent years because of the failure to make adequate provision for claims, especially by companies seeking to increase market share by offering low premiums.

Individual applications for insurance are assessed by underwriters, who first confirm an applicant's standard premium rate risk classification (e.g., "age 25, female, non-smoker, white collar"), and then consider other risk factors—most importantly, the applicant's current and expected future state of health. This may include assessment of an applicant's health information, family medical history, and any genetic test results, as well as relevant "non-medical" factors, such as the risks associated with hazardous occupations, extreme sports, and other pastimes. Application forms usually include a standard medical authority, which gives the insurer written consent to obtain full particulars of the applicant's medical history from his/her family doctor, including details of any clinical notes. Where there is the suggestion that a past, current, or potential medical condition may require further investigation (or the applicant is seeking an atypically large amount of coverage), this may be accomplished through a questionnaire, a report from the applicant's doctor, or a request for an independent medical examination from a general practitioner or a specialist.

Underwriters base their decisions on underwriting manuals—compiled by one or other of the six large international reinsurance companies operating in Australia. In some difficult cases, underwriters may seek specialist advice from doctors and reinsurers. The production and updating of underwriting manuals is a specialist, commercially sensitive, and costly task, involving insurance medical specialists, actuaries, underwriters, geneticists, and others. Reinsurers play a critical role in formulating basic underwriting manuals because of the large amount of data they obtain through their dealings with many insurance companies globally.

There are limited avenues for redress currently available for applicants dissatisfied with, or disadvantaged by, an underwriting decision. An applicant may approach the insurer concerned and request internal review. If the matter is not resolved, the applicant may lodge a formal complaint with a relevant agency, such as the Human Rights and Equal Opportunity Commission (HREOC). Critically, neither the Financial Industry Complaints Service (FISC, the industry scheme that deals with complaints about life insurance) nor Insurance Enquiries and Complaints Ltd (which handles complaints about general insurance matters) has jurisdiction to deal with complaints about premiums or underwriting.[17]

3.4 The Collection and Use of Genetic Information

IFSA's submission to the Inquiry noted:

> The use of family medical history is an integral part of the underwriting process. Family medical history has been used for over 100 years within the life insurance industry worldwide.... It is used to identify potential medical risks on the basis of the probability that the insurance applicant may be susceptible to certain risks due to a familial/hereditary link with his or her immediate family.[18]

Although the forms vary somewhat from company to company, applicants for risk-rated insurance typically are asked questions about family medical history: whether immediate family members, i.e., parents, brothers and sisters—living or dead—suffered from heart disease, stroke, high blood pressure, diabetes, cancer, or other familial disorders. As noted by IFSA, family medical history information has been used by insurers—and by doctors—as a means of assessing longevity and the degree of likelihood that an individual will develop a familial or inherited condition in the future. Of course, the most obvious and fundamental bit of genetic information—a person's sex—correlates strongly with longevity.

In October 2002, to assist the Inquiry, IFSA conducted a survey of its members to determine the significance of family medical history in underwriting. Sixteen insurers and reinsurers participated in the survey, which covered 7,949 applications for term life cover, disability insurance, trauma cover, or some combinations of these products. According to IFSA:

> Family medical history played a part in 558 (7.39%) applications. Of these, 349 applications showed a family medical history that was either not significant in the underwriting decision or resulted in a favourable underwriting decision (i.e. accepted at standard rates), when considered with other personal medical information. The remaining 209 (2.62%) applications received an unfavourable underwriting decision (resulting in a loading, exclusion, deferral or declining of insurance). In 106 of these applications the rating was *exclusively* attributable to the family medical history, while in the remaining 103 applications, the ratings

were based on a combination of family medical history and other medical and personal information.[19]

In recent times, the insurance industry also has been using genetic test information for underwriting purposes, where this is disclosed by the applicant—and most insurance company's questionnaires now ask directly about whether the person (or that person's close relatives) has undertaken any genetic testing. In 2001, prompted by the spotlight put on this area by the Inquiry, IFSA commissioned the Institute of Actuaries of Australia to survey, on a 6-monthly basis, all life insurance companies that sell term life insurance, total and permanent disability insurance, trauma insurance, disability income insurance, and business expenses insurance in Australia, to monitor both the volume of genetic tests disclosed in Australian life insurance applications and the progress of these applications through the underwriting process.

The Inquiry had available to it results disclosed during a 2-year survey period (e.g., the first four reporting periods, ending 31 May 2001, 30 November 2001, 31 May 2002, and 30 November 2002), during which time Australian insurers received a total of 235 applications containing a genetic test result. Of the 211 applications that were assessed, 98 were underwritten on standard terms, 58 were underwritten on non-standard terms, 26 were deferred, and 29 were declined. Of the 113 applications that were underwritten adversely, the genetic test result was cited as the major reason for the adverse decision in 27 cases (24% of adverse cases), while some other medical reason was offered in the remaining 69 cases (61% of adverse cases). Of the 235 genetic test results disclosed, haemochromatosis was by far the most commonly reported (170), followed by Huntington's disease (HD) (22), hereditary breast cancer (10), cystic fibrosis (CF) (8), Factor V Leiden (5), myotonic dystrophy (4), and a further 12 genetic conditions with only 1–3 reports each.[20] Placing these figures into some perspective, approximately 1.23 million new policies (excluding group life/superannuation products) were issued by life insurers in Australia in 2001.[21]

The most recent survey report available at the time of writing,[22] covering the period between 1 December 2003 and 31 May 2004, found a genetic test result reported in 100 cases (down from 135 applications in the preceding 6 months), out of 235,577 applications overall—or 0.04% for this period. Of course, as the science and technology develops and the associated costs decline, it is expected that genetic test information will become much more prevalent. Again, the overwhelming majority of tests in this survey period were for haemochromatosis, reported in nearly three quarters of the 100 applications, with the remainder divided among 17 different genetic tests.[23] In November 1998, haemochromatosis became the first genetic test to be included in the Medicare Benefits Schedule (MBS)—which means that patients get at least a 75% rebate on the scheduled fee—and it remains one of only a small number of genetic tests (outside of the comprehensive neonatal screening programme) to be listed in the MBS.[24] Victoria has established a Hereditary Haemochromatosis screening programme and, as discussed further below, clinical genetics services, major employers, and IFSA have combined to establish an innovative HaemScreen programme. In 94 out of the 100 applications reporting genetic test results, the underwriting process had been completed by the time of the survey, with 52 of the applications (55%) accepted at standard rates, and 42 (31%) accepted under non-standard terms and conditions.[25] Of the latter group, insurers cited the genetic test results as the main reason for the adverse decision in only 5 cases (1 of which resulted in a deferral).[26] A positive genetic test result was obtained in 18% of applications, and a negative result in 35%, while 46% indicated carrier status.[27] Even among the 17 applications disclosing positive test results for a genetic condition, only 2 were declined insurance coverage, while 6 were covered on standard terms and 7 on non-standard terms (with 2 deferrals).[28] Contrary to popular perception, very few applicants with positive test results for HD or hereditary breast cancer were declined insurance cover, although the imposition of a permanent premium loading was typical.

3.5 Industry Policy on the Use of Genetic Information

Prior to 1995, the life insurance industry in Australia had no articulated policy with respect to the use of genetic information for underwriting purposes. In the mid-1990s, the Life Investment and Superannuation Association (the precursor to IFSA) developed a draft policy on genetic testing, which was released to its members for consideration in June 1997. In early 1999, IFSA released an agreed draft industry policy, and applied to the ACCC for an authorization[29] in relation to a number of clauses in the policy that potentially could be construed as anti-competitive. IFSA argued that its genetic testing policy should be exempted on the basis that any anti-competitive aspects of the policy were outweighed by the public benefits arising from it.[30] Specifically, IFSA conceded that the draft policy might impede insurers from competing on the basis of price, in so far as it prohibited "preferred risk underwriting",—i.e., the practice of discounting premiums to persons who present less than standard risk. However, IFSA submitted that the primary purpose of the draft policy was to ensure that insurers did not compel or indirectly coerce applicants into undergoing genetic testing, which would cut across an applicant's "right not to know" about a latent genetic disorder or predisposition. The original application of IFSA was opposed by the Human Genetic Society of Australasia (HGSA), the Australian Medical Association (AMA), AHEC, and the federal Department of Health—all of whom sought concessions from the insurance industry aimed at minimizing the risk of discrimination against persons based on genetic testing—although mindful of the fact that the traditional questions about family medical history also amount to "genetic information." In its Draft Determination, issued 14 June 2000, the ACCC proposed *not* to grant an authorization for such arrangements, on the basis that

> the provisions of the IFSA draft policy were not likely to result in a public benefit, and that significant anti-competitive detriment would arise from a collective agreement to prevent the offer of lower than standard premiums based on genetic test results.[31]

In effect, the ACCC wanted insurance companies to have increased opportunities to *discriminate in favour* of persons with "good" genetic test results by offering them especially favourable rates, in theory stimulating a more competitive market. However, in November 2000, the ACCC granted IFSA a 2-year authorization, noting "the complex issues involved" and deciding to provide a "breathing space" during which the issues surrounding genetic testing could be debated and public policy developed. In this context, the ACCC expressly referred to the Government's announcement of the establishment of the ALRC-AHEC Inquiry.[32] The ACCC concluded:

> Ensuring IFSA's members do not require applicants for insurance to undergo genetic testing, and that applicants will not be indirectly influenced into undergoing such tests, is likely to result in benefit to the public. In particular, the Commission considers that there is public benefit in avoiding insurer-initiated coercion to undertake genetic testing.[33]

IFSA then further developed the draft policy and formalized it into an industry standard: "IFSA Standard 11.00—Genetic Testing Policy." In December 2002, when the initial 2-year authorization expired, the ACCC granted an interim authorization in relation to the relevant clauses. In October 2003, the ACCC—referring to findings and recommendations in ALRC 96—released a draft decision providing the IFSA policy with full authorization, noting:

> The ACCC continues to accept that there is a public benefit in life insurers not coercing individuals to undergo genetic testing. . . . While the ACCC is concerned that the arrangement may have a detrimental effect on competition it has concluded that the arrangement is likely to result in a net public benefit.[34]

The purpose of the IFSA Genetic Testing Policy is to specify standards for handling genetic test results[35] to be adopted by life insurers in the operation of their business.[36] IFSA members must certify compliance with the policy annually according to the terms of the IFSA Code of Conduct and Code of Ethics.[37] The key elements of the IFSA Genetic Testing Policy are as follows:

- Insurers will not initiate any genetic tests on applicants for insurance.
- Insurers may request that all existing genetic test results be made available to the insurer for the purpose of classifying the risk.
- Insurers will not use genetic tests as the basis of "preferred risk underwriting" (offering individuals insurance at a lower-than-standard premium rate).
- Members must provide their employees and authorized representatives with sufficient information and training so that they understand the content and meaning of the Standard so far as it relates to their particular jobs and responsibilities.

- Insurers will ensure that results of existing genetic tests are obtained only with the written consent of the tested individual.
- The results of a genetic test will be used only in the assessment of an insurance application with respect to the individual on whom the test was conducted.
- Insurers will ensure that strict standards of confidentiality apply to the handling and storage of the results of genetic tests.
- Insurers will provide reasons for offering modifications or rejections to applicants in relation to either new applications or requests for increases on existing policies.
- Insurers will have a competent and efficient internal dispute resolution system to deal with complaints relating to underwriting decisions involving a genetic test result.[38]

4. THE IMPACT OF PRIVACY AND DISCRIMINATION LAWS

Mutually rated insurance is based on a process of underwriting which involves differentiating among individuals on the basis of the risk that they would bring to the insurance pool if their application were accepted. For example, Australian life insurance companies almost always will ask for higher premiums from older applicants and from smokers than they do from younger applicants and non-smokers. Similarly, unfavourable health information—such as high blood pressure, high serum cholesterol or diabetes, or hereditary medical conditions or disorders—will have implications for underwriting. From one perspective, this process of differentiation constitutes a form of discrimination—it involves treating people differently on the basis of their age, disability, or genetic status. However, such discriminatory practices are largely exempt from the provisions of Australian anti-discrimination legislation. The exemptions recognize that differentiating between individuals is fundamental to the market in mutually rated insurance products—at least where the decision-making process is based on actuarial and statistical data or is otherwise reasonable.

4.1 Insurance and Genetic Privacy

The preceding chapter considers the general issues raised by the "New Genetics" for privacy laws and interests. Privacy issues also can arise specifically in relation to both mutually rated and community-rated insurance. For example, the Health Insurance Commission collects health data in the course of administering Medicare payments for medical services, and private health insurers collect health information in relation to pre-existing conditions. The privacy of health information held by health insurers is protected by a number of laws. Public sector organizations that administer programmes at the federal level, such as the Health Insurance Commission, are bound by the Information Privacy Principles under the Privacy Act 1988 (Cth) (Privacy

Act), as well as by guidelines issued by the Office of the Federal Privacy Commissioner (OFPC) pursuant to the National Health Act 1953 (Cth). Private sector health insurers are governed by the private sector provisions of the Privacy Act, which are discussed further below. Prior to 21 December 2001, the insurance industry was essentially self-regulating in relation to the principles governing the collection, storage, use, and disclosure of personal information. In a 1996 Information Paper on the privacy implications of genetic testing, the then Federal Privacy Commissioner found that "life insurance companies put considerable emphasis on protecting the confidentiality of personal information and complaints about improper handling of information do not appear to be a major focus of dissatisfaction."[39] Since 21 December 2001—when the Privacy Amendment (Private Sector) Act 2000 (Cth) came into force in relation to the private sector—the collection, use, storage, and disclosure of an applicant's or insured's personal information by private sector insurers has been regulated under the Privacy Act. Under these provisions, the National Privacy Principles (NPPs) apply to life insurers.[40] Several provisions in IFSA's Policy on Genetic Testing Policy are also directed to privacy issues. In addition to the matters listed above, the provisions include the following:

> Access to the results of genetic tests in a form identifiable to particular individuals will be restricted to the insurer's underwriters and reinsurers. The results will be made available to other third parties only with the written authorisation of the applicant/insured or in the normal course of discovery during legal proceedings.[41]

Submissions to the Inquiry did not indicate the existence of any major inadequacies in the regulatory framework for protecting the privacy of genetic information in insurance. The OFPC reported that it had received a number of complaints in relation to the information-handling practices of private sector insurers, but concluded that "the privacy protection framework for personal information across the private sector, including the insurance industry, is fundamentally sound," and there is a deepening awareness of privacy principles and appropriate personal information-handling practices across the insurance industry in Australia.[42] The Centre for Law and Genetics agreed, and observed:

> Notably, although there have been ongoing concerns about the use by insurers of genetic test information, few, if any, complaints have been heard regarding insurers' failure to adequately protect the privacy of this information.[43]

The Inquiry considered that the basic framework for privacy protection in the insurance context is satisfactory. However, it noted that the collection and use of genetic information by insurers does give rise to the need to ensure that applicants are adequately informed. Genetic information has some special characteristics, such as its predictive and familial nature, which need to be raised with, and considered by, applicants at the time of collection. While applicants have a duty to disclose relevant information to insurers, that duty only arises if the applicant decides to proceed with the insurance application. An applicant should be given sufficient information to enable the applicant to make an informed decision about whether to proceed. Consequently, the Inquiry recommended that insurers review their consent and medical authority forms to ensure that they contain sufficient information about the collection, use, and disclosure of genetic information to allow applicants to make an informed decision about whether to proceed with the application and consent to the collection of the information.[44] The Inquiry also recommended that the insurance industry approach the Federal Privacy Commissioner seeking a Public Interest Determination (in effect, an exemption or authorization) under the Privacy Act in relation to the long-standing practice of collecting family medical histories, since this may amount to a technical breach of the Act in so far as information about genetic relatives is collected and applied without their consent.[45]

4.2 Anti-Discrimination Legislation

As discussed in the preceding chapter, anti-discrimination legislation exists at the federal, state, and territory levels in Australia.[46] Despite some differences in detail, all of the legislation embodies the same basic paradigm for identifying unlawful discrimination, requiring that it must be based on one of the grounds or attributes set out in the legislation (such as sex, race, age, or disability); must fall within an area of activity specified in the legislation (such as employment or the provision of goods and services); must result in some harm or less favourable treatment; and must not be subject to an exception, exemption, or defence. At the federal level, the Sex Discrimination Act 1984 (Cth) (SDA), the Racial Discrimination Act 1975 (Cth) (RDA), the Disability Discrimination Act 1992 (Cth) (DDA), and the Age Discrimination Act 2004 (Cth) (ADA) contain provisions relevant to discrimination in insurance. All four acts make it unlawful to discriminate in the provision of goods and services. Subject to the other requirements identified above, it is generally unlawful to discriminate by refusing to provide a good or service, offering a good or service on altered terms or conditions, or by discriminating in the manner in which the good or service is provided.[47] "Services" are defined to include insurance services.[48] The DDA, the SDA, and the ADA all contain express exemptions relating to the provision of insurance, which allow insurers to discriminate in certain circumstances—where this is based on actuarial or statistical data upon which it is reasonable for the insurer to rely.[49] The RDA does not provide an exception for discrimination in insurance based on race. The RDA limits the information that insurers are permitted to use in underwriting applications for insurance, despite the actuarial relevance of the information. For example, insurers may not discriminate between applicants on the basis of race even though the life expectancy of indigenous Australians (especially males) is, tragically, markedly lower than for the population at large.

Following the decision of the High Court of Australia in *Australian Mutual Provident vs Goulden*,[50] the insurance provisions in state or territory anti-discrimination legislation may be subject to challenge on the basis that they are inconsistent with federal legislation that regulates how life insurers may determine premiums by reference to actuarial advice and prudent insurance practice. In that case the High Court found that the provision prohibiting disability discrimination in the provision of goods and services in the Anti-Discrimination Act 1977 (NSW) was invalid to the extent that it was inconsistent with the Life Insurance Act 1945 (Cth).[51] Because of the possibility that state legislation on this issue remains subject to challenge, future complaints of discrimination on the basis of genetic information in insurance are more likely to be brought under the DDA.[52]

4.3 The Disability Discrimination Act

Section 24(1) of the DDA makes it "unlawful for a person who, whether for payment or not, provides goods or services, or makes facilities available, to discriminate against another person on the ground of the other person's disability" by refusing to provide the goods and services or to make available the facilities, or by failing to do so in the same manner and on same terms and conditions as would apply to other persons. However, section 24(2) provides a general exception where it would impose an "unjustifiable hardship" on the provider. In addition, section 46 of the DDA recognizes the nature of (mutually rated) insurance and superannuation and provides a specific exception, meaning that discrimination in these industries is not unlawful where it is based upon actuarial or statistical data on which it is reasonable to rely (section 46(1)(f)), or where no such actuarial or statistical data is available and cannot reasonably be obtained—and the discrimination is reasonable having regard to any other relevant factors (section 46(1)(g)). In *QBE Travel Insurance vs Bassanelli*,[53] the Federal Court confirmed that the onus was on the insurer to demonstrate that the exception applies in the particular circumstances of the case. In relation to what actuarial or statistical data is "reasonable" to rely upon, the Court noted that this involves

> an objective judgment about the nature and quality of the actuarial or statistical data relied on. The actuary or statistician (or the data itself) may indicate that for whatever reason it would not be reasonable to rely upon it. It may be qualified, or be an insufficient sample for reliable use, or not be directly applicable to the particular decision. There may be other reasons why, on its face, it would not be reasonable to rely upon it. There may be actuarial or statistical data upon which it may be unreasonable to rely for other reasons external to the data being relied upon. The data may be incomplete, or out-of-date, or discredited, and the decision-maker ought, in the circumstances, to have known that.[54]

According to the *Guidelines for Providers of Insurance and Superannuation* issued by HREOC pursuant to the DDA, actuarial or statistical data upon which insurers reasonably may rely include such things as underwriting manuals, local data (e.g., census statistics), relevant overseas studies, and relevant domestic and international insurance experience.[55] Where there are no relevant statistics or actuarial data available, and these cannot reasonably be obtained, insurers are required to show that discrimination is "reasonable" if based on other factors. Some genetic disorders are so rare that it might take decades to collect statistically reliable data. HREOC has suggested a number of factors that insurers may seek to rely on, including medical opinion, opinions from other professional groups, actuarial advice or opinion, relevant information about the individual seeking insurance, and commercial judgment.[56]

4.4 Public Concerns about Genetic Discrimination in Insurance

The Inquiry was presented with limited verifiable evidence of the actual extent of any unlawful discrimination by the insurance industry based on genetic information. As noted above, the Barlow-Stewart and Keays studies reported nearly 50 (anonymous) allegations of discrimination—although it is not clear how many of these claims, even if factually correct, would fall within the existing statutory exemptions. As noted above, the survey performed by the Australian Institute of Actuaries on insurance applications has identified only a small number (and a very tiny percentage) of adverse underwriting decisions linked directly to genetic test information (as opposed to family medical history). The Inquiry also heard a number of anecdotal accounts, and received written submissions, from clinicians, genetic counsellors, and genetic support groups.[57] Taken together, these individual case studies provided the Inquiry with a valuable source of information about the way in which genetic information is used by insurers. The Inquiry noted that in some of these cases the insurer appeared to have acted on the basis of a misunderstanding of the genetic information provided and that some decisions may not have been consistent with anti-discrimination law. The case studies examined by the Inquiry indicated that the use of genetic information by insurers sometimes leaves an applicant with the impression that the underwriting decision was not well informed or fair—even if the insurer's actions were permitted by law. However, in most cases there appeared to have been a lawful decision by the insurer that the risk the applicant would bring to the insurance pool was too high to accept.[58] There is still considerable uncertainty about the nature and extent of discrimination in this area and a need for further detailed empirical research. This need should be satisfied by a federally funded "Genetic Discrimination Project."[59] Submissions received by the Inquiry identified a range of issues and problems related to the use of genetic information in underwriting. Significant concerns were expressed that allowing unlimited use of genetic information in this context could lead to the creation of a "genetic underclass" that perpetually would be denied access to insurance cover and other related benefits. Concern also was expressed about the negative impact that the use of genetic information by insurers may have on individual and public health outcomes. For example, David Keays expressed his view to the Inquiry:

> The cascading discrimination that can result from a genetic test has the potential to foster the creation of a genetic underclass. A group of people who already have the misfortune of inheriting genetic mutations, who then suffer discrimination at the hands of insurance companies, which then limits their opportunity and freedom. Furthermore, because genetic characteristics are passed from one generation to the next, so too is the discrimination that accompanies it.[60]

However, the Queensland Anti-Discrimination Commission commented:

> It is acknowledged that the contract of insurance is a private commercial relationship between the insured and an insurer and that insurers should not be expected to provide a social safety net for people. The issue of access to insurance for all is an issue of equity and is a matter for government. A socialised insurance system would involve significant cross-subsidies between different groups of policy owners and could risk escalating costs and reductions in participation rates as witnessed in the private health system.[61]

IFSA expressed the view that the use of genetic test information would not significantly impact on the number of individuals who would be uninsurable:

> Various community groups have expressed concern that the use of genetics in underwriting will result in a pool of individuals being unable to secure insurance cover, disadvantaging them financially.... The introduction of new testing technologies, such as genetic testing, does not in itself impact the underlying health of the population. It does not increase the number of people who are likely to develop severe health conditions in the future, and therefore does not impact the number of people who present such a high risk as to be uninsurable. Therefore, it is not expected to increase the number of people who are declined insurance.[62]

A number of submissions suggested that the potential for discrimination in insurance deters people from taking health-related genetic tests—a claim substantiated by the experience of several individuals who made submissions to the Inquiry. Health professionals stated that some patients hesitate to consult clinical genetics services due to the fear of negative consequences for insurance. As a result, some health professionals counsel patients to seek life insurance prior to undergoing genetic testing. Although the Inquiry did not receive any submissions from individuals directly stating that the fear of genetic discrimination had prevented them from participating in genetic research projects, there were submissions that suggested, in general terms, that whatever the reality, genetic discrimination

> is certainly *perceived* by many to be a problem. Indeed, the *fear* of discrimination is a significant issue because of the potential impact this may have on people's healthcare decisions, in particular, whether to undergo genetic testing and also in relation to their willingness to participate in genetic research.[63]

Members of the Familial Cancer Service at Westmead Hospital, Sydney, commented that patients had difficulty distinguishing between the various types of insurance, including health insurance.[64] It is possible that the level of concern about potential discrimination in insurance is based in part on the misapprehension that genetic information will impact on access to public healthcare or to private health insurance—a more realistic fear in the United States, which lacks a comprehensive public healthcare system and affordable, community-rated, private health cover. The majority of submissions that addressed this issue supported some degree of regulation of genetic test information in insurance to overcome negative consequences for patient health and medical research.

4.5 Adverse Selection and the Risk of Market Failure

A number of individuals and organizations argued that banning the use of genetic information in underwriting would give rise to "adverse selection," which would threaten the viability of the voluntary, mutually rated insurance market.[65] The Australian Prudential Regulation Authority (APRA) explained the phenomenon of adverse selection as follows:

> Genetic information may influence a person's desire to apply for insurance. A person who is aware of their genetic test results indicating that they are at high risk of an early death or disablement might find a life insurance policy an attractive proposition. Conversely, armed with favourable genetic test results, some people might choose not to take out insurance to cover their future risk for developing a particular condition. This is symptomatic of the inherent problem with insurance of adverse selection, where the demand for insurance is largest for individuals who are most likely to have a loss, more generally, or who expect their loss to be larger than average.
>
> The adverse selection problem is especially acute when buyers of insurance can conceal information that the insurer could use to evaluate the likelihood of loss, such as the information available from genetic tests undertaken. In this sense, genetic test information is no different from any other information relevant to an assessment of the insured's health or medical condition. APRA's concern is to ensure that life insurance companies are in a position to assess and accurately price the risks which they underwrite.
>
> The presence of asymmetric information also raises systemic implications. If more people with knowledge of their higher risk join the risk-sharing pool at too low a price relative to their likelihood of claim, then premiums would rise for all policyholders. This will result in insurance becoming generally less attractive to those who believe themselves to be relatively healthy and therefore less in need of insurance cover. This could lead to a shift in the average risk of people taking out life insurance, causing an upward spiral in premiums and risk across the industry.[66]

Not surprisingly, submissions from the British[67] and Australian insurance industries highlighted the concern about adverse selection. IFSA declared that it was

> opposed to the placing of restrictions on underwriting such that it undermines the right of access to all information relevant to the underwriting process including human genetic information known to the applicant. The undermining of this fundamental principle could lead to the destabilising of the system and threaten the commercial viability of this form of insurance.[68]

However, in a number of submissions commentators questioned the severity of the likely impact of denying insurers access to existing genetic information.[69] The Centre for Law and Genetics, for example, stated:

> Although these [adverse selection] arguments have frequently been made of the damaging effect for the industry if insurers are denied access to genetic test

> information for underwriting purposes, rarely have they been substantiated. There is in fact evidence (largely from the United Kingdom), to suggest that, whilst there are risks to insurers arising from adverse selection in the event that applicants have access to genetic test information that is not available to the insurer, the risks are greatest in respect of large policies. This research indicates that the risks arising from adverse selection in relation to small to average size policies would not be significant and certainly would not undermine the viability of the industry. This points to the desirability of distinguishing between large policies on the one hand, for which some measures to protect against adverse selection may be warranted, and small to average sized policies, in respect of which the industry could reasonably be expected to absorb the risks associated with adverse selection.[70]

A body of expert opinion in other countries suggests that adverse selection is unlikely to be significant in the current climate, at least where genetic test information alone is excluded.[71] Tony McGleenan, who was commissioned by the Association of British Insurers to conduct research into the impact of genetic information on the insurance industry, commented in his report:

> Actuarial modelling indicates that four factors are crucial in determining whether adverse selection based on genetic information will be damaging to a life insurance company:
>
> (i) If the results of the genetic test need not be disclosed to the insurer.
> (ii) If the possibility of the condition being present would not have been revealed in any event by other medical information, notably family history.
> (iii) If the additional mortality risk indicated by the genetic test is higher than that in the broad categories already used to classify risk in underwriting.
> (iv) If there is no therapeutic option to improve the healthcare prospects of someone with a positive genetic test.
>
> It must be said that currently, given the costs involved in genetic testing, these diagnostic procedures are usually only performed when clinically indicated for some phenotypic reason other than family history. Therefore, in most cases the condition outlined in (ii) above will not be satisfied. The market for genetic testing for the purposes of satisfying personal curiosity is extremely small and is likely to remain so.[72]

Angus Macdonald, a leading United Kingdom actuary, has noted:

> The most striking feature about this, often heated, debate is the almost total absence of numerical estimates of the cost implications. Actuarial modelling is beginning to provide such numerical estimates, in the first instance to the question of the costs of adverse selection if life insurers did not know genetic test results. The answers point to a sharp distinction between dominant single-gene disorders and multifactorial disorders. The former are rare enough that solutions outwith the free market should be sought, and (with some exceptions) the latter probably will not provide clear and reliable estimates of lifetime risk, distinguishable from lifestyle and environmental factors; they might therefore not meet criteria of accuracy and reliability such as those that govern discriminatory pricing in respect of disability.[73]

The United Kingdom's Human Genetics Commission (HGC) has concluded:

> [R]ecent [actuarial] modelling has shown that a moratorium that extended to family history (as well as genetic test results) would be likely to have a large impact on insurance premiums and affordable access to "essential" insurance.

> On the other hand, we have also heard that restricting access to family history information might have only a small impact on insurance premiums in most markets in comparison with the commercial variations that already exist. We do not at present recommend that the insurance moratorium should be extended to the use of family history information.[74]

4.6 A Moratorium on the Use of Genetic Information by Insurers?

There was some support in submissions to the Inquiry for a general prohibition on the use of genetic test information in insurance underwriting, either on an interim or permanent basis. For example, the Haemophilia Foundation of Victoria expressed the opinion:

> There was a strong and unanimous feeling that insurance companies should NOT have access to genetic information under ANY circumstance. While it is fair that they know of pre-existing conditions, a predisposition to a condition should not have to be declared, even if tests have been conducted and results known. No one has perfect genes![75]

The Centre for Law and Genetics noted:

> One of the key advantages of at least delaying the use of genetic test information for the purposes of insurance underwriting (e.g. through an industry moratorium) is that it permits time for the scientific and actuarial relevance of genetic tests to be established, thus addressing current concerns about the reliability and relevance of information currently used by the industry for underwriting purposes.[76]

Not surprisingly, IFSA strongly opposed any prohibition on the use of genetic information, arguing:

> The major disadvantage of a complete ban is that it undermines the basic principles of a voluntary, risk-rated insurance system. Such an approach exposes the industry to the risk of adverse selection and potentially destabilises the system. The main advantage of the approach is that it potentially provides greater access to life insurance to those who are aware of an unfavourable genetic test result. However, the industry believes this preferential treatment is inequitable, as other consumers bear the additional cost.[77]

4.7 Consideration of a "European Two-Tier" Approach

Some submissions urged the adoption of a "two-tier" system of risk-rated insurance, which would allow individuals to purchase coverage up to a specified monetary limit without any obligation to disclose adverse genetic information. Full disclosure would only be required with respect to applications for coverage that exceeds the threshold sum. In such a system, "genetic information" could be defined to include only genetic test information or extended to include family medical history. The two-tier system attracted some support in submissions on the basis that it would go some way to addressing consumers' concerns by providing access to a basic level of insurance regardless of genetic information. It was also suggested that it might meet insurers' concerns if the monetary limit was set below the level at which the effects of adverse selection might become apparent.[78] For example, the Centre for Law and Genetics recommended:

> A "ceiling" model along the lines suggested . . . is readily applicable to life insurance and could also be adapted to disability and related forms of insurance. Such an approach could be accommodated within existing insurance legislation (*Insurance Contracts Act 1984* (Cth)) as a qualification on the usual disclosure obligations: the alternative, and arguably preferable option, would be for this to be dealt with by way of an industry code or moratorium.[79]

A number of European countries have adopted various forms of the two-tier system. The type of genetic information protected varies between jurisdictions. In Sweden, the two-tier system applies to the use of genetic test results and family medical history, while in the United Kingdom the system applies only to genetic tests, defined as chromosomal cytogenetic tests and molecular DNA tests.[80] The method of implementation also varies. The United Kingdom insurance industry has opted for a self-imposed industry scheme to run for 5 years. In Ireland, a bill that included a moratorium on genetic testing for insurance purposes until 2010 and imposed a two-tier system with respect to the use of family medical history was introduced into Parliament in December 2001, but has since lapsed.[81] The monetary threshold varies significantly among countries. For example, the threshold for term life policies ranges from €60,000 (approximately A$110,000) in Sweden to £500,000 (approximately A$1.35 m) in the United Kingdom.[82] The differences appear to reflect variations in the insurance market and the type of genetic information protected under the threshold. In some countries with a two-tier system, the threshold initially was selected by reference to the average cost of housing—because life insurance is required in order to obtain a mortgage, something that is unknown in Australia. The monetary thresholds in Europe also vary depending on the type of insurance purchased. In the United Kingdom, for example, the limit for term life insurance is set at a higher level than other insurance products (e.g., trauma insurance and disability income protection insurance) because these other products are more vulnerable to the effects of adverse selection.[83]

There are two ways in which a two-tier system could be implemented in Australia: through industry codes or standards, or through legislative amendment (e.g., by altering the applicant's duty of disclosure in the Insurance Contracts Act 1984 (Cth)). It was noted that many superannuation funds provide a certain amount of life insurance to members without requiring the insurance to be fully underwritten. The Anti-Discrimination Commission of Queensland noted:

> [S]eparate insurance policies have now been replaced by personal insurance benefits attached to superannuation. Presently, most employees (other than those who are self-employed or employed in small businesses) are provided with automatic cover up to an automatic acceptance limit. Where employees require a greater amount of insurance, that extra cover is mutually rated. In our submission, the system of underwriting presently used for insurance benefits attached to superannuation provides a good example of a working "two-tier" system of insurance.[84]

In their submission, the Queensland Government argued that, if a two-tier system were to be recommended, it should apply only to genetic test results, and not to family medical history.[85] IFSA expressed the view that the introduction of a two-tier system would be impractical in Australia for a number of reasons:

> The size of the population in Australia compared to the population overseas where the two-tier system operates is significantly smaller. Thus, the costs of implementing a two-tier system in a small voluntary market are not justifiable (given the costs will outweigh any perceived benefits). The nature of the business sold in the Australian market is more risk focused and therefore the impact on price of any such introduction would be more significant.... The variable nature of Australian life insurance products compared with those offered in the overseas market would make it difficult to introduce a common two-tier system (like the overseas models) to apply across diverse and unique products.[86]

APRA, the insurance industry regulator, also expressed some concern:

> Obviously, the potential impact of such a proposal depends on the level of any threshold adopted. However, this has the potential to reintroduce adverse selection problems...and will lead to cross-subsidisation, in that one group of policyholders (e.g. those who have not undertaken a genetic test) may be subsidising the other group that have undertaken such tests.[87]

The appeal of any two-tier system also must depend upon its treatment of family medical history, as well as genetic test information. As noted above, underwriting is still overwhelmingly done on the basis of information disclosed through family medical history, rather than through genetic testing. The European two-tier approach deals poorly, or not at all, with family medical history. In fact, in some European countries that prohibit the use of genetic test information for underwriting purposes, an applicant is barred from using test results to show that he/she does *not* have the disease-related allele (e.g., for HD) that runs in the family. Thus, such persons—bizarrely and unfairly—may be denied insurance cover on the basis of a familial genetic condition or predisposition that they do not share.

5. THE INQUIRY'S PREFERRED APPROACH TO REFORM

The Inquiry recognized the range of genuine concerns raised by the use of genetic information in underwriting mutually rated insurance. However, for the reasons explained further below, the Inquiry concluded that a shift away from the fundamental principles of voluntary mutually rated insurance, based on parity of information between the applicant and the insurer, was not warranted at the present time. An insurance contract is a private commercial relationship between an insured and an insurer by which the former agrees to pay a regular premium in exchange for a payout on the occurrence of a defined event. Although insurance can provide insured persons and their families with significant financial support in adverse circumstances, private insurers should not be expected to provide a social safety net for Australians regardless of their genetic status—that function is more appropriately performed by the State, through the social security and public health systems. Statistics produced by the Insurance and Superannuation Commission in 1996 indicated that only about 30% of Australians had voluntary, mutually rated, life insurance. This suggests that Australians do not regard such insurance as an essential good, but rather as only one investment and financial services product to be considered among an array of products—most of which are not mutually rated by reference to genetic status—for providing individuals and families with financial security for the future. Any significant departure from a system of equality of information between applicants and the insured also raises important issues of equity. If high-risk individuals knowingly can join an insurance pool at standard rates, the increased claims by those individuals ultimately must be borne by others. In the absence of the sort of substantial government subsidy that operates in the private health insurance field, those higher costs will be borne by other persons in the insurance pool in the form of higher premiums. This gives rise to inequities because individuals in the pool are not contributing in accordance with the relative risk that they bring to the pool.[88]

Although the numbers of applications for life insurance involving genetic test information are currently quite small, as discussed above, it is important to adopt policies that are sufficiently robust to endure in the longer term. As genetic tests become cheaper and more widely used, and as our knowledge of the genetic basis of such common health problems as asthma, diabetes, heart disease and depression expands, the relevance of genetic test information is likely to grow. If insurers were denied access to that class of information in underwriting, the disparity in the information known to the applicant and the insurer would likewise grow, enhancing the prospect of market failure caused by adverse selection.[89] The legal principles upon which personal insurance is currently underwritten do not prevent an individual from obtaining insurance at standard rates merely because of his/her genetic status, so long as that status is unknown to the applicant. The present law targets decision-making on the basis of differential information; it does not target decision-making on the basis of underlying genetic status as such. In light of these considerations, the Inquiry formed the view that a basic departure from the fundamental principle underlying the market in voluntary, mutually rated personal insurance in Australia—namely, equality of information between the applicant and the insurer—could not be justified at this time.

The Inquiry noted that many of the community concerns raised in submissions relate to the manner in which insurers use, or are perceived to use, genetic information in underwriting, rather than the underlying duty of disclosure. The Inquiry concluded that these concerns could be addressed *without* departing from the basic principles of parity of information. However, over the last 10 years, many countries have begun to confront the challenges posed by the use of genetic information in underwriting. Different approaches have been taken in different jurisdictions, and some countries have experimented with a number of models within a relatively short period of time. The variety of responses suggests that this shared problem has no universal solution that is likely to commend itself to all. Account must be taken of important differences between insurance markets and between social objectives when comparing jurisdictions. Consequently, the Inquiry recommended that a proposed Human Genetics Commission of Australia (the "HGCA", as discussed in the preceding chapter) should be charged specifically with keeping under review the experience of the insurance industry in using genetic information in underwriting, both in Australia and overseas, in order to make recommendations to government at a later time, if the need arises.[90]

The Inquiry's rejection of genetic exceptionalism strongly influenced the recommendations ultimately made with respect to insurance underwriting law and practice. The Inquiry was not persuaded that there was a case for interfering with long-standing legal requirements that parties to an insurance contract make full disclosure of all material facts—which certainly would include known, significant risks of genetic disorder, whether this knowledge comes from family medical history or a genetic test. Many of these arguments ran along the lines that persons with a genetic disorder were being punished unfairly, in insurance terms, for something that was "not their fault." If the Inquiry had accepted arguments that Australia should join the United Kingdom in imposing a moratorium on the use of genetic information by insurers, someone with a genetic-linked cancer would be privileged for insurance purposes over someone with a non-genetic-linked cancer. And should a person with a genetic-linked disorder be privileged over, say, someone who had been severely injured in a car accident or in an industrial accident? Or privileged over someone who had suffered brain injury or another serious disability, having been the innocent victim of a criminal assault? Or privileged over someone who had developed depression because of stressful family circumstances or despair about the lack of world peace, rather than because of identifiable genetic factors?

While sympathetic to the human dimension, the Inquiry considered that such arguments muddled up the concepts of *fault* and *risk*—and only the latter is central to underwriting. The Inquiry indicated that it certainly had no philosophical objection to no-fault schemes or community rating; however, it was noted that such schemes cannot operate in the private marketplace without a heavy subsidy from the public purse.[91] The Inquiry did express a principled objection to recommending the imposition of a community-rating system, in effect, on the private, traditionally risk-rated, life insurance market *only* with respect to persons shielding adverse *genetic* health information.

6. IMPROVING POLICY AND PRACTICE IN INSURANCE UNDERWRITING

Having rejected a moratorium or the imposition of a two-tier system, the Inquiry turned its attention to developing a range of significant consumer-oriented safeguards and improved policies and practices for the insurance industry, aimed specifically at addressing the most prevalent concerns raised during public consultations and by submissions.

6.1 Scientific Reliability and Actuarial Relevance

As discussed above, Australian anti-discrimination laws relating to age, sex, and disability (but not race) provide an exception in relation to insurance underwriting. The effect of the exception is to enable insurers to discriminate lawfully where:

- The discrimination is based on actuarial or statistical data and is reasonable.
- In the absence of actuarial or statistical data, the discrimination is reasonable having regard to any other relevant factors.

In seeking to rely on genetic information to make distinctions among individuals for the purposes of underwriting, insurers must therefore be able to demonstrate either the actuarial or statistical basis of their decisions or the reasonableness of their actions. Where the scientific reliability or actuarial relevance of genetic information is doubtful, its use in underwriting may take insurers outside the scope of the exception and render their discriminatory conduct unlawful. Although questions of relevance and reasonableness often arise in relation to genetic information derived from genetic tests, the use of family medical history must be of much more concern, given its vastly greater use. For this reason, the UKHGC recommended that the government continue to monitor the evidence used by the insurance industry to justify its use of family medical history in underwriting.[92]

In establishing whether it is reasonable for insurers to rely on genetic information in underwriting, two main issues arise: (a) the scientific reliability of the genetic information; and (b) its actuarial relevance. The first factor relates to the link between the existence of a genetic mutation and the expression of a particular medical condition or disorder; the second relates to the link between the expression of disease and increased morbidity or mortality. The two factors are not necessarily causally linked in any particular case—a genetic test may be reliable in identifying whether or not a person carries a certain mutation associated with a genetic disease or disorder. However, it is another matter whether a person testing positive will, or will not, eventually get the disease (and when).

The Inquiry went to considerable lengths to explain, in an accessible fashion, the current state of knowledge in genetic science and medicine.[93] In particular, the existence of a genetic mutation for a disease does not lead inexorably to the development of that disease—except in a number of rare monogenic disorders.[94] To provide just one common example, the so-called breast cancer gene, BRCA1, is found in up to 1% of women in certain populations. Its presence is said to increase the risk of developing breast cancer by a factor of five. However, only 60–85% of women with a BRCA1 mutation will develop breast cancer during their lifetimes (i.e., 60–85% penetrance)—in other words, 15–40% of women with this mutation will *not* do so. There is a danger that, in inexpert hands, predictive genetic information may be given more weight than it deserves, and treated as if it were medical fact rather than a measure of probability. The Inquiry was concerned to learn whether the latest scientific research and medical knowledge are being promptly and accurately translated into actuarial manuals and utilized intelligently in making underwriting decisions. In its submission to the Inquiry, the Institute of Actuaries of Australia described the manner in which actuarial data is compiled over time whenever a new medical treatment or test is developed:

> In the early days statistics will be scanty. The development will be experimental at first. The impact of it on life rating factors will at that stage be based mostly on informed opinion. Only after scientific papers have been published will the development be put into widespread use. With familiarity, the development will be further refined and the results re-evaluated. This will lead to another round of medico-actuarial analysis, this time with a larger pool of statistics to work with. So the new development will work its way through a classic learning curve, with the level of confidence in it steadily growing. This is the way that life insurers have always assessed new medical information for use in underwriting. IAAust sees no reason why insurers would not follow the same pattern with genetic information.[95]

Despite the modest use of genetic test information to date, many submissions expressed unease with the insurance industry's ability to accurately interpret and use genetic test information. The New South Wales (NSW) Privacy Commissioner maintained: "Evidence indicates that the insurance industry generally does not yet have the information which would be needed to make actuarially sound use of genetic test results."[96] In its submission, the HGSA argued:

> There is inadequate scientific data for interpreting the majority of genetic tests for the purposes of insurance underwriting at this time. The interpretation of data needs to be undertaken by experts in the area, based on published data. It often takes many years following the discovery of a gene to understand the significance of a result, and sometimes even then specific results cannot be interpreted with certainty.[97]

The Centre for Law and Genetics stated:

> In many cases, insurers would probably be able to justify their decisions to load premiums or decline cover on the basis of actuarial or statistical data. But given the broad range of genetic conditions and the increasing number of genetic tests that are available, serious concerns are being raised about the reliability of the actuarial data that is currently being used by insurers to make their underwriting decisions, raising doubts about the lawfulness of their decision-making. Indeed, many have argued that there is presently insufficiently reliable actuarial, statistical or other data available to allow use of genetic test information for underwriting purposes.[98]

However, IFSA expressed the following view:

> [T]he insurance industry's current use of genetic information in underwriting has sufficient actuarial and statistical basis.... In examining the impact of genetic test results on the level of risk, underwriters generally rely on existing statistical

> data and research drawn from previous experience; medical research and expert actuarial advice; and in particular underwriting guidelines and ratings manuals of international reinsurance companies. Extensive actuarial and statistical analysis of data over many years is used to formulate such risk ratings and guidelines. The review and modification of these ratings and guidelines is an ongoing process applying actuarial and statistical analysis to the latest published medical research.[99]

IFSA pointed to its new policy about underwriting people testing positive for haemochromatosis as an example of the way the industry has moved to deal creatively and sensibly with genetic test results. As noted above, most of the life insurance applications disclosing a genetic test result involved the test for haemochromatosis—a genetic condition that causes an overload of iron in the blood, and can be life-threatening, but is easily (and altruistically) treatable if the person avoids the build-up of iron by becoming a regular blood donor. Working with Genetic Health Services Victoria and the Murdoch Childrens Research Institute's pilot genetic screening programme, HaemScreen, IFSA developed an industry statement which makes clear that, for the vast majority of people tested in the HaemScreen programme there will be no adverse impact on their life, disability, or trauma insurance. For the 1 in 300 Australians found by HaemScreen to be at high risk of developing haemochromatosis, there will be no impact on their application for life insurance, as long as there is no evidence of significant medical problems caused by the condition.[100]

A common view expressed to the Inquiry was that considerable comfort would be given to consumers about scientific and actuarial reliability if there was independent expert oversight of the use of predictive genetic tests by the insurance industry.[101] For example, the Anti-Discrimination Board of NSW's submission was typical in expressing the following view:

> Without an adequate independent mechanism for evaluating the scientific reliability and actuarial relevance of genetic information, an onerous burden will fall to individuals to lodge complaints under anti-discrimination legislation in order to test the actuarial relevance of the genetic information upon which the insurers seek to rely and the accuracy of the interpretation of that information in the underwriting process. To allow the scientific reliability and actuarial relevance of predictive genetic test information to be determined on a case by case basis is totally inadequate to address the complexities of determining the use of genetic information when applied to risk rating for insurance purposes.[102]

Similarly, the Centre for Law and Genetics argued:

> The prospects of ensuring that accurate and reliable information is uniformly available to agents and brokers would be greatly enhanced if this responsibility was shared between the insurance industry and government, through the work of an expert committee established for the specific purpose of evaluating the scientific and actuarial relevance of genetic tests proposed for use by the insurance industry in setting insurance premiums, along the lines of the *Genetics and Insurance Committee* (GAIC) established in the United Kingdom.[103]

The Inquiry agreed, and recommended that the proposed HGCA should be asked to provide independent, expert advice about whether particular genetic tests should be used in underwriting mutually rated insurance, having regard to their scientific reliability, actuarial relevance, and reasonableness.[104] As the intention is that the HGCA will be an advisory and standards-setting body, but not a regulator, it would not directly "ban" the use or interpretation of any genetic test; however, its advice and standards obviously would be given great weight by industry regulators and any court or tribunal testing whether an insurer had operated within the "scientifically and actuarially reliable" exception to anti-discrimination laws. During the Inquiry, IFSA indicated that it "would support the proposed HGCA's role in reviewing and approving tests as being suitable for medical diagnostic, therapeutic or predictive purposes in Australia on the understanding that they can then also be used for underwriting,"[105]. But IFSA and the Institute of Actuaries Australia[106] both warned against the creation of a de facto moratorium in case of a long delay before the HGCA or an equivalent body is established. Both also suggested that this proposal could be implemented effectively through industry codes, such as by amending IFSA's Genetic Testing Policy to prohibit the use of genetic tests that had been considered and rejected by the HGCA and to prohibit the use of new genetic tests until they had been considered and approved by the HGCA.[107] The Acting Disability Discrimination Commissioner agreed, expressing his view:

> Government, the public and industry should be able to expect insurance to be properly regulated by insurance law and industry mechanisms in the first instance, with discrimination law providing a safety net or check on these mechanisms if necessary rather than needing to be the first resort on any issue.[108]

The Acting Disability Discrimination Commissioner also noted that it would be possible to reflect any changes by amending the *Guidelines for Providers of Superannuation and Insurance* issued by the HREOC.[109] The Inquiry agreed that its recommendations about the role of the HGCA in relation to the use of genetic test information in underwriting should be implemented through the development or amendment of relevant industry codes. This approach allows flexibility in a rapidly developing area. The insurance industry peak bodies have demonstrated a willingness to work with government and stakeholders to improve industry practices through self-regulation—but this situation should be kept under review by the HGCA.[110] However, the Inquiry differed with the industry's view that, where a genetic test is reliable enough to be used by the medical profession, it should necessarily be available for use by insurers. For example, the Therapeutic Goods Administration (TGA) evaluates some goods used in genetic tests for quality, safety, and efficacy, among other things. Although the TGA may comment generally on the use of specific tests in clinical settings, this evaluation does not extend to whether the test is appropriate for use in a particular clinical situation. This decision is made on a case-by-case basis by the medical professional arranging the test. The TGA approval process involves an examination of the scientific reliability of a particular test—e.g., it examines whether genetic test A gives a reliable result for genetic mutation B—but it does not consider the actuarial significance of test results.

6.2 Family Medical History

As discussed above, insurers have been using family medical history for underwriting purposes for over 100 years. Even today, despite the growing importance of genetic testing, family medical history comprises the vast majority of "genetic" information collected and used by insurers. Standard life insurance application forms in Australia ask questions aimed at identifying whether the applicant's immediate family members (limited to biological mother, father, and siblings—known collectively as "first-degree" relatives) have been diagnosed with, or have died from, a number of medical conditions that medical research has identified as having a strong familial link.[111] It is instructive that the UKHGC recommended that the voluntary moratorium on the use of genetic *test* information should *not* be extended to cover family medical history. This recommendation was based on economic modelling, which indicated that the exclusion of family medical history from underwriting was likely to have a significant impact on insurance premiums.[112] Reinsurance manuals provide guidance to insurers about how to translate family medical history into underwriting decisions. For example, an applicant with no family history of colorectal cancer is assigned a 2% lifetime risk of developing colorectal cancer at some stage in his life. If one "first-degree relative" has had colorectal cancer, this translates into a 6% lifetime risk of the applicant developing the disease; however, this jumps to a 10% risk if the relative was less than 45 years of age when first diagnosed—and a premium loading of up to 50% would likely be required for insurance cover. Two first-degree relatives with colorectal cancer translates to a 17% lifetime risk of developing the condition, and the near certainty of loadings.[113] In their submission, the NSW Anti-Discrimination Board argued that the use of family medical history, whether or not such information amounts to "genetic information,"

> should be subject to greater scrutiny to determine whether or not the information used in the underwriting process is scientifically reliable and actuarially relevant. The independent body we propose above should play a role in evaluating the scientific reliability and actuarial relevance of both genetic and non-genetic information.[114]

The Inquiry noted that insurers have had lengthy experience with the collection and actuarial analysis of statistical data based on family history. However, the use made of family medical history is in some ways more abstract and subjective than genetic test information. In particular, problems may arise because of the quality of the data collected about genetic relatives or the lack of medical understanding about the genetic influences on common diseases. It was recommended that insurers, through their peak bodies (and in consultation with the HGCA and the Institute of Actuaries), should develop and publish industry policies on the use of family medical history in underwriting to ensure that, where such information is relied upon by insurers, it is scientifically reliable, actuarially relevant, or otherwise reasonable.[115] Specifically, these policies should provide guidance for insurers on the following matters:

– The relationship between family medical history and other factors used to assess risk, so that the former is only given its due weight
– The relationship between family medical history and genetic test information, particularly where a genetic test result is negative
– The proximity of the blood relationship between the applicant and his/her family members that justifies collection of family medical history
– The need, if any, for verifying diagnoses of family members and the procedures for doing so.

Following this recommendation, IFSA established a working group to review the industry's guidelines and practices with respect to the collection and use of family medical history. Draft guidelines were released to insurers and other stakeholders (including the ALRC) for discussion and comment in late 2004, and were set to be finalized as industry policy in 2005.

6.3 Duty to Provide Reasons for Adverse Decisions

The extent to which an applicant is provided reasons for an adverse underwriting decision is currently regulated in three ways:

1. Section 75 of the Insurance Contracts Act imposes a duty on insurers to give applicants written reasons for an unfavourable underwriting decision, where requested in writing to do so.
2. Section 107 of the DDA enables the President of HREOC to require an insurer to disclose the source of the actuarial or statistical data on which a discriminatory act was based.
3. Articles 11 and 12 of IFSA's Genetic Testing Policy require all underwriting decisions involving a genetic test, whether or not the test was a significant factor in the decision, to be thoroughly documented, so that adequate information can be provided to the applicant on request.[116]

The first and second methods apply to underwriting decisions irrespective of whether they utilize genetic information. The third is specific to genetic test information (e.g., to the exclusion of family medical history). The Inquiry found that there was community dissatisfaction with the adequacy of the reasons provided by insurers for unfavourable underwriting decisions, and the mechanisms for obtaining such reasons. For example, the NSW Anti-Discrimination Board stated:

> We strongly disagree with the view... that the current methods of risk assessment using genetic information are sufficiently transparent and accountable to the public because the DDA provides consumers with the capacity to lodge a complaint and this in turn would mean that the insurer may be required to provide evidence in support of their underwriting decision. We do not consider that it is acceptable for insurance companies to require individuals to lodge a complaint before such information is provided to consumers. In our view, consumers should have the right to access adequate information about the basis for the insurer's decision and the actuarial or statistical evidence on which the insurer has relied in making that decision. It is only with such

information that consumers can determine whether to challenge the decision under anti-discrimination legislation.[117]

Transparency and accountability of decision-making has the benefit of building public confidence in the way in which insurers use genetic information in underwriting and would be likely to generate a better decision-making process. It would also create checks and balances by providing consumers with the means of ensuring that the discriminatory acts of insurers fall within the terms of the statutory exemptions. The reasons provided must be effective for the purposes of consumer understanding and possible review—and they may fail to be so if an insurer provides either too little information or too much. A bare statement that an applicant has been denied insurance because of his/her family history of a particular genetic disorder is unlikely to satisfy a consumer's wish to understand the basis of an adverse decision. On the other hand, the provision of vast quantities of raw statistical or actuarial data is unlikely to offer an applicant any better understanding. The Inquiry recommended that section 75 of the Insurance Contracts Act be amended to clarify the nature of the information that must be provided to applicants on their request. The reasons provided by insurers should be clear and meaningful and explain the actuarial, statistical, or other basis for the decision. In order to ensure that applicants are aware of their right to request reasons, it was also recommended that the peak associations for the insurance industry develop mandatory policies requiring their members to inform applicants of their statutory entitlement to reasons for an adverse underwriting decision.

This should ensure that an applicant's right not to know is respected because reasons will not be given to an applicant unless they have been requested. It would also limit the cost to insurers because it is likely that reasons will not be required in every case. It was noted that, in some cases, the information to be provided to applicants might be sensitive because of the inclusion of data about expected morbidity or mortality. Insurance industry peak bodies should develop policies on appropriate mechanisms for providing reasons to applicants where sensitive information is involved. In some cases it may be appropriate to provide information to the applicant's nominated medical practitioner rather than directly to the applicant, as is already common practice in the industry. The Inquiry also recommended that industry policies dealing with the provision of reasons for adverse decisions based on genetic test information should be further developed to cover the provision of reasons for decisions based on family medical history.[118]

6.4 Review and Appeal Mechanisms

The Inquiry heard that the review and appeal mechanisms available to insurance applicants who received adverse decisions were inadequate. At present, applicants are limited to: (a) seeking internal review by the insurer; (b) lodging a complaint with IFSA in relation to an alleged breach of the Genetic Testing Policy; or (c) lodging a complaint of unlawful discrimination with HREOC. As noted above, existing external review processes—the Financial Industry Complaints Service (FICS) and Insurance Enquiries and Complaints Ltd (IEC)—do not currently have jurisdiction to consider complaints relating to premiums or underwriting decisions.[119] A complaint of unlawful discrimination based on the use of genetic information by an insurer can be brought before HREOC, which has the power to investigate and conciliate complaints under the DDA. Of the total 452 complaints received by HREOC in relation to alleged unlawful discrimination under the DDA during the period 2001–2002, 15 complaints (3.3%) were received in relation to insurance and superannuation,[120] but none of these related to the use of genetic information in insurance.[121] If HREOC terminates a complaint of alleged unlawful discrimination because, for example, it cannot be conciliated, the complainant may apply to have the matter considered by the Federal Court of Australia or the Federal Magistrates Court.

In the United Kingdom, the Association of British Insurers (ABI) has established the Genetic Testing–ABI Code of Practice Adjudication Tribunal, which can receive and adjudicate complaints of alleged breaches of the ABI Genetic Testing Code of Practice for life insurance and some forms of general insurance.[122] The Swedish Insurance Federation informed the Inquiry that a review board had been established by statute in Sweden to investigate complaints with regard to the use of genetic information in underwriting, using a mechanism that is independent of the insurer who made the underwriting decision.[123] The Inquiry agreed that there is a gap in the avenues for review and appeal currently available to applicants for insurance where genetic information has been used in underwriting. It recommended that the best way forward would be to expand the existing external dispute resolution schemes (FICS and the IEC) to provide an industry-based mechanism for investigating and adjudicating disputes about underwriting decisions based on genetic information. The Inquiry specified that these processes must be:

- Timely and efficient
- Carried out by suitably qualified individuals with a demonstrated understanding of insurance law and anti-discrimination law, underwriting practice, and clinical genetics
- Binding on the insurer but not on the complainant
- Available with respect to a substantial majority of complaints, having regard to the monetary sum in question[124]

6.5 *Education and Training*

There was significant evidence before the Inquiry that participants in the insurance industry—and particularly those "at the coalface" providing advice directly to applicants, such as agents and brokers—did not have an adequate understanding of genetic information and its implications for insurance. The Centre for Law and Genetics stated:

> Anecdotally one hears accounts which suggest that the information available to agents and brokers on this subject may be less than adequate, or even if adequate, is not well understood by the agents and brokers, and that this, in turn, is reflected in the quality and accuracy of the information that they are able to provide. Indeed, it has been suggested that advice given by agents and brokers may inappropriately deter individuals who have obtained unfavourable genetic test results or who have a family history of genetic disease from even applying for insurance, on the mistaken belief that their application will not be accepted.[125]

There was widespread agreement that better education and training about genetics was required throughout the process, from agents and brokers[126] through to the underwriters and actuaries who assess applications. The Inquiry recognized that the insurance industry was already active in this area, but there was still work to be done—and it made a number of recommendations directed at enhancing industry, professional, and community education in this area.[127]

7. CONCLUSION

As discussed in the preceding chapter, the Inquiry rejected notions of genetic essentialism or genetic determinism, or the incorporation of these notions into policy or practice (however unwittingly).[128] Similarly, the Inquiry was careful not to develop policy and practice based on any notions of "genetic exceptionalism." Among other things, this strongly influenced the recommendations made with respect to insurance underwriting law and practice. For example, the Inquiry was not persuaded that there was a case for interfering with long-standing common law and statutory requirements of full disclosure, which underpin the underwriting process for risk-rated insurance—for to do so would privilege persons with genetic risks above all others who bring non-genetic medical risks to the insurance pool. Instead, the Inquiry did recommend a range of significant consumer-oriented reforms: that insurers must develop and publish sound policies for handling family medical history information (vastly more prevalent than genetic test information); refine their actuarial processes and utilization of cutting-edge scientific information, if they are to justify the exemption currently granted under anti-discrimination laws; improve internal industry education and processes in relation to dealing with predictive genetic information; provide reasons in writing for any adverse underwriting decision; and establish an independent, effective new mechanism to review such decisions (whereas, at present, dissatisfied consumers basically must go to the courts for redress).[129] Thomas Murray, Chair of the Human Genome Project's first Ethical, Legal, and Social Issues Working Group and currently head of the Hastings Center (for bioethics) in New York, has written that the Inquiry's rejection of genetic exceptionalism in this context is

> the single most courageous and wise judgment in the report. Genetic information remains mysterious and threatening to many. Our judgment is easily skewed by its novelty and our suspicions of its occult powers. Yes, genetic information can

> be misused either through misunderstanding or malevolence. ALRC 96 offers cogent and thorough recommendations to guard against both.[130]

Similarly, Sandy Raeburn, a leading British medical geneticist, currently the head of clinical genetics in Oman, commended "the excellent report of the ALRC—for the most clear and least biased description of genetics and insurance ever produced."[131] The Inquiry recognized the need to develop flexible approaches that can respond to the rapid changes in science and technology, and a broad mix of regulatory strategies tailored to the needs and circumstances of each context—*not* "one size fits all" solutions, or "Big Law." This meant that the Inquiry was not afraid to take a firmly interventionist approach in the labour relations context,[132] recommending strong legal restrictions on the collection or use of any genetic information in relation to job applicants or employees,[133] to guard against the danger of creating a "genetic underclass" in Australia of people fit and willing to work, but with some predisposition that may be used to rule them out.

> It is important to ensure that regulatory structures, and the anti-discrimination framework in particular, are adequate to protect people from inappropriate use of genetic information in employment, both now and in the future.[134]

However, with respect to risk-rated private insurance, the Inquiry did not favour intrusive government intervention, preferring instead to call upon the industry and rely on the market to provide more effective regulation; greater adherence to scientific and medical advances (and their actuarial implications); more transparency; and greater responsiveness to legitimate consumer interests and concerns. This certainly does not mean that the insurance industry "got off lightly." The Inquiry's recommendations will require insurers, for the first time, to develop and publish an industry policy on the collection and use of family medical history; detail the scientific and actuarial basis for *every* adverse underwriting decision; and provide an accessible, independent forum to have these decisions reviewed.[135] This attracted little or no media attention at the time ALRC 96 was released. However, the comprehensive package of recommendations aimed at the insurance industry, and the industry's own willingness to take a progressive stance in this area, should prove to be a powerful force for altering and improving industry practices in the public interest.

NOTES

1 Australian Law Reform Commission, 2003. *Essentially Yours: The Protection of Human Genetic Information in Australia* (ALRC 96).

2 Who later served on the Inquiry's Advisory Committee.

3 Barlow-Stewart received 703 anonymous responses, in which there were 43 cases of alleged discrimination. Keays conducted interviews with five other persons who had reported instances of alleged genetic discrimination: see Barlow-Stewart, K. and Keays, D. 2001. Genetic discrimination in Australia. *Journal of Law and Medicine* 8: 250, 251–252.

4 Including those for haemochromatosis, inherited breast cancer, inherited bowel cancer, familial melanoma, Alzheimer's disease, Huntington's disease, and hyperlipidemia, ibid., 252.

5 There also were three reported cases of alleged genetic discrimination in employment; two cases in which respondents reported being required to undertake genetic testing as part of the application and selection process for a job; and two claims of individuals being discriminated against in the provision of healthcare services, ibid., 254.

6 Ibid., 253.

7 Under the Trade Practices Act 1974 (Cth), organizations that engage, or propose to engage, in certain anti-competitive business arrangements or conduct that could breach the Act may apply to the ACCC for authorization of such arrangements or conduct. The ACCC may grant authorization where the public benefit of the subject arrangements or conduct outweighs the public detriment, including the anti-competitive detriment. If granted, an authorization provides immunity from legal proceedings under the Act with respect to the arrangements or conduct.

8 Australian Prudential Regulation Authority, 2002. *General Insurance Trends September Quarter 2002.*

9 Private Health Insurance Administration Council, Industry performance, available at <www.phiac.gov.au/circularspublications/publications/AR_registered_health/part_a1/index.htm>, cited 20 February 2003.

10 According to information supplied by IFSA to the Inquiry in January 2002, the approximate average level of cover for term life insurance in Australia is $235,000.

11 According to IFSA, the approximate average level of cover for disability income insurance in Australia is $3,700 per month.

12 According to IFSA, the average level of cover for trauma insurance in Australia is $165,000.

13 Australian Life Underwriters and Claims Association Inc., *Submission G300*, 10 January 2003.

14 Ibid., *Submission G244*, 19 December 2002.

15 *Carter versus Boehm* (1766) 3 Burr 1905, 1909 (Mansfield, L. J.).

16 Marks, F. and Balla, A. 1998. *Guidebook to Insurance Law in Australia*, 3rd edn. Sydney: CCH Australia.

17 Financial Industry Complaints Service, 2002. Rules, Melbourne, Rule 15; Insurance Enquiries and Complaints Ltd, The General Insurance Enquiries and Complaints Scheme: Terms of Reference, available at <www.iecltd.com.au/index2.html>, cited 20 February 2003 [4.2].

18 Investment and Financial Services Association, *Submission G244*, 19 December 2002.

19 Ibid.

20 ALRC 96, ibid., Table 25-1.

21 Figures provided by the Australian Securities and Investments Commission (ASIC).

22 Institute of Actuaries Australia, 2004. *IFSA Genetic Test Survey Report—Period 7: 1 December 2003–31 May 2004*. Sydney: Institute of Actuaries Australia, 30 August 2004.

23 Ibid., 10, Table 3.

24 These include genetic tests for: haemochromatosis; Factor V Leiden; fragile X (A) syndrome; antithrombin III, protein C and protein S deficiencies; acute myeloid, lymphoid or promyelocytic leukaemia; and certain chromosome studies.

25 Ibid., 16–17, Table 10.

26 Ibid., 4–5.

27 Ibid., 12–13, Table 6.

28 Ibid., 17, Table 11. Table 14 cross-references the underwriting results by the disorder tested for and the type of insurance cover requested.

29 Under the Trade Practices Act 1974 (Cth) section 88(1), concerning arrangements that may have the effect of substantially lessening competition, within the meaning of section 45 of the Act.

30 Trade Practices Act 1974 (Cth) sections 90(7)–90(8). See the view of the Trade Practices Tribunal (adopted by the ACCC) regarding the practical application of the test: *Re Media Council of Australia (No. 2)* (1987) ATPR 40, 48, 418.

31 Australian Competition and Consumer Commission, *Draft Determination re Application for Authorisation Lodged by Investment and Financial Services Association (IFSA) in Relation to the Implementation of a Draft Policy on Genetic Testing* (2000).

32 Australian Competition and Consumer Commission Media Release, 2000. *ACCC Authorises Life Insurance Bar on Genetic Testing*, 22 November.

33 Australian Competition and Consumer Commission, 2000. *Determination re Applications for Authorisation Lodged by Investment and Financial Services Association (IFSA) in Relation to Clauses 2 and 4 of Its Draft Policy on Genetic Testing*, 15.

34 ACCC, 2003. *ACCC's Draft Decision Maintains Life Insurance Bar on Genetic Testing*, Media Release 21 September 2003, available at <http://www.accc.gov.au/content/index.phtml/itemId/385323>, cited 9 October 2003.

35 The current policy does not extend to genetic information obtained from family medical histories.

36 There is no equivalent policy in place in relation to the general insurance sector.

37 IFSA, 2001. *Code of Ethics and Code of Conduct*. The Code states that, in the event of non-compliance, the IFSA Board may impose a range of disciplinary measures including public or private censure, suspension from membership, or expulsion. However, as IFSA is not a regulator, it has indicated that its monitoring of compliance will be done with a "minimum of formality."

38 IFSA, *IFSA Standard 11.00 "Genetic Testing Policy"* (2002).

39 Federal Privacy Commissioner, 1996. *The Privacy Implications of Genetic Testing*. Sydney: OFPC, 40.

40 The Insurance Council of Australia was the first private sector organization to develop a privacy code and to have it approved and listed on the Register of Approved Privacy Codes under section 18BG of the Privacy Act. The Code is based on the General Insurance Information Privacy Principles, with some additions and modifications to meet the new legislative requirements. The General Insurance Information Privacy Code was approved on 17 April 2002.

41 IFSA, *IFSA Standard 11.00 "Genetic Testing Policy"* (2002).

42 Office of the Federal Privacy Commissioner, *Submission G143*, 22 March 2002; and *Submission G294*, 6 January 2003.

43 Centre for Law and Genetics, *Submission G048*, 14 January 2002.

44 ALRC 96, ibid., Recommendation 28–1. The Inquiry noted that such a review also would provide an opportunity to ensure that consent and medical authority forms are consistent with the NPPs, any approved privacy codes and IFSA's Genetic Testing Policy, where applicable.

45 Ibid., Recommendation 28–3; see discussion at paragraphs 28.49–28.66.

46 Each state and territory in Australia has its own anti-discrimination regime and each Act contains its own insurance exception; see: Discrimination Act 1991 (ACT) section 28; Anti-Discrimination Act 1992 (NT) section 49; Anti-Discrimination Act 1977 (NSW) section 49Q; Anti-Discrimination Act 1991 (Qld) sections 74 and 75; Equal Opportunity Act 1984 (SA) section 85; Anti-discrimination Act 1998 (Tas) section 44; Equal Opportunity Act 1995 (Vic) section 43; Equal Opportunity Act 1984 (WA) section 66T.

47 Sex Discrimination Act 1984 (Cth) section 22; Racial Discrimination Act 1975 (Cth) section 13; Disability Discrimination Act 1992 (Cth) section 24; and Age Discrimination Act 2004 (Cth) section 24, which are general provisions applying to the supply of goods and services, including insurance.

48 And related matters, such as banking, superannuation, and the provision of grants, loans, credit, or finance; see: Sex Discrimination Act 1984 (Cth) section 4(1); Racial Discrimination Act 1975 (Cth) section 3(1); Disability Discrimination Act 1992 (Cth) section 4(1); and Age Discrimination Act 2004 (Cth) section 5.

49 Disability Discrimination Act 1992 (Cth) section 46; Sex Discrimination Act 1984 (Cth) section 41; Age Discrimination Act 2004 (Cth) section 37.

50 *Australian Mutual Provident Society vs Goulden* (1986) 160 CLR 330.

51 This Act was repealed and replaced with the Life Insurance Act 1995 (Cth).

52 For a detailed discussion of the High Court's decision and its implications see Otlowski, M. 2001. *Implications of Genetic Testing for Australian Insurance Law and Practice*. Hobart, Australia: Centre for Law and Genetics, University of Tasmania, 19–21.

53 *QBE Travel Insurance vs Bassanelli* (2004) 137 FCR 88.
54 Ibid., 95.
55 Human Rights and Equal Opportunity Commission, *Guidelines for Providers of Insurance and Superannuation*, Revised 2005, available at <http://www.hreoc.gov.au/disability_rights/standards/Insurance/insurance_adv.html#4.2>.
56 Ibid.
57 ALRC 96, ibid., paragraphs 26.20–26.30.
58 Some of these cases also pre-dated the adoption of IFSA's Genetic Testing Policy.
59 A large Australian Research Council grant was awarded to Professor Margaret Otlowski (University of Tasmania), Dr. Sandra Taylor (University of Queensland), and Dr. Kristine Barlow-Stewart (NSW Genetics Education Unit) to conduct research into the nature and extent of genetic discrimination in Australia. For further information about aims and methodology, see the Genetic Discrimination Project's website at <http://www.gdproject.org/contact/index.php>.
60 Keays, D. *Submission G152*, 14 April 2002.
61 Anti-Discrimination Commission Queensland, *Submission G214*, 2 December 2002.
62 IFSA, *Submission G049*, 14 January 2002.
63 Genetic Discrimination Project Team, *Submission G252*, 20 December 2002.
64 Kirk, J. *Submission G096*, 30 January 2002.
65 Raeburn, S. *Submission G033*, 2 January 2002; Institute of Actuaries of Australia, *Submission G105*, 7 March 2002; Investment and Financial Services Association, *Submission G244*, 19 December 2002; Association of British Insurers, *Submission G053*, 15 January 2002; Australian Prudential Regulation Authority, *Submission G279*, 31 December 2002; Australian Life Underwriters and Claims Association Inc., *Submission G300*, 10 January 2003.
66 Australian Prudential Regulation Authority, *Submission G279*, 31 December 2002.
67 Association of British Insurers, *Submission G053*, 15 January 2002.
68 IFSA, *Submission G244*, 19 December 2002.
69 Centre for Law and Genetics, *Submission G048*, 14 January 2002; Human Genetics Society of Australasia, *Submission G050*, 14 January 2002; Keays, D. *Submission G152*, 14 April 2002; Richards, F. *Submission G044*, 14 January 2002; Otlowski, M. *Submission G159*, 24 April 2002; Anti-Discrimination Board of NSW, *Submission G157*, 1 May 2002; Liddell, K. *Submission G147*, 10 April 2002; Office of the Privacy Commissioner (NSW), *Submission G118*, 18 March 2002; MacMillan, J. *Submission G015*, 19 November 2001; *Confidential Submission G066CON*, 10 January 2002.
70 Centre for Law and Genetics, *Submission G048*, 14 January 2002.
71 Harper, P. 1997. Genetic testing, life insurance, and adverse selection. *Philosophical Transcripts of the Royal Society of London 352* (*B series*) 1063; Macdonald, A. 1999. Modeling the impact of genetics on insurance. *North American Actuarial Journal* 3 (83); MacDonald, A. 1997. How will improved forecasts of individual lifetimes affect underwriting? *Philosophical Transcripts of the Royal Society of London 352*(*B series*) 1067; MacDonald, A. 2003. *Human Genetics and Insurance Issues*, Genetics and Insurance Research Centre, available at <www.ma.hw.ac.uk/~angus/papers/aberdeen.pdf>, cited 18 February 2003; MacDonald, A. 2002a. *Genetics and Insurance: What Have We Learned So Far?* MacDonald, A. 2002b. Genetics and health costs: some actuarial models. *Law, Probability and Risk* 1 (97).
72 McGleenan, T. 2002. *Insurance and Genetic Information*. London: Association of British Insurers.
73 MacDonald. 2002b, ibid.
74 Human Genetics Commission, 2002. *Inside Information: Balancing Interests in the Use of Personal Genetic Data*. London: Human Genetics Commission, 124.
75 Haemophilia Foundation Victoria, *Submission G145*, 25 March 2002.
76 Centre for Law and Genetics, *Submission G048*, 14 January 2002.
77 IFSA, *Submission G049*, 14 January 2002.
78 See Otlowski, M. 2001. *Implications of Genetic Testing for Australian Insurance Law and Practice*. Hobart, Australia: Centre for Law and Genetics.
79 Centre for Law and Genetics, *Submission G048*, 14 January 2002.
80 Association of British Insurers, *Submission G053*, 15 January 2002.

[81] Disability Bill 2001 (Ireland). See the Irish Parliamentary website: Parliament of Ireland, *Disability Bill 2001*, available at <www.irlgov.ie/bills28/bills/2001/6801/default.htm>, cited 18 March 2003.

[82] The lower tier amount in the UK initially was set at £250,000, because this represented the average London mortgage at that time.

[83] Association of British Insurers, *Submission G053*, 15 January 2002.

[84] Anti-Discrimination Commission Queensland, *Submission G214*, 2 December 2002.

[85] Queensland Government, *Submission G161*, 16 May 2002.

[86] IFSA, *Submission G244*, 19 December 2002.

[87] APRA, *Submission G279*, 31 December 2002.

[88] See comments by Ralph, L. 2000. In Senate Legal and Constitutional Legislation Committee. *Inquiry into the Provisions of the Privacy Amendment (Private Sector) Bill 2000*, The Parliament of Australia, 35. See also Pokorski, R. quoted in Lemmens, T. 2000. Selective justice, genetic discrimination, and insurance: should we single out genes in our laws? *McGill Law Journal* 45: 347, 384.

[89] See Butler, J. 2003. Adverse selection, genetic testing and life insurance—lessons from health insurance in Australia. *Agenda* 10 (1): 73–89; and Heaney R. and Pitt, D. 2003. Impact of genetic testing on life insurance. *Agenda* 10 (1): 61–72.

[90] ALRC 96, ibid., Recommendations 26–1 and 26–2.

[91] Such as currently operates with respect to private health insurance in Australia, which has required a public subsidy of over $2 billion per annum to maintain community rating at premium levels sufficiently attractive to maintain a reasonable pool.

[92] Human Genetics Commission, 2002. *Inside Information: Balancing Interests in the Use of Personal Genetic Data.* London: Human Genetics Commission, 124. In establishing whether it is reasonable for insurers to rely on genetic information in underwriting, two main issues arise—the scientific reliability of the genetic information and its actuarial relevance. The first factor relates to the link between the existence of a genetic mutation and the expression of a particular disorder; the second relates to the link between the expression of disease and the increased morbidity or mortality.

[93] ALRC 96, ibid., Chapters 2–4 and 10.

[94] Huntington's disease (HD) is an example of a condition with high penetrance approaching 100%. Those who test positive for the HD mutation almost always will develop the disease if they live long enough. However, even for HD, some people may develop the disease very late in life, or die of something else before they manifest symptoms. Similarly, for instance, it is possible to speak of the penetrance of each particular mutation (or combination of mutations) causing cystic fibrosis (CF). For the mutation known as "DF508," the penetrance is very high—about 99%. For other alleles, the penetrance is lower—but this calculation is also dependent upon the definition of the disease. See ALRC 96, ibid., paragraphs 2.24–2.27 and Table 2.1.

[95] Institute of Actuaries of Australia, *Submission G105*, 7 March 2002.

[96] Office of the Privacy Commissioner (NSW), *Submission G118*, 18 March 2002.

[97] Human Genetics Society of Australasia, *Submission G050*, 14 January 2002.

[98] Centre for Law and Genetics, *Submission G048*, 14 January 2002.

[99] IFSA, *Submission G244*, 19 December 2002.

[100] Murdoch Childrens Research Institute, IFSA, and Genetic Health Services Victoria, 2001. World first on genetic testing and insurance, Media Release, 10 September 2001, available at <http://haemscreen.com/PressRelease1.htm>; IFSA, *Gene Testing for Haemochromatosis: Will it Impact on Your Insurance?* Sydney.

[101] Haemophilia Foundation Victoria, *Submission G201*, 25 November 2002; Dominello, A. and others, *Submission G222*, 3 December 2002; Institute of Actuaries of Australia, *Submission G224*, 29 November 2002; Centre for Genetics Education, *Submission G232*, 18 December 2002; Genetic Support Council, Western Australia, *Submission G243*, 19 December 2002; Human Genetics Society of Australasia, *Submission G267*, 20 December 2002; Department of Health, Western Australia, *Submission G271*, 23 December 2002; Australian Prudential Regulation Authority, *Submission G279*, 31 December 2002; Androgen Insensitivity Syndrome Support Group, Australia, *Submission G290*, 5 January 2003; Acting Disability Discrimination Commissioner, Human Rights and Equal Opportunity Commission, *Submission G301*, 16 January 2003.

102 Anti-Discrimination Board of NSW, *Submission G157*, 1 May 2002.
103 Centre for Law and Genetics, *Submission G048*, 14 January 2002.
104 ALRC 96, ibid., Recommendation 27–1.
105 IFSA, *Submission G244*, 19 December 2002.
106 Institute of Actuaries of Australia, *Submission G224*, 29 November 2002.
107 Institute of Actuaries of Australia, *Submission G224*, 29 November 2002; Investment and Financial Services Association, *Submission G244*, 19 December 2002.
108 Acting Disability Discrimination Commissioner, Human Rights and Equal Opportunity Commission, *Submission G301*, 16 January 2003.
109 Human Rights and Equal Opportunity Commission, *Guidelines for Providers of Insurance and Superannuation*, available at <www.hreoc.gov.au/disability_rights/standards/Insurance/insurance_adv.html>, cited 19 February 2003.
110 ALRC 96, ibid., Recommendation 26–2.
111 IFSA, *Submission G244*, 19 December 2002. The insurer does not ask for family history information relating to the applicant's children or their uncles, aunts, cousins, or more distant relatives.
112 Human Genetics Commission, 2002, ibid.
113 ALRC 96, ibid., paragraph 27.51: the source of the risk ratings is the *Gerling Global Reinsurance Manual.*
114 Anti-Discrimination Board of NSW, *Submission G157*, 1 May 2002.
115 ALRC 96, ibid., Recommendation 27–4.
116 The Explanatory Notes which accompany the Policy state that members will inform applicants "in a clear and meaningful way" of the reasons for the decision; reasons may be given to the applicant's doctor in appropriate cases; and members will include information on how an applicant can lodge a complaint in relation to the decision.
117 Anti-Discrimination Board of NSW, *Submission G157*, 1 May 2002.
118 Of course, the interest of consumers in obtaining adequate information about adverse underwriting decisions is not confined to underwriting based on genetic information. The NSW Anti-Discrimination Board (ADB) made this point in its submission when referring to the findings of its report into Hepatitis C–related discrimination: NSW Anti-Discrimination Board, 2001. *C-change: The Report of the Enquiry into Hepatitis C Related Discrimination.* Sydney: NSW Anti-Discrimination Board. The ADB expressed support for legislative amendments that would compel insurers to provide consumers with access to adequate information in relation to *all* unfavourable decisions, a view shared by the Institute of Actuaries of Australia—but outside the Inquiry's Terms of Reference.
119 Financial Industry Complaints Service, 2002. Rules, Melbourne, Rule 15; Insurance Enquiries and Complaints Ltd, The General Insurance Enquiries and Complaints Scheme: Terms of Reference, available at <www.iecltd.com.au/index2.html>, cited 20 February 2003.
120 Human Rights and Equal Opportunity Commission, 2002. *Annual Report 2001–2002.* Sydney: Human Rights and Equal Opportunity Commission.
121 Once a complaint has been lodged, HREOC has the power to require an insurer to provide actuarial or statistical data in accordance with section 107 of the DDA.
122 Association of British Insurers, 1999. *Genetic Testing: ABI Code of Practice.* London: Association of British Insurers, Pt 5. Relevant provisions of the Code of Practice are set out in ALRC 96, ibid., paragraph 27.119.
123 As of March 2003, the board had not yet received a complaint.
124 ALRC 96, ibid., Recommendation 27–9.
125 Centre for Law and Genetics, *Submission G048*, 14 January 2002.
126 Who now must meet certain training and competence requirements to be licensed under the *Financial Services Reform Act 2001* (Cth); see also Australian Securities and Investments Commission, *Policy Statement 146 Licencing: Training of financial product advisers*, available at <www.asic.gov.au/asic/pdflib.nsf/LookupByFileName/PS146.pdf/$file/PS146.pdf>, cited 22 January 2003.
127 ALRC 96, ibid., Recommendations 27–10 and 27–11. The proposed HGCA also was charged with "assistance with the development and coordination of community, school, university, and professional education about human genetics": ALRC 96, ibid., Recommendation 5–2.

[128] Ibid., especially paragraphs 3.64–3.77 on the "Dangers of genetic essentialism."
[129] Ibid., Part G, especially the recommendations in Chapters 26–28.
[130] Murray, T. 2003. Essentially yours: a review. *Reform* 83 (Spring): 47, 50.
[131] Ibid.
[132] See ALRC 96, ibid., Part H.
[133] Ibid., Recommendation 30–1.
[134] Ibid., paragraph 30.51.
[135] Without binding the complainant, who could still approach HREOC or the courts.

MARYANNE AITKEN AND SYLVIA METCALFE

THE SOCIAL IMPERATIVE FOR COMMUNITY GENETIC SCREENING: AN AUSTRALIAN PERSPECTIVE

In 10 years from now when we go for our driver's licence, could we be asked to provide a quick cheek brush sample so that our DNA can be analysed to look for some important variations? For example, a variation in a gene that causes hypertrophic cardiomyopathy (HCM) that is associated with heart attack and sudden death.[1,2] This has obvious and serious implications if a person is driving. If you do have this variation and are considered to be at high risk, it is possible to be fitted with a tiny monitor under your skin that can detect such an attack before it happens.[3] Perhaps in future a person with the HCM gene variant who is considered to be at high risk will only be granted a driver's licence on the condition that such a device is fitted. The licensing authority could also test for a gene variant associated with drug addiction,[4,5] to enable them to predict those drivers who they say will be more likely to take illicit drugs and drive erratically and cause more accidents. It could be argued that this information could save hundreds of lives and millions of dollars by keeping such individuals off the road. The issues surrounding population genetic screening are complex and will be discussed in the following sections. The scenario presented above may seem a futuristic one, but as indicated below, much has happened in the field of genetic testing and screening so rapidly, perhaps it is not so far-fetched.

1. A BRIEF HISTORY OF GENETICS

In the late 19th to early 20th century the plant breeding experiments of the monk Gregor Mendel attracted the attention of scientists such as Francis Galton and Charles Darwin. In 1910 Thomas Hunt Morgan's work on Drosophila showed that genes determine inherited traits and that they reside on chromosomes.[6,7] In 1944 Oswald Avery and his colleagues proved that DNA (not protein, as previously thought) is the hereditary material in most living organisms.[8] In 1950 Douglas Bevis described how amniocentesis could be used to test a foetus for Rh-factor incompatibility.[9] This prenatal

Michela Betta (ed.), The moral, social, and commercial imperatives of genetic testing and screening. The Australian case, 165–184.

sampling technique has been used from the 1970s onwards in testing for a number of genetic disorders. In 1953 James Watson and Francis Crick published the structure of DNA.[10] In 1956 as chromosome staining techniques improved, Joe Hin Tijo and Albert Levan found that humans have 46 chromosomes, not 48 as previously thought.[11] In 1959 Jeromé Lejeune discovered that people with Down syndrome have an extra chromosome 21.[12] By the 1960s genetics had become a medical subspecialty, and Victor McKusick published *Mendelian Inheritance in Man* in 1966 citing 1,500 inherited disorders.[13] In 1978 the first human gene, insulin, was sequenced.[14] The 1980s saw the discovery of many genes associated with *rare* single gene disorders cloned and genetic testing for these disorders became available, e.g., cystic fibrosis in 1989.[15] In the 1990s genes associated with more *common* disorders such as breast cancer, haemochromatosis, and deafness were discovered. In 1991 Mary-Claire King published evidence that there is a mutation in a gene, BRCA1, associated with an inherited form of breast and ovarian cancer.[16] Having a mutation in this gene does not, however, confer a 100% risk of having breast and/or ovarian cancer. The mutation is not 100% *penetrant*, but is in fact approximately 60% penetrant, meaning that there is a 60% chance that the mutation carrier will develop breast cancer in her lifetime.[17] Thus the use of the term "susceptibility" or "high risk" when referring to these mutations. Recently we have seen the discovery of high-prevalence mutations associated with more common, *complex* diseases, e.g., diabetes and heart disease (see Table 1).

However, it has become clear that these mutations are not enough in themselves to ensure disease onset and there are likely to be several other gene changes as well as environmental and social factors that contribute to the onset of disease. Hence the term complex disorders, to denote those disorders that are common, usually familial, and multifactorial.[30] This brief history reveals how quickly the practice of human genetics has changed. *Medical* genetics originally focused on rare disorders caused by alterations in chromosome numbers or single genes, emphasizing diagnosis and treatment of existing conditions, usually in children. The genetic information pertaining to these conditions (if it was available) was definite and unchangeable and directly affected the individual and/or the family. More recently, the dramatic shift from a child focus (e.g., mainly congenital disorders) to an adult focus, often associated with susceptibility testing in healthy individuals, has raised different implications for family members. In February 2001 came the completion of the first draft of the map of the human genome.[31] Now there are well over 16,000 entries in McKusick's (online) *Mendelian Inheritance in Man*.[32]

2. SCREENING IN AUSTRALIA IN 2006

There are several screening programmes established in Australia at a national level, e.g., "BreastScreen," mammographic breast screening for women over 50 years of age,[33] and screening for cervical cancer.[34] There are no national

Table 1. Examples of genetic markers associated with susceptibility to common complex conditions

Condition	Gene variant	Known risks	Intervention
Thrombosis	Factor V Leiden[18]	Surgery, trauma, immobility, oral contraceptive pill, pregnancy, smoking	Avoidance of risk factors, anticoagulant therapies in some high-risk cases[19]
Emphysema	Alpha1 antitrypsin[20]	Smoking, lung irritants	Avoidance of smoking and lung irritants, neonatal screening [21]
Hypertension	Adducin [22,23]	Salt	Reduce salt intake, specific antihypertensives
Hyper-cholesterolemia	LDL receptor apoB-100[24]	Cholesterol	Decrease cholesterol intake, targeted drug therapy
Osteoporosis	Vitamin D Receptor(VDR)[25]	Calcium and vitamin D deficiency and lack of weight-bearing exercise	Specific dietary modification and exercise advice
Type II diabetes	Several[26,27]	High-calorie diet, inactivity	Presymptomatic lifestyle advice
Coronary heart disease	ApoE4[28,29]	Smoking (specifically)	Avoid smoking

genetic screening programmes, and those endorsed by State governments vary due to differences in funding, policy, and local emphasis.

2.1 Antenatal Screening

Generally, pregnant women are offered screening for blood group, thalassaemia and foetal chromosomal and structural anomalies.[35] Table 2 shows the screening tests for foetal chromosomal and structural anomalies, offered in the first and second trimester of gestation, that are available in Australia. Again, the availability and level of government funding of these tests differs in each State.

2.2 Newborn Screening

Newborn screening occurs in every State in Australia; however, different conditions are screened for in each State. Most programmes screen newborns for phenylketonuria, congenital hypothyroidism, and cystic fibrosis, and may or may not include galactosaemia and up to 30 other metabolic conditions identified by tandem mass spectrometry.[36,37]

2.3 Cascade Screening

Fragile X syndrome is the most common inherited form of intellectual disability. Generally, if an individual is found to have the gene change associated with this syndrome, the family is referred to a genetic service for counselling, and testing should preferably be offered to the extended family.[38,39] The same is true when a child with cystic fibrosis is detected via newborn screening. Detection of carriers allows families to make informed decisions regarding family planning. There is no programme to routinely test individuals for fragile X syndrome or cystic fibrosis carrier status, and only those with a family history or relatives of known carriers are tested.

2.4 Carrier Screening

Screening of healthy, low-risk individuals to determine if they carry a single gene change for a particular genetic condition is not widely accepted practice in Australia. Carrier screening programmes for Tay–Sachs disease operate in New South Wales and Victoria in conjunction with the Jewish Community.[40,41] Programmes for cystic fibrosis carrier screening operate alongside Tay–Sachs disease screening in schools[42] or from private laboratories.[43]

There is worldwide agreement that screening for disorders must follow certain guidelines; a summary of these is presented in Box 1.[44] Note that informed consent for screening was not a feature when these guidelines were

Test	Gestation (weeks)	Percentage of pregnancies with Down syndrome detected[b]	Advantages	Disadvantages
Nuchal translucency screening (ultrasound)[c]	11–13	75%	Early screen and therefore early diagnosis Detection of some foetal abnormalities Benefits relating to early scan Accurate dating Diagnosis of multiple pregnancy	Will detect some affected pregnancies that may spontaneously miscarry
Combined first trimester screening (ultrasound and blood test)	10–12 (blood test) 11–13 (ultrasound)[c]	85–90%	Detection of early pregnancy failure Detection of some foetal abnormalities	Will detect some affected pregnancies that may spontaneously miscarry
Second trimester maternal serum screening (blood test)	14–20 (15–17 ideal)	70–75%[d]	Available to women presenting in second trimester	Later screening test Inaccurate dates can result in inaccurate risk calculations. A dating scan should be considered if dates are uncertain
Second trimester foetal anomaly scan (ultrasound)	16–20	<40%	Detection of neural tube defects and other structural anomalies	Later screening test

[a] The cost of many of these procedures is covered by the public health system in Australia; however, there are regional and state differences in availability and cost to the patient, especially for first trimester screening.

[b] This is an average detection rate across all age groups. Detection rate increases with increasing maternal age.

[c] If nuchal translucency measurement is performed by an accredited operator.

[d] Assumes use of the quadruple test (four analytes) and ultrasound dating.

published in 1969. However, in 1975 guidelines were published specifically for genetic screening programmes and these include considerations of consent, setting for screening, best time to screen, confidentiality of results, follow-up, and deciding on new genetic screening programmes.[45] Genetic screening raises critical issues that do not arise from traditional public health screening programmes. Firstly, screening for a genetic condition has implications for all blood relatives. Secondly, having a genetic condition or the potential to develop that condition may lead to discrimination and, finally, there is no current cure or treatment for most single gene conditions. In spite of this, the information about a condition or the potential to develop that condition can be useful for lifestyle and reproductive reasons. Even though there are hundreds of genetic conditions that could be screened for, there is every reason to approach genetic screening with caution and in a systematic way including all stakeholders in the development process.

Box 1. Criteria for screening for a disorder

- The disease must be an *important* health problem; it must be severe and/or common.
- The disease must be *preventable* or treatable by acceptable methods.
- The screening test must be *simple, safe, reliable, and acceptable.*
- *Education and counselling* facilities must be generally available.

2.5 Lessons from Genetic Screening

There are obvious benefits of genetic screening (see Box 2); however, there are also potential harms. Firstly, a screening procedure is never 100% effective. There will always be a (small) number of false negatives (people with the disorder that are not detected) and false positives (people without the disorder who are declared to have the disorder). Secondly, an ethical dilemma arises when a government provides screening for a disorder to decrease the incidence of affected individuals. Is the government also bound to provide the best and most up-to-date care for families who choose to bear children with this disorder?[46] Thirdly, problems arise when health professionals and screened individuals are unclear about the meaning of results. This is why the provision of appropriate information and availability of counselling is crucial. The other crucial component of a successful screening programme is the involvement of the target community and all relevant stakeholders in the development and implementation of the programme. When direction and philosophy are lacking from a screening service, major misconceptions can occur—e.g., the sickle cell anaemia carrier screening programmes in the 1960s and 1970s in the United States.

Box 2. Screening for PKU
The genetic disorder phenylketonuria (PKU) has a devastating and progressive course with intellectual and physical manifestations. If this disorder is identified in the newborn period, the child can be treated immediately and is able to live a normal, healthy life. Newborn screening for this disorder has been implemented in Australia for the last 30 years.

Screening programmes were established, funded by State Governments, for African-Americans who were entering schools, new jobs, and the armed forces. The corollary of this was that people with sickle cell trait (e.g., carriers) were often discriminated against in the work force and by insurance companies because they were labelled as having a disease.[47] Hampton and colleagues in 1974 studied a cohort of children identified as having sickle cell trait, whose relatives described the trait as a disease that had grave physical manifestations.[48] The relatives also thought that "affected" children should be on vitamin supplements and required rest, and therefore were unable to participate in normal daily activities. The screening programe was eventually ceased; however, this did little to minimize the discrimination and stigma attached to being a carrier of the sickle cell trait. In reality, people who have sickle cell trait are often at an advantage as shown in Box 3.[49]

Box 3. Possible selective advantage associated with traits

Condition	**Proposed advantage to a carrier**
Sickle cell anaemia	Protection against malaria
Thalassaemia	Protection against malaria
Tay–Sachs disease	Protection against tuberculosis
Cystic fibrosis	Protection against gastroenteritis

2.6 Wading into the Gene Pool

Discussions about screening and selection often lead to the question of the effects of changing the gene frequencies in the population. Is it possible that genetic screening and treatment will prevent natural selection by protecting the unfit, thereby increasing the number of bad genes in the population? Most of our genes code for health; however, every person carries at least five lethal recessive mutations. The *prevalence* of people with chronic congenital and genetic problems may increase because treatment is improved but the *birth incidence* does not necessarily rise.[50] Relatively few congenital malformations are inherited in a Mendelian fashion, and therefore they will not be passed on to offspring. In addition, if a person has an autosomal recessive condition, two copies of the gene change are required for a person to be affected. Hence, it is unlikely that the offspring will have the same condition unless the partner is a carrier or has the same condition. Screening and selection *do* reduce the frequency of severe autosomal dominant and X-linked disorders where a person needs only one copy of the gene change to be affected by the condition. In this case, the gene change will not be passed on unless people choose to reproduce.[51] There is little evidence that primary healthcare and medical genetics are "bad" for the human gene pool. On the contrary, there is evidence that replacing natural selection with improved care for people with and without disabilities actually reduces the incidence of genetic disease.[52]

2.7 Susceptibility Screening

Genetic susceptibility or predisposition is caused by alterations in genes that contribute to the chance of developing a condition (e.g., cancer). Other factors may also contribute to risk. An individual who has a genetic predisposition may never develop the condition (i.e., have reduced penetrance). Several examples of gene variants associated with genetic conditions are seen in Table 1. It is possible that healthy individuals could be screened and given a risk value for developing any one of these conditions. However, it is vital that research continues before such screening programmes are established. The genetic risk can be substantially modified by other genetic, social, and environmental factors. The example in Box 4 is of a gene variant associated with Alzheimer disease and illustrates the complexity of genetic susceptibility.[53–58]

Box 4. ApoE variants and Alzheimer disease

- A susceptibility gene, ApoE, has been identified for Alzheimer disease.
- The ApoE gene has three forms (alleles) (ApoE2, ApoE3, and ApoE4). Everyone has two copies of the gene and can have either two identical forms (e.g., ApoE2/ApoE2) or a combination of two alleles (e.g., ApoE3 and ApoE4).
- An individual's risk of developing Alzheimer disease is related to the combination of ApoE forms they carry. Those individuals with one or two copies of the ApoE4 allele are at increased risk of developing Alzheimer disease; however, 50% of all Alzheimer disease cases do not have a copy of ApoE4.
- Ongoing research is attempting to clarify the significance of ApoE in causing Alzheimer disease.
- Testing for ApoE status for Alzheimer disease has been the subject of debate. To date, local collaborative groups and international bodies have recommended that ApoE not be used for diagnostic or predictive testing for Alzheimer disease.

Susceptibility screening of healthy individuals may have repercussions for their psychological as well as somatic health. There is discussion in the literature about the "worried well" and the "unpatients" who are informed of their increased susceptibility for a genetic condition and perceive themselves as already diseased or damaged in some way.[59–61] There is also the possibility that a person will be stigmatized and discriminated against. Even though there is a great deal of information, as evidenced by the example of ApoE, genetic risk assessments for multifactorial conditions will not actually predict the future with any certainty.

2.8 Pharmacogenomics

Several of the drugs prescribed for common conditions may only be effective in 25–75% of cases. Further to this, some drugs may cause severe side effects and even result in death. A study conducted in the 1990s in United States reported that approximately 2 million people are hospitalized each year resulting from adverse drug reactions and up to 100,000 people per year die from these reactions.[62] The questions as to why some drugs are effective for some individuals while being harmful to others is partially answered by genetics. Genetic variation is responsible not only for our differences in height and weight and colouring but also for our capacity to metabolize drugs. The drug metabolism pathway involves several genes coding for receptors, transporters, metabolizing enzymes, and excretion.[63] The science of pharmaco*genetics* utilizes genetic variation to pinpoint individuals who will respond to a particular drug and those who either will not respond or will have an adverse reaction. Pharmaco*genomics* refers to the general study of many different genes in a person's genome that determine drug behaviour. The pharmacogenomic future is one where a person would be screened for a host of gene variants before being prescribed medications. This concept of "individualized prescribing" will save money and lives and is set to become an integral part of medical practice.[64,65] This is a form of genetic screening that will initially be undertaken in a medical context. It is important to recognize that the issues surrounding the other forms of genetic screening will also apply in this situation. For example, a person with a gene variant indicating they will respond to a certain drug may still have an adverse reaction due to the presence of another variant or caused by other environmental factors such as poor nutrition, or a medical condition.[66] Also, the information about one person's pharmacogenomic profile is relevant for other family members. Again there is a possibility that people discovered to be non-responders to particular drugs may be discriminated against.[67,68] Discrimination may also occur due to lack of drug development for particular ethnic minority groups who do not have common variants (orphan alleles).[69]

3. PUBLIC ATTITUDES TO GENETIC SCREENING IN AUSTRALIA

3.1 Attitudes to Screening

As mentioned above, there are several genetic screening programmes operating, none of which is mandatory. Other non-genetic screening programmes that are voluntary have consistent uptake rates. For example, awareness of mammographic breast screening for women over 50 years of age is nearly 90%[70] and uptake of the programme is around 50%,[71] while participation in the national cervical cancer screening programme is 64%.[72]

3.2 Attitudes to Genetics and Genetic Information

The first Australian study to address this issue reported that a multipronged awareness campaign targeting health professionals and the general public did little to raise knowledge and to change attitudes to genetics. Most participants, although supportive of genetics as it relates to health, had low levels of interest unless the information was directly relevant to the individual or an affected family member.[73]

Other surveys have found that generally Australians accept genetic technologies, especially as they relate to health and medicine,[74] although problems related to privacy and informed consent are still unresolved. A report from the Australian Law Reform Commission and the Australian Health Ethics Committee in 2003[75] makes several recommendations regarding the privacy issues around genetic information. This report was a collaborative effort involving several stakeholders in this area. It is a consensus view on the importance of protecting a person's genetic information while at the same time ensuring communication of that information for the health and well-being of that person and other family members.

3.3 Attitudes to Newborn Screening

The newborn screening programmes in Australia are managed State by State and, although carried out routinely, they involve a consent process whereby people may "opt out."[76] It is estimated that more than 95% of newborns are screened in Australia.[77] However, the experience from one centre is that only 27% of women indicated that they knew the newborn screening test had been performed on their child.[78] Hence, there are obvious issues for informed consent.

3.4 Attitudes to Antenatal Screening

Women interviewed at their first antenatal visit had very limited knowledge of Down syndrome and the diagnostic and screening tests available.[79] In another study the majority of women were in favour of first trimester screening for Down syndrome rather than second trimester screening.[80] Both studies found that even though women were provided with information on Down syndrome and the diagnostic and screening tests available, their knowledge was still poor. This is corroborated by another survey of women, indicating that they have a very positive attitude towards diagnostic and screening tests; however, their understanding is very limited.[81] In addition, most women who are eligible for prenatal diagnosis (due to maternal age) but decline such testing will accept non-invasive screening procedures.[82] More recently, a study conducted with women postnatally reported that most women were aware they had screening or testing for Down syndrome during their pregnancy and 45% of women had declined screening or testing for Down syndrome.[83] These figures indicate that awareness is improving and that some of these women were able to make an informed choice about antenatal screening for Down syndrome.

3.5 Attitudes to Carrier Screening

Tay–Sachs disease carrier screening programmes have been implemented in Sydney and Melbourne where the highest proportion of Ashkenazi Jewish people reside. The carrier programme was facilitated in conjunction with the Jewish community and carried out at Jewish schools in both sites and has had high uptake and is well accepted. Attitudinal surveys have shown that for programmes to be effective, there must be communication, education, and counselling services available.[84] Population carrier screening for cystic fibrosis has thus far been carried out in schools and piloted in the primary care setting.[85–87] Overall knowledge was good and attitudes towards testing were positive. Anecdotally it has been reported that parents of children with cystic fibrosis detected via newborn screening commonly express concerns that couples are not screened routinely before or during pregnancy.[88]

4. THE IMPLEMENTATION OF COMMUNITY GENETIC SCREENING PROGRAMMES

4.1 Experience of a Screening Programme for Genetic Susceptibility in Victoria, Australia

From 2001 to 2004, over 11,000 people were screened for their risk for haemochromatosis via the HaemScreen programme.[89,90] HaemScreen was run in Victoria, Australia, offering genetic screening to adults in a workplace, university, or sports club setting. Haemochromatosis is an iron-overload disorder, whereby iron accumulates in the body and can lead to liver damage, diabetes, and cardiomyopathy. The iron overload is easily preventable by giving blood regularly to eliminate excess iron. A person identified with two copies of the gene change C282Y (a C282Y homozygote) was identified as being at increased risk and is offered follow-up with clinical monitoring and venesection if required. In Australia, studies have shown that approximately 50% of homozygotes will develop iron overload manifesting in organ damage.[91] However, in other settings these findings have not been duplicated[92] and penetrance of haemochromatosis is controversial.[93,94] Screening for haemochromatosis is a good model for a genetic screening programme as it fits the criteria set out in Box 1. HaemScreen was a pilot programme with 3 years of funding received from State government and philanthropic organizations. The programme is outlined in Box 5.

Box 5. Outline of HaemScreen pilot programme for haemochromatosis screening
– Approach workplace, university, or sporting club via director – Enlist aid of Human Resources Department and/or healthcare staff – Inform and recruit participants via email, posters, written materials – Participants attend education session: 10 minute video or talk – Answer knowledge and attitudes questionnaire – Cheek brush sample taken – Follow-up questionnaire and non-attenders questionnaire – Homozygotes identified as "high risk" and followed up – C282Y heterozygotes and wild-type homozygotes notified as being at "low risk"

The education session covers the clinical aspects of haemochromatosis, inheritance, penetrance, the concepts of high risk and low risk, prevention and insurance, and testing issues. The major outcomes of this programme were:

- On average 5–10% of potential participants attended the session.
- 97% of those attending gave a cheek brush sample.
- Rates of participation were higher in smaller workplace settings, e.g., up to 100%, and where the settings were contained, e.g., university lecture theatres, post seminar.
- Knowledge of the cause and treatment of haemochromatosis was high after education session.

Data suggest that the negative influences on uptake of this screening programme include practical reasons: people did not know the sessions were on or they were too busy at work. Other reasons were that they had low iron, or anaemia, that they were healthy, or that they already gave blood. The positive influences on uptake of predictive genetic screening were that the testing was free, convenient, and that the condition is preventable "so why wouldn't you have the test?"

4.2 Experience of Surveying the Secondary School Community about Genetic Susceptibility Screening "HaemSchool"

Using haemochromatosis as the model, the secondary school community in Victoria, Australia, were surveyed about their knowledge and attitudes to screening.[95] This project was referred to as HaemSchool and screening was not offered in this setting. Participants included students, staff, and parents.

The overall response to the suggestion of a genetic screening programme for haemochromatosis susceptibility was positive, with the students being more positive after the education session but still remarkably positive even before the condition was explained to them.

To sum up, it seems that in Australia at least genetic susceptibility screening for a preventable condition is acceptable to the community, both in the workplace and in educational institutes (schools and universities). There are issues that need to be addressed, first and foremost, such as the penetrance of the C282Y mutation, the health economic measures, and feasibility. However, at present in Victoria, this programme meets the screening criteria which requires that the condition be common, testing cheap and simple, treatment available, testing acceptable to the community, and education and counselling available.

5. THE FUTURE

As discussed above the possibilities for genetic screening have increased exponentially in the last decade. The clinical, social, and public health benefits of these opportunities will be the focus of research for the next few decades.[98,99] Other advances in antenatal screening are also imminent (see Box 6). At present, screening for chromosomal anomalies and neural tube defects takes place when the woman is in the first or second trimester. This screening procedure gives an indication as to whether the pregnancy is at an increased or decreased risk of a particular condition. To determine this with certainty the woman must undergo invasive testing procedure of chorionic villus sampling or amniocentesis. In future, possibilities for non-invasive diagnosis of genetic conditions in the first 12 weeks of pregnancy would mean earlier identification of affected pregnancies and improvement of care. Diagnosis of genetic conditions before the embryo is transplanted into the womb—pre-implantation genetic diagnosis—is available to some families. However, this involves the couple having in vitro fertilization procedures and hence has the expense and the low success rates associated with these assisted reproductive technologies.[100] Earlier, non-invasive detection would be preferable, as the low success rates for pregnancy and the risks of miscarriage associated with invasive procedures are absent.

Box 6. Future possibilities for early diagnostic testing for genetic conditions
– Karyotyping and DNA analysis of foetal cells present in maternal blood[96] – Sequencing of foetal RNA in maternal serum[97]

Screening for susceptibility genes whereby interventions could reduce the incidence of common disorders is a public health possibility (see Table 1). As stated previously, this kind of genetic information refers to a predisposition. A positive screening result indicates that an individual is at an increased risk, but may never develop the condition. Eventually, laboratories will be able to screen for all these with a simple cheek brush sample or finger prick onto a DNA chip. These chips are 1–2 cm^2 and could include sequences for hundreds of single-gene disorders and susceptibilities.[101] These screening scenarios raise issues about the confidentiality of genetic information and who should be allowed access. There is also the issue of individuals' right to know and not to know information about themselves. Health and life insurance companies may demand genetic information, as may employers, leading to discrimination on the basis of one's genetic constitution. Screening may expose genetic information pertaining to other family members and may have profound effects on health and society in unforeseen ways.[102]

6. RESEARCH, EDUCATION, AND COUNSELLING ARE THE KEYS

To avoid negative consequences of genetic screening, a multidisciplinary approach must be taken. Consultation, research, education, and counselling are essential components prior to, and throughout, any screening programme. In fact, the social imperative is to *include* these components and monitor potential and existing programmes to ensure they meet the screening criteria and have the support of the community. To foster this approach we must promote public dialogue of human genetics and technology and involve the public in deliberations over its use.[103] Public education campaigns, responsible journalism, and not overstating genetic findings,[104] in addition to the education of health professionals and other scientists working in different areas, can address this.[105,106] There must also be an emphasis on multidisciplinary efforts at undergraduate and postgraduate levels and for continuing professional education.

7. CONCLUSIONS

In conclusion, it is clear that dialogue with all stakeholders during the negotiation and planning phase of genetic screening programmes is critical as is documented for any healthcare programme.[107] A multidisciplinary team is necessary with strengths in the clinical, logistical, education, consumer, epidemiology, health promotion, laboratory, psychosocial, and health economic arenas. Education and counselling must be available. Genetic screening must be voluntary and participants must make informed choices. The way forward is to conduct research to measure acceptance, awareness, and clinical and public health significance.[108,109] The examples used above of HaemScreen and HaemSchool provide models for screening for a preventable disorder that is acceptable to the community. The HaemSchool study reported only the attitudes of the school community. Screening for haemochromatosis is not being offered to secondary school students; however, the school community sees genetic screening for haemochromatosis as an acceptable option. Finally, it is important to consider the value in learning to live with an uncertain future and the value in learning to live with disability. Consideration must be given to the value for society in participating in strategies enabling people to overcome disability or for society to change structures and policies to be inclusive. The ideal is to provide an opportunity for informed choice while simultaneously respecting individual differences.

Acknowledgements

The authors would like to acknowledge the collaboration of other key researchers who are participants in the multidisciplinary team and whose work and ideas contributed to this chapter, namely Martin Delatycki, Alexandra Gason, Clara Gaff, Jane Halliday, Veronica Collins, and Katie Allen.

NOTES

1 Marian, A. J. and Roberts, R. 1995. Recent advances in the molecular genetics of hypertrophic cardiomyopathy. *Circulation* 92: 1336–1347.
2 Ly, H. Q., Greiss, I., Talakic, M., Guerra, P. G., Macle, L., Thibault, B., Dubuc, M., and Roy, D. 2005. Sudden death and hypertrophic cardiomyopathy: a review. *Canadian Journal of Cardiology* 21: 441–448.
3 Crespo, E. M., Kim, J., and Selzman, K. A. 2005. The use of implantable cardioverter defibrillators for the prevention of sudden cardiac death: a review of the evidence and implications. *American Journal of the Medical Sciences* 329: 238–246.
4 Nestler, E. J. 2001. Psychogenomics: opportunities for understanding addiction. *The Journal of Neuroscience* 21: 8324–8327.
5 Nestler, E. J. 2004. Molecular mechanisms of drug addiction. *Neuropharmacology* 47 (Suppl. 1): 24–32.
6 Morgan, T. H. 1910. Sex-linked inheritance in Drosophila. *Science* 32: 120–122.
7 Morgan, T. H., Sturtevant, A. H., and Muller, H. J. 1915. *The Mechanism of Mendelian Heredity*. New York: Holt, Rhinehart & Winston.
8 Avery, O. T., MacLeod, C. M., and McCarty, M. 1944. Studies on the chemical nature of the substance inducing transformation of pneumonococcus types. *Journal of Experimental Medicine* 79: 137–158.
9 Bevis, D. C. 1952. The antenatal prediction of haemolytic disease of the newborn. *The Lancet* 1: 395–398.
10 Watson, J. D. and Crick, F. H. C. 1953. Molecular structure of nucleic acids: a structure for deoxyribose nucleic acid. *Nature* 171: 737–738.
11 Tijo, H. J. and Levan, A. 1956. The chromosome numbers of man. *Hereditas* 42: 1–6.
12 Lejeune, J., Gautier, M., and Turpin, M. R. 1959. Etude des chromosomes somatiques de neuf enfants mongoliens. *Comptes Rendus de l'Académie des Sciences* (*Paris*) 248: 1721–1722.

[13] McKusick, V. A. 1966. *Mendelian Inheritance in Man; Catalogs of Autosomal Dominant, Autosomal Recessive, and X-Linked Phenotypes*. Baltimore, MD: Johns Hopkins Press.

[14] Bell, G. I., Pictet, R. L., Rutter, W. J., Cordell, B., Tischer, E., and Goodman, H. M. 1980. Sequence of the human insulin gene. *Nature* 284: 26–32.

[15] Riordan, J. R., Rommens, J. M., Kerem, B., Alon, N., Rozmahel, R., Grzelczak, Z., Zielenski, J., Lok, S., Plavsic, N., Chou, J. L. et al., 1989. Identification of the cystic fibrosis gene: cloning and characterization of complementary DNA. *Science* 245: 1066–1073.

[16] Friedman, L. S., Ostermeyer, E. A., Szabo, C. I., Dowd, P., Lynch, E. D., Rowell, S. E., and King, M. C. 1994. Confirmation of BRCA1 by analysis of germline mutations linked to breast and ovarian cancer in ten families. *Nature Genetics* 8: 399–404.

[17] Wooster, R. and Weber, B. L. 2003. Breast and ovarian cancer. *New England Journal of Medicine* 348: 2339–2347.

[18] Price, D. T. and Ridker, P. M. 1997. Factor V Leiden mutation and the risks for thromboembolic disease: a clinical perspective. *Annals of Internal Medicine* 127: 895–903.

[19] De Stefano, V., Martinelli, I., Mannucci, P. M., Paciaroni, K., Chiusolo, P., Casorelli, I., Rossi, E., and Leone, G. 1999. The risk of recurrent deep venous thrombosis among heterozygous carriers of both factor V Leiden and the G20210A prothrombin mutation. *New England Journal of Medicine* 341: 801–806.

[20] Primhak, R. A. and Tanner, M. S. 2001. Alpha-1 antitrypsin deficiency. *Archives of Diseases in Childhood* 85: 2–5.

[21] Sveger, T. and Thelin, T. 2000. A future for neonatal alpha1-antitrypsin screening. *Acta Paediatrica* 89: 259–261.

[22] Ferrandi, M. and Bianchi, G. 2000. Genetic mechanisms underlying the regulation of urinary sodium excretion and arterial blood pressure: the role of adducin. *Acta Physiologica Scandinavia* 168: 187–193.

[23] Li, Y., Thijs, L., Kuznetsova, T., Zagato, L., Struijker-Boudier, H., Bianchi, G., and Staessen, J. A. 2005. Cardiovascular risk in relation to alpha-adducin Gly460Trp polymorphism and systolic pressure: a prospective population study. *Hypertension* 46: 527–532.

[24] Goldstein, J. L. and Brown, M. S. 2001. Molecular medicine: the cholesterol quartet. *Science* 292: 1310–1312.

[25] Ralston, S. H. 2002. Genetic control of susceptibility to osteoporosis. *Journal of Clinical Endocrinology and Metabolism* 87: 2460–2466.

[26] van Tilburg, J., van Haeften, T. W., Pearson, P., and Wijmenga, C. 2001. Defining the genetic contribution of type 2 diabetes mellitus. *Journal of Medical Genetics* 38: 569–578.

[27] Barroso, I. 2005. Genetics of type 2 diabetes. *Diabetic Medicine* 22: 517–535.

[28] Humphries, S. E., Talmud, P. J., Hawe, E., Bolla, M., Day, I. N., and Miller, G. J. 2001. Apolipoprotein E4 and coronary heart disease in middle-aged men who smoke: a prospective study. *Lancet* 358: 115–119.

[29] Humphries, S. E., Hawe, E., Dhamrait, S., Miller, G. J., and Talmud, P. J. 2003. In search of genetic precision. *Lancet* 361: 1908–1909.

[30] Hirschhorn, J. N. 2005. Genetic approaches to studying common diseases and complex traits. *Pediatric Research* 57: 74R–77R.

[31] Lander, E. S., Linton, L. M., Birren, B., Nusbaum, C., Zody, M. C., Baldwin, J., Devon, K., Dewar, K., Doyle, M., FitzHugh, W., Funke, R., Gage, D., Harris, K., Heaford, A., Howland, J., Kann, L., Lehoczky, J., LeVine, R., McEwan, P., McKernan, K., Meldrim, J., Mesirov, J. P., Miranda, C., Morris, W., Naylor, J., Raymond, C., Rosetti, M., Santos, R., Sheridan, A., Sougnez, C., Stange-Thomann, N., Stojanovic, N., Subramanian, A., Wyman, D., Rogers, J., Sulston, J., Ainscough, R., Beck, S., Bentley, D., Burton, J., Clee, C., Carter, N., Coulson, A., Deadman, R., Deloukas, P., Dunham, A., Dunham, I., Durbin, R., French, L., Grafham, D., Gregory, S., Hubbard, T., Humphray, S., Hunt, A., Jones, M., Lloyd, C., McMurray, A., Matthews, L., Mercer, S., Milne, S., Mullikin, J. C., Mungall, A., Plumb, R., Ross, M., Shownkeen, R., Sims, S., Waterston, R. H., Wilson, R. K., Hillier, L. W., McPherson, J. D., Marra, M. A., Mardis, E. R., Fulton, L. A., Chinwalla, A. T., Pepin, K. H., Gish, W. R., Chissoe, S. L., Wendl, M. C., Delehaunty, K. D., Miner, T. L., Delehaunty, A., Kramer, J. B., Cook, L. L., Fulton, R. S., Johnson, D. L., Minx, P. J., Clifton, S. W.,

Hawkins, T., Branscomb, E., Predki, P., Richardson, P., Wenning, S., Slezak, T., Doggett, N., Cheng, J. F., Olsen, A., Lucas, S., Elkin, C., Uberbacher, E., Frazier, M., Gibbs, R. A., Muzny, D. M., Scherer, S. E., Bouck, J. B., Sodergren, E. J., Worley, K. C., Rives, C. M., Gorrell, J. H., Metzker, M. L., Naylor, S. L., Kucherlapati, R. S., Nelson, D. L., Weinstock, G. M., Sakaki, Y., Fujiyama, A., Hattori, M., Yada, T., Toyoda, A., Itoh, T., Kawagoe, C., Watanabe, H., Totoki, Y., Taylor, T., Weissenbach, J., Heilig, R., Saurin, W., Artiguenave, F., Brottier, P., Bruls, T., Pelletier, E., Robert, C., Wincker, P., Smith, D. R., Doucette-Stamm, L., Rubenfield, M., Weinstock, K., Lee, H. M., Dubois, J., Rosenthal, A., Platzer, M., Nyakatura, G., Taudien, S., Rump, A., Yang, H., Yu, J., Wang, J., Huang, G., Gu, J., Hood, L., Rowen, L., Madan, A., Qin, S., Davis, R. W., Federspiel, N. A., Abola, A. P., Proctor, M. J., Myers, R. M., Schmutz, J., Dickson, M., Grimwood, J., Cox, D. R., Olson, M. V., Kaul, R., Shimizu, N., Kawasaki, K., Minoshima, S., Evans, G. A., Athanasiou, M., Schultz, R., Roe, B. A., Chen, F., Pan, H., Ramser, J., Lehrach, H., Reinhardt, R., McCombie, W. R., de la Bastide, M., Dedhia, N., Blocker, H., Hornischer, K., Nordsiek, G., Agarwala, R., Aravind, L., Bailey, J. A., Bateman, A., Batzoglou, S., Birney, E., Bork, P., Brown, D. G., Burge, C. B., Cerutti, L., Chen, H. C., Church, D., Clamp, M., Copley, R. R., Doerks, T., Eddy, S. R., Eichler, E. E., Furey, T. S., Galagan, J., Gilbert, J. G., Harmon, C., Hayashizaki, Y., Haussler, D., Hermjakob, H., Hokamp, K., Jang, W., Johnson, L. S., Jones, T. A., Kasif, S., Kaspryzk, A., Kennedy, S., Kent, W. J., Kitts, P., Koonin, E. V., Korf, I., Kulp, D., Lancet, D., Lowe, T. M., McLysaght, A., Mikkelsen, T., Moran, J. V., Mulder, N., Pollara, V. J., Ponting, C. P., Schuler, G., Schultz, J., Slater, G., Smit, A. F., Stupka, E., Szustakowski, J., Thierry-Mieg, D., Thierry-Mieg, J., Wagner, L., Wallis, J., Wheeler, R., Williams, A., Wolf, Y. I., Wolfe, K. H., Yang, S. P., Yeh, R. F., Collins, F., Guyer, M. S., Peterson, J., Felsenfeld, A., Wetterstrand, K. A., Patrinos, A., Morgan, M. J., Szustakowki, J., de Jong, P., Catanese, J. J., Osoegawa, K., Shizuya, H., Choi, S., and Chen, Y. J. 2001. Initial sequencing and analysis of the human genome. *Nature* 409: 860–921.

32 OMIM Online Mendelian Inheritance in Man 2004, available at <www.ncbi.nlm.nih.gov/entrez/query.fcgi?db=OMIM>.

33 Barratt, A. L., Cockburn, J., Redman, S., Paul, C., and Perkins, J. 1997. Mammographic screening: results from the 1996 National Breast Health Survey. *Medical Journal of Australia* 167: 521–524.

34 Australian Institute of Health and Welfare 2000. Cervical screening in Australia 1997–1998. *AIHW Catalogue No. 9. Canberra: AIHW, 2000: 36*, available at <http://www.aihw.gov.au/publications/can/csa97-8/csa97–8.pdf>.

35 HGSA Policy 2004. Antenatal screening for Down's syndrome and other fetal aneuploidy, available at <http://www.hgsa.com.au/ >.

36 Wilcken, B. M. 2003. Does every baby get a newborn screening test? *Medical Journal of Australia* 179: 400–401.

37 Wilcken, B., Wiley, V., Hammond, J., and Carpenter, K. 2003. Screening newborns for inborn errors of metabolism by tandem mass spectrometry. *New England Journal of Medicine* 348: 2304–2312.

38 HGSA Guidelines 2003. Guidelines for testing for fragile X syndrome, available at <http://www.hgsa.com.au/>.

39 Turner, G., Robinson, H., Wake, S., Laing, S., and Partington, M. 1997. Case finding for the fragile X syndrome and its consequences. *British Medical Journal* 315: 1223–1226.

40 Gason, A. A., Sheffield, E., Bankier, A., Aitken, M. A., Metcalfe, S., Barlow-Stewart, K., and Delatycki, M. B. 2003. Evaluation of a Tay-Sachs disease screening program. *Clinical Genetics* 63: 386–392.

41 Barlow-Stewart, K., Burnett, L., Proos, A., Howell, V., Huq, F., Lazarus, R., and Aizenberg, H. 2003. A genetic screening programme for Tay-Sachs disease and cystic fibrosis for Australian Jewish high school students. *Journal of Medical Genetics* 40: 45.

42 Ibid.

43 Sydney Ultrasound for Women 2002, available at <http://sufw.com.au/>.

44 Wilson, J. M. and Jungner, G. 1968. *Principles and Practice of Screening for Disease*. Geneva: World Health Organization.

[45] National Research Council (U.S.). Committee for the Study of Inborn Errors of Metabolism. 1975. *Genetic Screening: Programs, Principles, and Research.* Washington, DC: National Academy of Sciences.

[46] Collins, V. and Williamson, R. 2003. Providing services for families with a genetic condition: a contrast between cystic fibrosis and Down's syndrome. *Pediatrics* 112: 1177–1180.

[47] Beutler, E., Boggs, D. R., Heller, P., Maurer, A., Motulsky, A. G., and Sheehy, T. W. 1971. Hazards of indiscriminate screening for sickly. *New England Journal Medicine* 285: 1485–1486.

[48] Hampton, M. L., Anderson, J., Lavizzo, B. S., and Bergmen, A. B. 1974. Sickle cell "nondisease." A potentially serious public health problem. *American Journal of Diseases of Children* 128: 58–61.

[49] Rotter, J. I. and Diamond, J. M. 1987. What maintains the frequencies of human genetic diseases? *Nature* 329: 289–290.

[50] Modell, B. and Modell, M. 1992. *Towards a Healthy Baby: Congenital Disorders and the New Genetics in Primary Care.* Oxford: Oxford University Press, 358–359.

[51] Mueller, R. F. and Young, I. D. 2001. *Emery's Elements of Medical Genetics,* 11th edn. Edinburgh: Churchill Livingstone, 372.

[52] Modell and Modell, ibid., 359–361.

[53] Mayeux, R., Saunders, A. M., Shea, S., Mirra, S., Evans, D., Roses, A. D., Hyman, B. T., Crain, B., Tang, M. X., and Phelps, C. H. 1998. Utility of the apolipoprotein E genotype in the diagnosis of Alzheimer's disease. Alzheimer's Disease Centres Consortium on Apolipoprotein E and Alzheimer's Disease. *New England Journal of Medicine* 338: 506–511.

[54] Farrer, L. A., Cupples, L. A., Haines, J. L., Hyman, B., Kukull, W. A., Mayeux, R., Myers, R. H., Pericak-Vance, M. A., Risch, N., and van Duijn, C. M. 1997. Effects of age, sex, and ethnicity on the association between apolipoprotein E genotype and Alzheimer disease: a meta-analysis. APOE and Alzheimer Disease Meta Analysis Consortium. *Journal of the American Medical Association* 278: 1349–1356.

[55] Yip, A. G., Brayne, C., Easton, D., Rubinsztein, D. C., and Medical Research Council Cognitive Function Ageing Study. 2002. Apolipoprotein E4 is only a weak predictor of dementia and cognitive decline in the general population. *Journal of Medical Genetics* 39: 639–643.

[56] Panegyres, P. K., Goldblatt, J., Walpole, I., Connor, C., Liebeck, T., and Harrop, K. 2000. Genetic testing for Alzheimer's disease. *Medical Journal of Australia* 172: 339–343.

[57] Post, S. G., Whitehouse, P. J., Binstock, R. H., Bird, T. D., Eckert, S. K., Farrer, L. A., Fleck, L. M., Gaines, A. D., Juengst, E. T., Karlinsky, H., Miles, S., Murray, T. H., Quaid, K. A., Relkin, N. R., Roses, A. D., St George-Hyslop, P. H., Sachs, G. A., Steinbock, B., Truschke, E. F., and Zinn, A. B. 1997. The clinical introduction of genetic testing for Alzheimer disease. An ethical perspective. *Journal of the American Medical Association* 277: 832–836.

[58] Bird, T. D. 2005. Genetic factors in Alzheimer's disease. *New England Journal of Medicine* 352: 862–864.

[59] Jonsen, A. R., Durfy, S. J., Burke, W., and Motulsky, A. G. 1996. The advent of the "unpatients". *Nature Medicine* 2: 622–624.

[60] Broadstock, M., Michie, S., and Marteau, T. 2000. Psychological consequences of predictive genetic testing: a systematic review. *European Journal of Human Genetics* 8: 731–738.

[61] Davison, C., 1996 in *The troubled helix. Social and psychological implications of the new human genetics*, edited by T. Marteau and M. P. M. Richards, Cambridge University Press, Cambridge, pp. 317–330.

[62] Phillips, K. A., Veenstra, D. L., Oren, E., Lee, J. K., and Sadee, W. 2001. Potential role of pharmacogenomics in reducing adverse drug reactions: a systematic review. *Journal of the American Medical Association* 286: 2270–2279.

[63] Mueller, R. and Young, I. 2001. *op.cit.* pp. 169–170.

[64] Collins, F. S. 1999. Genetics: an explosion of knowledge is transforming clinical practice. *Geriatrics* 54: 41–47.

[65] Roses, A. D. 2000a. Pharmacogenetics and the practice of medicine. *Nature* 405: 857–865.

66 Evans, W. E. and Relling, M. V. 1999. Pharmacogenomics: translating functional genomics into rational therapeutics. *Science* 286: 487–491.

67 Roses, A. D. 2000a. *op.cit.*

68 Roses, A. D. 2000b. Pharmacogenetics and future drug development and delivery. *Lancet* 355: 1358–1361.

69 ibid.

70 Glasziou, P. P. and Irwig, L. M. 1997. Mammographic screening in Australia. *Medical Journal of Australia* 167: 516–517.

71 Barratt, A. L. et al. 1997. *op.cit.*

72 Australian Institute of Health and Welfare 2000. *op. cit.*

73 Walpole, I. R., Watson, C., Moore, D., Goldblatt, J., and Bower, C. 1997. Evaluation of a project to enhance knowledge of hereditary diseases and management. *Journal of Medical Genetics* 34: 831–837.

74 Dietrich, H. and Schibeci, R. 2003. Beyond public perceptions of gene technology: community participation in public policy in Australia. *Public Understanding of Science* 12: 381–401.

75 Australian Law Reform Commission Report 96. 2003. Essentially Yours: The *Protection of Human Genetic Information in Australia* <http://www.austlii.edu.au/au/other/alrc/publications/reports/96/ALRC96.rtf/>. Australian Government Printers.

76 Wilcken, B. M. 2003. *op.cit.*

77 Metz, M. P., Ranieri, E., Gerace, R. L., Priest, K. R., Luke, C. G., and Chan, A. 2003. Newborn screening in South Australia: is it universal? *Medical Journal of Australia* 179: 412–415.

78 Suriadi, C., Jovanovska, M., and Quinlivan, J. A. 2004. Factors affecting mothers' knowledge of genetic screening. *Australian and New Zealand Journal of Obstetrics and Gynaecology* 44: 30–34.

79 Mulvey, S. and Wallace, E. M. 2001. Levels of knowledge of Down's syndrome and Down's syndrome testing in Australian women. *Australian and New Zealand Journal of Obstetrics and Gynaecology* 41: 167–169.

80 Mulvey, S. and Wallace, E. M. 2000. Women's knowledge of and attitudes to first and second trimester screening for Down's syndrome. *British Journal of Obstetrics and Gynaecology* 107: 1302–1305.

81 Rostant, K., Steed, L., and O'Leary, P. 2003. Survey of the knowledge, attitudes and experiences of Western Australian women in relation to prenatal screening and diagnostic procedures. *Australian and New Zealand Journal of Obstetrics and Gynaecology* 43: 134–138.

82 Halliday, J. L., Warren, R., McDonald, G., Rice, P. L., Bell, R. J., and Watson, L. F. 2001. Prenatal diagnosis for women aged 37 years and over: to have or not to have. *Prenatal Diagnosis* 21: 842–847.

83 Suriadi, C. et al. 2003. *op.cit.*

84 Gason, A. et al. 2003. *op.cit.*

85 Gordon, C., Walpole, I., Zubrick, S. R., and Bower, C. 2003. Population screening for cystic fibrosis: knowledge and emotional consequences 18 months later. *American Journal of Medical Genetics* 120A: 199–208.

86 Barlow Stewart, K. et al. 2003. *op.cit.*

87 Wake, S. A., Rogers, C. J., Colley, P. W., Hieatt, E. A., Jenner, C. F., and Turner, G. M. 1996. Cystic fibrosis carrier screening in two New South Wales country towns. *Medical Journal of Australia* 164: 471–474.

88 Collins, V., Halliday, J., Kahler, S., and Williamson, R. 2001. Parents' experiences with genetic counseling after the birth of a baby with a genetic disorder: an exploratory study. *Journal of Genetic Counseling* 10: 53–72.

89 Nisselle, A. E., Delatycki, M. B., Collins, V., Metcalfe, S. Aitken, M. A. du Sart, D., Halliday, J., Macciocca, I., Wakefield, A., Hill, V., Gason, A., Warner, B., Calabro, V., Williamson, R., and Allen, K. J. 2004. Implementation of HaemScreen, a workplace-based genetic screening program for hemochromatosis. *Clinical Genetics* 65: 358–367.

[90] Delatycki, M. B., Allen, K. J., Nisselle, A. E., Collins, V., Metcalfe, S., du Sart, D., Halliday, J., Aitken, M. A., Macciocca, I., Hill, V., *et al.* 2005. Use of community genetic screening to prevent HFE-associated hereditary haemochromatosis. *Lancet* 366: 314–316.

[91] Olynyk, J. K., Cullen, D. J., Aquilia, S., Rossi, E., Summerville, L., and Powell, L. W. 1999. A population-based study of the clinical expression of the hemochromatosis gene. *New England Journal of Medicine* 341: 718–724.

[92] Beutler, E., Felitti, V. J., Koziol, J. A., Ho, N. J., and Gelbart, T. 2002. Penetrance of 845G→A (C282Y) HFE hereditary haemochromatosis mutation in the USA. *Lancet* 359: 211–218.

[93] Gertig, D. M., Hopper, J. L., and Allen, K. J. 2003. Population genetic screening for hereditary haemochromatosis. *Medical Journal of Australia* 179: 517–518.

[94] Imperatore, G., Pinsky, L. E., Motulsky, A., Reyes, M., Bradley, L. A., and Burke, W. 2003. Hereditary hemochromatosis: Perspectives of public health, medical genetics, and primary care. *Genetics in Medicine* 5: 1–8.

[95] Gason, A. A., Aitken, M. A., Metcalfe, S. A., Allen, K., and Delatycki, M. B. 2004. Genetic susceptibility screening in schools: attitudes of the school community towards hereditary haemochromatosis. *Clinical Genetics* 67: 166–174.

[96] Jackson, L. 2003. Fetal cells and DNA in maternal blood. *Prenatal Diagnosis* 23: 837–846.

[97] Ng, E. K., Tsui, N. B., Lau, T. K., Leung, T. N., Chiu, R. W., Panesar, N. S., Lit, L. C., Chan, K. W., and Lo, Y. M. 2003. mRNA of placental origin is readily detectable in maternal plasma. *Proceedings of the National Academy of Sciences of the United States of America* 100: 4748–4753.

[98] Beskow, L. M., Khoury, M. J., Baker, T. G., and Thrasher, J. F. 2001. The integration of genomics into public health research, policy and practice in the United States. *Community Genetics* 4: 2–11.

[99] Halliday, J. L., Collins, V. R., Aitken, M. A., Richards, M. P. M., and Olsson, C. A. 2004. Genetics and public health - evolution, or revolution? *Journal of Epidemiology and Community Health* 58(11):894–9.

[100] Ouhibi, N., Olson, S., Patton, P., and Wolf, D. 2001. Preimplantation genetic diagnosis. *Current Women's Health Reports* 1: 138–142.

[101] Lockhart, D. J. and Winzeler, E. A. 2000. Genomics, gene expression and DNA arrays. *Nature* 405: 827–836.

[102] Kerr, A. and Shakespeare, T. 2002. *Gene politics : from eugenics to genome*. New Clarion press, Cheltenham.

[103] Dietrich, H. and Schibeci, R. 2003. *op.cit.*

[104] Bubela, T. M. and Caulfield, T. A. 2004. Do the print media "hype" genetic research? A comparison of newspaper stories and peer-reviewed research papers. *Canadian Medical Association Journal* 170: 1399–1407.

[105] Metcalfe, S., Hurworth, R., Newstead, J., and Robins, R. 2002. Needs assessment study of genetics education for general practitioners in Australia. *Genetics in Medicine* 4: 71–77.

[106] Newstead, J., Delatycki, M. B., and Aitken, M. A. 2002. Haemochromatosis and family testing, what should a GP do? *Australian Family Physician* 31: 533–537.

[107] Crawford, M. J., Rutter, D., Manley, C., Weaver, T., Bhui, K., Fulop, N., and Tyrer, P. 2002. Systematic review of involving patients in the planning and development of health care. *British Medical Journal* 325: 1263.

[108] Halliday, J. et al. 2004. *op.cit.*

[109] Beskow, L. M. et al. 2001. *op.cit.*

ENZO A. PALOMBO AND MRINAL BHAVE

GENETICALLY TRANSFORMED HEALTHCARE: HEALTHY CHILDREN AND PARENTS

Recent developments in the fields of molecular biology and genetics have led to great advances in our understanding of how our genetic material, DNA, controls and determines our individual characteristics. With increasing awareness of the benefits that these developments will bring, particularly improved and novel medical treatments, there is no doubt that there will be positive impacts on the healthcare of adults and children. We must, nonetheless, be conscious of the fact that society is concerned about the ethical implications of some aspects of these technologies. In particular, rapid developments in the areas of genetic screening, cloning, and other reproductive technologies have the capacity to bring amazing outcomes, but they are also capable of dividing society. This review will examine the areas of genetic screening, genetic counselling, and related ethical, legal, and social issues from the Australian perspective.

1. INTRODUCTION

Molecular biology emerged 50 years ago when Watson and Crick proposed their model for the structure of deoxyribonucleic acid (DNA),[1] a model that was exquisite in its simplicity, yet powerful in its implications. Finally, a structure was able to reveal how a seemingly unimpressive molecule could possess the necessary characteristics to control the functions of living cells while enabling this information to be passed onto subsequent generations. The advent of molecular biology has transformed practically all life science disciplines.[2] In fact, the classical structure of DNA, with its familiar double helix, has come to represent modern medical science, particularly genetics, and the diverse field of biotechnology. Indeed, many prestigious biomedical institutions incorporate the double helix into their insignia as an indication of the central role this molecule plays in our understanding of life. A significant scientific achievement was recently fulfilled with the completion of the draft sequence of the human genome,[3] an accomplishment that is set to

Michela Betta (ed.), The moral, social, and commercial imperatives of genetic testing and screening. The Australian case, 185–200.

revolutionize the way in which we are able to diagnose, treat, and hopefully cure many of the diseases that currently afflict humans. However, with the promise of better medical interventions comes the concern that the new genetic information age will bring a variety of controversial issues that will need to be addressed by society. These issues are beyond the scope of the scientific technologies and will manifestly involve input from experts in ethics, the law, and the behavioural sciences.

2. WHAT IS "GENETIC TESTING"?

Almost all information about a person's health and physical well-being can fall under the broad category of "genetic information." As defined by the Investment and Financial Services Association (IFSA), the peak body representing life insurance bodies in Australia, a genetic test is "the direct analysis of DNA, RNA, genes or chromosomes for the purpose of determining inherited predisposition to a particular disease or group of diseases, but excluding DNA, RNA, gene or chromosome tests for acquired disease."[4] For the purposes of genetic testing, the actual genetic samples could be tested directly, or the biological products of genes, e.g., certain proteins, could be utilized.

2.1 Genetic Testing Methods

Depending upon the nature of the condition being tested, the testing methods include cytogenetic tests (which can identify abnormal karyotypes, e.g., chromosome sets with unusual numbers of chromosomes or major chromosomal rearrangements or defects) on adult cells or cells of foetal origin (such as the amniotic fluid or the chorionic villi), and biochemical tests on an adult's blood. However, molecular diagnostic tests on DNA from cells of adult or foetal origin are required where the condition or disease is caused by minor variations in DNA that cannot be detected at the chromosome level. Collectively, there are approximately 220 medical genetic tests available through various laboratories[5] and the number is continually updated, as there are numerous tests under development. The previous chapter by Aitken and Metcalfe outlines the guidelines generally followed for genetic screening in Australia. This chapter focuses on prenatal and early diagnoses and addresses the rationale behind the testing methods for some common genetic conditions.

3. PURPOSES OF GENETIC TESTS

Genetic testing is commonly divided into three major categories, based upon the main purpose it is carried out for, e.g., medical testing, identification testing, and kinship testing. Of these, the latter two categories of testing are generally conducted for the purposes of forensic or genetic (e.g., blood) relationship identification, and examine certain properties of the non-coding DNA, e.g., sections of DNA not associated with any particular genetic effects or functions, and will not be covered here. Medical testing is the area making significant impact on adult and child health as it concerns parts of DNA that encode essential products such as proteins, and will be the focus of this discussion. This type of testing can be further subdivided into the following broad categories.

3.1 Diagnostic and Carrier Testing

Diagnostic testing is conducted on a person already showing symptoms of a disease, to confirm the existence of a specific suspected genetic disorder. Although such diagnosis can generally play no direct role (except effective disease management) in the health outcome for the person already exhibiting the symptoms, it serves a very important role in making the person concerned and his/her family members aware of their own genetic condition or potential carriers status (discussed below) and of the possibilities of their own children being (or not being) affected. This, in turn, plays a significant role in allowing them to make informed reproductive choices and be better prepared emotionally and/or financially. A diagnostic test can also provide peace of mind to parents by clarifying the cause of a child's condition and allowing them to make any treatment or lifestyle changes early on.

Carriers of a condition are individuals who have mutations in one of the two copies of the relevant gene, making this copy non-functional; however, the mutant copy in the case of these types of diseases is recessive, e.g., unable to cause the disease in the presence of the other, normal copy of the gene. One must have mutations in both copies of the gene concerned to express the disease; hence carriers generally do not suffer from the disorder and are thus unaware that they carry such a mutation or that they may pass it onto their children, who may then exhibit the disease if they also inherit another such copy from the other parent. The testing for carrier status thus allows one to assess whether or not he/she is indeed a carrier, and the chances of passing their defective copy onto their child, or make informed reproductive decisions, such as a prenatal or pre-implantation diagnosis, or considering egg or sperm donations, or adoptions.

3.2 Prenatal or Pre-implantation Testing

Although most children are born healthy, about 4% are born with defects that will require major medical treatment.[6] Prenatal diagnostic tests are used to identify some of these defects. As mentioned above, a number of genetic disorders can already be tested, and in Australia, access to these tests is through a number of clinical genetics services in each State and Territory.[7] The vast amount of data generated by the Human Genome Project and the rapid developments in DNA technologies will no doubt increase the application of DNA testing.[8] These developments will undoubtedly impact on prenatal screening, in terms of the number of tests that can be performed simultaneously, the accuracy of tests, and the rapidity with which results will be obtained. This is exemplified by developments in two of the most common prenatal screens carried out in Australia, those for Down syndrome and cystic fibrosis (CF; discussed below). As maternal age in pregnancy is increasing in Australia (median age = 29 years and 16% of pregnant women are older than 35 years), the number of women taking part in prenatal screening programmes is on the rise.[9] Further, a new application of molecular diagnostics, e.g., pre-implantation genetic diagnosis, can now be carried out in specialized reproductive technology clinics. These tests are applied to embryos created by in vitro fertilization (IVF), for the purpose of selecting for implantation those embryos that have a high chance of successful pregnancy and normal development.[10]

The testing is performed by removal of one or two cells from an eight-cell stage embryo; this process is not known to harm the embryo development. The excised cells are then tested for irregularities on specific chromosomes, or their DNA can be extracted, amplified by the polymerase chain reaction (PCR; an in vitro laboratory method used to produce many copies of a specific sequence of DNA) and tested for the appropriate mutation(s). The diagnosis may also involve sex determination of the embryo, as the sex of an individual plays a critical role in certain X-linked genetic disorders. This will allow high-risk couples to select embryos without the genetic defect, or of the appropriate sex, to be implanted. Due to their enormous potential to improve children's health, such assisted reproductive techniques are likely to become more common in the next few years. An indication of this trend is provided by the recent example of pre-implantation screening of an embryo to avoid an inherited immune deficiency disorder, the hyper-IgM syndrome (a rare genetic immunodeficiency disorder). The embryo was created by IVF for a Tasmanian couple in order to provide a healthy sibling as bone marrow transplant donor for an affected child.[11]

3.3 Screening Testing

Genetic screening is performed on large, select sections of the population, including the majority of people who are healthy and not at risk of a particular genetic disorder. One such major screening programme in Australia, as in most developed countries, is the screening of newborns for certain metabolic disorders including phenylketonuria, which is the most common inherited metabolic disorder affecting nervous system development. It is characterized by the inability to correctly break down the amino acid phenylalanine, leading to an abnormal breakdown product, phenylketone, which affects brain development. Treatment involves a low-phenylalanine diet. Since many of these disorders are treatable or manageable if detected early, such screening programmes worldwide have resulted in saving of many otherwise at-risk lives and betterment of quality of life of children, Australia being no exception. Over the last 40 years since the inception of general newborn screening programmes, starting with phenylketonuria, further tests have been added over periods of time, e.g., tests for congenital hypothyroidism, CF, and a number of errors of amino and fatty acid metabolism.[12] The potential advantages of extending such screening programmes to other diseases also appear to be appreciated increasingly, as exemplified by discussions and pilot studies on the testing for hereditary haemochromatosis (discussed later).

3.4 Predictive or Pre-symptomatic Testing

This type of testing is performed on a person who does not have any symptoms of the suspected disorder at the time of testing, in order to determine whether or not he/she has the mutation which may result in a later onset of this condition (predictive testing), or where the genetic history of the family members suggests he/she may have the genetic basis for the disorder but not yet the symptoms (pre-symptomatic testing). This is a controversial area of genetic testing, particularly the testing of children for adult onset conditions for which no medical treatment exists.[13] While recognizing the lack of evidence-based research on these issues, the Human Genetics Society of Australasia (HGSA) has implemented a number of policies and guidelines that relate to these areas. Pre-symptomatic testing is defined as "a genetic test performed on a person who has a family history but no symptoms of a specific disorder at the time of testing, to determine whether or not the mutation for that disorder (known to be present in the family) has been inherited."[14] A positive result indicates that the person is almost certain to develop the disorder at some time in the future, provided they live long enough. Huntington disease and familial adenomatous polyposis are examples of disorders that are suited to this type of testing. Predictive testing is defined in the same way in that the test determines if a particular mutation has been inherited. However, in contrast to pre-symptomatic testing, a positive test is only indicative that the person has an increased probability, rather than certainty, of developing the disorder at some time in the future, if they live long enough. Examples of such tests are those that detect mutations in BRCA1 and BRCA2 for breast cancer and MLH1 and MSH2 for colon cancer. Genetic counselling plays an important role in pre-symptomatic and predictive testing, and exploring the reasons why testing has been requested is a particularly important question.

Predictive testing of children is a special situation that requires additional considerations. Most predictive tests are offered to individuals over the age of 18 years (which is accepted as being the legal age for independent decision-making in Australia), although predictive testing can be offered to minors when "testing provides preventative options which are of direct benefit to the child."[15] In fact, HGSA guidelines implicitly recommend that children should "only have predictive testing when the resulting information will be used to help with their health management in the immediate future, and not simply because parents wish to know." Prior to the child turning 18, parents have the legal authority to make most medical decisions on behalf of their child. However, where predictive testing of children is sought, the child should be made aware of this and participate in genetic counselling.

3.5 Research Testing

This type of testing involves "systematic analysis of genetic information to advance medical or scientific knowledge about how genes influence the health of individuals and populations."[16] Simply put, this is the stage where medical scientists are trying to make the connections between clinical observations of a person and the genetic profile of this person or his/her family, to understand the structure and function of the gene involved and the defects in it, develop new predictive diagnostic tests for the disease, and manage the clinical condition better. When sufficient data is collected, the research would be shared with peers and extended to a larger scale. Most of the gene discovery research and new molecular diagnostic tests would need to go through this stage before they become well established. All of these testing categories have made, and are making, significant contributions to the improved healthcare in Australia; some examples of these will be discussed below.

4. EXAMPLES OF GENETIC DISEASES COMMONLY TESTED FOR IN AUSTRALIA

4.1 Down Syndrome

Down syndrome is the most common inherited cause of intellectual disability, accounting for up to 15% of such cases in Australia, with an incidence of 1.2 in 1,000 live births in Australia.[17] Although screening of high-risk individuals is recommended, it is appropriate that pregnant women of all ages be tested.[18] Screening methods include ultrasound and measurement of the levels of placental protein markers in serum and the calculated risk is based on maternal age, with the recognition that the risk of Down syndrome increases with advancing maternal age.

Over the last decade, nuchal translucency ultrasound (which detects fluid beneath the skin in the head and neck region of the developing foetus; the amount of fluid is usually increased in Down syndrome), performed in the first trimester (at 11–13 weeks), has become an alternative screening strategy. If the risk resulting from this testing is greater than 1 in 300, further testing by chromosome analysis after chorionic villus sampling or amniocentesis will be offered. Recognizing the need for continuing assessment of the centres offering this service, a national training, accreditation, and audit programme has been funded by the Commonwealth Department of Health and Ageing.

4.2 Cystic Fibrosis

CF is a recessively inherited disease in Caucasians that affects the exocrine glands leading to production of thick mucus secreted into the lungs and gut. One in 2,500 babies is affected[19] with life expectancy varying between teenage and 50 years. The majority (95%) of CF cases are detected by newborn screening, with the remainder by clinical features.[20] Elevated levels of salts in the sweat and CF gene mutation tests are used to detect or confirm the condition, and newborn screening can also detect carriers (1 in 25 Australians are carriers). Prenatal testing (at 11 weeks gestation) is suggested for carrier couples. New developments in DNA and related molecular technologies and application of these to foetal cells are likely to become the primary mode of screening in the next decade,[21] including the testing and diagnosis of Down syndrome and CF. It is possible to extract foetal DNA free from maternal plasma within 10–14 days after conception and this material can be analysed by conventional PCR. The presence of maternal cells may limit this technology to screening rather than diagnostic applications.[22] A newer technique, multiplex fluorescent PCR, is more sensitive than conventional PCR and is able to carry out multiple diagnoses simultaneously from a single cell.[23] This technique can be applied to the detection of common chromosomal trisomies (as in Down syndrome) and single-gene defects (such as in CF).[24] Although neonatal screening has been the conventional method of detection for CF, antenatal screening is considered a way of giving couples a choice about pregnancy options. Making CF screening available to all couples, regardless of carrier risk, is recommended by the American College of Obstetricians and Gynecologists. There are no similar recommendations by Australian professional bodies and screening is targeted to those with a family history. The ethical issues regarding screening must also be considered given that the process involves DNA sampling, testing, and storage and there is currently no rebate from the Australian public health system.[25] Couples should receive appropriate prenatal genetic counselling including information about the risk of being a carrier, the test limitations, possible test outcomes and options for prenatal testing if both parents are carriers.

An important issue for CF screening, related to the ethnic diversity of the Australian population, is to determine which genetic mutation to screen for. For example, although the ΔF508 mutation (which causes CF) accounts for 75% of Caucasian carriers, it is only present in 28% of carriers of Ashkenazi Jewish origin.[26] Screening can be targeted if there is a family history of CF with a known mutation. Otherwise, screening can be tailored to the ethnic background of the prospective parents. Screening for multiple mutations increases the carrier detection rate significantly. However, as CF is known to be caused by a myriad of other mutations,[27] the task of ruling in or out each one of these is currently impractical, thus raising the possibility of false-negative diagnoses in a small number of cases. Technical advances such as inexpensive multiplexing will certainly aid in the unequivocal diagnosis of CF and other such diseases with diverse origins.

4.3 Tay–Sachs Disease and Fragile X Syndrome

An understanding and acceptance of the potential of genetic tests appears to be increasing, as exemplified by the selective carrier screening programme for Tay–Sachs disease. This disease is a debilitating, incurable disorder of the central nervous system that causes blindness, degeneration of nerve cells, paralysis, and seizures, leading to death in early childhood. It is caused by a recessive genetic condition, the frequency of carriers being 1 in 300 in the general population but about 1 in 30 in Ashkenazi Jews. The screening programme for carriers of Tay–Sachs was initiated in Sydney and involves screening and education of students at private Jewish high schools[28] and is now conducted on a wider scale.[29] Similarly, all Australian States conduct early childhood screening of individuals with intellectual disabilities, to identify those with fragile X syndrome, a fairly common disorder with a complex genetic basis that can affect either males or females, causing developmental delays and mental retardation.[30] The screening for affected individuals and carriers of this condition can assist families in expanding the screening to other family members and making informed choices regarding further pregnancies.

4.4 Hereditary Haemochromatosis

Hereditary haemochromatosis is a serious iron overload disorder, caused by a person having two copies of a gene with a mutation. However, it is also a treatable disorder, making it an ideal candidate for population genetic screening. One in 200 Australians is homozygous for this mutation (e.g., carry two copies of the mutated gene), and since the identification of the molecular basis for the defect in 1996, the genetic testing for hereditary haemochromatosis has been increasing rapidly, to about 30,000 tests per year.[31] However, there are uncertainties regarding whether or not a person who is homozygous for this condition will actually develop the disease, and the disease is preventable with a relatively easy strategy involving frequent blood donations by at-risk individuals, to avoid iron overload. Therefore, there is debate as to whether or not the screening for hereditary haemochromatosis should be expanded to the population at large, and a pilot study is underway to investigate the potential of such testing[32]. Additional information on this condition can be found in the previous chapter (Aitken and Metcalfe).

4.5 Genetic Counselling

Advances in genetic knowledge in recent years, stimulated by audacious undertakings such as the Human Genome Project, have led to an increased understanding of how genetics contributes to health and disease.[33] While public awareness of scientific advances has been encouraging, there is less awareness of the related ethical and legal implications.[34] These issues will be explored in detail below. The "new genetics" offers hope of new prospects for the diagnosis of genetic diseases, patient management, and alerting individuals and families of potential disease. As such, medical practitioners need to be aware of the new technology and give patients every support in understanding the implications for their own health and that of their children. A general practitioner is the first point of contact for individuals with most clinical conditions, and they are either treated here or referred to specialists. However, unlike infectious diseases, the genetic disease condition or the carrier status of a person has implications for the whole family as well. Thus the general practitioner clearly plays a significant role in influencing the health outcome for the whole family and future generations and would be expected to have appropriate knowledge of genetics, "molecular medicine," and the process of access to genetic diagnosis clinics and counsellors. However, according to a pilot study of general practitioners in Victoria, Australia, conducted through a collaboration between the Victorian State Government and several other institutes, general practitioners themselves were underprepared to take on this new challenge in medical practice and requested strengthening of education in several areas.[35]

A document has now been compiled for the use of general practitioners[36] that outlines the genetic education strategy designed for their role and provides them with information in all areas such as specific disease conditions, collecting family history, talking to families and contacts for diagnostics and gentic counselling. There is no doubt that such initiatives are indicative of the government's desire to offer world-class healthcare in Australia. One important link between patients and medical practitioners in Australia is the clinical geneticist. Patients who require diagnosis, management, genetic testing, and genetic counselling are referred to a clinical geneticist, who has undergone specialist training in a broad range of areas including adult and paediatric disorders, cancer, dysmorphology, reproduction, neurology, theoretical genetics, counselling theory and practice, ethics, laboratory experience, and research.[37] In Australia, clinical genetic services are provided through a network of metropolitan and regional clinics that operate in particular geographical regions. These regions are New South Wales and Australian Capital Territory, Queensland, South Australian and Northern Territory, Victoria and Tasmania, and Western Australia. Genetic counselling is an integral part of the clinical roles provided by a clinical geneticist. This will involve offering information and advice to patients, including the features of the disorder, how it is inherited, the risk of developing the disorder or passing it onto children, and ways to prevent or improve the outcome of the disorder.[38] Given the sensitive nature of the information that is provided to patients, genetic counselling raises many ethical issues. Confidentiality and privacy are major issues and the practitioner–patient relationship is subject to statutory and common-law duties.[39] Specific legislation exists in the Australian Capital Territory, New South Wales, and Victoria. However, other ethical issues that should be considered include (1) undertaking formal consent procedures; (2) ensuring patients understand the consequences of proposed genetic testing; (3) consideration of the possible stigma and discrimination associated with diagnosis; (4) making the patient aware of predictive or carrier testing options; and (5) the procedures involved with approaching other family members who may be at risk.

5. ETHICAL AND LEGAL AND SOCIAL ISSUES

The explosion of genetic knowledge in recent years has raised concerns about the possible misuse of this information.[40] Currently, it is possible to easily test and screen for numerous genetic conditions; however, the capacity to treat and cure these diseases is limited. Although the information is uniquely personal, it has implications for other family members (parents, siblings, children, and the unborn) or individuals within wider ethnic groups, as well as for a number of other issues such as employment and health or life insurance.

5.1 Privacy Issues

Concerns about the privacy of personal genetic details (e.g., the linking of health records by computerization) and the potential for discrimination may result in a general reluctance for individuals to undergo predictive genetic testing.[41] This is in spite of evidence suggesting that anxiety and depression is reduced in people who choose to undergo genetic testing compared to those who prefer not to know.[42] A recent initiative in Victoria, where free screening for haemochromatosis (a condition that can be prevented if treated appropriately) was offered, resulted in a low level of response.[43] Perhaps concerns exist that an individual's tissue or DNA may be "banked" for future use as new mutations are recognized; additional testing could be done, for example, for Alzheimer's disease.[44] People fear that their tissue could be retained in databases to be used in genetic research without consent or used in forensic investigations.[45] In other situations, such as the diagnosis of Huntington's disease, an individual may simply not wish to know their genetic destiny. The privacy of genetic information and the impact of genetic information on insurance coverage and costs as well as employment issues are also causes for concern and are being discussed at the Australian Federal Government level. The Australian Privacy Act does not include genetic samples and a number of gaps have been identified. The Australian Law Reform Commission (ALRC), which conducts inquiries into areas of law reform at the request of the Attorney-General of Australia, is recommending that these matters be addressed, and that an individual has access to bodily samples of his/her first-degree relatives, for the express purposes of testing, diagnosis, or treatment of a disease or preventing a serious threat to life.[46]

5.2 Cost and Patenting Issues

The cost of a number of diagnostic tests to confirm a clinical observation or a predictive or asymptomatic test for persons closely related to someone with the disorder are covered under the Australian public health insurance scheme, for which a citizen or a permanent resident of Australia is eligible. However, the costs to the government and/or to individuals could rise due to a number of factors such as the expense of the tests themselves, the labour-intensive nature of many of the tests, indirect costs such as funding for new equipment and additional counselling services, the patent rights of companies on the technology required for the diagnoses, and possibly insurance issues.[47,48] Patenting laws have been initiated in most countries due to their obvious benefits such as pumping of private funds into encouragement of innovations and research and development ventures. However, patenting by biotechnology companies of information such as functionally proven gene or protein sequences (not the DNA sequence per se), or specialized diagnostic techniques or drugs, are seen as a major factor that could push upwards the costs of such tests (or treatments) or the insurance premiums. A number of reasons have been identified for such views, e.g., opportunistic behaviour by patent-holders through monopoly or oligopoly of licensed laboratories that can carry out a test, significant profit margins, or limits attached to the type of testing conducted. For example, testing in Australia for those genes associated with breast or ovarian cancer susceptibility may be limited to the conditions laid down by the licence holder, and may result in higher costs and limited information for data collection.[49] The ALRC has been looking into both sides of this issue and has identified a number of factors that may affect Australian healthcare and recommended a number of solutions including the use of government's purchasing power to regulate medical genetic testing.[50]

5.3 Health and Life Insurance Issues

While an intensive debate has occurred over this issue, there is no proof that genetic discrimination could be happening in Australia, at the level of provision and costs of life insurance coverage. However, there is anecdotal and unverified evidence of numerous cases of genetic discrimination in relation to employment and insurance.[51] Under the current policy on genetic testing adopted by IFSA, a national organization representing life insurance companies in Australia, an individual requesting life insurance is currently not required to *undergo* a genetic test.[52] Australian life insurance companies have also undertaken initiatives to ensure that there is no negative impact on an individual wishing to take a genetic test, that the results of the genetic test of an applicant are not considered for assessing another family member's risk, and that cost benefits of an early (or negative) diagnosis and early treatment or prevention strategies are considered as well. However, some life insurance providers may require the applicant to disclose the results, if known to them, of a genetic test they or their family member(s) might have undertaken *previously*. Thus, there are some discrepancies between the privacy law and the demands of life insurance providers. The recent review of genetic privacy and insurance by the ALRC recommends that this issue be addressed "by examining industry practice and the operation of anti-discrimination laws."[53] The issue of genetic discrimination by insurance companies needs to be watched closely over the next several years.

5.4 Scientific Reliability Issues

Like any other scientific method, the results of genetic tests have a small degree of uncertainty, in spite of extensive measures taken to avoid these. Factors that lead to such situations include sample contamination, incorrect sample labelling, the inherent limitations of techniques such as the PCR, which can occasionally generate errors in the DNA sequence, shortcomings of testing procedures, or result misinterpretation. The consequences of these factors might lead to occasional false-positive or false-negative results, which can both be equally traumatic for the family concerned. These risks can be reduced by further automation at sample-handling stages or through the introduction of multiple tests to confirm a diagnosis.

5.5 Ethnicity or Cultural Issues

It is well known that certain genetic diseases have non-uniform distribution in different ethnic groups in terms of their frequency of occurrence or the nature of disease-causing mutations. For example, people of Anglo-Saxon origin have a higher frequency of being carriers for CF, while those of the Mediterranean and Asian regions have a greater frequency of being carriers of thalassaemia disorders. In fact, the nature of some mutations in CF or hereditary haemochromatosis is also ethnicity-related.[54] These aspects help the medical practitioners assess the risk probabilities for a particular group and provide appropriate patient education or request appropriate diagnostic tests, and are now being identified as being important in healthcare, as Australia's society becomes more and more multicultural.[55]

5.6 Other Social Concerns

The implications of some genetic testing extend to the whole family, genetic relatives/ancestors or an ethnic group. A test may end up revealing family secrets, such as non-paternity, misattributed parentage, adoption, and the use of assisted reproductive technologies. Should genetic information be considered private, or is it shared information that other family members have the right to know, as it may have implications for their own health? Genetic tests provide results of "possibilities" but not always certainties. All those with a positive test for a certain mutation may not develop the disease, and there would be varied degrees of symptoms and age of onset. There is also the issue of some people being unable to understand the statistics or technical details of the diagnosis. There is a risk of society ending up with a "genetic underclass" of healthy people, who may develop the disease in the future. There may also be a basic flaw in attaching so much significance to genetic data. Should it differ from other sorts of health or medical information? Other lifestyle factors, such as smoking, nutrition, and certain occupations also have important implications for future health. If genetic data are accepted as a separate indicator, the health system will be required to create two categories of diseases: genetic or non-genetic, even though many diseases will not fit clearly into either. Social attitudes might change, leading to expectations that people with genetic susceptibilities pay for their own and their children's health costs, rather than society sharing the costs as it does now. Other societal disputes may also arise, resulting from genetic tests to confirm or refute the ethnic background of an individual.

6. CONCLUSIONS AND FUTURE DIRECTIONS

Use of genetic information for genetic intervention is an aspect that has enormous potential in disease treatment, but requires further discussions. Genetic intervention involves somatic cell gene therapy, where a genetic disorder caused by a recessive condition can be "treated" by augmentation of the person's affected system by the introduction of cells carrying functional copies of the gene concerned. This approach is used rarely, due to a number of limiting factors such as the need for extremely specialized medical and laboratory facilities and personnel, the individual nature of the treatment, and the costs. However, the potential of this treatment is exemplified by its use for treating a rare genetic disorder, adenosine deaminase deficiency, which leads to an extremely compromised immune system. Patients with this disorder have been treated by gene therapy successfully in the United States,[56] and as a number of the above-discussed genetic conditions (e.g., CF and Tay–Sachs disease) caused by recessive mutations in single genes, it is expected that we would see various techniques and more frequent applications of gene therapy in the future. This might be considered a *band-aid* approach, as it can only help the person concerned and not provide a permanent cure for the next generation, and there have been instances of adverse effects in some of the trials.[57] However, the alternative, germ-line gene therapy (e.g., augmenting the reproductive cells with the functional gene), is not acceptable or desirable, due to society's reluctance to readily accept this technology and/or insufficient understanding of the irreversible nature of this approach and the many social, ethical, moral, and legal issues associated with it. New and rapid developments in technologies such as therapeutic and, potentially, reproductive human cloning will further challenge the ethics and morals of the "new genetics."

NOTES

1 Watson, J. D. and Crick, F. H. C. 1953. A structure for deoxyribonucleic acid. *Nature* 171: 737–738.

2 Stent, G. S. 1995. The aperiodic crystal of heredity. *Annals of the New York Academy of Sciences* 758: 25–31.

3 Mattick, J. S. 2003. The human genome and the future of medicine. *Medical Journal of Australia* 179: 212–216; The Human Genome. 2001. *Nature* 409: 745–952; The Human Genome. 2001. *Science* 291: 1145–1434.

4 Investment and Financial Services Association. 2002. IFSA Standard No. 11.00. Genetic testing policy, available at <http://www.ifsa.com.au>.

5 Human Genetics Society of Australasia. 2004, available at <http://www.hgsa.com.au>, cited 20 February 2004.

6 Gaff, C., Newstead, J., and Metcalfe, S. 2003. The genetics file: a resource for general practitioners. Victorian Department of Human Services, available at <http://murdoch.rch.unimelb.edu.au/GF/pages/GeneticsFile.asp>.

7 See note 5.

8 Trent, R. J. A, Williamson, R., and Sutherland, G. R. 2003. The "new genetics" and clinical practice. *Medical Journal of Australia* 178: 406–409.

9 McLennan, A. 2003. Advances in prenatal screening. *Australian Family Physician* 32: 107–112.

10 Monash IVF. 2003, available at <http://www.monashivf.edu.au>, cited March 2004.

11 The Age. 9 March 2003. Boy's survival depends on unborn brother, available at <www.theage.com.au>.

12 Genetic Health Services Victoria, available at <http://www.genetichealthvic.net.au>, cited March 2004.

13 Savulescu, J. 2001. Predictive genetic testing in children. *Medical Journal of Australia* 175: 379–381.

14 See note 5.

15 Ibid.

16 Australian Law Reform Commission (ALRC). 2003. ALRC Report 96: *Essentially Yours: The Protection of Human Genetic Information in Australia*, 321–331, available at <http://www.alrc.gov.au>.

17 Glasson, E. J., Sullivan, S. G., Hussain, R., Petterson, B. A., Montgomery, P. D., and Bittles, A. H. 2002. The changing survival profile of people with Down's syndrome: implications for genetic counselling. *Clinical Genetics* 62: 390–393.

18 See note. 9.

19 Ibid.

20 See note 6.

21 See note 9.

22 Ibid.

23 Findlay, I., Matthews, P., and Quirke, P. 1998. Multiple genetic diagnoses from single cells using multiplex PCR: reliability and allele dropout. *Prenatal Diagnosis* 18: 1413–1421.

24 See note 9.

25 Ibid.

26 Ibid.

27 Sudbery, P. 1998. *Human Molecular Genetics*. Essex, England: Addison Wesley Longman, 100–102.

28 Barlow-Stewart, K., Burnett, L., Proos, A., Howell, V., Huq, F., Lazarus, R., and Aizenberg, H. 2003. A genetic screening programme for Tay-Sachs disease and cystic fibrosis for Australian Jewish high school students. *Journal of Medical Genetics* 40: e45, available at <http://www.jmedgenet.com>.

29 Ibid., 12.

30 Ibid., 16, 615–636.

31 Gertig, D. M., Hopper, J. L., and Allen, K. J. 2003. Population genetic screening for hereditary haemochromatosis. *Medical Journal of Australia* 179: 517–518.

32 Ibid.; Gertig, D. M., Fletcher, A., and Hopper, J. L 2002. Public health aspects of genetic screening for hereditary haemochromatosis in Australia. *Australia New Zealand Journal of Public Health* 26: 518–524; Barlow-Stewart et al., ibid.

33 Haan, E. A. 2003. The clinical geneticist and the "new genetics." *Medical Journal of Australia* 178: 458–462.

34 Otlowski, M. F. A. and Williamson, R. 2003. Ethical and legal issues and the "new genetics." *Medical Journal of Australia* 178: 582–585.

35 See note 16.

36 See note 6.

37 See note 33.

38 Ibid.

39 Thomson, C. J. H. 2003. Confidentiality and privacy: beyond legal duties. *Medical Journal of Australia* 178: 252–253.

40 See note 34.

41 Ibid.

42 Lynch, E. L., Doherty, R. J., Gaff, C. L., Macrae, F. A., and Lindeman, G. J. 2003. "Cancer in the family" and genetic testing: implications for life insurance. *Medical Journal of Australia* 179: 480–483.

43 See note 34.

44 Panegyres, P. K., Goldblatt, J., Walpole, I., Connor, C., Liebeck, T., and Harrop, K. 2000. Genetic testing for Alzheimer's disease. *Medical Journal of Australia* 172: 339–343.

45 Spencer, C. A. 2004. Genetic testimony: a guide to forensic DNA profiling. Upper Saddle River, NJ: Pearson Prentice-Hall.

46 See note 16, 261–288.

47 Ibid., 321–331; 739–755.

48 Australian Law Reform Commission (ALRC), 2004. Gene patents and the healthcare system. In: *Final Report Alrc 99: Genes and Ingenuity: Gene Patenting and Human Health*, available at <http://www.alrc.gov.au>.

49 Walpole, I. R., Dawkins, H. J. S., Sinden, P. D., and O'Leary, P. C. 2003. Human gene patents: the possible impacts on genetic services healthcare. *Medical Journal of Australia* 179: 203–205.

50 See note 48.

51 Otlowski, M. F., Taylor, S. D., and Barlow-Stewart, K. K. 2002. Major study commencing into genetic discrimination in Australia. *Journal of Law and Medicine* 10: 41–48.

52 See note 4.

53 See note 16, 739–755.

54 See note 6; note 8; note 27.

55 Meiser, B., Eisenbruch, M., Barlow-Stewart, K., Tucker, K., Steel, Z., and Goldstein, D. 2001. Cultural aspects of cancer genetics: setting a research agenda. *Journal of Medical Genetics* 38: 425–429; note 6; note 8.

56 Mattick, J. S. 2003. The human genome and the future of medicine. *Medical Journal of Australia* 179: 212–216.

57 Ibid.

SUSAN PENNICUIK

THE AUSTRALIAN LAW REFORM INQUIRY INTO GENETIC COMMISSION TESTING - A WORKER'S PERSPECTIVE

1. INTRODUCTION

In 2003, the Australian Law Reform Commission (ALRC) and Australian Health Ethics Commission (AHEC) released the report of their joint Inquiry, *Essentially Yours: The Protection of Human Genetic Information in Australia* (ALRC 96) (the Inquiry).

The terms of reference of the Inquiry were to consider how best to:

- protect privacy
- protect against unfair discrimination and
- ensure the highest ethical standards in research and practice.[1]

According to the Commission "the major challenge for the Inquiry [was] to find a sensible path that meets twin goals: to foster innovations in genetic research and practice that serve humanitarian ends and to provide sufficient reassurance to the community that such innovations will be subject to proper ethical scrutiny and legal control."[2] This was a major challenge indeed. Providing reassurance to the community and, given past experience, protecting the rights and privacy of workers, individually and/or collectively, would be very difficult to achieve.

I am generally supportive of the recommendations of the Inquiry, including: the establishment of a Human Genetics Commission in Australia (HGCA); amendments to *privacy* and *disability discrimination* legislation to better protect individuals' genetic information; and the harmonization, by the Australian States and Territories, of information and health privacy legislation as it relates to human genetic information. This chapter looks more closely at the recommendations of the Inquiry as they apply to the employment relationship. Issues considered include the inherent requirements of jobs, privacy and the potential for misuse of information and discrimination, occupational health and safety (OHS), occupational health surveillance, and workers' compensation. The issues associated with genetic testing and data collection are sensitive and complex. An extremely cautious approach must be taken to the

Michela Betta (ed.), The moral, social, and commercial imperatives of genetic testing and screening. The Australian case, 201–210.

collection and use of such information. In the workplace context, in particular, the rights of the individual must take precedence, at least until a compelling case has been made for the benefits of a different approach.

2. EMPLOYMENT AND PRIVACY OF GENETIC INFORMATION

In the final report the Inquiry recommends (Recommendation 30-1) that: "Employers should not collect or use genetic information in relation to job applicants or employees, except in the limited circumstances where this is consistent with privacy, anti-discrimination, and occupational health and safety legislation." I am not been convinced that there are any "limited circumstances" that would justify permitting employers to collect, use, or keep genetic information about employees or job applicants, or to require them to provide such information to employers. The fundamental issue, as always in the employment relationship, is that of a relative power imbalance. Employers, who hold the power to employ or not to employ, may be interested in collecting, holding, and using information—particularly health information—about employees, even if it bears little or no relevance to the actual work to be performed. Employees, as is their right, are often reluctant to provide such information, or have it collected from them, for privacy reasons, and/or for fear of the information being used to discriminate against them. While it might be argued that genetic testing of employees or prospective employees should be permitted with the "informed consent" of the individual, this does not take into account the nature of the power relationship between an employer and an employee, particularly where testing is required as part of the pre-employment process. Forced to choose between submitting to a test or foregoing a job, many employees will "choose" the former, with those most likely to do so being those with the least knowledge of the issues involved and with the least financial ability to refuse such a request from an employer or prospective employer.

Many employers hold a great deal of sensitive information about their employees, including health information. Unfortunately, Australian privacy laws do not prevent an employer passing on information about a past or current employee to another employer or prospective employer. This is a major shortfall of the Privacy Act as it applies to the private sector. Many employers see the use of sick leave or workers' compensation claims by prospective employees as an indication of their suitability for employment, even though these are legitimate employee entitlements, the taking of which does not indicate any lack of commitment to the job. It appears that there is potentially some trade in such information, as was seen when a small company established an internet site and invited employers to submit names and details of employees who took, in their view, excessive sick leave. The plan was to charge prospective employers a fee for access to the database. While this project appeared to involve some breaches of the Privacy Act by the employers providing the information (although there is also an exemption for small business under the Privacy Act), it does indicate the high level of interest in the subject of employee absenteeism. There can be little doubt that genetic information, if obtainable by employers, would be circulated to prospective employers and potentially to others, particularly in the private sector. Therefore, the Privacy Act should be amended to remove the current exemption for employee records, at least for sensitive information, particularly health information including genetic information. Also important is the right of employees to choose not to find out genetic information or, where they have this information, to keep it private. This right should override any interests employers might say they have in that information. Therefore, I support of Recommendations 34-1 and 34-2 of the Inquiry, that the "Commonwealth should amend the *Privacy Act* to ensure that employee records are subject to the protections of the Act, to the extent that they contain genetic information."

3. POTENTIAL FOR MISUSE OF GENETIC INFORMATION AND FOR DISCRIMINATION

If genetic testing of employees or prospective employees by employers is allowed, it could well be misused in a number of significant ways. Firstly, testing could be used to screen out employees who might have only a slightly higher predisposition to acquire a particular condition than the general population. Many employers would not distinguish between a predisposition and a certainty, and the possibility of false negatives and positives might not be taken into account. For example, a genetic predisposition to alcoholism could rule out an employee who, in fact, did not drink alcohol. Secondly, genetic testing could be seen and used as a cheaper and easier alternative to addressing hazards in the workplace. Ironically, this could increase the risk to employees and the public, given that genetic testing cannot determine, for certain, who will or will not develop any given condition. Thirdly, genetic testing could potentially be used by employers to screen out employees whose genetic predisposition has no direct relationship to work, but who the employer might conclude, whether rightly or wrongly, are likely to take considerable time off work. An example of this could be an employee carrying a gene, such as for Tay–Sachs, which could result in a future child having the disease. It might then be inferred that the parent of a very sick child would not be a reliable employee and so should not be employed.

Employers could find themselves required by insurers to minimize risk by not employing people with predispositions to disabling conditions, or face higher workers' compensation premiums. Collection of genetic information could also affect general workplace salary continuance insurance arrangements, which are currently offered to all employees in some workplaces. If such testing and data collection became widespread, it could very well lead to the development of an"under class," whose employers, assuming they were employed, would be unwilling to invest in their training and development, or to offer them long-term advancement opportunities. This would take the discrimination against employees who have made workers' compensation claims, for example, which is already a problem, to far greater lengths. The application of anti-discrimination legislation in Australia to employees who do not have a current impairment is uncertain, to say the least. Therefore I support Recommendation 31-1 of the Inquiry, that the commonwealth should amend disability discrimination human rights and equal opportunity and industrial relations legislation to provide that, except where it is reasonable to do so, the assessment of the ability of an employee to perform the inherent requirements of a job should not include an assessment of whether he/she may be unable to perform the inherent requirements in the future on the basis of his/her genetic status. The provision 'except where it is reasonable to do so', is problematic because it has not been shown by any example or argument, where or when it would be reasonable to do so.

An employee who is dismissed as a result of the findings of genetic testing might be able to take legal action to seek redress, however, without specific provisions prohibiting terminations based on genetic information, each case would have to be treated on its particular circumstances, so that clear principles would not necessarily be developed. It should also be noted that while such a remedy might be available for employees, no provisions exist in relation to a failure to employ a person, or otherwise discriminating against an employee in his/her employment, short of termination. A similar position applies under the various Australian state and territory anti-discrimination and industrial relations laws. A genetic predisposition is not a certainty, or even a probability, and a person may never develop the condition for which they may have a predisposition. As it is impossible to prove a negative, it may well be that such a circumstance might arise in the future, although that cannot be a justification for discrimination or denial of opportunity today.

There is a high risk of job applicants or employees being coerced into submitting to genetic or other testing. Despite good intentions about prior informed consent, the reality is that most employees and job applicants are not in an economic position where they can realistically refuse their consent. There is also a danger of covert genetic testing using samples obtained without permission. Sanctions against this behaviour need to be severe. The potential for abuse of genetic information by employers and/or others is high, and the redress, if any, to the employee or job applicant will need to be pursued by them after the event, when discrimination has already occurred. This clearly places employees and job applicants at a disadvantage. Legislation to allow one party (employers) to collect private and potentially sensitive information about another party (employees or job applicants) should not be drawn up on this basis, when the strong likelihood is that its main effect would be to enable misuse of the information.

4. INHERENT REQUIREMENTS OF THE JOB AND RELATED ISSUES

It is difficult to see how a genetic predisposition to acquiring a condition in the future, which may never happen, is relevant to the ability of a person meeting the inherent requirements of a job today. The definition in law of "inherent requirements" of a job should refer only to the current ability of an employee or prospective employee to perform the work. Therefore, the assumptions behind Recommendation 31-2 of the Inquiry are questionable as they would allow "where genetic information is used to assess an applicant or employee's ability to perform the inherent requirements of a job, employers should develop clearly defined job descriptions that identify these inherent requirements . . . [and] . . . develop policies to ensure that genetic information is used for these purposes only in relevant and reasonable circumstances." Similarly, Recommendation 31-3, that "The Commonwealth should amend the anti discrimination legislation to prohibit an employer from requesting or requiring genetic information from a job applicant or employee except where the information is reasonably required for a purpose that does not involve unlawful discrimination, such as ensuring that a person is able to perform the inherent requirements of the job," is also highly questionable in that it has not been shown, nor is it currently possible to show, that the possibility of a person acquiring a condition in the future has any bearing on his/her ability to perform the inherent requirements of a job in the present time.

This issue highlights the difference between genetic testing, and ordinary employment-related "medicals." While these have discriminatory implications, used properly, "medicals" can allow for conditions to be identified and, if possible, treated. In the case of genetic testing, by contrast, there is generally no more than an increased possibility, not a certainty, of a person acquiring a condition that could create a problem in the workplace in the future. Consequently, the issuing of guidelines in relation to the use of genetic information in employment is problematic as is the appropriateness of Recommendation 31-4: that guidelines dealing with the collection and use of genetic information in employment should be developed. Screening out workers from particular jobs because of possible, future conditions is wrong in principle and from a practical point of view. For example, would all prospective employees with a predisposition be excluded, or only those above a certain level? How would those decisions operate in the labour market; i.e., would the attitude of employers to employees with particular predispositions vary according to how easy or difficult it was to attract suitable labour?

5. OCCUPATIONAL HEALTH AND SAFETY

I am very sceptical of Recommendation 32-1 of the inquiry, that the HGCA "should establish procedures to assess and make recommendations on whether particular genetic tests should be used in employment for screening for susceptibility to work-related conditions including whether:

- there is strong evidence of a clear connection between the working environment and the development of the condition;
- the condition may seriously endanger the health or safety of employees; and
- the test is a scientifically reliable method of screening for the condition."

I am is not aware of any situation in which genetic testing at work could be justified on OHS grounds. None of the examples given during the Inquiry, or anywhere else, indicate that a need for such testing exists. In every case cited, action by employers to eliminate and reduce hazards—as they are required to do under OHS law, even if this involves some expense—is the preferred and more effective way of addressing OHS concerns. Although proponents of genetic testing may try to justify it in terms of protecting workers' health and safety, this is a reversal of the most basic OHS principles: (1) that employers are responsible for providing a safe and healthy workplace and safe systems of work; and (2) that work should be made safe for workers, not the other way around. Similarly, it is also difficult to support Recommendation 32-2 of the Inquiry, that "The HGCA and the Australian Safety and Compensation Commission (ASCC) should . . . develop national guidelines for the conduct of genetic screening for susceptibility to work-related conditions."

In Australia there are at least 2,750 work-related deaths each year, or more than 50 deaths every week. This is known to be a significant underestimation, as data on the nature and extent of work-related death, injury, and disease in Australia is based largely on compensation statistics. Estimates put the true figure anywhere between 4,000 and 8,000 deaths per year. These deaths, injuries, and diseases are a result of hazards in the workplace, not the genetic make-up of workers. Australia continues to suffer such high rates of workplace deaths, injuries, and diseases because not enough is being done by employers to remove hazards or by governments to enforce the health and safety laws. Genetic testing of job applicants and employees will do nothing to alleviate this situation, but *will* put workers at risk of discrimination. Australian OHS legislation places a duty of care on employers to provide a safe workplace and safe systems of work. Employers are required to conduct "risk assessments" to identify OHS hazards, assess the risks, and implement the "hierarchy of controls" in order to control the risks. The primary emphasis is on prevention by the elimination of hazards from the work environment. I believe that any form of workplace testing of employees will simply provide yet another way for employers to avoid conducting proper risk assessments and applying the hierarchy of controls to OHS risks.

A number of theoretical arguments were put forward in the Inquiry for a possible "need" to test for genetic susceptibility, such as that people with a certain genetic deficiency may be more susceptible to lung disease if exposed to dusty work environments, or the claim that a genetic trait affecting susceptibility to carpal tunnel syndrome may have been found. As stated above, OHS laws place a duty of care on employers to remove hazards and risks from the work environment. Workplaces should be free from dust, so that all workers are protected from asthma, obstructive lung conditions, and/or cancer due to exposure to hazardous dusts. Carpal tunnel syndrome, or occupational overuse syndrome (OOS), arises when working conditions, such as workload, intensity, and pace of work are too high, hours worked are too long, and number of breaks are too few. Work can be organized so that workers are not exposed to hazardous agents or conditions, without the need to discriminate against people who, it is claimed, may be susceptible to the condition. Regrettably, the Inquiry goes even further in recommending—Recommendation 32-5—that the HGCA and ASCC should collaborate with other stakeholders to develop national guidelines for the collection and use of genetic information from applicants and employees "for the protection of third party safety." Recommendation 32-5 does ask that such guidelines "should indicate that genetic information from an applicant or employee should not be collected or used for the protection of third party safety if the danger can be eliminated or significantly reduced by other reasonable measures taken by the employer" and that where this is not possible, genetic information should be collected or used only where:

- the applicant or employee's condition poses a real risk of serious danger to the health or safety of third parties and.
- there is a scientifically reliable method of screening for the condition.

As previously argued in the context of OHS generally, it is difficult if not impossible to see how the possibility of a person developing a condition at some time in the future could affect the safety of any third persons now, and so Recommendation 32-5 is entirely unnecessary. The focus of workplace health and safety must be on hazard removal, not on a mathematical calculation of risk based on genetic testing. Only one or two highly exceptional examples of any genetic condition that could possibly affect a person's ability to do their job safely were cited in the Inquiry report. As one submission noted: "We have not had (catastrophic events) that have resulted, from a person's sudden manifestation of an undiagnosed genetic condition".

6. MEDICAL OR HEALTH SCREENING AND OCCUPATIONAL HEALTH SURVEILLANCE

I strongly oppose health surveillance involving genetic testing being carried out at the discretion of employers. Genetic testing does not test for existing impairment and no case has been put forward to show where genetic testing would assist in meeting OHS obligations. The collection of genetic information by employers should be prohibited, except in exceptional circumstances of legitimate health surveillance of groups of workers, not individual workers, to test whether exposure to workplace hazards is adversely affecting their genetic health. Such health surveillance should occur only under the supervision of the relevant regulatory authority and within the existing framework of the ASCC Schedule 3 for Health Surveillance and *National Guidelines for Health Surveillance*, provided under the National Model Regulations for the Control of Workplace Hazardous Substances. The *National Guidelines for Health Surveillance* specify if and when particular accredited tests may be applied for particular occupational exposures. Genetic testing could, if deemed appropriate by ASCC, be added to the range of monitoring tools. Therefore, I would give qualified support—see further for Recommendation 32-4—for the development of a national code of practice for the conduct of genetic monitoring of employees exposed to hazardous substances in the workplace. Under this code of practice, genetic monitoring of employees should be conducted only where:

- there is strong evidence of a connection between the working environment and the development of the condition.
- the condition may seriously endanger the health or safety of employees.
- and there is a scientifically reliable method of screening for the condition.

It cannot be assumed that occupational health surveillance is always benign. Health surveillance involves monitoring the adverse effects of hazardous agents on the health of working people who are exposed to them. The union movement has reluctantly agreed that health surveillance may be necessary in certain circumstances, in order to alert workers, employers, and government agencies to potential adverse health outcomes from such exposures. However, health surveillance must be conducted under strict provisions with regard to the confidentiality of personal health information and with associated obligations on the part of employers to control exposures and with a view to taking preventive action if problems are identified. Employers should not be provided with, or hold any personal results of, work place health surveillance—whatever type of monitoring or testing is used. These must be retained by the medical practitioner, with worker access to his/her own personal results and health information. Medical Practitioners should be independent and not directly engaged by the employer, so that the confidentiality of personal health information may be assured. Aggregate results of occupational health surveillance may be provided to employers, employee representatives, and OHS authorities, so as to ascertain the health impacts of exposures and to assist in determining what type of preventive action is required.

7. WORKERS' COMPENSATION

Although the Inquiry did not look in detail at the issue of workers' compensation, there is a concern that genetic information about employees could be used by employers and/or insurers to deny or reduce workers' compensation claims on the grounds of a person's alleged genetic predisposition to certain conditions. The provision for the use of family history under some workers' compensation schemes is already problematic as family history is not unequivocally predictive of a person developing any condition or disease. All workers, and/or their families, should be entitled to compensation for a work-related death, injury, or illness, whatever their family history or genetic make-up. Therefore, HGCA has to develop a policy regarding the appropriate use of genetic information in the assessment of workers' compensation claims.

8. CONCLUSIONS

The use of genetic testing and/or the collection of genetic information for employment purposes has the potential to create enormous personal difficulties for employees and their families with wider social ramifications. At present, the dangers associated with permitting genetic information to be available to employers are obvious and serious, while the case for any beneficial effect, if it exists at all, has not been demonstrated. The Inquiry acknowledged that it did not have a single concrete example of a circumstance in which permitting employers to collect data would be "reasonable and relevant." The only examples provided were so exceptional (and unconvincing) that to propose national regulations to cover them is totally out of proportion. Yet, inexplicably, the Final Inquiry still made recommendations allowing for the collection of genetic information based on spurious OHS grounds. Given that the only cases that came to the attention of the Inquiry involved attempted or actual inappropriate use of genetic information by employers, the risk is that, in the absence of a general prohibition, employers would apply their own test of "reasonable and relevant," leaving each case to be determined through litigation after the fact, should the employee or job applicant have the knowledge and (less often) the resources to challenge the employer's action. In light of the current, inadequate protection offered by Australian federal or state anti-discrimination or industrial relations legislation, it is recommended the enactment of specific legislation prohibiting discrimination in relation to employment based on:

1. An employee or prospective employee's refusal to submit to genetic testing or to disclose genetic information
2. Any genetic information about the employee held by the employer about the employee or prospective employee.

Employers and prospective employers should be prohibited from requiring, requesting, collecting, or disclosing information derived from genetic testing of current or prospective employees. Notwithstanding any legislative controls that may be put in place, there has, to date, been no demonstrated need to allow employers to collect, or otherwise receive, genetic information about job applicants or existing employees. Genetic testing in the work environment could only be justified on the grounds of significant public interest. There is no evidence any public interest justification exists, or is likely to exist in the future, to allow employers to collect genetic information about employees or job applicants. It would be more prudent and sensible to legislate for a total prohibition on employer use of such information, with the ability for this to be further reviewed should there be changes in science or other relevant circumstances.

NOTES

1 ALRC, Executive Summary.
2 Ibid.

SUZANNE JAMIESON

GENETIC INFORMATION AND THE AUSTRALIAN LABOUR MOVEMENT

1. INTRODUCTION

While the Australian labour[1] movement has not yet had to fight any cases of discrimination against union members or of any other employment matter on the basis of genetic information, it is concerned about the implications of the scientific development and its possible uses (and abuses) by employers. It would be more accurate to note that most concern remains limited to the highest forums of the trade union movement, i.e., inside the Australian Council of Trade Unions (ACTU), which is the sole national peak body to which most trade unions are affiliated. As we shall see below, some other individual unions are concerned by the issue, but it does not constitute a high priority matter. This is also true of employer associations in Australia.[2] A relative lack of concern across Australian society in relation to genetic screening, and the wider use of personal genetic information and the possible abuses of human rights arising from that use, must also be reported. If any real concern is general amongst Australians, it is probably limited at this stage to matters of genetic engineering in food-related matters.

A great many institutions of the Australian State may be potentially involved in the playing out of the issues aired in the Inquiry and its various documents. It is useful to note here that the Australian polity consists of a federal government situated in Canberra and six state (or provincial) governments and a further two territory governments. The Australian Constitution allocates legislative powers between the centre and the periphery and in some areas such as workplace relations and anti-discrimination there are both state and federal laws in operation. These laws do not operate simultaneously with respect to any individual worker, but a web of state and federal laws may operate to regulate the employment of any one worker, creating something of a minefield for the uninitiated. As an example, the author,who works full-time in a university is governed in workplace terms by a federal certified agreement (collective labour contract negotiated by the trade union), while occupational health and safety (OHS) matters and workers compensation issues are governed by state (New South Wales) law. In the event of seeking

Michela Betta (ed.), The moral, social, and commercial imperatives of genetic testing and screening. The Australian case, 211–220.

redress in matters of discrimination, either state or federal legislation (but not both) could be utilized. This is not available to all workers with a discrimination grievance. For example, a worker employed by the state government in New South Wales would be constrained if workplace discrimination occurred in the state legislation alone.[3] It is clear that potentially issues around genetic information may have complex legal outcomes.

It should also be noted here that while a significant amount of anti-discrimination legislation exists at federal and state levels, there is no over-arching Bill of Rights similar to those operating in the countries from which Australia drew its inspiration for much of its human rights legislation. The very recent joint Inquiry by the Australian Law Reform Commission (ALRC) and the Australian Health Ethics Committee (AHEC) conducted in 2001–2003, while raising matters of enormous legal, political, industrial, and ethical importance, did not become a huge talking point amongst the Australian public.[4] The generally deregulationist conservative Federal government to whom the ALRC reported is not likely to rush to implement all of the suggested reforms and, as we shall see below, a large number of issues in the general area of employment/discrimination are the subject of wildly differing views between employers and employees and their trade unions. Presumably there is still a long and tortuous road to travel before the majority of ALRC recommendations see the light of day in implementation. Some implementation has of course already occurred in the areas of information and health privacy law, human genetic databases, human tissue collections, genetic counselling and medical education, insurance in genetic information and sport, and identification of deceased persons. Additionally, in the area of discrimination law the Disability Discrimination Act 1992 is currently being reviewed by the national Productivity Commission (a federal government agency with a roving brief to look at economic issues) with a view to amending the definition of disability to include discrimination based on genetic status.[5] But of course any recommendations made by the Productivity Commission will have to face the usual parliamentary processes and are not assured of success. The composition of the Australian Senate at the time of writing[6] would seem favourable to such a development as it is dominated by non-government parties, but the lower House of Parliament (the House of Representatives) dominated by the government of the day may not see this as such a great priority.

This chapter will provide a brief sketch of the nature of Australian industrial relations and the position in which the trade union movement now finds itself. Some attention will also be paid to the regulation debate, which not only touches industrial relations but also most areas of government activity, and the way in which that debate may impinge on the outcomes of the Inquiry. This will be followed by a review of the perspectives put to the ALRC Inquiry by the ACTU and individual trade unions and a summary of survey work carried out for this chapter looking at developments since the Inquiry and how trade unions are responding to what remains a potential rather than an actual threat. Finally an attempt will be made to predict what may happen in the future, especially should genetic testing in the pre-employment period become usual.

2. AUSTRALIAN INDUSTRIAL RELATIONS AND THE LABOUR MOVEMENT

Australian industrial relations[7] have been notable for the historical intervention by the State since the adoption of Conciliation and Arbitration as the preferred method of settlement for industrial disputes by the Australian Constitutional Convention in Melbourne in 1898.[8] Successive interpretations of the Constitution and the Conciliation and Arbitration Act 1904 and its successors[9] ensured that trade unions would be central to the settlement of industrial disputes and in the establishment of industrial awards that not only recorded the terms of the settlement of those disputes but also laid down the legally enforceable minima of working conditions such as wages, hours of work, uniforms, and other matters. As we saw above, OHS and workers compensation issues are largely in the domain of governments other than the federal government. Several state governments have also historically adopted systems of conciliation and arbitration to regulate labour relations and set legally enforceable employment minima. Employer associations are also able to be registered (just as are trade unions) and to act as parties to awards.

Since 1996, however, the role played by the Australian Industrial Relations Commission[10] has been cut back by the openly anti-regulationist and anti-union conservative federal government. Decentralization of industrial relations since the beginning of the 1990s and the liberalization of the Australian economy since the 1980s has seen a shift in power very much in the favour of employers. Added to the demise of the Prices and Incomes Accord of 1983–1996, which was essentially a social contract between the ACTU and the federal Labor government and had seen the trade union movement involved in most government thinking of an economic or social nature, the labour movement is no longer automatically at the centre of Australian political life. The ACTU was established in 1927 as the prime representative and peak body of the trade union movement, and by the mid-1980s it was the only union peak body. The vast majority of Australian trade unions is affiliated to it. Like the wider union movement it has historically close ties to the Australian Labor Party.[11] While acting as a principal social partner during the Accord years,[12] it also turned increasing attention in terms of time and resources to the decline in union membership density in the years after 1990,[13] although density had been falling for some time before this as we see below. Trade unions first appeared in the 1850s and are as such a long-standing part of the Australian industrial scene, being critical to the creation of the Australian Labor Party in 1891 and in the events leading to the adoption of Conciliation and Arbitration into the Constitution.[14]

Trade union membership in Australia is dropping as is the case in most countries.[15] In 2002 total union membership in Australia stood at 1,834,000 persons, which represented just 23% of all employees.[16] In 1990 the total membership number had stood at 2,660,000 and 41% of all employees. Looking further back to 1982 (to the time immediately before the advent of the Accord), the respective figures were 2,567,000 and 49% of the total employed workforce.[17] There is some evidence that the so-called organizing strategy is beginning to bear fruit.[18] A pessimistic view of developments would interpret these strategies as being most successful in halting the faster decline in membership density rather than halting absolute decline. There is no one simple explanation for this decline[19] but reasons include structural changes in the Australian economy, increasing individualization amongst the Australian population, anti-union government policies, and imperfect union policies and leadership. So at a time when the labour movement in Australia is apparently fighting for its very survival in an increasingly hostile economic and political environment, it is perhaps not surprising that seemingly inappropriately little attention is being paid to possible threats posed by the use/abuse of personal genetic information by employers. The nature of the response by the labour movement to this issue is taken up below, but first we turn to a brief examination of the wider debate about the role of regulation in Australian society and the appropriate role for the State, a debate played out not just with respect to genetic information but also to industrial relations and the relationship between business and the wider community.

3. A WORD ON REGULATION MATTERS

The debate around regulation is intensely political and much written about.[20] It would be true to suggest that the regulatory State, which grew out of, and developed contemporaneously with, the rise of modern Capital, is very much in retreat. The traditional command/control form of regulation is out of favour and calls for reflexive, responsive, or smart regulation are in vogue.[21] That does not mean, however, that the leading writers in this area are calling for deregulation of commercial life in Australia but that there is significant support for self-regulation in spite of local and overseas corporate collapses and other events[22] occurring in a questionable ethical context. An Australian, Christine Parker, notes that rhetoric has a lot to do with the popularity amongst governments for the deregulation of business but that "the actual quantum of legislation or regulations affecting business has not actually decreased in most developed countries."[23] It was a strong theme in the submissions received from the Australian Chamber of Commerce and Industry (ACCI) that the cost of further regulation of Australian business was something that needed to guide the deliberations of the Inquiry, and that further regulation should only occur where a demonstrated need for it could be established, where there was evidence of the failure of existing regulation, or where the benefits of further regulation outweigh the potential costs to business.[24] Before the ALRC Inquiry report was published, the leading Australian writer in the area of genetic information and employment issues,

Margaret Otlowski, made it clear that some form of regulation to protect the rights of employees was necessary.[25] Regulation was recommended by the Inquiry, but to the satisfaction of neither employer nor trade union groups. To Otlowski this was evidence of the Inquiry's claim that the recommendations "represent a compromise of competing interests."[26]

4. THE INQUIRY

The origins of the joint Inquiry conducted by the ALRC-AHEC go back at least to 1992 when a House of Representatives committee looked at the privacy issues associated with genetic testing. This issue was taken up by the federal Privacy Commissioner in 1996 and in 1998 a private member's Bill attempted to adopt the United States' approach to some extent although it included bans on the use of genetic test material in all employment situations. This exercise failed but by then the social issue of how to prevent the new science from colliding with civil rights was firmly on the political agenda.[27] The Inquiry would eventually produce not just the Issues Paper[28] but also a Discussion Paper in August 2002 and the Final Report in March 2003.[29] The Final Report provided significant background scientific material on genetic information for the non-scientific community. It also noted that the use of genetic information did not as yet appear to be a significant problem in the Australian workplace.[30] In saying that, it also noted the current ability of Australian employers to use this material in recruitment (subject of course to the existing anti-discrimination and privacy laws) where they believed this information may be relevant in determining whether a potential employee had the capacity to perform the inherent requirements of the job or that this information might be relevant to OHS obligations imposed on employers under other legislation.[31] The implication for screening out potential employees who might carry an increased susceptibility to a particular disease or workplace hazard was at the core of the trade union concerns about the misuse of genetic information and was recognized by the Inquiry.[32] The Inquiry specifically rejected the contention that genetic material could not be used at all in the employment arena but that an appropriate balance between the interests of employers and those of employees must be struck.[33]

The Inquiry recommended the establishment of a human genetic advisory body to be called the Human Genetics Commission of Australia[34] and that a range of legislative and non-legislative measures be adopted including significant amendments to the various anti-discrimination statutes while avoiding wherever possible the creation of entirely new laws.[35] Employers according to the Inquiry should, within the limits of other laws (e.g., anti-discrimination and privacy statutes) and suggestions made in the report, be able to continue to use genetic information but with the consent of the worker (or potential worker) and in a transparent way.[36] With respect to OHS the Inquiry rejected a ban on the use by employers of genetic information, but instead urged the preferential elimination of environmental risks by reasonable measures.[37] This carefully articulated halfway house between employer and trade union desires satisfied no one.

5. LABOUR MOVEMENT RESPONSES

The ALRC-AHEC Inquiry between 2001 and 2003 attracted only five individual responses from trade unions[38] and a significant submission from the ACTU. No doubt many smaller trade unions did not see the need to make a submission when the ACTU was known to be making a submission, which at that time did not reveal real evidence of abuse of worker civil liberties by employers in the area of genetic information or testing. As we saw above, only the ACCI made a submission on behalf of employers, although a number of organizations that clearly employ labour made submissions (e.g., church-based health services, medical colleges, and government departments) but these appear to have been mainly about non-employment issues. It may be that there will be more trade union activities in 2006 when the empirical work undertaken pursuant to the Genetic Discrimination Project conducted by Otlowski and her team and funded by the Australian Research Council will be published,[39] which may well reveal further evidence of genetic discrimination.[40] The ACTU submission to the Inquiry [41] limited itself to issues concerned with the employment relationship, making it clear that it could see no circumstances where employees could be assisted by employer access to the genetic information relating to the employees. In particular it noted that with respect to workers' health and safety no case could be made for blaming workers' genetic make-up for work-related illnesses and injuries when responsibility fell squarely on the control of hazards in the workplace by employers. The submission went on to specifically recommend the adoption of legislation at federal and state level prohibiting employment discrimination based either on the employee's refusal to submit to genetic testing or to disclose such information, or on the basis of information held by the employer about the employee or potential employee. The submission went on to make clear the ACTU's opposition to exemptions in any such legislation whereby the "inherent requirements of the job" could be used to exclude any employee unless shown on balance to be beneficial to employees. Mandatory testing of current or potential employees was specifically rejected by the ACTU. It further recommended that the federal Privacy Act 1988 be amended with respect to the current exemption afforded to employee records "at least for sensitive information." The ACTU concluded:

> The ACTU submits that an extremely cautious approach should be taken to the use of such information and that in the workplace context, in particular, the rights of the individual must take precedence, at least until a compelling case has been made out for the benefits of a different approach.[42]

As noted above, the ACTU ultimately believed that the ALRC proposals did not go far enough and the major employer association, the ACCI, believed the proposals went too far down the road of regulation before significant problems have developed.[43] In general, the submission put by ACCI[44] saw a potential need for employers to be able to access employees' genetic information, particularly in the case of giving effect to OHS obligations. This was not clarified in their submission. A major critique of further regulation ran through the submission, drawing on arguments ranging from the non-failure of existing regulation to the cost to business of further regulation. An acknowledgement was clearly made that sensitivity to the privacy needs of individual workers must be shown.

In August 2004 the author undertook to follow up developments amongst the trade unions to see if the use of genetic information by employers had become a problem in their eyes since the publication of the ALRC final report in March 2003. Unequivocally it can be reported that very little has changed in the intervening 18-month period. A documentary survey of the 16 largest affiliates of the ACTU's 46 affiliates revealed virtually no policy or interest in the issue of genetic information and no current alerts to their members.[45] Only the New South Wales Nurses' Association had any detailed policy on the issue, and one might assume that had more than a little to do with the fact that the membership of that union may be expected to have a better understanding of the science involved and, by extension, of the legal and industrial issues associated with genetic testing.[46] It is clear from the Position Statement that the Association understands the potential positives that can come from the use of genetic information in the area of health, but it is equally clear that genetic information can be used in a discriminatory way and moreover that the information should never be used in recruitment.[47] This was followed up with interviews with senior officials of those trade unions that had made submissions to the Inquiry where those senior officials were also geographically available in New South Wales.[48] This methodology was chosen because those unions had already shown some interest in the issue during the time of the Inquiry, to the extent that they had made submissions when it was known that the ACTU would do this on behalf of all affiliated trade unions. In all cases, however, it emerged that no case of misuse of genetic information by employers appears to have occurred that has been reported to these trade unions.

In fact, there did not appear to be any evidence that Australian employers were using genetic information at all. Of course this must be read in the light of low levels of union membership and the fact that every known act of discrimination in our society/workplaces does not result in a complaint. And, of course, where potential workers believes they may have been discriminated against in recruitment on the basis of their genetic status, they may not yet be a member of the trade union to whom they might ordinarily complain about workplace conditions when there is an employment relationship on foot. What was reported by several of the interviewees was that increasing surveillance of employees on drug and alcohol grounds seems to be occurring and increasing resort to psychological testing of employees prior to recruitment (even for manual jobs) seems to be widespread. While no actual evidence of genetic information discrimination was reported,[49] in all interviews the union respondents believed that on the basis of the drug/alcohol and psychological screening, genetic screening or use of information was on the horizon. It might be that in a historical period when the employer seemed to have the ascendancy in Australia, trade unions were feeling particularly under threat and more than a little paranoid. In the absence of another federal Labor government there does not seem to be much chance that trade union dissatisfaction with the outcomes of the Inquiry will get a second hearing.

6. CONCLUSIONS

Unless the ARC-funded Genetic Discrimination Project led by Otlowski and her team reveals evidence of genetic discrimination on a mid-to-large scale, calls for immediate further regulation are not likely to emerge. The Australian labour movement remains implacably opposed to the use of genetic information in recruitment or in any other stage of the employment relationship. But the *Realpolitik* of the use of genetic information in Australia has probably been better articulated by the ALRC Inquiry, and that an intermediate position of compromise with appropriate safeguards for the civil rights of workers is the most likely outcome when the use of genetic information becomes mainstream. Old style command and control regulation is not likely to happen. Given the likely continued loss of membership strength and influence by the trade union movement in Australia and an uncertain countervailing social contract with a future Labor government in Canberra, a compromise position is the best outcome for which the trade unions could hope.

NOTES

1 Here I have adopted the use of the generic term and spelling of LABOUR, which usually connotes the trade union movement in Australia. Advocates of spelling reform long ago adopted LABOR for the title of the largest affiliate of the Australian Council of Trade Unions, that is the New South Wales Labor Council, and the social-democratic party most closely associated with the trade union movement is the Australian Labor Party.

2 As we shall see below employers as represented through their employer associations do not seem to be too involved in the question of genetic information, testing, or screening at this stage if their responses to the various stages of the recent Australian Law Reform Commission Inquiry into Human Genetic Information is a reliable guide where only the peak body, the Australian Chamber of Commerce and Industry (ACCI), made a submission on behalf of Australian employers, see, for example, Submissions G170 and G308.

3 That is the Anti-Discrimination Act 1977.

4 The author should admit at the outset that she participated in the Inquiry on the Advisory Committee to the Joint Inquiry.

5 See the ALRC online, available at <www.alrc.gov.au.>, cited 27 August 2004.

6 August 2004.

7 For a good general overview see Lansbury, R. and Wailes, N. 2004. Employment relations in Australia. In: Bamber, G., Lansbury, R., and Wailes, N. (eds.), *International and Comparative Employment Relations—Globalisation and the Developed Market Economies*. Crows Nest, New South Wales: Allen & Unwin.

8 For detailed narrative and analysis on this development see generally Macintyre, S. and Mitchell, R. (eds.), 1989. *Foundations of Arbitration—The Origins and Effects of State Compulsory Arbitration 1890–1914*. Melbourne: Oxford University Press.

9 Industrial Relations Act 1988 and Workplace Relations Act 1996. It was only in the 1988 Act that a form of non-union agreement, the so-called Enterprise Flexibility Agreement, was introduced paradoxically and amidst great criticism by the Australian Labor Party government. After the change of government in 1996, the incoming conservative government introduced non-union agreements on an individual and collective basis.

10 The successor since 1989 of the Commonwealth Court of Conciliation and Arbitration (1904–1956) and the Australian Conciliation and Arbitration Commission (1957–1989).

11 The former President of the ACTU, R. J. L. Hawke, became Prime Minister in 1983 after having negotiated the Accord immediately before the election of the new government. Two other former presidents of the ACTU now sit on the Opposition front benches in the federal parliament.

12 The Accord was a national social compact negotiated by the Australian Labor Party and the ACTU that operated between 1983 and 1996 which, essentially saw the trade union movement trade off wage increases for improvements in the social wage.

13 See especially Briggs, C. 1999. *The rise and fall of the ACTU: maturation, hegemony and decline*. Unpublished PhD thesis, University of Sydney.

14 See above in paragraph 1 of this section.

15 Peetz, D. 1998. *Unions in a Contrary World: The Future of the Australian Trade Union Movement*. Cambridge: Cambridge University Press.

16 Australian Bureau of Statistics, Trade Union Members, Australia, Cat 6325.0.

17 Ibid.

18 The so-called organizing model was developed in the United States and seeks to empower grass-roots union members to be able to defend and represent themselves to a large extent. This is to be distinguished from the so-called servicing model whereby the full-time paid officials. For an insightful discussion of these issues, see Cooper, R., Lansbury, R., and Westcott, M. 2003. Labour revitalization in Australia. In: Cornfield, D. and McCammon, H. (eds.), *Labor Revitalization*. Oxford: Elsevier.

19 Griffin, G. and Svensen, S. 1996 The decline of Australian Union density: a survey of the literature. *Journal of Industrial Relations* 38: 505–547.

20 A particularly useful discussion of regulation from an Australian perspective is to be found in Gunningham, N. and Johnstone, R. 1999. *Regulating Workplace Safety: Systems and Sanctions*. Oxford: Oxford University Press. Other perspectives may be found in Picciotto, S. 2002. Introduction: reconceptualising regulation in the era of globalisation. *Journal of Law and Society* 29: 1–11.

21 Gunningham and Johnstone, ibid.

22 Clarke, F., Dean, G., and Oliver, K. 2003 *Corporate Collapse: Accounting, Regulatory and Ethical Failure*. Cambridge: Cambridge University Press.

23 Parker, C. 2002. *The Open Corporation—Effective Self-Regulation and Democracy*. Cambridge: Cambridge University Press, 13.

24 Australian Chamber of Commerce and Industry. 2003. *Submission to the ALRC-AHEC Joint Inquiry on the Protection of Human Genetic Information*.

25 Otlowski, M. 2002. Employers' use of genetic test information: is there need for regulation? *Australian Journal of Labour Law* 15: 1–39.

26 Otlowski, M. 2003. The ALRC-AHEC report on the protection of human genetic information in Australia: implications for the employment sector. *Australian Journal of Labour Law* 16: 370–380.

27 See ALRC-AHEC, 2001. *Protection of Human Genetic Information—Issues Paper*, ALRC, 59–61.

28 Ibid.

29 For example, ALRC-AHEC, 2002. *Protection of Human Genetic Information—Discussion Paper*. ALRC and ALRC-AHEC, 2003. *Essentially Yours—Report on The Protection of Human Genetic Information in Australia*, ALRC.

30 ALRC-AHEC, 2003. ibid., 782.

31 For example, New South Wales Occupational Health and Safety Act 2000.

32 ALRC-AHEC, 2003, ibid., 766.

33 Ibid., 767–770. Note the different approach in the private member's Bill of 1998 mentioned above.

34 Ibid., 211–213.

35 Ibid., Chapter 31.

36 Ibid., 783.

37 Ibid., 815.

38 For example, from the Australian Manufacturing Workers Union (AMWU), the Australian Nursing Federation (ANF), the Construction Forestry Mining and Energy Union-Construction and General Division (CFMEU), the New South Wales Nurses' Association (NSWNA), and the Police Federation of Australia (PFA).

39 Otlowski, M. 2003, ibid., 373.

40 It should be noted here that while no further evidence of genetic information discrimination was revealed by the trade union respondents to the author (see below in this section), evidence of this has been reported by Dr. Barlow-Stewart in ALRC-AHEC, 2001. *Protection of Human Genetic Information—Issues Paper*, ALRC, 61.

41 *Protection of Human Genetic Information*. January 2002, *Submission G037*.

42 Ibid., 6.

43 See Otlowski, M. 2003, ibid., 380.

44 January 2003, *Submission G308*. untitled.

45 The unions surveyed in this way were the Association of Professional Engineers, Scientists, and Managers, Australia, Australian Education Union, Australian Manufacturing Workers' Union, Australian Nursing Federation, Australian Workers' Union, Communications Electrical and Plumbing Union, Community and Public Sector Union, Construction Forestry Mining and Energy Union, Finance Sector Union, Liquor Hospitality and Miscellaneous Workers Union, National Tertiary Education Union, National Union of Workers, New South Wales Nurses' Association, Rail Tram and Bus Union, Shop Distributive and Allied Employees Association, and the Transport Workers' Union.

46 This Policy (Position Statement) was reviewed at the 2002 Conference with no significant changes and may form the basis of other union policies should genetic testing become a widespread industrial issue.

47 Position Statement, ibid., p. 1.

48 These trade unions were the Australian Manufacturing Workers Union (AMWU), Communications Electrical and plumbing Union (CEPU), Construction Forestry Mining and Energy Union (CFMEU), and the New South Wales Nurses Association (NSWNA).

49 See note 41.

ASTRID H. GESCHE

PROTECTING THE VULNERABLE: GENETIC TESTING AND SCREENING FOR PARENTAGE, IMMIGRATION, AND ABORIGINALITY

As healthcare professions, law enforcement agencies, governments, employers, insurance companies, and others rush to utilize genetic information about individuals with whom they interact or have relationships, conflict may arise between different stakeholders. In such circumstances, it may be the function of ethics to balance competing interests and activities, explore alternatives and options, and protect the vulnerable from harm. Ethics may explore and advise on issues of the moral life, but sometimes it needs the backup of constructive policy developments and the investigative, protective, and guiding forces of the law to achieve a more mutually beneficial outcome. This chapter on DNA kinship testing is an example of such merging of forces, namely ethics, policy, and law to protect the vulnerable. It portrays the effects of unethical behaviour on three different stakeholders and makes some recommendations on how to re-establish and protect the moral life.

Genetic kinship testing can create multiple vulnerabilities, all of which can be experienced on an individual, societal, and cultural level. Parentage testing stands as an example where vulnerability to an individual is created by not observing proper consent procedures; genetic identity testing for immigration purposes discusses identity fraud and the potential harm to society; and, lastly, DNA kinship testing of Australia's Aboriginal and Torres Strait Islander peoples demonstrates that it is appropriate to sometimes let the sociocultural triumph over the biological.

1. DNA PARENTAGE TESTING

"Children suffer dad's vengeance"[1] and "Not my son, claims dad"[2]—two recent headlines in the media, two DNA paternity tests, two families in turmoil. A court in Melbourne, Australia, set a precedent by awarding Liam Magill $70,000 in damages, after a DNA test confirmed that one of his children was not his biological child. Magill paid maintenance to his former wife from 1992 to 1999.[3] However, in June 2005, the case was

Michela Betta (ed.), The moral, social, and commercial imperatives of genetic testing and screening. The Australian case, 221–236.

dismissed on appeal by the Supreme Court of Victoria.[4] In the second case, a similar story unfolded. Warren Lucas, a Hobart (Tasmania) bricklayer, ended his marriage after he learnt from another woman that his now 24-year-old child is not his biological child and a DNA test confirmed her story. He too claimed damages,[5] but the case was later settled out of court.[6] In Australia, an estimated 3,000 paternity tests are carried out each year.[7] The number of undetected cases may be much higher. Most paternity tests are sought privately, with the Family Court ordering only a small proportion of these.[8] Eighty-four per cent of children tested are aged 12 years and younger, with an average age of 6.3 years and a median age of 2.5 years.[9] Why do individuals seek out parentage testing? In most cases, DNA parentage testing is performed to establish a genetic relationship between a presumed father and a child. A man may be suspicious that he may not be the biological father of the child who is supposed to be his offspring. If he is paying child support or is seeking custody, he may want to confirm that the child is his. In another scenario, a woman may wish to confirm that her husband or partner is really the biological father of her child. In a third case, a child may seek to establish whether there is a biological link to one or both parents for reasons of identity, family medical history, child support, inheritance, or immigration. Similarly, a child conceived by artificial reproductive technology involving sperm donation may ask for parentage testing in order to obtain more information about his/her genetic identity, ancestry, and family medical history.[10]

Thus, at the centre of DNA parentage testing are children and their families. DNA parentage testing is a form of kinship testing that compares a series of DNA markers in a child with those of another person, usually the child's father. Parentage testing has two possible outcomes, which can be interpreted as: "No, you are definitely not biologically related to the child" or "Yes, you are almost certainly the father." Parentage testing differs from other types of genetic testing (medical, forensic) in that it is a biological test conducted primarily for *social* reasons. Unlike other types of genetic testing, DNA parentage testing usually neither fulfils a diagnostic/therapeutic function nor is it associated with the need to identify a victim of crime. The main function of parentage testing is to confirm or refute paternity. Parentage testing requires sensitivity with regard to the various interests and priorities of fathers, mothers, and children, and the different social and biological relationships that exist in today's families. In earlier times, the family was defined as the legal relationship between a man and a woman. Fatherhood was assumed by the relationship of the man to the mother, because biological paternity could not be proven. The significance of a father–child relationship was primarily a social, not a biological, one. Biological relatedness only began to gain in importance with the introduction of ABO blood group testing.[11] Although demonstrating blood group compatibility between a father and a child was an improvement, its meaningfulness was still very limited, since the majority of people are either blood group A or O. Even when one included other antigen markers on blood cells, such as the Rhesus

(Rh) factor, the tests could not give reliable answers. This uncertainty changed with the advent of DNA paternity testing. DNA analysis can establish with much greater certainty whether parent and child are biologically related. Biological parentage is starting to assume prominence over social parenthood in matters of child custody, child support, inheritance, and so forth.

The psychological impact of paternity testing can be profound. When testing confirms that the male is the biological father of the child tested, formerly suspicious fathers no longer need to be suspicious and can continue being a father to their child. In these cases, there are beneficial outcomes. However, if paternity testing reveals that no biological relationship exists between the male and the child, the potential harms can be serious and far-reaching. Harms can result in several ways. In cases where paternity cannot be confirmed, learning about the test results can be emotionally painful and fuel anger and resentment in fathers as well as older children. It can rupture and destroy established father–child or man–woman relationships; it can stigmatize and discriminate. While the event can have profound implications for both parents, the person who potentially suffers the most is the child being tested. However, the possible negative outcomes for the child are seldom acknowledged. If the test result shows that the child is not the biological offspring of the person requesting parentage testing, the child may lose not only a father but also the wider paternal family. The loss can be traumatic and bewildering for the child, especially when the child's immaturity may make it difficult for him/her to comprehend the issue and the resultant fallout. The child might feel abandoned twice, first by the person the child knew as father and again by the person the child never knew as father—his/her biological father. Furthermore, every time a doctor takes the family medical history, the child will be reminded that half of that history is unknown to him/her. This may cause embarrassment or anxiety. The child may feel resentment towards the mother for bringing about the predicament. Finally, paternal abandonment can lead to economic disadvantage and can profoundly impact on the child's present and future well-being. Numerous other examples could be listed.

The moment a parent takes a biological sample from the child without proper consent for paternity testing, the child becomes a vulnerable person. While a child may not understand the test's implications at a young age, the ramifications of the test may possibly stay with the child for many years to come. Apart from the more obvious harms mentioned above, there may be other, less obvious ones, such as those that might arise when genetic samples and test records are stored in the laboratory archives of the testing laboratories (as discussed in chapter 4). If these archives become inchoate genetic databases, it may create additional future harms, such as loss of genetic privacy and autonomy. This is of special concern, since the vast majority of children tested are minors who are dependent on their parents to make the best choices for them. In cases where consent on behalf of the child is only forthcoming from one parent but not from the other, the child may not only become vulnerable but also feel disempowered and defenceless at the same time. At the centre of DNA paternity testing lies the issue of consent. From 2001 until 2003, the Australian Law Reform Commission (ALRC) and the Australian Health Ethics Committee (AHEC) held a joint inquiry (the "Inquiry") into genetic testing. Both the ALRC and the AHEC are independent Commonwealth government organizations. The ALRC responds to requests by the federal Attorney-General to inquire into certain topics and make recommendations for law reform, if necessary.[12] The AHEC responds to requests by Australia's National Health and Medical Research Council (NHMRC)[13] to inquire into ethical issues regarding research involving humans, promoting ethical standards and developing relevant ethical guidelines. In February 2001, the ALRC and the AHEC were asked by the Attorney-General and by the Minister for Health and Aged Care to jointly examine mainly four areas of human genetic information:[14,15]

1. How to protect the privacy of genetic samples and genetic information?
2. How to prevent unfair discrimination from the use of genetic samples and genetic information?
3. How to balance different ethical considerations that attach to both and maintain high ethical standards of conduct in a number of different contexts?
4. Are changes to the current regulatory framework required?

The inquiry was completed in May 2003 and a final 1,200-page report tabled in the Australian Parliament. Of the 144 recommendations made in the report, it is expected that the majority will eventually be adopted either fully or partially.[16] Amongst others, the Inquiry considered whether legal protection was required for genetic sampling and testing that takes place without the knowledge or consent of the person from whom the sample was taken.[17] In the context of parentage testing, informed consent is an important ethical consideration. In 2000, the *Sydney Morning Herald* reported that in non-accredited laboratories at least 80% of all tests were conducted without the knowledge and consent of the mother[18] and the child. The concept of consent is fundamental in ethics. In order to give informed consent, a person must be fully informed about the purpose, method, risks, and possible outcomes of the test. Furthermore, a person's consent must be voluntary and be obtained without coercion or any other form of inducement or influence. A person should also have the right to withdraw his/her consent at any time. These prerequisites to consent are all based on a person who is competent and who comprehends the information. The question arises: When is a child competent to understand parentage testing and its implications? In Australia, a child is deemed competent and mature at age 18. A grey zone exists for children between 12 and 18 years of age. In this age cohort, some children may comprehend the nature and the implications of testing better than others and may be able to give their consent to genetic testing.[19] The Inquiry recommended that in this age group assessment of maturity and voluntariness should be conducted by an independent professional family and child counsellor, a psychologist, or a social worker. However in their response, the Australian government in 2005 rejected the suggestion and recommended that for consistency reasons the Family Law Act should be followed, which makes its determinations according to what is in the best interest of the child.[20]At the other end of the spectrum are children younger than 12 years. This age group comprises the majority of children who undergo genetic parentage testing. Children at that age are not regarded competent enough to consent to testing.

Currently, the Family Law Court requires only *one* parent to give consent.[21] In the ALRC-AHEC report's view, in future, *both* parents have to give their consent.[22] This acknowledges that both share the responsibility to act in the best interest of their child. In the interim, the amending Family Law Regulations 2004 (Cth), which commenced operation on 23 December 2004, should prescribe that a parent or guardian must swear or affirm that he/she consents to the taking of a genetic sample from a child. Considering the many potential serious repercussions, the ALRC-AHEC report recommended to make genetic testing without the consent of either the person being tested, or, in the case of minors, without the consent of *both* parents, a new criminal offence.[23] In its response, the government accepted the recommendation.[24] Criminal liability will also attach to any person or corporation that conducts genetic parentage testing without lawful authority.[25] The ALRC-AHEC final report provided the following rational.

Firstly, non-consensual genetic testing can lead to the disruption or destruction of family relationships and "harmony," "may compromise significant interests" that merit protection under the law, and does not respect the autonomy of the person or his/her individual freedom.[26] The latter is the foundation for protecting privacy and providing the grounds for remedies for the harm caused by any breaches of privacy. Secondly, existing legislation does not provide sufficient protection against the non-consensual collection and testing of genetic samples. One reason is that section 16E of the Privacy Act 1988 (Cth)[27,28] (Privacy Act) exempts the collection of personal information and samples for "personal, family or household affairs."[29] A further set of privacy measurements are set out in the National Privacy Principles (NPPs),[30] which regulate how private sector organizations can collect, store, use, and disclose personal information. However, it was found that neither the Privacy Act nor the NPPs were adequate for dealing with genetic testing.[31]

At present, individuals use both accredited and non-accredited laboratories for parentage testing. Often parents send genetic samples for parentage testing to offshore testing laboratories to avoid embarrassment and to keep the testing secret. The new criminal offence will extend to offshore testing,[32] which means that parents can no longer submit non-consensual evidence of paternity tests to any courts or to any other organizations in Australia as proof of parentage without the risk of being prosecuted. The new legislation will also seek to address weaknesses in the current laboratory procedures. Accreditation to conduct DNA paternity tests is obtained from the National Association of Testing Authorities (NATA),[33] a body that lays down quality laboratory standards and procedures. The ALRC-AHEC report made the following recommendations: In future, laboratories that conduct DNA paternity tests should have protocols and procedures in place that:[34]

- Confirm the identity and written informed consent of both parents
- Ensure that individuals are made aware of the availability of pre- and post-testing counselling
- Introduce protocols and procedures, which protect the integrity of the sample within the chain of custody
- Lead to improved laboratory protocols regarding reporting of results, the storage of information and samples, record keeping, and quality control mechanisms varied widely in quality and quantity

DNA parentage test kits are also available on the free market ("direct parentage test kits") and so far have not been subjected to much scrutiny. This is unlikely to change. Since these tests are not used for therapeutic use, they do not fall under the Federal Therapeutics Goods Administration (TGA) regulatory oversight. Thus neither quality assurance nor legal and ethical standards can currently be assured when individuals access parentage test kits by mail order from foreign laboratories via the Internet. The ALRC Report 96 recommends that only paternity tests that have been conducted by a NATA-accredited laboratory in accordance with NATA accreditation requirements, and that comply in full with the Family Law Act 1975 and the Family Law Regulations, should be admissible in proceedings.[35] Furthermore, by making genetic testing without consent a criminal offence, the Inquiry ensured that individuals would no longer be able to present these test results in legal proceedings in Australia.[36] DNA parentage testing is a form of kinship testing. Kinship testing is useful not only to confirm or dismiss parentage but also to verify the identity of a person.

2. GENETIC TESTING FOR IMMIGRATION PURPOSES

In Australia two different migration programmes exist: the general migration programme, which covers skilled migration, family migration, and special eligibility migration; and the humanitarian programme, which covers refugees and special humanitarian cases. Most of the streams have further sub-streams. For example, the family stream applies to partner migration, child migration, parent migration, and "other family" migration.[37] Under these arrangements, several immediate relatives (dependent children, spouse, and parents) of a person who has permission to live in Australia can apply for family reunification. Family reunification also applies to the offshore special humanitarian strand of the humanitarian programme. Here, not only immediate family members but also other members of the family unit may be considered, such as orphaned child relations, individuals who come to Australia in order to care for Australian relatives, or legally adopted children. Even children who have not been legally adopted might be able to obtain a visa, if they are recognized as adoptees by "customary" means. Despite these flexible interpretations of family, some individuals who do not, or cannot, satisfy the requirements for a visa for one of the two categories mentioned above resort to illegitimate means to enter and live in Australia. The most common methods of illegal migration into Australia are either to overstay a tourist visa or to arrive in Australia by plane or sea, using false travel and other documents.[38] A less public, but also common, method to enter Australia is identity fraud. Identify fraud is practised all over the world and has become a major national and international problem.[39] Australia has not been immune from these developments, which are costing the Australian community over $1.1 billion per year.[40] Identity fraud occurs when people pretend to be a close family member of an already accepted immigrant living in Australia, or when they assume another person's identity when seeking asylum, or when they arrive in Australia with falsified passports. Other instances have involved women and child trafficking.[41] Sometimes identity fraud remains undetected for a long time. For example, a 2003 investigation revealed that a certificate validation between the Westpac Bank and the New South Wales Registry of Birth, Death, and Marriages resulted in the finding that 13% of the birth certificates did not match the records held in the registry.[42] One way to ascertain whether documents are genuine or not or to establish and verify family relationships is DNA genetic testing. In the Australian migration context, genetic testing has three different purposes, as shown in Table 1.

In Australia, only the first two, parentage/kinship testing and health testing, are used. The third application, DNA biometric identification, is currently under general consideration and may be used in the future.[43] When documentary evidence is either absent or suspicious, the Department of Immigration and Multicultural and Indigenous Affairs (DIMIA) can suggest, but not demand, genetic testing to prove an applicant's identity.[44] However, requesting genetic testing for identification purposes is rare in Australia.[45] In the family stream, DIMIA ordered merely 206 tests in 2001–2003, representing only about 0.5% of the total family migration intake.[46] Most requests are for parentage tests. Other tests establish wider kinship ties[47] or check the relationship between a sponsor and an applicant.[48] DIMIA rarely uses genetic testing to establish identity. This appears to be different from the view held in the Australian community. A recent survey

Table 1. The three different contexts of genetic testing for migration purposes

Type of DNA Testing	Purpose
Parentage and kinship	Confirms family relationships
Health	Supports health assessment
Biometric identification	Uncovers identity fraud

exploring the attitudes of Australians towards genetic testing shows that while 75–77% of respondents would reject genetic testing for themselves (especially with regard to employment or insurance), one in three of this group would support genetic testing for migrants. The authors of the report caution, however, that this may be more indicative of respondents' view on migrants than a "principled position on genetic testing."[49] With regard to the processes, procedures, and standards that should be adhered to when proposing and conducting genetic testing,[50] DIMIA's *Procedures Advice Manual* gives detailed information and guidance. The procedures state that officers should inform the person to be tested as to why the tests are needed, what the procedure entails, and why the tests are conclusive.[51] However and significantly, the manual does not recommend that applicants be counselled on the possible *implications* of genetic testing, an omission the Inquiry found to be problematic.[52,53] It means that persons might not be aware of the possible negative effects of parentage or kinship testing, such as the fracturing or break up of family relationships, the abandonment of children as was outlined in section 1 on parentage testing, or the discovery of adultery—a finding that can be life-threatening for some women from certain ethnic backgrounds. In response to the weaknesses identified, the Inquiry recommended a number of changes, such as:[54,55,56]

- Revising and improving existing DIMIA procedures and their formulation
- Considering potential social and psychological consequences of kinship testing
- Informing applicants about counselling before and after testing[57]
- Improving privacy protection measures of genetic samples
- Exploring legislative backing for genetic testing for immigration purposes

While kinship testing for immigration purposes may be regarded as helpful in establishing the identity of individuals or for clarifying family relationships, it may not be regarded as helpful in other circumstances, e.g., when suggested to establish ethnicity.

3. INDIGENOUS AUSTRALIANS AND DNA KINSHIP TESTING

The Aboriginal people are thought to have arrived in Australia about 40,000–50,000 years ago. Hundreds of tribal groups occupied the continent, each with their own language, laws, and customs. Now, as then, Australia's indigenous peoples have a profound sense of belonging to the land, to fauna and flora, and to their clan and ancestral lineage. They feel connected to the land and all living things through the *Dreamtime*, the spiritual force that explains and sustains life. They see themselves as the custodians of an ancient land and of ancient rituals and codes of conduct preserved and passed on through legends and songs. The first Europeans who arrived in Australia had little understanding and respect for the indigenous populations of Australia. Because they thought them primitive and viewed them with curiosity, they devised a policy of protective separation. This policy required many Aborigines to live on missions. It was thought that this arrangement would protect them from the negative influences of European settlement, such as alcohol, disease, and family breakdowns. The policy of protection was superseded by a policy of assimilation. Assimilation intended to integrate Aborigines into European life. The policy sought to reduce the tension that had built up between Europeans and Aborigines by educating, training, and "socializing" indigenous people. It was especially directed at children.[58] As part of this policy, an estimated one in three[59] to one in ten children[60] were forcefully removed from their families and brought up and educated like white children of European settlers.

The outcomes of both policies were negative. A young Aboriginal woman describes the short- and long-term effects of both policies on her and her community's life as follows:

> I may never know what it's like to be black, but I know what it's like to be Aboriginal. Even now I struggle with that... even with such a strong background in knowing what my culture is about I still fear that I haven't experienced what a lot of people—say my brother, who's very dark skinned, and my mother—have experienced, and does that take away from my validity to be able to speak as a young Aboriginal woman?
>
> This kind of conditioning, I think, is inherent in a lot of Aboriginal people, and in our forefathers, and has come down through policies that were implemented during the times when our parents and our grandparents were on missions, because they were divided up into half-castes and quarter-castes. That was the way that they separated our communities, and people with lighter skin were treated differently. They were treated as special. They could assimilate into the non-Aboriginal community, and this has caused a lot of resentment within our own communities. This was their way of turning our communities and our families against each other, and regardless of whether this is something that we acknowledge now, it's still part of our conditioning, and the way that we think when we look at other people.[61]

Today's policy is directed towards self-determination, advocating a separate political infrastructure and special Aboriginal programmes and services.[62] Bridging the divide between Aborigines and non-Aborigines remains difficult on many levels. Economically, Australian indigenous populations, including the Torres Strait Islander peoples, still belong to the most disadvantaged groups living in Australia. Their living standard remains far below that of other Australians, despite the fact that equal opportunity legislation by the Federal Government introduced special services and targeted programmes to improve their living conditions. Two of these targeted services and programmes are the special Community Housing and Infrastructure Program (CHIP), which granted around $120 million in 2001–2002 for housing[63], and the Aboriginal and Torres Strait Islander Study Assistance Scheme (ABSTUDY), which provides government funding to Aboriginal and Torres Strait Islander students for schooling and tertiary study. In

2000–2001, it made an extra $158 million available in financial assistance for 50,451 eligible students.[64] Special government services and programmes can only be accessed when recipients prove that they are Aboriginal and Torres Strait Islander people. Since the beginning of White settlement in Australia, there have been 67 definitions of "Aboriginal."[65] Early attempts focused mainly on descent. When mixed unions between Aboriginals and European settlers became more complex, a system of "quantum of blood" was introduced in an attempt to indicate how substantial the indigenous proportion of the genetic material was.[66] While Johnston (1991) argues that classifying a person as "Aboriginal" was often a political and strategic decision for both sides, usually to gain some administrative, economic, or political advantage,[67] others provide a different view. In a submission to the United Nations Committee in 2003 on the Rights of the Indigenous Children, the Aboriginal and Torres Strait Islander Social Justice Commissioner writes:

> Control of Aboriginal people through definitions of Aboriginality, and through associated policies, historically amounted to a denial of the citizenship or equality rights of Indigenous people in Australia.... Historically, attacks on the identity of Aborigines have taken many forms but the ultimate aim has not been the denial of identity per se but the denial of other associated rights.[68]

In the early 1980s, the Constitutional Section of the Commonwealth Department of Aboriginal Affairs recommended that a set of three criteria be used to define a person as being Aboriginal:[69]

- Biological relatedness (descent)
- Self-identification as Indigenous or Torres Strait Islander
- Community acceptance of the individual as belonging to their community

This definition was cognisant of the fact that Aboriginal people have an understanding of relatedness that goes beyond the linear genealogical understanding of Europeans and that recognizes the complex, equally important social and cultural kinship ties. Reed (1969), who had an intimate knowledge of the customs and particularities of indigenous people, described such non-linear close family relationship as follows:

> All brothers were equivalent to each other, and sisters to each other. Thus a mother's sister was regarded as equivalent to a mother and was so called. However, the first degree of kinship existed between mother's brothers, not with sisters. Similarly, a father's brother was a father, therefore the sons of [a] father's brothers were also brothers, not as we know them, cousins. Conversely, a nephew who [sic] was the son of a brother and not a nephew but a son.[70]

In addition, within extended families and regional clusters of families, adoptions are a very common practice and adoptees become full family members. Asking an Aboriginal or Torres Strait Islander person to prove his/her genetic descent in order to access special programmes and services has remained controversial to this day.[71] As pointed out by De Plevitz and Croft in 2003,[72] no other disadvantaged group in Australia is required to fulfil a similar three-part test before being able to access government benefits. The three-part test for Aboriginality can be seen as one of *inclusion*, in the sense that a person is included in the pool of potential beneficiaries of programmes and services once he/she meets the prescribed criteria. It can also be seen as a test of *exclusion*. One such example occurred in 2002, when an individual was excluded from playing an active part as an Aboriginal person in Aboriginal political life. In Tasmania, a person who wanted to qualify to stand as candidate to be elected to the Regional Council of the Aboriginal and Torres Strait Islander Commission (ATSIC)[73] had to fulfil the requirements of the Aboriginal and Torres Strait Islander Commission Act 1989 (Cth) (ATSIC Act)[74] and provide evidence that he/she was a *biological* descendent of "an Aboriginal race of Australia." When the Tasmanian Aboriginal Corporation (TAC) doubted the indigenous heritage of an applicant, the applicant called for a DNA test so that he could prove to them his Aboriginality and have their decision to exclude him overturned.[75] However, should and can genetic testing be used to establish Aboriginality or is Aboriginality a social and political construct rather than a biological reality? There seems to be no scientific basis for "race." From a genetic perspective, DNA sequencing of the human genome seems to demonstrate that there is no biological basis for "race." All humans are 99.9% identical. In fact, Lewis[76] asserts that two individuals each belonging to a different "race" are in reality genetically more similar than two members of the same race: "Very few, if any, gene variants are unique to a racial or ethnic group." Within the 0.01% remaining variation, there is only a 5% variation between "races."

Even if there would be a genetic test for "Aboriginality" or "Torres Strait Islander," such a test would have two important limitations in practice. The first and most obvious one would be a biological one, in that appropriate population-specific alleles or valid reference samples for comparison are difficult or impossible to obtain. The second limitation would be sociocultural in character. Given the complex understanding of family in Aboriginal life as described above, especially in relation to adopted children from within extended families,[77] genetic inheritance is not always applicable or appropriate. Humans might all be genetically related, but they are also embedded in a number of ever-increasing circles of cultural, social, and political relationships, one influencing the other, none existing in isolation. Demanding proof of genetic relatedness for the purpose of accessing special programmes and services could be damaging to the personal self-worth, could interrupt group cohesion, and could lead to discrimination. It could also exclude some individuals, who always believed that they were of Aboriginal or Torres Strait Islander descent. Learning that they are not may not only be emotionally and socially destructive but also potentially humiliating and harmful. Using genetic testing as means to establish ethnic affiliation does not appear to be in the best interest of indigenous peoples, because it can isolate, make exceptional what is not, and discriminate. In the case of deceased people, it may also offend tribal morals. In fact, classifying humans according to race is contrary to international human rights principles, as reflected in Article 1.2. and Article 3 of the International Labour Organisation's Indigenous and Tribal Peoples Convention (1989).[78]

Australia's indigenous peoples are no doubt a disadvantaged group and may need to be compensated for past wrongs. However, the use of a "race"-based classification system is questionable, if not paternalistic, inequitable, and discriminatory. Given these historical events, the present scientific realities, and the still uneasy relationship that exists between non-indigenous and indigenous populations to this day, the Australian Institute of Aboriginal and Torres Strait Islander Studies (AIATSIS) suggested that the right to define identity issues and community belonging should remain with the indigenous peoples themselves. Alternatively, indigenous peoples could work together with the legal fraternity to establish "frameworks that are appropriate and relevant for Aboriginal and Torres Strait Islander peoples."[79] Recognizing a lack of scientific basis for race and the sensitivity of the issues, the Inquiry rejected genetic testing to prove indigenous identity and stated that under no circumstances should a person be required to undergo genetic testing to prove or disprove his/her Aboriginality. Such request would constitute racial discrimination against an Aboriginal person. It recommended that the Aboriginal communities themselves should determine matters related to Aboriginal identity[80] in their own way according to their own communities, institutions, and consultation processes.[81] This recommendation transfers autonomy back to the peoples where it belongs. It is an acknowledgement that biological tools, such as genetic testing, are not always appropriate to achieve social, political, and economic goals.

4. CONCLUSION

This chapter by necessity emphasized the possible negative sides of genetic testing, but we should not dismiss the profound positives that are already with us or are waiting on the horizon, especially for medicine and human health. This chapter closed with an illustration of the triumph of the sociocultural over the biological. Genes may have blindly steered us along an evolutionary path to humanness, but our sociocultural development has freed us from instinct and opened our eyes to justice so as to become the creators of our own past, present, and future humanity.

NOTES

1 Sweetman, T. 2004. Children suffer dad's vengeance. *The Courier-Mail*, 2 July 2004, 17.

2 Healy, K. 2004. Not my son, claims dad. *Sunday Herald Sun*, 27 June 2004, available at <http: //www.heraldsun.news.com.au/printpage/0,5481,9965262,00.html>, cited 18 July 2004.

3 Sweetman, ibid.cit.

4 *Magill v Magill* [2005] VSCA 51 (17 March 2005).

5 Healy, ibid.cit.

6 Ritchie, K. 2005. *Court Overturns Paternity Judgement*. Transcript. Thursday, 17 March, Radio National, 5.10 pm, available at <http://www.abc.net.au/pm/content/2005/s1326090.htm>, cited 17 September 2005.

7 Smith, D. 2000. Mothers kept in the dark on paternity tests. *The Sydney Morning Herald*, 27 March 2000, In: Australian Law Reform Commission, *ALRC 96: Essentially Yours: The Protection of Human Genetic Information in Australia*, 2003, Section 35.44, available at <http://www.austlii.edu.au/au/other/alrc/publications/reports/96/>, cited 5 April 2004.

8 ALRC 96, ibid., section 35.44.

9 Ibid., section 35.156 mentions 103 cases in 2000–2001.

10 Paternity testing can also be used to prove maternity. But these cases are rare. This might be the case where a child has been separated from his/her mother shortly after birth, or where maternity needs to be proven in the context of immigration.

11 Sussman, L. N. 1976. *Paternity Testing by Blood Grouping*. Springfield, MA: Thomas. For a diagrammatic explanation see: Natural Toxins Research Center. Classnotes. *Blood Group Antigens: The History Behind the Blood Group in Humans*. Kingsville, TX: A&M University, available at <http: //ntri.tamuk.edu/ immunology/blood.html>, cited 19 July 2004.

12 Opeskin, B. 2002. Ten signposts to better law reform in relation to human genetic information. Conference Paper. Einshac and the Istituto di Psicolgia Conference, Rome, 21–22 March, available at <http://www.alrc.gov.au/events/speeches/BRO/20020322.htm>, cited 8 July 2004.

13 The National Health and Medical Research Council (NHMRC) is an independent statutory authority that allocates Commonwealth funding for medical research, provides guidelines and advice on matters relating to human health, healthcare, public and medical health research, and health ethics, and promotes community debate on certain issues. National Health and Medical Research Council Act 1992. Section 7, available at <http: //scaleplus.-law.gov.au/ html/pasteact/0/379/0/ PA000130.htm>, cited 7 July 2004.

14 ALRC 96, 2003, ibid., Terms of Reference.

15 Opeskin, ibid..

16 Ibid.

17 ALRC 96, 2003, ibid., section 12.1.

18 Smith, D. 2000. Mothers kept in the dark on paternity tests. *The Sydney Morning Herald*, 27 March 2000. Cited in ALRC 96, 2003., ibid., section 35.159.

19 However, a court can overrule the child's decision if it finds the decision as not to be in the interest of the child. But most people who ask for paternity testing of their offspring shy away from the court system, because they fear losing and humiliation, because they perceive the family court to be biased against males, and because of costs. However, costs can be kept to a minimum by applying not to a court but instead to a Federal Magistrate, who will assess the application and determine whether the person has an "honest, bona fide and reasonable doubt as to the child's parentage." ALRC 96, 2003. ibid., sections 35.149 and 35.151.

20 Australian Law Reform Commission and Australian Health Ethics Committee Report. Essentially Yours: The Protection of Human Genetic Information in Australia. Government Response to Recommendations, 2005. http://www.ag.gov.av/agd/www/agdhome.nsf/HlDocs/DFC5F37153385647CA2570CA0076BC77? Open Document, 20 March 2006.

21 Essentially Yours (2003), op.cit. section 35.157.

22 Ibid., section 35.170.

23 Ibid., Recommendations 12–1. and 12–2.

24 Government Response to Recommendations, 2005, op. cit. response to recommendation 12.1.

25 Essentially Yours (2003), op. cit., section 12.55.

26 Ibid., sections 12.14–12.16 and 12.

27 Commonwealth ("Cth").

28 Privacy Act 1988, available at <http://www.privacy.gov.au/publications/privacy88_030504.pdf>, cited 20 July 2004. The Privacy Act 1988 provides a privacy framework for Commonwealth agencies and agencies residing in the Australian Capital Territory. It also applies to private sector organizations earning more than $3 million annually, health service providers, and small businesses, which trade in personal information. The Act covers primarily the "collection, use and disclosure, quality and security of personal information." Lawlink NSW, available at <http://www.lawlink.nsw.gov.au/lawlink/privacynsw/ll_pnsw.nsf/ pages / PNSW_03_fedprivact>, cited 6 August 2004.

29 Essentially Yours, 2003, op. cit., section 35.116.
30 Australian Government, Attorney-General's Department, 2001/2003. National Privacy Principles, available at <http://www.law.gov.au/WWW/AGDHOME.nsf/AllDocs/RWP4F5346B13D041F55CA256BB40023EB65?OpenDocument>, cited 10 July 2004.
31 Essentially Yours, 2003, op. cit., section 12.23.
32 Ibid., section 12.2.
33 National Association of Testing Authorities, Homepage, available at <http: //www.nata.asn.au/>, cited 20 July 2004.
34 Essentially Yours, 2003, op. cit., sections 11.25–11.49 and Recommendations 11-1–11-4.
35 Essentially Yours, 2003, op. cit., recommendation 35–4.
36 Ibid., Recommendation 35–101.
37 Department of Immigration and Multicultural and Indigenous Affairs. Migrating as a family member, available at <http://www.immi.gov.migration/family/index.htm>, cited 25 July 2004.
38 Graycar, A. 2000. Human smuggling. Speech presented at: Symposium on Human Smuggling. Centre for Criminology. The University of Hong Kong. 19 February 2000, available at <http://www.aic.gov.au/conferences/other/graycar_adam/2000–02-humansmuggling.html>, cited 18 July 2004.
39 Graycar, A. 2002. Identity-related fraud: risks and remedies. Institute of Criminology Conference Paper, available at <http://www.aic.gov.au/conferences/other/graycar_adam/2002–04-idfraud.pdf>, cited 10 July 2004.
40 Australian Government. Attorney-General's Department, 2004. Development of biometrics for border control. Media release, available at <http://www.ag.gov.au/www/budget Home2004.nsf/Web+Pages/E7E7B479D869E837CA256E91000A03E3?OpenDocument>, cited 10 July 2004.
41 No reliable statistical data are available. For an overview on trafficking in the sex industry, see Hearn, J. 2003. *Trafficking and the Sex Industry: From Impunity to Protection.* Current Issues Brief No. 28 2002–2003. Commonwealth of Australia, available at <http://www.aph.gov.au/library/pubs / cib/2002–03/03cib28.pdf>, cited 12 July 2004.
42 Cuganesan, S. and Lacey, D. 2003. Identity fraud in Australia: an evaluation of its nature, cost and extent, available at <http://www.austrac.gov.au/publications/identity_fraud/identity_fraud_extract.pdf>, cited 11 July 2004.
43 Essentially Yours, 2003, op. cit., section 37.3.
44 Department of Immigration and Multicultural and Indigenous Affairs, 2004. DNA Testing, available at <http://www.immi.gov.au/migration/family/dna.htm>, cited 26 July.
45 While DIMIA rarely uses genetic testing to establish identity, Salleh (2005) reports that a recent survey exploring the attitudes of Australians towards genetic testing seems to indicate that a substantial proportion (37%) of the Australian public would agree with genetic testing on immigrants, even though more than half would not want to undergo genetic testing for employment or insurance purposes themselves. Salleh, A. 2005. Support for DNA tests on migrants. ABC Science Online, 15 August 2005, available at <http://abc.net.au/science/news/health/HealthRepublish_1436435.htm>, cited 17 September 2005.
46 Essentially Yours, 2003, op. cit., section 37.16.
47 Ibid., section 37.17.
48 Ibid.
49 Barlow-Stewart, K., Treloar, S., and Taylor, S. 2004. Knowing your genetic information—Freedom, burden or power. Paper presented at a workshop sponsored by the Academy of the Social Sciences in Australia, Canberra, 7–8 June, available at <http://www.assa.edu.au/policy/papers/2004/ genetic.pdf>, cited 18 September 2005.
50 Department of Immigration and Multicultural and Indigenous Affairs, *Procedures Advice Manual* (*PAM3*) (1994–2002), DIMIA, Canberra Div 1.2 r 1.12, Member of the Family Unit. Cited in ALRC Report 96, 2003, ibid., section 37.12.
51 Essentially Yours, 2003, op. cit., section 37.30.
52 Ibid., section 37.35.
53 Ibid., Recommendation 37–1.
54 Ibid., section 37.13.

55 Ibid., Recommendation 37–2.
56 Ibid., section 37.36.
57 Ibid., section 37.62.
58 Johns, G. 2003. The gulf between aboriginal policies and aboriginal people in Australia, available at <http://www.bennelong.com.au/papers/Articles/chile/GaryJohnsChile.pdf>, cited 18 July 2004.
59 National Inquiry into the Separation of Aboriginal and Torres Strait Islander Children from their Families (Australia). *Bringing them home*. Human Rights and Equal Opportunity Commission, Sydney, 1997, Chapter. 2. Cited in De Plevitz, L. and Croft, L. 2003.. Aboriginality under the microscope: the biological descent test in Australian Law. *QUT Law & Justice Journal*, 3 (1): 13, available at <http: //www.law.qut.edu.au/about/ljj/ editions/v3n1/ deplev_ full.jsp>, cited 17 July 2004.
60 Australian Bureau of Statistics. 1994. *Characteristics of the Aboriginal and Torres Strait Islander Population*. Family and culture. 1997. Catalogue 4190.0, Canberra: AGPS. Cited in De Plevitz and Croft, ibid.
61 Aboriginal and Torres Strait Islander Social Justice Commissioner, Human Rights and Equal Opportunity Commission of Australia. 2003. *Submission to the United Nations Committee on the Rights of the Child for their Day of General Discussion on the Rights of Indigenous Children: Issue 1: Identity and culture*, available at <http://www.hreoc.gov.au/social_justice/croc/sub1.htm>, cited 15 July 2004.
62 Johnsky. 2003, op. cit., Johns believes that there is no guarantee that this approach will be successful either, believing that it may be divisive and again lead to separation.
63 Trewin, D. 2003. *Year Book Australia*. Australian Bureau of Statistics, Canberra: Commonwealth of Australia, 247.
64 Ibid., 300–301.
65 Royal Commission into Aboriginal Deaths in Custody, *National Report* (1991), Commonwealth of Australia: Canberra [11.12.5], cited in Essentially Yours, 2003, op. cit., Chapter 36, p. 3.
66 Australian Law Reform Commission. *The Recognition of Aboriginal Customary Laws*, Report 31. 1986, Australian Government Publishing Service: Canberra [89].
67 Johnston, E. 1991. Royal commission into aboriginal deaths in custody. *National Report*. Commonwealth of Australia: Canberra [11.12.20]. Cited in ALRC 96, 2003, op. cit.
68 Aboriginal and Torres Strait Islander Social Justice Commissioner. 2003, ibid.
69 Australian Government. Department of the Parliamentary Library. 2000–2001. The definition of aboriginality. Research Note, Number 18, available at <http://www.aph.gov.au/library/pubs/rn/2000–01/01rn18.pdf>, cited 18 July 2004.
70 Reed, A. W. 1969. *An Illustrated Encyclopaedia of Aboriginal Life*. Brookvale: Literary Productions, 132.
71 De Plevitz, L. and Croft, L. 2003, op. cit.
72 Ibid.
73 ATSIC was created by the Australian Federal Parliament in 1992 in order, amongst others, to advise the minister on Aboriginal and Torres Strait Islander matters, and to formulate, implement, and monitor programmes for Aboriginal and Torres Strait Islander people; Aboriginal and Torres Strait Islander Act 1989 (Cth), available at <http://www.austlii.edu.au/au/legis/cth/consol_act/aatsica1989478/s7.html>, cited 17 July 2004.
74 Essentially Yours, 2003, op. cit., section 36.23.
75 Bevilacqua, S. 2002. Aboriginality under the microscope, *Sunday Tasmanian*, 17 February 2002, 6–7. Cited in De Plevitz, L. and Croft, L. 2003, op. cit.
76 Lewis, R. 2003. *Human Genetics: Concepts and Applications*, 5th edn. New York: McGraw-Hill, 7.
77 Australian Institute of Aboriginal and Torres Strait Islander Studies, *Submission G286*, 16 December 2002. Essentially Yours, op. cit., section 36.63.
78 Office of the High Commissioner of Human Rights. 1989. Convention (No. 169) concerning indigenous and tribal peoples in independent countries. Entered into force on 5 September 1991, available at <http: // www.unhchr.ch/html/menu3/b/62.htm>, cited 12 July 2004.

[79] Australian Institute of Aboriginal and Torres Strait Islander Studies. *Submission G286*, 16 December 2002. Cited in Essentially Yours, 2003, op. cit., page 2.

[80] Essentially Yours, 2003, op. cit., section 36.71.

[81] Ibid., section 36.74.

LYN TURNEY

ESSENTIALLY WHOSE? GENETIC TESTING AND THE OWNERSHIP OF GENETIC INFORMATION

In March 2003, following extensive public consultation, the Australian Law Reform Commission (ALRC) and the Australian Health Ethics Committee (AHEC) produced their final report entitled: *Essentially Yours: The Protection of Human Genetic Information in Australia* (ALRC-AHEC, 2003). The Commission made many recommendations according to the main theme encapsulated in the title that clearly preserve the right of individuals to ownership of their own genetic information. In doing so, the Commission endorsed the universal application of the broad ethical values of "protecting the integrity of the person, human dignity, autonomy and the individual's right to consent"[1] to all forms of genetic testing, including paternity testing. However, they also acknowledge that the information revealed through genetic testing not only applies to individuals but also has implications for families, kinship, and racial groupings and for populations. Each of these mainly social groupings comprises individuals with distinct often conflicting rights and interests. This chapter provides an overview of the broader legal, ethical, and social issues associated with genetic testing, specifically in relation to the ownership of the information revealed. It outlines individual, group, and collective investments in the knowledge that genetic testing reveals, arguing that genetic information, except perhaps in the context of forensic profiling, is never entirely individual information. It then takes paternity testing as a specific but exceptional case of genetic testing that illustrates the complexities involved in applying existing ethical and legal frameworks to genetic information about the primary relationship between father and child. The popularly canvassed notion of mandatory paternity testing at birth is examined as an example of the collision of individual, family, and collective interests.

Michela Betta (ed.), The moral, social, and commercial imperatives of genetic testing and screening. The Australian case, 237–246.

1. GENETIC TESTING AND INFORMATION ABOUT THE INDIVIDUAL

The most common use of genetic screening and testing is for identifying medical conditions. Testing in this context is primarily conducted to assess individual information about health, i.e., the diagnosis of a genetic disease and the potential for either developing a disease or being a carrier of a disease condition. Ethical and legal issues are framed around individual autonomy and the individual's right to know about their health status, their right to consent to testing, and their right to privacy in relation to any genetic information collected. One of the main concerns for individuals is finding out through testing that they are carrying the gene or genes for a serious disease that they will inevitably get but which is untreatable.[2] Added to this is the predictive nature of genetic tests, their unique ability to indicate the propensity for developing a particular disease in the future. Although the person diagnosed with a suspect gene may not actually develop the disease and be in good health, any information about genetic disease status has consequences for future decisions around partnering, reproduction, work, and finances. Furthermore, when the individual is informed of their predisposition to a particular disease, they are likely to join the ever-increasing ranks of the "worried well," people who become overly absorbed in monitoring health and lifestyle to ward off the possibility of ill health in the future. Alternatively, such knowledge may lead to individuals taking a fatalistic approach: rather than attempting to reduce risks by changing behaviour, they tempt fate in the belief that a genetic condition is hardwired and totally beyond their control[3]. Sociologist Evan Willis[4] highlighted a further concern about the social effects of individual decisions made in antenatal screening and testing procedures. The collective effect of individual decisions about whether or not to abort a foetus with certain disease conditions is effectively eugenic in outcome because it rules out whole categories of people who are medically deemed to be defective. Furthermore, these seemingly individual decisions are in essence contributing to a change in the nature of the kind of society we are, one that is increasingly less tolerant of people with disabilities and less supportive of parents who choose *not* to abort a defective, high-cost, and resource-intensive child when they have the opportunity to do so.

Individual testing for both dominant and recessive disorders inevitably reveals information about the genetic status of other family members. What this means is that someone who tests positive also finds out that other family members could be at risk of developing or passing on a serious genetic disorder. What rights and responsibilities does a person have to disclose such information? What right does a relative have *not* to know? The revelation of this information also presents a problem for geneticists and genetic counsellors who are privy to information about serious diseases that will affect other family members, especially in situations where early intervention can prevent degeneration and death. There is clearly an ethical conflict between preventing harm and the person's right to confidentiality, privacy, and ownership of genetic information. Perhaps the most individual of all genetic tests is genetic profiling, which is used for forensic purposes to match samples that profilers suspect or expect will be from the same person. This technology matches banding patterns of an individual's DNA against another sample, perhaps collected at a crime scene. The test is conducted on non-coding or "junk" DNA, which, erroneously it seems, was thought by scientists to contain no health information but which contains repetitive coding sequences unique to each individual. The test is simpler and quite different from the one used in medical testing but, because of the ubiquity of DNA, there are concerns that the samples potentially could be used in other ways to reveal medical information. Despite objections about privacy from civil libertarians, there is widespread public acceptance of the use of genetic profiling techniques in the identification of criminals or human remains.[5] The main ethical and legal concerns, especially in the context of "dragnet" testing of a specified and entire population defined by residency or occupation, are ensuring the deletion from the database of information about non-criminals incidentally tested, or those innocently caught up in a dragnet operation. Nonetheless, genetic data banks for DNA data matching are generally considered to be a positive advancement in crime detection and prevention.

2. GENETIC DATA BANKS AND POPULATION-BASED INFORMATION

The building of genetic data banks for medical purposes is somewhat more contentious as it raises different legal and ethical issues. As the ALRC-AHEC report pointed out, genetic samples can be tested for conditions other than that for which the material was collected. This means that once an individual has had any DNA test done, that sample can be used as a permanent record of the person's entire genome, one that contains unique identity and very private health information. Unless these samples can be protected from unauthorized use, their very existence allows the potential for others to use them for further testing in relation to the entire range of disease conditions, for research purposes and for population level information. For example, the Guthrie blood test, used to detect a common genetic disorder PKU, has been conducted since the 1970s on all Australian newborn babies making it a huge, permanent, and scientifically valuable data bank.[6] Although all young people born in Australia under the age of 35 have their genetic information stored in a database, most of them would be unaware that it exists or that it is used for research. In the state of Victoria, for example, Genetic Health Services Victoria, a private non-profit organization that legally owns the screening cards of more than 2 million children, was investigated regarding the release of excess DNA samples from this database to researchers[7]. Although samples were de-identified and the data used for beneficial health research, its very existence raises concerns about privacy and ownership of genetic information, lack of knowledge about, and consent to, the use of samples for purposes other than that for which they were given and collected. It also raises issues about its potential use for genetic health surveillance, something fiercely debated in Europe when the Icelandic government passed legislation authorizing the establishment of a national health database sponsored financially by private enterprises through DeCode Genetics Inc. In this project, health-related data were (and continue to be) collected from the entire population of public and private patients in Iceland when they have medical treatment. The project raised ethical questions about informed consent, the power of government, and the rights of the patient. It especially brought to light an emerging conflict of interest for the clinician, whose imperatives to collect data for research may be at odds with his/her duty of care to the patient.[8]

3. GENETIC TESTS, CONFIDENTIALITY, AND THIRD PARTY ACCESS TO INFORMATION ABOUT GENETICS

Because an individual's DNA can be extracted at the cellular level from physical traces, such as sweat, saliva, or hair, there are concerns about third party usage of genetic information, particularly by health insurance companies and the workplace.[9] The ALRC-AHEC accepts that the interests of insurers are likely to (and should?) dominate any attempt to balance the rights of individuals to health and other insurance cover because they hold the trump card in their determination of whom to insure. However, the potentiality of creating a genetic underclass of uninsured is likely to cause a serious social problem.[10] On the basis of genetic information, including predisposition to a disease, some people are likely to be denied access to both health and housing insurance, the social, financial, and ethical ramifications of which are serious. The situation in relation to workplace access to genetic information, on the other hand, is somewhat less clear according to the ALRC-AHEC. The report points out that there are different and competing interests among employer, employee, and the public in relation to genetic screening, monitoring, and testing in the workplace. There are obvious advantages to the employer in testing to avoid costs associated with unhealthy workers and to demonstrate a duty of care by protecting their workers under mandated Occupational Health and Safety (OHS) legislation. However, the employee has an interest in the protection of his/her bodily integrity, as well as private and familial information, and is likely to be powerless to refuse testing prior to being accepted into employment. Conversely, testing information might empower individual workers to refuse "high-risk" employment. Finally, the ALRC-AHEC points out that public interest may be served through routine genetic monitoring of heart health, drug and alcohol consumption of people (such as pilots and surgeons) in positions that hold responsibility over the health, safety, and well-being of consumers, clients, or patients. Again, this points to the problem of how best to balance individual rights to ownership of genetic information with group and public interests.

4. TESTING RELATIONSHIPS BETWEEN PARENTS AND A CHILD

In contrast to genetic testing used to uncover information about a person's health or to identify an individual's specific genome for forensic purposes, DNA parentage testing checks biological relationships *between* people: between parents and a child. The most common form of these tests is the genetic paternity test. Paternity testing is a particular instance of a range of identity tests that determine relationships between people for immigration, succession to estates, identification of human remains, or racial inclusion or exclusion. The test itself shares more similarity with forensic testing than medical testing. It is a special case of genetic testing that reveals information about paternity as a biological fact normatively expected to coincide with the social role of fatherhood. As such, it reveals biological information about the relationship of a man to a child, whereas testing the mother provides no new information. Although children have the greatest stake in a paternity test conducted to reinforce or deny a primary relationship, in most cases they are too young to give an informed consent to being tested against their father's DNA. The ALRC-AHEC report, in applying the same principles as with medical testing, has recommended that paternity testing should not be conducted without the consent of both parents. It made this recommendation on the assumption that paternity testing disrupts intact family relationships. In practice, except in the case of incidental discovery of non-paternity through genetic carrier screening,[11] paternity testing is usually actively resorted to in conditions of acrimonious relationship breakdown and further contextualized in a volatile and highly politicized social context.[12] This being the case, parents are unlikely to come to a consensus decision about the child's best interest.

5. MANDATORY PATERNITY TESTING AT BIRTH AND THE INTERESTS OF THE CHILD

To avoid the problems associated with knowing the best interests of a child when parents are most unlikely to agree with each other, mandatory paternity testing at birth is commonly put forward in the Australian context as a clear-cut, routine way of determining paternity. It is seen by fathers and mothers caught up in "paternity fraud" scenarios as well as by experts and members of the general public as a relatively non-problematic, child-centred way of averting the issues associated with the potential discovery of non-paternity before a child reaches an age of understanding. However, one of the main problems associated with the discovery of misattributed paternity at this time in a child's life is that it intervenes in an intact parental relationship, perhaps at the happiest time of that relationship. Here, a routine test conducted at birth would reveal confidential biological, social, and relational information that medical personnel would have to convey—knowledge that is highly likely to cause the breakdown of a relationship and dissipation of a family at the cusp of its formation. Although there is no question that a child deserves to know the truth about genetic paternity, mandating the revelation of non-paternity at this vulnerable point in his/her life arguably is detrimental to the child's social well-being. Where testing reveals non-paternity, a baby is denied the possibility of the security and social support of the father he/she would have had in the absence of compulsory testing at birth. This is not to argue that a child should be denied knowledge of their biological origins but that it is difficult to reconcile the interests of the child being served by legislating mandatory testing at the time of birth, especially since he/she cannot yet comprehend truths about paternity. It may, however, be a better strategy to encourage rather than mandate testing at birth. Where there is a possibility of paternal confusion, free, voluntary, and non-judgemental testing could be offered to couples at birth along with supportive counselling. This, together with a broader social acceptance that pregnancy can happen to any sexually active heterosexual person, might allow space, unclouded by double standards, for a man to know about his non-paternity so that he can make a choice at the birth of a child whether or not he goes ahead and becomes a father to the child.

6. TESTING MORAL RELATIONSHIPS BETWEEN PARENTS

At the heart of paternity testing is the presence or absence of a biological relationship between a man and his child. Although the child is central to the reasons for testing, too often the test itself becomes focused on financial, fidelity, and trust relationships between the parents. The effect of this is to marginalize the child as the product of the mother's infidelity whose interests in having a father becomes either irrelevant or of secondary concern. This being the case, there is little doubt that the purported need for universal mandatory testing at birth to check paternity is premised on an assumption that women are likely to be dishonest about paternity with the intention to deceive. It also rests on the questionable postulation that while fathers are said to be never entirely sure of paternity, women always know. In reality, although men are sometimes deceived about paternity, most men *are* certain about it. Conversely, and against conventional wisdom, there are situations where women themselves are uncertain about paternity. This may occur because the woman has indeed been unfaithful, but uncertainty also occurs when there is a short time frame between relationships, overlaps between the end of a relationship and the beginning of a new one or where a relationship disintegrates for a period of time and then resumes[13]. All of these are tenuous or emerging relationships that are unlikely to withstand an open discussion about prior or intervening sexual activities. Indeed, men are similarly unlikely to risk a budding and promising relationship in this way, given that any penetrative sex is potentially productive. Mandatory testing at birth thus intervenes as a check on a woman's fidelity, but importantly, testing for fidelity abrogates trust in relationships, is an insult to all women, and extends and validates the questionable practice of infidelity testing, i.e., testing physical traces, such as a condom, to check a partner's "faithfulness"[14] as if testing were a natural and normative response to suspicion.[15] In practice then, a mandated test at birth to check biological paternity and infidelity would be an unnecessary intrusion into the private lives of couples. The idea underpinning mandatory testing at birth is premised on the criminal model, the dragnet principle, that in testing an entire population, you can identify the good from the bad and catch and punish the latter.

7. PATERNITY DATA BANKS AND MEN'S RIGHTS

Perhaps more important than individual rights and obligations around mandatory testing, though, is the accumulation of a database that would record the genetic profile of every man, woman, and child at the birth of a child. Quite apart from the sheer cost of testing and storing such information, there would be concerns about how such a database would be managed and protected against both authorized and unauthorized use. If concerns are raised about the Icelandic study in relation to the powers of governments over population medical history, there are potentially greater problems associated with either government or private control over a database containing identity information about all men, women, and children. This would be particularly the case for men and their legal and ethical rights around paternity. In calling for mandatory testing at birth, people are inadvertently advocating for a criminal-like database that allows potential paternity to be checked at any time against a previously taken DNA sample. The Australian Family Court, Legal Aid, and Child Support Agency spend a good deal of time and resources pursuing biofathers to submit to testing when they have denied, or are unaware of, paternity. Also, taxpayers are increasingly disinclined to pay for social service provision for single mothers and their children. Should governments decide that the common good is served by overriding an individual's right to bodily integrity, privacy, and ownership of their genetic information, men accused of paternity could be treated in the same manner as potential criminals. Whether a woman names a presumed father or refuses to do so, it would be a relatively simple matter to take the child's sample and run it against the database until a father is identified. Potentially, PKU samples of men under the age of 35 could be used now.[16] If it were legitimated through legislative means, this could be done without the necessity for the consent of either the man or the mother. It would be seen to be conducted in the interests of the "common good." Coercive and cost-effective measures could thus potentially be used as an efficient solution to rectify the problem of fathers defaulting on their financial paternal obligations.

8. ESSENTIALLY WHOSE?

Data banks, as valuable repositories of population genetics, perhaps present the greatest challenge of all to individual ownership of genetic information. They are valuable because they contain profiles of individuals as well as profiles of entire populations and can thus be employed in a variety of ways for the good of humankind. But the very thing that makes them valuable also presents a threat to the autonomous individual. The potential benefits to cost-cutting governments of a data bank of identity information on all men in Australia are obvious. When construed as potentially absconding fathers, all men become legitimate targets of scrutiny; so, should paternity testing be mandated at birth, the ownership of genetic information clearly would not rest with individual men. Because paternity testing tests relationships between a man and a child, the information it produces also belongs to the child whether or not it confirms or denies paternity. Moreover, paternity information has the potential to destabilize and reorganize the family unit and affect broader kinship groupings. It also has the power to legally change paternal responsibility and thus has social and policy implications. The genetic paternity test then is essentially a social, legal, and moral test as much as a biological one. Although this makes paternity testing unique in comparison to other screening and testing procedures discussed above, the issue of contested ownership of genetic material does resonate across all types of testing, including medical testing. The question then perhaps is not "Who owns genetic information?" but how much emphasis should we place on it, how should we interpret what it means to us, and what should we do or allow to be done about it? Because of the ubiquity and stability of DNA, any samples collected contain both health and identity information, regardless of the initial reason for sample collection. The above discussion highlights the ways in which the full range of genetic testing and screening technologies presents a challenge to individual ownership and protection of genetic information.

Genetic knowledge also belongs to families, kinship, and racial groupings and, more contentiously, to populations, governments, researchers, and other organizations. The issue of what to do about genetic information beyond its individual use and application is problematic because it is unlike any other medical or identity information. Genetic information unequivocally links individuals to others but also uniquely and precisely defines and identifies every aspect of the individual. As such it confronts a range of established legal and ethical guidelines that have traditionally focused on individual rights and interests. Customary law and conventional ethics may very well prove to be irrelevant when applied to genetic information. The challenge for lawyers, ethicists, and social scientists may be to entirely re-evaluate and rewrite the rules of policy, law, and ethics to innovate ways in which we might take advantage of genetic information while, at the same time, minimizing the harms associated with contested ownership.

NOTES

[1] ALRC-AHEC, 2003. *Essentially Yours: The Protection of Human Genetic Information in Australia*. Canberra: Australian Law Reform Commission/Australian Health Ethics Committee, 861.

[2] Pilnick, A. 2002. *Genetics and Society: An Introduction*. Buckingham and Philadelphia: Open University Press.

[3] Senior, V., Martineau, T. M., and Peters, T. J. 1999. Will genetic testing for predisposition for disease result in fatalism? A qualitative study of parents' responses to neonatal screening for familial hypercholesterolaemia. *Social Science & Medicine* 48 (12): 1857–1860.

[4] Willis, E. 2002. Public health and the "new" genetics: balancing individual and collective outcomes. *Critical Public Health* 12 (2): 139–151.

[5] Australian Centre for Emerging Technologies and Society. 2003. *Swinburne National Technology and Society Monitor*. Hawthorn: Swinburne University of Technology, available at <http://www.swin.edu.au/sbs/acets/monitor/2003MonitorFULL.pdf>.

[6] Phenylketonuria (PKU) is an inherited genetic disorder that prevents normal breakdown of protein in food. Around 2% of people are carriers of the recessive gene for PKU. The DNA sample from the PKU test is also used to identify other inherited diseases at birth, such as cystic fibrosis (CF), so the samples collected are potentially a repository of valuable population health information. Phillips, G. 2003. Guthrie cards. *Catalyst—ABC TV Science*. 29 May 2003. Print version available at <http://www.abc.net.au/catalyst/stories/s867619.htm>, cited 11 August 2005.

[7] Noble, T. 2004. Genetic company owns up to faults. *The Age*, Melbourne, 3.

[8] Chadwick, R. 1999. The Icelandic database—do modern times need modern sagas? *British Medical Journal* 319 (7207): 441–444.

[9] ALRC-AHEC, 2003, ibid., 651–855.

[10] Pilnick, ibid., 85.

[11] Turney, L. 2005a. The incidental discovery of nonpaternity through genetic carrier screening: an exploration of lay attitudes. *Qualitative Health Research* 15 (5): 620–634.

[12] Turney, L. 2004. Power, knowledge and the discourse of "paternity fraud." *International Journal of the Humanities* 2(1): 223–231.

[13] Turney, L. 2005b. Paternity Secrets: Why women don't tell. *Journal of Family Studies* 11 (2): 227–245.

[14] Wroe, D. 2002. The hazards of dealing with seeds of doubt. *The Age*, Melbourne, 3.

[15] Anderlik, M. R. and Rothstein, M. A. 2002. DNA-based identity testing and the future of the family: a research agenda. *American Journal of Law & Medicine* 28 (2/3): 215–232.

[16] Philips, ibid., 1. The police in Western Australia have already wrongfully accessed the database, an action that led to a Perth hospital destroying all previously collected samples and only storing them for a maximum 2 years. Philips, G. 2003, 1.

III. FUTURE PERSPECTIVE

MICHELA BETTA

SELF-KNOWLEDGE AND SELF-CARE IN THE AGE OF GENETIC MANIPULATION

In this final chapter, we will explore the centrality of ethical practices in the knowledge culture. In the course of this analysis, I will try to describe the opportunities evoked by the "new genetics" as a practice that strengthens the autonomy and well-being of the self. Here I will argue that social life can be improved or even made possible through practices informed by ethics rather than by law. A life guided by ethical practices bases on two fundamental pillars: self-care or the need to care for the self; and self-knowledge or the need to know the truth about oneself. An analysis of the shift that may lead from control to self-governance seems an unavoidable task if we are to understand the condition of possibilities of cultural changes. Changes do not simply target individuals. They go through them investing the body, its spiritual dimension, and its resources, and conversely, they are made possible by the individual's needs to expand. The philosophy of limits belongs to metaphysics. The need for a recreation of the self questions the notion of those limits, revealing the post-metaphysical elements present in our time. A perspective that focuses on the individual as a conscious decision-maker can also be seen as an attempt to understand the new genetics from a different perspective, moving away from biopolitics and its disciplinary devices, and directing our attention towards an analytic of power that reinforces the role of the individual, as an ethical subject, in social relations. This book opens with the statement that it is technology and scientific advancements that revolutionize society and culture. Now it appears safe to say that, although science and technology or better scientists and inventors do bring new forms and objects into perspective, they do not fully understand what they do. Put another way, scientists and inventors not only cannot solve the ethical dilemmas they cause but they do not even know how to pose such problems. Here different actors are required who are capable of identifying the processes through which changes occur and assemblages emerge, substituting previous crystallizations of powers. Therefore, it is worth exploring whether, during this shift, the individual can strategically position herself/himself between the imperative of control and the imperative of freedom.

Michela Betta (ed.), The moral, social, and commercial imperatives of genetic testing and screening. The Australian case, 247–256.

1. THE ETHICAL SUBJECT—A HISTORICAL EXCURSION

For many centuries science has been attracted to the mysteries of life in an attempt to unveil them and so claim to be the sole interpreter of life processes. Science is now claiming the additional role of being a shaper or creator of postmodern society through subtle biomanipulations of the vital processes of our bodies. It seems that the body and its resources are moving again towards the centre of our thinking. This is not to say that it did not play a central role before the "advent" of new genetics. As Foucault reminds us in his monumental work, the body has always been an object of scientific analysis and speculations and a knowledge component of western culture. This has been true since the emergence of modern science and modernity, when, according to Foucault (1989),[1] the human being "begins to exist within his organism, inside the shell of his head, inside the armature of his limbs, and in the whole structure of his physiology." This is the moment at which western culture's scientific mode of being puts an end to metaphysics—a shift that represents only the negative side of a more complex event, namely the appearance of the individual as a "knowing subject and the object of knowledge." In the 18th century the conceptualization of the body as a "machine" led to the possibility of the body being opened to mechanical rearrangement and tuning, and further to the idea of "political anatomy" where the small features of life become subject to close analysis. Such intervention, which Foucault calls "discipline," transformed individuals into "cases." The cases are later converted into "case notes." It is true that through this work on the individual "the body loses its mystery" (Burrel 1998); but it never remains the sole governor of the existence of the individual. This because it is not the body as such that becomes the target and the medium of discipline. The contrary is probably true, that it is the soul that becomes objectified and, for that very reason, capable of capturing the body. In Foucault's (1977) words: "The soul is the effect and instrument of a political anatomy; the soul is the prison of the body." If biopolitics and biopower had only taken the body as the sole reference of their practices in order to become the essential mode of governing individuals and the species since the 18th century, it would not have taken two centuries to install the governing strategies that have led to the present time. There would have been no need to display the subtle politics of belonging and exclusion so well known to us. To govern a body is not a difficult task. But when the body is more than its resources, functions, desires, and needs, its governance is more difficult, sometimes even impossible, without working hard on the individual/s.

We have seen this happen in the bourgeois culture with its self-affirmative style and bodily politics differentiating it from the aristocratic culture, so much preoccupied with its ancestors, and in demonstrating the continuity of the bloodline. To aristocracy the past was more important than the present. The future existed only in terms of alliances and family strategies capable of assuring continuity and legitimacy based on aristocratic blood. In modernity, the blood of the aristocracy turns into the health and genetic patrimony of the bourgeoisie to which the descendants and their health were of fundamental importance. Sexual exclusivity, guaranteed by the family structure, would create the condition for proper legitimacy. The future, offspring and genealogy, was more important than the past. As Foucault (1998) argues, "the bourgeoisie's 'blood' was its sex." But to reach this stage a complex system of affirmation and governance of the body of the individual and the body of the population was necessary. The body was instrumental in the emerging modern society and for its social disciplines/policies, and biopolitics was the strategy that shaped new devices for the governing of the individuals and their private lives as well as the population and the generations. Consequently, there were rigorous interventions against promiscuity and strict governance over sexuality. Sexuality must be understood here as the discourse that installs the condition for guaranteeing the reproduction of the species. But it must be understood as a way of initiating a process leading to self-knowledge too. Especially when sexuality was understood in terms of a secret, of something lying somewhere in the depth of the body that had to be unveiled or "discovered" in order to be properly understood and governed. Here psychoanalysis must be understood as the way in which the emerging modern elite tried to discover their own sexuality, the secret of its moral and immoral desires, and the way of governing them through a discursive practice targeting the self, the care of the self and of the species. Psychoanalysis had the task of "alleviating the effects of repression," of course for those who where in the social position to refer to it. It will take long before psychoanalysis turns into a governing practice for the mass.[2]

The entrance of sexuality into the political discourse surrounding the population as well as the health and safety of the generations, however, was not such an inevitable phenomenon. Why sexuality and not something else, say, sport or diet? Indeed diet had been one of the main preoccupations of antiquity, especially of old Greek and Roman medicine. The dietetics of alimentation, alimentary abstention and fasts, as well as alimentary prescriptions, represent the fundamental mode of expression of an entire civilization and its practices. Such practices were challenged daily by the fragility of the human body and the danger of sexual practice, causing philosophers and physiologists to praise the "positive effects of sexual abstention." In his 1988 book *The Care of The Self: The History of Sexuality 3*, Foucault[3] describes the concerns that antiquity placed on the care of the self, as a practice that would allow the individual to create a system of self-governance capable of increasing his/her use of the bodily resources and, at the same time, to play a more productive role in public life. The preoccupation with one's own physical and mental health must therefore not be understood as a retreat to privacy, as perhaps suggested by Starkey and McKinlay (1988),[4] who argue that the practices of self-care were located in the "interstices of power." Undeniably, Foucault uses that expression, but he does this in the best Foucauldian style. The interstices of power have to be understood as a sort of local and peripheral knowledge, something that escapes the codification of established/official knowledge-power. He never speaks of the interstices of power in terms of a place where hidden practices of the care of the self can be displayed. In one of his 1976 lectures at the *Collège de France*, Foucault (2003) underlines that power exists through networks and individuals who are never inert or consenting targets of power. In other words, power "passes through" individuals; it is not applied to them.

In *The Care of the Self*,[5] Foucault expressly says that, in ancient times, one of the most important aspects of the activity devoted to oneself was that it constituted not an exercise in solitude, but a true "social practice." The care of the self takes form in more or less institutionalized ways; it reflects an intensification of "social relations." The benefits of the cultivation of the self are not just private. The notion of the care of the self is a key element in a political life that aims at establishing a system capable of putting the self in the condition of knowing how to properly conduct oneself; only through this self-knowledge will the individual be capable of leading others. "The art of governing oneself becomes a crucial political factor," because it will constitute oneself as an ethical subject with regard to the social, civic, and political activities of the communities in which the self is embedded. But how is the practice of the care of the self displayed, and how does it work on the individuals? There are two central elements of the ethics of self-care: the body and the soul. Body and soul are interrelated in so far as the problems affecting the former have negative effects on the latter. The practices of the self culminate in one point—at which the ills of the body and those of the soul can "communicate with one another and exchange their distresses." Here Foucault discovers an important "truth"—in the ancient culture the soul does not "operate" as the prison of the body, but it is an accomplice that can help create an ethical subject or undermine this operation. Modernity will transform it into the privileged platform on which discipline and control shape the bodies of the organized and working society.

In ancient culture, the practices of self-care bring ethics and medicine closer than ever. The increased medical involvement in the cultivation of the self found expression in a particular and intense form of attention to the body. "Between medicine and ethics, there is the inducement to acknowledge oneself as being ill or threatened by illness." What seems to happen in the art of an existence preoccupied with oneself is the emergence of a discipline that does not derive from surveillance and normalizing power, but from a desire to cultivate the self in order to better perform in public life. It is a change in the perspective that gives individuals their power back, which will make them strong enough to respond to political challenges; in other words, the leading principle will lie in self-knowledge. Improvement will be assessed through "testing procedures" capable of demonstrating what virtues have been acquired as well as the degree of maturity reached by the individual in the process leading up to self-governance. The necessity to organize and manage one's personal life through the body seems, at this stage, less an attempt to radicalize control over oneself than an intensification or a "disparagement of the body" in a context in which organism, soul, health, environment, and circumstances (the interrelation between body and environs) contributed to the success or failure of the attempt to create an ethical individual. The liaison between ethics and medicine happens to facilitate this bodily disparagement. In antiquity, sexuality was considered the criterion by which the care of the self is tested, representing the limit, the dimension in which the weakness of the soul and the temptation of the body can be tested and repaired. Sexuality represents the risk dimension: if exercised in excess or at the wrong moment, it could put the physical and mental health under serious pressure. Conversely, diet and alimentation represent the way by which one cares for one's own well-being and, consequently, for the soul. Therefore, self-restraint or even abstinence in sexual matters, which is equivalent to a specific self-governance, is considered the perfect system. This cultivation of the self is inherent in a regimen medicine.

As noted earlier in the chapter, it will take European societies a very long time to replace these practices revolving around food and alimentary regimes with sex and sexuality, and the governance of desire. But as soon as this shift occurs, different technologies of the self will appear in the social and cultural landscape. In his article "Technologies of the Self" (1988)[6], Foucault reminds us that "as there are different forms of care, there are different forms of self." And therefore the different accent that modernity poses on the technologies of the self contrasted with that of antiquity and produced a different ethical self, although it represents an improvement compared with the technologies of the self that take place in Christian society, in which the individual is expected to deny the self and demonstrate complete obedience to someone else. In this text Foucault makes a very interesting remark with regard to an inversion of patterns in the politics of the self. In the past, one had to take care of oneself in order to have knowledge of oneself, while in modernity knowing oneself constitutes the fundamental principle of self-care. The consequence of the past turns into the fundamental principle in modernity. But what sort of hierarchy is emerging from the new assemblages that we have identified in the chapters of this volume? Are we taking care of ourselves in order to get more knowledge about ourselves, or are we applying the principle "know thyself" in order to take care of ourselves in a society that has lately been described as a knowledge society? Another striking remark made by Foucault (1988), while describing past ethical practices towards oneself, is that "permanent medical care is one of the central features of the care of the self. One must become the doctor of oneself."

2. SELF-IMPROVEMENT AND THE CARE OF THE SELF

How can we now link these notions and practices with the genetic practices and trends already manifest in our time? In their remarkable 2004 article "Human growth hormone and the temptation of biomedical enhancement",[7] Peter Conrad and Deborah Potter speak of genetic enhancement as one of the self-improvements inherent in our culture. The two authors elaborate on the meaning of genetic enhancement by differentiating between treatment, enrichment, and enhancement as such. This differentiation is made necessary by the very definition of health which has to be understood as "socially situated, flexible, and may ultimately be a mirage."[8] Conrad and Potter engage in a debate that we have encountered in chapter 1 on human nature and liberal eugenics, and maintain that the line dividing biomedical therapy and enhancement is a fine one. Developing a definitional grid that differentiates between normalization, repair, and performance edge, the two authors describe the forms that enhancement can take in a society that is "moving toward a new notion of normality." Through normalization the body is successfully repositioned according to personal or cultural expectations. An example here could be plastic surgery or genetic enhancement for aesthetical reasons. Through practices aiming at repairing parts of the body, genetic enhancement "takes the current body to places where it no longer exists." Finally, the two authors describe intervention or enhancement that work on the spirit and describe drugs such as Prozac, Paxil, and Ritalin.

A fundamental line of reasoning taken by Conrad and Potter is that the enhancement is not inherent in the biomedical composition, "but in when and how the intervention is used." Here the article takes a little turn. It seems that the authors have not successfully managed to link their premises with their analysis. On the one hand, they maintain that the "social forces driving biomedical enhancement are strong," including science, medicine, commerce, and culture, while on the other, they argue that biomedical enhancements are "inherently conservative." This statement somewhat contradicts their initial assumptions in which they suggest that genetic enhancements reposition the body or take it "where it has never been before." How can a practice that installs something new be conservative? It would be different if, instead of genetic enhancement we had cloning. Indeed, cloning can safely be described as a conservative practice that reproduces, or intends to reproduce, a given genotype. It was the philosopher Hans Jonas who first formulated this criticism in his 1987 book *Technik, Medizin und Ethik*.[9] In fact, cloning does not introduce anything new into cloned life, otherwise one could hardly speak of cloning. A cloned life subjected to alterations diverging from the matrix is undoubtedly a new life form or a new bodily assemblage. Undeniably, Conrad and Potter have identified new practices of the care of the self, but they fail to understand the ethical value of these practices and related attitudes; in other words, they become too normative while judging people's action according to an old definition of life.

Other commentators have adopted a more relaxed stance. Powell and Biggs (2004),[10] for example, describe biomedical and information technologies as devices that allow a "re-coding of the body," especially of the ageing body. The physical recomposition of the bodily components goes hand in hand with a re-creation of the self through diet and physical exercise. This intervention on the bodily level is flanked by a cultivation of the mental capacity through narrative therapies. Narrative counselling is currently experiencing a renaissance in gerontology, especially in ultra-modern societies such as Canada. As the authors stress, "a 'healthy age' is seen to be the result of prudent self-care. A healthy old age signifies that one has lived a 'moral life' that not only has its own rewards, but relieves others of any obligation to care." Seen from this perspective the notion of the technologies of the self must be understood as "capable of accommodating the complexity of the 'subject'." The importance of counselling in our culture has also been underlined by Julie Brownlie (2004), who looks at this practice as an interaction through which the person acquires his/her identity as a resistant. The author does not specifically target the role of genetics in this process, but her approach is interesting in that she reminds us that identity emerges from a process of resistance, and is therefore fundamentally related to the social context of therapeutic counselling. It seems that counselling will play an important role in a culture where genetic manipulation, testing, and screening will intensify the practices leading up to self-knowledge and self-care. Perhaps the time has come in which knowing oneself and caring for oneself are merged into a uniform principle. In the culture reflected in this practice there is no room for a revendication of the right to ignorance or not to know.

NOTES

1. Foucault, M. 1989 [1969]. *The Archaeology of Knowledge*. London: Routledge, 274–318.
2. This phenomenon has exhaustively been explored in Rose, N. 1989. *Governing the Soul of the Private Self*. London/New York: Free Association Books.
3. Foucault, M. 1988. *The Care of the Self: The History of Sexuality*, Vol. 3. London: Allen Lane.
4. Starkey, K. and McKinlay, A. 1998. Afterword: deconstructing organization—discipline and desire. In McKinley, A. and Starkey, K. (eds.) *Foucault, Management and Organization Theory*. London: Sage, 230–241.
5. Foucault, *The Care of the Self*, ibid., 39–68, 81–144.
6. Foucault, M. 1988. Technologies of the self. Martin, L. H., Gutman, H., and Hutton, P. H. (eds.), *Technologies of the Self: A seminar with Michel Foucault*. Amherst: The University of Massachusetts Press, 16–49, specifically 18–22, 31–49.
7. Conrad, P. and Potter, D. 2004. Human growth hormone and the temptations of biomedical enhancement. *Sociology of Health & Illness* 26 (2): 184–215, specifically 185–187, 200–210.
8. The two authors draw on studies that go back to the 1950s, and specifically refer to Dubos, R. 1959. *Mirage of Health*. New York: Harper & Row.
9. Jonas, H. 1987. Technik, Medizin und Ethik. Praxis des Prinzips Verantwortung. Frankfurt, Suhrkamp. I refer to p. 195 of the German version.
10. Powell, J. L. and Biggs, S. 2004. Ageing, technologies of self and bio-medicine: a Foucauldian excursion. *International Journal of Sociology and Social Policy* 24 (6): 17–29, specifically 20–21, 24.

IV. CONCLUSION

From the works collected in this volume, *The Moral, Social, and Commercial Imperatives of Genetic Testing and Screening*, emerges a unique analytical framework that embeds the "new genetics" in four interrelated fields:

1. Genetic enhancement and morality
2. Genetic commerce and law
3. Genetic policies and privacy
4. Genetic knowledge and ethics

In those major fields genetics and diagnostic knowledge of (healthy) individuals appear at the same time as a threatening reality and as advancing options. The chapters have illustrated the conflicting interests characterizing the shift from scientific practices predicting certainty (also the certainty of the limits) to a science predicting probabilities through testing. In fact, it seems appropriate to speak of a new science and new scientific practices, because the forms of life made possible by the genetics of the 21st century are undoubtedly different from those of the past. Some will perhaps smile at this, and say that it is normal that the present differentiates itself from the past. But what this book shows beyond any doubt is that this is not a differentiation based on chronological developments. What is called the "new genetic" does not simply add a new layer to the biological strata of complex life. Instead, it seems appropriate to say, the entire structure becomes reorganized through practices that target completely new possibilities. This means that not only will the physical body (desires) go through different forms of shaping and adaptations but also the social body (society) in which it is placed, and with these two the mental body (the will) as well.

As illustrated by the authors, there are four forms of "intervention." In chapter 1 Michela Betta has described genetic enhancement and the limits and possibilities that individuals and societies will attach to it. In the course of this exploration, it has emerged that moral imperatives seem to impede rather than advance a fair discussion of the propositions made by genetic science and its new testing practices. However, at the same time, the current bioethical reflection also seems insufficient to address all possible consequences of the genetic enhancement policies discussed by the proponents of liberal eugenics. But if moral philosophy is struggling to keep its

Michela Betta (ed.), The moral, social, and commercial imperatives of genetic testing and screening. The Australian case, 257–264.

position in the debate, and bioethics still has a few methodological problems to solve, how can we reach a balance between imperative and choice? An attempt to address this question has been undertaken in chapter 13, in which Michela Betta has looked at desires from an ethical perspective, one which puts the conscientious individual at the centre of his/her actions. The exploration has showed that it is through "true" knowledge of the self that the individual will be able to build the conditions of possibility for social life in a culture very much determined by new forms of interconnected scientific practices and self-care. How? By reinforcing self-discipline, asserting social belonging, and reaffirming trust towards the axes of science and commerce. Trust is currently missing or is too tenuous to work successfully. This is what unmistakably emerges from the chapters in the Australian Case. The idea that there might be a genetic explanation of crime has fascinated the legal mind for centuries. Now, with the entrance of the genome into the crime scene, this fascination seems to acquire additional substance. But does it not represent the same hopes of the past in new clothes? This is what Richard Hil and Richard Hindmarsh have explored in chapter 3, underlining the need to be cautious in matters related to crime and violence, as the social environment might still be the nurturing humus of the criminal mind. Attempts to separate the technical problem "crime" from the net of social practices and discourses reveal a "bio-utopian" design that uses science to address the insufficiencies of social policies and politics, loading too many responsibilities that belong to the public sphere on the scientists' shoulders. Suspicion towards criminology and its operational crime agencies has also been expressed by Astrid Gesche (chapter 4) in spite of the demonstrated possibility that, in some cases, DNA fingerprinting might contribute to an explication of criminal offences. But is this wish to explain crimes through genetics, as highlighted by Hil and Hindmarsh, just another form of big hope? And where is this big hope leading us to in terms of policies? Gesche has described the emergence of new criminal genetic databases linked to genetic information, unveiling the many expectations attached to them as well as the power given to them to create transparent human beings—as the result of data and information collected over the years with or without their consent and matched according to the needs of public and social safety. The author has highlighted an extremely productive legislative mind that seems to have been led to such a degree by prevention that sometimes one does not really know how to process the control mechanism already put in place by the legal profession and political class.

The visible hand of the law also emerges in chapter 5 by David Weisbrot and chapter 6 by David Weisbrot and Brian Opeskin, but this time it seems that the law has restrained itself from adding new legislation to that already in existence. In fact, the two authors have reassured us that claims for "absolute rights" and "big law" have been rejected by the Australian Law Reform Commission, which resisted calls for a new genetic privacy legislation and incisive intervention in the insurance industry. According to Weisbrot and Opeskin the Inquiry was careful not to develop policy and practice based on any notions of genetic exceptionalism. This approach strongly influenced the recommendations regarding privacy protections and anti-discrimination laws, as well as insurance underwriting law and practice. Weisbrot (chapter 5) has underlined the efforts made by the Commission to assert the personal rights of the individual by reinforcing existing laws, but avoiding new legislative steps. In this revisited law scenario, the notion of the "informed consent" has fundamentally been revitalized, as no genetic tests or collection of genetic samples, use of them, and revelation of genetic information should occur without the explicit consent of the individual involved. The intention behind this "limited" intervention is to make existing rules more flexible in order to address changed social patterns. These cautious strategies put Australia worldwide at the forefront, as they demonstrate its ability to look towards the future without hysteria. This is a style that differentiates it from countries such as Italy, Germany, and the United States in which modernization is always accompanied by fundamentalist debates questioning the constitution or the very existence of the State. Chapters 5 and 6 are important for another reason. They clearly give us an idea of the intense debate that has taken place during the Inquiry. The narrative emerging from their chapters tells many stories about the conflicting interests surrounding the issue of genetic testing and screening related to privacy and informed consent.

The informed consent emerges from these chapters as a good compromise between the interests of science and society and those of the individual. In chapter 4 Gesche has argued that one should move away from primarily signing forms, suggesting that the consent process should become a "meaningful *process* of information sharing and negotiation." In her chapter on the vulnerable members of society (chapter 11) Gesche has also questioned genetic testing for ethnic reasons, which, in her opinion, are intrusive and show disrespect for tradition and other forms of belonging beyond genetic truth. This is of course a new way of looking at consensual practices that reposition the individual in emerging assemblages and negotiating spaces. In the negotiating culture even educational strategies targeting the need to test individuals and screen social groups, as MaryAnne Aitken and Sylvia Metcalfe (chapter 7) remind us, would remain ineffective without a clear and informed consent given by the individual under non-coercive power. The two authors are conscious of the risks involved in the "new genetics"; as scientists, they know that science works best when it acts in harmony with society and the people to whom it needs to prove its scientific truths. In fact, science cannot work against people, it only can work for them. Otherwise, who would appreciate and admire it? Concerns about public participation and involvement also emerge from the chapter by Enzo Palombo and Mrinal Bhave (chapter 8). These two scientists, too, are concerned with general consensus in genetic healthcare and the creation of proper conditions for an ethical performance of science. Then what else is science doing, if not trying to create options for society? It is reassuring to see genetic scientists address the very sensitive question of consensus and equal participation in matters related to genetic testing and screening.

How can we then explain the mistrust towards science? In chapter 2 Michela Betta has touched on a taboo by discussing the notion of scientists as entrepreneurs. Are we, is society, prepared to accept that scientists can commercially use their inventions and extrapolate from them wealth and social positions? Has the old relationship between science and commerce become more dangerous with the advent of the new genetics? The chapter displays controversial positions regarding the entrepreneurial science by showing how bodily parts such as the umbilical cord blood can turn into raw material in which one can invest money. Is this a problem? The chapter leaves this question open, and avoids the risk of a precipitous answer, because the trend seems to anticipate that we will see more and more entrepreneurs in medical science than ever before. However, this trend is not necessarily due to the fact that universities have no money to support science, but more importantly to the changing patterns of wealth and knowledge creation. But if universities are no longer the depositaries of innovation and revolutionary knowledge, and commerce is still too sceptical towards genetic revenues, on what cultural platform will emerging scientific options be displayed and how will they be embedded in the social context? It seems that the cultural shift we are witnessing will have serious repercussions on business and economy too, and that new forms of wealth creation and distribution will probably contribute to an overcoming of current corporate structures.

The pressure on traditional industry sectors is already palpable. In chapter 6 on private health and life insurance Weisbrot and Opeskin argue that insurance contracts are private contracts embedded in the free market economy, and that therefore they cannot be seen as social policies. Any attempt by governments to legislate differently would transfer social responsibility from the government to the private economy. Consent and fair exchange of information about genetic predispositions and genetic tests results between the parties, namely the insurance industry and the individual seeking an insurance contract, has always guaranteed and will guarantee best practice and fair treatment. But of course not everybody agrees with this approach. Sue Pennicuik (chapter 9) has argued that the ALRC-AHEC have been soft on the employers, while Suzanne Jamieson (chapter 10) has described the recommendations made by the ALRC-AHEC as a halfway house between the interests of the employers and the trade unions. According to these two authors, this reveals the commercial pressure under which the ALRC and AHEC stood at the time of their Inquiry. The most controversial reply to the ALRC and AHEC Inquiry and its recommendations has been formulated by Ly Turney (chapter 12), who has rejected the Commission's line of reasoning by arguing that it is still unclear to whom genetic information belongs. By so doing she has questioned the very essence of the notion of private information. Turney has suggested that there is no private information in the genetic culture, especially in the context of genetic testing for parentage reasons.

Does this mean that the private nature of genetic information is becoming an obsolete concept in a culture where knowledge and self-knowledge are turning into a public resource? In chapter 13 Michela Betta has asked more questions than provided answers to a scenario in which the notion of life as a singular noun is seriously questioned by cultural practices that make it necessary to speak of forms of life—all of which are legitimate and perfectly embedded in a culture that reminds us of the ancient Greco-Roman practices of the care of the self in terms of self-discipline, diet, and all sorts of educational, social, and medical enhancements. From this perspective, genetic testing and screening in the 21st century can also be understood as a self-quest, an attempt to discover what we are beyond our wishes and desires—beyond what we would like to be.

INDEX

International Library of Ethics, Law, and the New Medicine

1. L. Nordenfelt: *Action, Ability and Health.* Essays in the Philosophy of Action and Welfare. 2000 ISBN 0–7923–6206–3
2. J. Bergsma and D.C. Thomasma: *Autonomy and Clinical Medicine.* Renewing the Health Professional Relation with the Patient. 2000 ISBN 0–7923–6207–1
3. S. Rinken: *The AIDS Crisis and the Modern Self.* Biographical Self-Construction in the Awareness of Finitude. 2000 ISBN 0–7923–6371–X
4. M. Verweij: *Preventive Medicine Between Obligation and Aspiration.* 2000 ISBN 0–7923–6691–3
5. F. Svenaeus. *The Hermeneutics of Medicine and the Phenomenology of Health.* Steps Towards a Philosophy of Medical Practice. 2001 ISBN 0–7923–6757–X
6. D.M. Vukadinovich and S.L. Krinsky: *Ethics and Law in Modern Medicine.* Hypothetical Case Studies. 2001 ISBN 1–4020–0088–X
7. D.C. Thomasma, D.N. Weisstub and C. Hervé (eds.): *Personhood and Health Care.* 2001 ISBN 1–4020–0098–7
8. H. ten Have and B. Gordijn (eds.): *Bioethics in a European Perspective.* 2001 ISBN 1–4020–0126–6
9. P.-A. Tengland: *Mental Health.* A Philosophical Analysis. 2001 ISBN 1–4020–0179–7
10. D.N. Weisstub, D.C. Thomasma, S. Gauthier and G.F. Tomossy (eds.): *Aging: Culture, Health, and Social Change.* 2001 ISBN 1–4020–0180–0
11. D.N. Weisstub, D.C. Thomasma, S. Gauthier and G.F. Tomossy (eds.) *Aging: Caring for our Elders.* 2001 ISBN 1–4020–0181–9
12. D.N. Weisstub, D.C. Thomasma, S. Gauthier and G.F. Tomossy (eds.): *Aging: Decisions at the End of Life.* 2001 ISBN 1–4020–0182–7
    (Set ISBN for vols. 10–12: 1–4020–0183–5)
13. M.J. Commers: *Determinants of Health: Theory, Understanding, Portrayal, Policy.* 2002 ISBN 1–4020–0809–0
14. I.N. Olver: *Is Death Ever Preferable to Life?* 2002 ISBN 1–4020–1029–X
15. C. Kopp: *The New Era of AIDS.* HIV and Medicine in Times of Transition. 2003 ISBN 1–4020–1048–6
16. R.L. Sturman: *Six Lives in Jerusalem.* End-of-Life Decisions in Jerusalem-Cultural, Medical, Ethical and Legal Considerations. 2003 ISBN 1–4020–1725–1
17. D.C. Wertz and J.C. Fletcher: *Genetics and Ethics in Global Perspective.* 2004 ISBN 1–4020–1768–5
18. J.B.R. Gaie: *The Ethics of Medical Involvement in Capital Punishment.* A Philosophical Discussion. 2004 ISBN 1–4020–1764–2
19. M. Boylan (ed.): *Public Health Policy and Ethics.* 2004 ISBN 1–4020–1762–6; Pb 1–4020–1763–4
20. R. Cohen-Almagor: *Euthanasia in the Netherlands.* The Policy and Practice of Mercy Killing. 2004 ISBN 1–4020–2250–6
21. D.C. Thomasma and D.N. Weisstub (eds.): *The Variables of Moral Capacity.* 2004 ISBN 1–4020–2551–3
22. D.R. Waring: *Medical Benefit and the Human Lottery.* An Egalitarian Approach. 2004 ISBN 1–4020–2970–5

International Library of Ethics, Law, and the New Medicine

23. P. McCullagh: *Conscious in a Vegetative State? A Critique of the PVS Concept*. 2004 ISBN 1–4020–2629–3
24. L. Romanucci-Ross and L.R. Tancredi: *When Law and Medicine Meet: A Cultural View*. 2004 ISBN 1–4020–2756–7
25. G.P. Smith II: *The Christian Religion and Biotechnology*. A Search for Principled Decision-making. 2005 ISBN 1–4020–3146–7
26. C. Viafora (ed.): *Clinical Bioethics*. A Search for the Foundations. 2005 ISBN 1–4020–3592–6
27. B. Bennett and G.F. Tomossy: *Globalization and Health*. Challenges for health law and bioethics. 2005 ISBN 1–4020–4195–0
28. C. Rehmann-Sutter, M. Düwell and D. Mieth (eds.): *Bioethics in Cultural Contexts*. Reflections on Methods and Finitude. 2006 ISBN 1–4020–4240–X
29. S.E. Sytsma, Ph.D.: *Ethics and Intersex*. 2006 ISBN 1–4020–4313–9
30. M. Betta (ed.): *The Moral, Social, and Commercial Imperatives of Genetic Testing and Screening*. The Australian Case. 2006 ISBN 1–4020–4618–9